PRAISE FOR THE WRITER'S IDEA BOOK

In a field crowded with disappointing tomes, what a joy to open *The Writer's Idea Book* and find vast regions of opinion and experience mined for creative fodder. As much fun to read as it is to use.

— JANET FITCH, AUTHOR OF *WHITE OLEANDER*

The Writer's Idea Book is a fascinating, no-nonsense, sit-your-butt-down-and-work approach invaluable to all writers hoping to stretch their imaginations, deepen their understanding of experience, and explore their moral visions. Not since John Gardner's *The Art of Fiction* has there been such a useful and informative and comprehensive resource book. In fact, if writers have only one book about writing on their shelves, it should be this one.

— LAURA HENDRIE, AUTHOR OF *STYGO* AND *REMEMBER ME*

Jack Heffron's *The Writer's Idea Book* is the literary equivalent of attending the Actor's Studio. Wise, entertaining, and inventive, the book liberates beginning and advanced writers alike, helping them get to the heart of their story.

— DAVID MORRELL, AUTHOR OF *FIRST BLOOD*
AND *BROTHERHOOD OF THE ROSE*

What an inspiring book! The Writer's Idea Book does exactly what it sets out to do—offer writers at all stages of their careers a seemingly endless variety of ideas to noodle around with, explore, and ultimately make their own. Jack Heffron's voice is so nurturing, funny, and wise that, as he guides you along the writer's path, you'll feel as though you've made a new best friend.

— JANICE EIDUS, AUTHOR OF *THE CELIBACY CLUB* AND *URBAN BLISS*

The Writer's Idea Book is an excellent workbook for people interested in any kind of writing. The advice is helpful and practical, without making grand promises or arousing inflated expectations in the writer. I recommend it highly.

— JOANNE GREENBURG, AUTHOR OF *I NEVER PROMISED YOU*
A ROSE GARDEN AND *WHERE THE ROAD GOES*

Every writer out there will benefit from *The Writer's Idea Book*. Whether you are just starting out, are immersed in a project, or simply feeling stuck, Jack Heffron has an idea to help you along. This is a book to keep close at hand as you will be referring to it often!

— ANN HOOD, AUTHOR OF *THE PROPERTIES OF WATER*
AND *SOMEWHERE OFF THE COAST OF MAINE*

10TH ANNIVERSARY EDITION

THE WRITER'S

idea

BOOK

10TH ANNIVERSARY EDITION

THE WRITER'S
idea
BOOK

HOW TO DEVELOP GREAT IDEAS FOR
FICTION, NONFICTION, POETRY, & SCREENPLAYS

JACK HEFFRON

WD
WRITER'S DIGEST
BOOKS
WritersDigest.com
Cincinnati, Ohio

For more resources for writers, visit www.writersdigest.com.

To receive a free weekly e-mail newsletter delivering tips and updates about writing and about Writer's Digest products, register directly at www.writersdigest.com/enews.

15 14 13 12 11   5 4 3 2 1

Distributed in Canada by Fraser Direct

100 Armstrong Avenue

Georgetown, Ontario, Canada L7G 5S4

Tel: (905) 877-4411

Distributed in the U.K. and Europe by F&W Media International
Brunel House, Newton Abbot, Devon, TQ12 4PU, England
Tel: (+44) 1626-323200, Fax: (+44) 1626-323319
E-mail: postmaster@davidandcharles.co.uk

Distributed in Australia by Capricorn Link
P.O. Box 704, Windsor, NSW 2756 Australia
Tel: (02) 4577-3555

Edited by Scott Francis
Cover designed by Terri Woesner
Interior designed by Josh Roflow
Production coordinated by Debbie Thomas

DEDICATION

For Michael and Nick,
and for Amy

ACKNOWLEDGMENTS

Given that this book is actually three books in one (different versions of two of them published years ago) I have a lot of people to thank. For this edition, I'm grateful to the folks at Writer's Digest who made it possible: Phil Sexton, Kelly Messerly, Suzanne Lucas, and Scott Francis, my editor. Without Scott's cool hand—and saintly patience—I don't know that the book would have been completed. Previous editors at Writer's Digest who provided advice and encouragement on the earlier books are Michelle Howry, Meg Leder, and Donya Dickerson, who all remain treasured friends.

I also need to thank my colleagues—and very dear friends—at the Writing it Real Conference, Sheila Bender and Meg Files. They have taught me many lessons about the craft of writing and have been some of the most important friends in my life. Meg and Sheila are the best—in so many ways. The conferees who have attended the conference through the years also deserve thanks because they, too, have offered no end of encouragement and insight, not to mention wonderful company. There have been too many to list each of them, but I must give special mention to Betty Schafer because she's, well, special.

Thanks to my good friends and great writers Mark Garvey, Brad Crawford, Elissa Yancey, and John Kachuba, who have been supremely valued sounding boards for ideas and projects through the years and have been the best of friends. Rhonda Sandberg, a gifted teacher of writing and a special friend, has provided much support and insight through the writing of these books, and I'm deeply grateful to her for all she's done.

Of course, no one suffers through the writing of a book as much as our families, and mine has always supplied no end of support and patience. Thanks to Mary, Joe, and Anne Marie Heffron; my niece, Mercedes; as well as to Kara and Katie; and to Gette, Joey, Christian, and Mia.

Jack Heffron is the author of a number of books and has ghostwritten several others. He worked in publishing for many years as an editor and has edited hundreds of books. He has taught at the University of Alabama and currently teaches in the journalism program at the University of Cincinnati. His writing has won numerous awards and appeared in magazines and literary journals. He was a founding editor of *Story* magazine, which twice won the National Magazine Award. He is currently a regular contributor to several print and online publications, and he works in advertising. He lives in Cincinnati, Ohio.

TABLE OF CONTENTS

PART IV: EVALUATING IDEAS

PART V: BETTER IDEAS

AUTHOR'S FOREWORD TO THE NEW EDITION

It's tough for me to believe that ten years have passed since the first edition of *The Writer's Idea Book* was published. I remember writing it as if it was, well, not yesterday but not all that long ago. At that time I didn't imagine it would still be around a decade later, and since that time I have heard from many writers who found something valuable in its pages—some exercise that launched a rewarding project. Those letters and e-mails are always gratifying to receive.

I've learned much since that first edition, through the process of putting words on the page, as well as from teaching. At the time when the original edition was published, I had just begun teaching at what became an annual writers conference with two amazing colleagues—Sheila Bender and Meg Files. And we're still doing it. What began as the Colorado Mountain Writer's Conference has evolved into the Writing It Real Conference, produced through Sheila's online magazine by the same name. Through the years, I've learned from Sheila and Meg, as well as from the hundreds of writers who have come to the conference, each with a story to tell.

One lesson I've learned is that the exercise that tickles our fancy is not always the one that sparks the best writing. Sometimes we reap the most results from an exercise that forces us to struggle, to push a bit harder. Writers at all levels of experience tend to go toward the path of least resistance, but often we need the resistance in order to find the material we most need to explore.

Sometimes, frankly, the starting point doesn't matter much at all. The initial challenge presented by an exercise can be merely a gateway—a means to accessing deeper, richer material. After our imaginations connect with that material, we must leave the first inspiration behind, which, of course, is not always easy to do.

In her essay "Notes for Young Writers," author Annie Dillard explains: "Usually you have to rewrite the beginning—the first quarter or third or whatever it is. You'll just have to take a deep breath and throw it away ... once you finish the work and have a clearer sense of what it is about. Tear up the runway; it helped you take off, and you don't need it now. This is why some writers say it takes 'courage' to write. It does. Over and over you must choose the book over your own wishes and feelings."

As you write your way through this book, keep these thoughts in mind. It *is* a journey that requires courage. And faith. Sometimes a piece of writing takes its own sweet time in revealing itself to us. If we're truly engaged by the material—even if on some days we feel more doubt than faith—then we need to push on, believing that a discovery will reward our patience and our trust.

In short, you can begin anywhere. Close your eyes, flip open the book, and jab a page with your finger. Then begin with the nearest exercise. You might, as some of my students have done in the past, let out a loud groan, thinking you have nothing to say in response to the prompt. That might be just the one you need to do. Give it a try.

In this edition of the book you'll find many new exercises. I've also added some new chapters, covering topics that hadn't occurred to me when I was writing the original. You'll also find some revised and expanded chapters from the follow-up book, *The Writer's Idea Workshop*. That book focuses on developing and jump-starting projects already under way. My hope is that you'll find enough here to spark any number of projects from poems to screenplays to short stories and personal essays to novels and memoirs.

I'm looking forward to taking that journey with you. I don't promise that it will be easy. In fact, I can pretty much guarantee that it won't be. Writing well requires a commitment. Like most any skill you can name, writing requires a lot of practice. It also requires a lot of reading. Without reading the best writing you can find, and studying that writing to discover what qualities make it special, you'll have a tough time progressing in your own work.

But as I tell my students, if it were easy we wouldn't get to feel so darn special about ourselves as writers. I tell them to recall the scene in the movie *A League of Their Own*, when Dottie Hinson, played by Geena Davis, quits the baseball team, saying that the game is simply "too hard." Her manager, Jimmy Dugan, played by Tom Hanks, responds, "It's supposed to be hard. If it wasn't hard, everyone would do it. The hard is what makes it great."

The same is true about writing. "The hard," however, doesn't mean it can't be fun. In fact, it's probably the most fun when we break through some obstacle, feeling the "writer's high," losing ourselves in the world of the piece. Suddenly our everyday world falls away, and our imaginations cartwheel from word to word, image to image sentence to sentence.

My hope is that this book creates many such moments for you. In fact, if you're willing to face the "hard" part, I guarantee that it will.

INTRODUCTION

Writing is an act of hope.

It is a means of carving order from chaos, of challenging one's own beliefs and assumptions, of facing the world with eyes and heart wide open. Through writing, we declare a personal identity amid faceless anonymity. We find purpose and beauty and meaning even when the rational mind argues that none of these exist.

Writing, therefore, is also an act of courage. How much easier is it to lead an unexamined life than to confront yourself on the page? How much easier is it to surrender to materialism or cynicism or to a hundred other ways of life that are, in fact, ways to hide from life and from our fears? When we write, we resist the facile seduction of these simpler roads. We insist on finding out and declaring the truths that we find, and we dare to put those truths on the page.

To get ideas and to write well, you have to risk opening yourself. In her book *When Things Fall Apart*, Buddhist teacher Pema Chödrön writes of this risk:

> When we regard thoughts and emotions with humor and openness, that's how we perceive the universe. ... We begin to find that, to the degree that there is bravery in ourselves ... and to the degree that there is kindness toward ourselves, there is confidence that we can actually forget ourselves and open to the world.

There must be that softness, that openness. Rather than making us weak, it makes us confident and fearless. The more confident we grow, the more open we can allow ourselves to be. If you can write even when your life seems dark and bleak, even if all you can write is "Life sucks," then you have the hope and courage necessary to keep moving, to persevere as an artist. In perseverance you will find your creative self.

Writing also is an act of joy and celebration. With it we say that life is worth preserving, worth exploring in all its facets, and to do it well we must have fun. It must be approached with a sense of play, of risk and experiment, openness and laughter. Throughout his book *Fiction Writer's Workshop*, Josip Novakovich entreats the reader to "have fun." This is not a catchphrase. It's an important piece of writing advice.

GETTING IDEAS

Most writers have more ideas than they can explore in a lifetime—subjects and situations that someday will be short stories and novels, memoirs and poems and screenplays, bits of scene, a great zinger of a line, characters, moments of loss and triumph to capture on the page. This book will help you explore those ideas and help you generate new ones. It will help you push deeper into your ideas to plumb their possibilities. The book is organized in four sections that follow the process of creation: warming up, deciding what you want to write about and beginning to generate ideas, finding a form for those ideas, developing those ideas. But you should feel free to open the book anywhere and find a prompt that interests you. If you respond to enough of the prompts, you will generate ideas for many new projects. You also can use the prompts to find new ways of seeing projects already underway. You might be stuck, for example, on a way to develop a minor character in your novel. Find a prompt that focuses on character and follow it. Then put the character into your novel.

A FEW POINTS TO KEEP IN MIND

In many of the prompts I use the word *story*. By *story*, I mean any sort of narrative—short story, short-short story, narrative essay, memoir, narrative poem, novel, script, even blog or journal entry. Rather than repeat all of these forms again and again, I use story as a shorthand word. Work in whatever form interests you. I do suggest that you try your hand at a few forms rather than sticking to just one. A new form can suggest all sorts of new possibilities and can provide a fresh context for your ideas. Sometimes I use the word *piece* to mean any type of writing—any "piece of writing."

Next, I've tried to vary gender-specific pronouns. Sometimes I use *she*; sometimes I use *he*. I've done this in an arbitrary way. If there are more of one than another, this is purely accidental. In my experience, I've found that writers can be either male or female, and I've tried to acknowledge that fact in as unobtrusive a way as possible.

As you can see from the introduction, the tone of the book will vary, from high-minded to playful to downright cranky. As for the content of the book, I hope you find it useful, that it sparks a great many ideas that lead to satisfying projects. Unfortunately, I can offer no hidden formulas, no *secrets* in this book. I don't know that any exist. The secrets to getting ideas aren't really secrets. Open your mind and heart. Open your eyes and ears. Take risks. Trust your talent and your instincts. Be willing to see your ideas—and your life and the world around you—in new ways. Be patient. Be positive. Don't be distracted by the opinions of others, real or imagined. Don't worry about getting published—that's a whole new topic, and one worth investigating if that's your goal, but it's a needless and potentially harmful distraction when you're writing. Don't worry about "getting better" or fret about whether you're really any good. Read a lot. Write a lot.

Most of all, as I said earlier, have fun. Your sense of freedom and play will infuse your writing with energy, and that energy will make your words enjoyable to read. And you'll be having fun, which is an end in itself. You'll be learning about yourself and about others. You'll have a place to nurture yourself and explore your ideas. You'll have a place to investigate things in all their maddening ambiguity, to seek and find your own opinions and truths. You will expand your powers of empathy as well as your understanding of life. In empathy and understanding, we find compassion, for others and for ourselves. We grow. With those goals in mind, let's begin.

Part I

INVITING
ideas

CHAPTER ONE

MAKING YOUR WAY TO SCHENECTADY

It is good to have an end to journey toward; but it is the journey that matters, in the end.

—URSULA K. LE GUIN

If you've been writing for any length of time, you've been asked this question by well-meaning friends and family: "Where do you get your ideas?" Perhaps you've even developed a stock, smart-ass reply, such as Robin Hemley's: "Joyce Carol Oates gives me her extras." Ray Bradbury had one, too: "I get them from the Schenectady Center for Ideas."

If you're feeling kind, you might reply, "Dunno," with a shrug. "Everywhere, I guess. They just sort of come to me." And you'd probably be telling the truth. But even this straightforward pooh-poohing of any grand source of ideas won't demystify the creative process for your listener. Instead, she'll probably be awed, convinced that your self-effacing response is a sign of genius.

"She's so creative," you will hear—and probably feel like the biggest fraud since Barnum and Bailey.

Unfortunately, there is no magic elixir we can brew to conjure ideas from the air, and though we've been told we're "so creative" since we were sucking on Tinker Toys, we often don't feel creative at all. Our ideas seem stale. Or we feel stuck, unable to get a pleasing voice on the page. Or we feel blocked on a particular project.

If only there were a real center for ideas in Schenectady. Oh, frabjous day—we'd write every morning and evening, pouring forth words of divine beauty.

But before we get to specific idea prompts, let's look at some general truths about writing more creatively, ways to keep your mind fresh and your imagination fertile. You possess the resources, you know you do, to come up with many good ideas. It's simply a matter of tapping into them and trusting them and understanding how your creative self works. To achieve these goals, you will need to help your creative self function at its best by shaping the way you perceive your writing and by structuring your life to write.

SHOW UP

Showing up is the main thing. Get to the desk regularly. You'll find you have no end of ideas if you can make writing a regular habit. Remember Woody Allen's famous observation that 80 percent of being successful in life is just showing up. We all know this is true. The writers we admire—or envy—might be geniuses whose talent dwarfs our own, but more often they're people who show up, with seven-hundred-page novels they've been rising at five to write every morning for the past year. You think, *I'm as talented as Anne. I could have done that.* But alas, you have no seven-hundred-page novel. You have six novels, varying from twenty-five to sixty pages. They're in a drawer or file cabinet, or even still in computer files. Is the culprit writer's block? A dearth of ideas? Cruel and fickle fortune? Nope. If you want to write, you must begin by beginning, continue by continuing, finish by finishing. This is the great secret of it all. Tell no one.

PROMPT: Writer Thomas McGuane goes to his study at a certain time every day and stays there for a scheduled length of time. He sits at his desk. "I don't have to write," he explains, "but I can't do anything else." Try his approach for a week, scheduling a specific period of time during which you must sit at your desk or wherever you write. You don't have to write, but you can't do anything else.

ACKNOWLEDGE THE DIFFICULTY

People, like me, say, "Just show up," as if it were the easiest thing in the world to do. It's not. It's hard. Why? Because writing creatively can be hard. Yes, it can empower you and free your spirit and can be a source of great joy, but it's not always easy. Sometimes we just don't feel creative. We're tired or bored. Also, as I said in the introduction, and many more brilliant folks than me have said before: Writing is an act of courage. Sometimes it's just too scary to face the page. Or too frustrating: We've worked hard, and still our skills seem small, our writing clumsy, our ideas foolish and hackneyed. Who needs it? Our friends get along just fine without opening the vein every day to pour their blood onto the page. They have more time to do things—have fun, enjoy themselves.

So if you fall away from your schedule, if you wake up at 5 A.M. but pop the snooze button six times rather than getting out of bed, don't beat yourself up. Telling yourself, "I'm lazy," "I have no willpower," "I'm not a writer," won't help you become a writer. That approach will convince you, instead, that you're a lazy loser with neither willpower nor talent. Such a person ain't flinging back the covers at 5 A.M., striding to the coffeemaker. Such a person stays in bed. Give yourself positive messages.

PROMPT: List the positive messages you have received about writing or about any creative undertaking. What did people say? How did they say it? Then write about times when you felt good about your writing, such as when a great idea zipped into your mind or when you finished a project that turned out well. Keep these messages and memories handy. When you're feeling stale or want to berate yourself about your work, read about what you've done in the past and know you can do it again.

PROMPT: Acknowledge that writing is hard. Write it down. Then write about how you're going to make writing happen. How will you find the balance in yourself to combine willpower with relaxation, stubbornness with joy? Write about how you've struck this balance in the past, with writing, a sport, a musical instrument—anything you've done.

PROMPT: If the McGuane approach mentioned previously doesn't work for you, create a writing schedule for the next three weeks. Start with five minutes per day. Add five minutes to every writing session. Note on your schedule how you're doing.

PROMPT: If you're blessed to have a friend or two who also struggles to write, create a schedule—maybe as a Google Doc—on which you check in every day, noting with a simple X next to the date that you did or did not write. Miss enough days and you'll feel the need to start adding those Xs. Doesn't matter how long you write or how much you write, the key is keeping it in your mind, forcing yourself to "touch" it on a regular basis. If you don't have friends who could join you in the program, do it for yourself.

Like many things, writing becomes a habit. If you do it, you just keep doing it. If you want to break a habit—smoking, watching television, eating chocolate—instead of trying to will yourself past the habit, cultivate the habit of *not* doing it. Get in the habit of not not writing. Sounds like psychobabble? All right, phrase it however you'd like.

But it's one way to reframe the situation. I learned this from a friend who quit smoking. He told me he did it, gradually, by cultivating the habit of not smoking. True, this took willpower. But he started by not smoking in his car, then not smoking right before going to bed. The same can happen with writing! Start small. Start cultivating the habit of not not writing.

If this refraining approach doesn't work for you, don't worry about it. It probably sounds a little weird. But it does eliminate the structured, even puritanical implications of disciplining yourself. It takes from your hand the *I should be writing* stick with which we are tempted to beat ourselves. It keeps discipline in a more positive, nurturing context. A positive mind-set is important for sustaining joy in your writing. If you turn it into a teeth-grinding test of your willpower, you'll lose the fun. If you lose the joy and the fun, why bother?

PROMPT: Collect some motivational statements about writing or about creativity or about perseverance. Choose ones that speak directly to your needs or beliefs, and post them where you write. You can find a number of these statements in this book. Use them to keep yourself writing.

JOY AND GRATITUDE

There's no question that only through regular writing will you generate a lot of good ideas. But joy and fun are important, too. We must find a balance. As writers, we know what the "writer's high" feels like, the sense of elation we feel when we're cooking on a project. The world and all of its problems melt away. Our lives have purpose, direction, meaning. We feel our passions rise within us. We tap into thoughts and emotions, and feel restored. As Annie Dillard said, "It is life at its most free."

PROMPT: Write about a time when your creativity flowed, perhaps when you were immersed in a project or when you spent a few hours at a coffeehouse scribbling in your journal. Try to describe the feeling. Describe, too, the circumstances—the time of day, the location, your mood before beginning. In this exercise, try to get to know your creative self a bit better.

PROMPT: Celebrate your creative self, the writer inside you. Write about how writing is an important part of your life. Write about the pleasure it brings. Write about your gratitude in possessing such a gift. Shakespeare once wrote the following:

> This is a gift I have, simple, simple; a foolish extravagant spirit, full of forms,
> figures, shapes, objects, ideas, apprehensions, motions, revolutions . . . .
> But the gift is good in those in whom it is acute, and I am thankful for it.

Though it may sound stupid, cultivate gratitude even for the obstacles that stand in the way of your writing, the ones that sometimes impede your ideas and creativity. Recent psychological studies show that these obstacles actually aid creativity.

Difficult to believe? Consider: Have you ever suffered from too much time to write? Though we all wish we had much more time to spend writing, sometimes when we receive such a gift, we find the well is dry. We don't feel creative. When we're snatching a desperate hour here and there, before work, during the kids' baseball practices, then the ideas seem to flow. We find a way to make it happen, and that fuels our imaginations.

Successful author Nicholson Baker (his books *The Mezzanine*, *U and I* and others are some of my favorites) said that, through the years, he has turned down teaching jobs because he feared that his life would be too easy—an undemanding schedule and a regular paycheck would lessen his need to write. He wouldn't be motivated enough to write regularly or to complete projects.

So instead of cursing your obstacles, be grateful for them. In chapter two, we'll discuss enemies of creativity, and you'll notice they share a common quality: They all exist inside us. Obstacles outside ourselves only make us more creative.

PROMPT: Reframe your view of the obstacles in your life that impede your writing. Make a list of these obstacles. Then, next to each one, write about how you can overcome the obstacle and how it might be used as a tool for creativity.

PROMPT: Research a few inventions. Write about the circumstances of the inventions: How were they discovered or made? What obstacles did the inventors overcome? If you want, write an essay about an inventor or invention.

Now is the time to be more creative. Today. Trust that there is no better time, that no time in the future will offer you more of what you need. I often hear people talk about a time when they will be able to write—when they retire, when the kids are grown and gone, or when they can quit their moonlighting job. Postponing your writing life is like postponing a new diet. It can be an excuse for never starting. My advice: Start now, if only in a limited way. A time in the future may exist that will hold fewer obstacles, but these can be dealt with today, and, as we've discussed, removing all the obstacles can hurt creativity. There's an old saying about life that applies to writing:

> Happiness is not a destination. It is a companion we can choose to accompany us on our journey.

You're not going to be a writer someday. You're a writer today. Discipline yourself to write and take time to enjoy writing. Do it a lot. Have fun with it. Begin now.

CHAPTER TWO

ENEMIES OF CREATIVITY

What is needed is, in the end, simply this: solitude, great inner solitude.

—RAINER MARIA RILKE

Getting ideas, as we've discussed, is largely a matter of showing up. Waiting for inspiration is a loser's game, because without a work in progress, even if you're only doing some personal journaling and the work in progress is you, ideas that arise will have no context. They won't be recognizable as ideas. Or, they'll be great ideas for a novel or article that will never be written. And so, at writers conferences and workshops, teachers will say the key is "Just do it."

And they're right. But "Just do it" is a slogan for shoes. And slogans work because they make things seem easier than they, in fact, are. If just doing it were simply a matter of deciding, anyone *could* do it. But sticking to a schedule goes beyond will. As we discussed in the previous chapter, it's a matter of consciously developing a writing habit.

But there are enemies to that habit, dark forces that keep us from writing creatively. Read this chapter to find out who they are—as if you didn't already know. Each has its strengths and weaknesses and all can be beaten. The key is awareness. Recognize the force at work against you. Recognition is a large part of the battle against these nefarious foes.

THE PROCRASTINATOR

What a great word: *procrastinator*. All of those crashing consonants. The Procrastinator sounds like the name of a comic book supervillain. This guy should be kicking Spiderman's butt all over New York.

Instead, he's at my house. And your house. He's convincing us we will write, yes we will, and we'll get started next week. Absolutely. No exceptions this time, no way. Well. Next week may not be ideal because there's a big meeting at work on Tuesday, which means all of those reports have to be finished, and Wednesday is parent-teacher night, and then there's soccer practice and the appointment with the eye doctor and something has to be done before the first freeze with that tree branch hanging over the garage. But the week after, no problem. We're all over it.

This is the voice of The Procrastinator. He's merciless. Very tough to beat. He can hit you with excuses so good your priest, minister, mother, and therapist would absolve you of your decision not to write. They'd even write a note for you. If you want, write your own, just like you used to do in grade school in your best Mom handwriting.

How does your excuse sound? Does it ring false in your ears? Will the muse believe this excuse? Like a clever truant, make a dozen of these notes, and when you miss a day or a week or whatever your schedule calls for, write a note to the muse explaining why. Look at your excuse on the cold white paper. Does it justify not writing? This strategy can keep The Procrastinator at bay.

But maybe your excuse really is valid. Stuff comes up. It really does. We all have worthwhile reasons not to write, and if we're not writing, we're not creating new ideas. If you made a list right now for why you can't write, or couldn't write the last time your schedule said you should, I'll bet you can come up with at least five reasons, three of them excellent.

PROMPT: The next time you skip a writing session, write five reasons, three of them excellent, for why you must skip. These reasons are The Procrastinator's power. Now, one by one, take back the power by writing a sentence or two explaining why each excuse is not good enough or how schedules could be shifted, arrangements made, to allow you to write some other time.

By using these strategies, you can defeat The Procrastinator. Today. That's the key. Don't delay. Have you ever had a friend tell you that she's starting a diet "on Monday"? Usually she's crunching through a mouthful of Doritos at the time. Yep. Monday. That's when she's starting. Meanwhile, you couldn't be more sure that the diet will fail. You just know it. Why? Because the postponement shows the lack of commitment and desire necessary to make a diet work.

The Procrastinator feeds on delay. To vanquish him, start now. If only for five minutes. Then do five minutes tomorrow, until you're churning out ideas and writing pages. Go ahead, start now. Write a scene from your current story. Pull an unfinished poem from your files and tinker with it. Write anything. Make a list of your favorite foods or a list of your favorite friends, then explain why you like them. List ten things you hate about the holidays and explain why. Describe in detail the most romantic evening of your life. Open this book to nearly any page and follow the prompt. Do it now.

Really. Right now. Go. What are you still doing here?

THE VICTIM

All of us are, at times in our lives, victims. Life can be cruel. And we use the role of victim to stop being creative. We give up control of our creative selves because

- our families don't understand or appreciate us.
- our bosses are demanding and fill our lives with stress.
- our children are demanding and fill our lives with stress.
- our finances are a mess.
- our mates are insensitive to our needs for space to create.
- our cars refuse to run properly.
- our neighborhoods are noisy and overrun with children.

As with The Procrastinator and his excuses, The Victim makes some valid points. The key is taking back the power. In her book *Awakening the Warrior Within,* Dawn Callan speaks of "owning your victim self" as a way of finding one's inner warrior. How? Stop complaining about the forces victimizing you. Stop making your lack of a creative life the fault of someone or something other than yourself. Any or all of the reasons on the list above might be true for you. But when you hear yourself complaining about them, hear the voice of The Victim. And, as with The Procrastinator, know that The Victim is inside you, under your control.

PROMPT: List the most common and frequent reasons you give for not spending enough time being creative. Next to each entry on the list, note who is in control of that situation. Now write a short plan for taking back control. It may require some tough admissions and a little creativity, but you're taking the first step toward opening your creative side.

THE WRITER'S IDEA BOOK

PROMPT: Recognize victim talk when you hear it. Don't condemn yourself for it, just recognize what it is. Then stop. Take control. Give yourself a place to be creative again.

Taking back control is a wonderfully empowering experience. When you beat your victim self, you feel a sense of victory and you know that anything is possible. You *can* finish that novel. You *can* finish that screenplay. It really *is* within your power. I've seen it happen so many times as a teacher at our annual conference. One year, a writer shows up with a little bit of writing and a lot of excuses why she doesn't have more completed on the project. The next year, a new person, but one who looks just like the old person, shows up and she's got an entire draft of a book she's been struggling to write (or not write) for years.

THE TALKER

Speaking of talk, this enemy just can't shut up. You've cooked up a great idea for a screenplay or an essay or you've made a revelation about your protagonist that will give your novel a much-needed new dimension—then The Talker takes over. She has to tell everyone in your writing group. She tells your mate. Or your mother. Or anyone at work who will listen. The Talker is an expert at squandering the creative nest egg. By the time you sit down to put this idea into action, it's dead, or at least not as zesty as it seemed to be a few days ago.

The Talker needs attention. The Talker needs validation. The Talker would rather talk about an idea than confront its complexities and obstacles. The Talker wants the glory but none of the hard work that really lies at the heart of all creative efforts. The Talker is a bit of a coward, frankly, a narcissist, a layabout. If you want to develop your ideas to their full potential and to see a work through to completion, take control of The Talker. When writers tell me they can't help it, or that they *need* to talk it all out first, my advice is simple: Whenever you're talking about a work in progress, don't. Just shut up. Really. The story you're writing is a secret. Anne Tyler takes a somewhat gentler approach:

> It makes me so uncomfortable for them. If they're talking about a plot idea, I feel the idea is probably going to evaporate. I want to almost physically reach over and cover their mouths and say, "You'll lose it if you're not careful."

Writing is a private act. It is a way of communing with our imaginations, our subconscious minds, our secret lives. Bringing in a third party is almost always a bad idea.

The sense of intimacy and revelation are lost, and you end up making small talk. By preserving the privacy of the creative process, you preserve the excitement of that intimacy. Getting back to that intimacy becomes a guilty pleasure, and it keeps the tension high. Ideas will spawn more ideas and you'll find yourself, and your project, rolling right along. Novelist Jay McInerney describes it this way:

> I find it helps to remove myself, as much as possible, from the world of daily life. Living in New York, it's tough to block out the din of the city. So I go away. I try to find a tree house somewhere and pull the ladder up behind me. Once I have begun to believe in my alternate fictional universe, I can come and go from the tree house. But it's a fragile state in the beginning.

Some writers simply think it's a jinx to talk about a work in progress. One writer I know was working on a novel for months and yet refused to even refer to the project as "a novel." She called it "this thing I'm working on" until, after more than a year, she finished it. She took care to avoid letting The Talker get so much as a toe in the door.

The best illustration of this process is also an admittedly silly one that I've used in classes and workshops for a number of years. It involves a TV commercial for grape juice. (Stick with me on this.) The commercial opened by demonstrating the way the competition made its grape juice—a rather primitive and cartoonish illustration of a big boiling vat of purple liquid. Above the boiling vat, smoke wafted into the air, and within the smoke sparkled little purple gems of flavor. Lost flavor. Flavor gone forever. Next, the illustration changed to show the sponsor's process. The vat of burbling purple stuff looked the same, but there was a cap on top of the vat, an inverted funnel with a pipe on the end that channeled the smoke (complete with sparkling purple gems of flavor) back into the vat, thus giving more flavor to the juice.

I can't believe this is how it's really done. But the ingenious ad person had created a good illustration of how The Talker can hinder the creative process. The Talker lets the steam out of your work, making it less rich and interesting. Your glistening purple gems of ideas are lost forever. Don't let that happen.

PROMPT: Remember some writing projects that were great at the start but stalled or remain unfinished. Write down why they weren't completed. Did you talk away any of them? Remind yourself when you're discussing a story in progress or an idea for a piece you've yet to begin that it's best to keep quiet. Tell yourself you'll talk about it after the next scene is written, then try to wait for the scene after that one.

THE WRITER'S IDEA BOOK

PROMPT: If you really want to share the excitement of a new idea with someone, write an e-mail, explaining everything you want to share. Then put that e-mail in a folder and save it for later. Don't send it. Not yet.

THE CRITIC

The biggest surprise I've found about The Critic is that he strikes every writer. As a young apprentice, I always thought that publishing a few stories would calm The Critic, that I'd gain the confidence to know that I was good and wouldn't be plagued by doubt and frustration. Since then, I've learned that's not the way it works. I've met esteemed writers, award winners, authors of best-selling books who still hear the voice of The Critic. As you get your chops and collect publications, your confidence grows but never to the point that The Critic is silenced. And maybe that's good, unless it's keeping you from writing, unless behind your chair The Critic is wailing an off-key version of Linda Ronstadt's classic "You're No Good."

In his book *Darkness Visible,* esteemed author William Styron discusses his nearly overwhelming feelings of self-doubt as he flies to Paris to accept an award. Despite tremendous reviews for her first novel, *A Bigamist's Daughter,* National Book Award-winner Alice McDermott still had such doubts about her ability that she considered quitting writing to attend law school.

The Critic is sometimes personified as a wicked English teacher from high school—Mrs. Crabass. She of the narrowed eyes and prodigious behind, she whose autocratic and hard-hearted insistence on rules of grammar and composition stripped us of our ability to let go, have fun, and be creative. Alas, she ruined us, or nearly so, and we must fight her at every turn.

Maybe. For some reason, I often hear a false note in this characterization. The majority of English teachers I've known and know would weep ecstatic tears if a student showed so much as a hint of an original thought. The Critic is, in fact, within us. We have, perhaps, absorbed the voice, from a teacher or a parent, or created the voice from our mythic personification of The Editor, who mocks with relish our feeble attempts at meaningful narrative. Once again, the voice of The Critic is our own voice. In fact, if we'd absorbed the lessons of composition from our English teachers, we may have fewer doubts about our ability.

The point here is not to "stop your whining." The Critic is a fearsome adversary, no question. And even after your flight to Stockholm to accept the Nobel Prize in literature, after you win the favor and admiration of readers everywhere, that voice still will be there. Publication and praise help, no doubt. As you practice, you will gain confidence, allow yourself to experiment, even risk looking—gasp—stupid.

But the real growth comes from inside, where The Critic resides. In an interview I conducted with author David Guterson, he spoke of this process:

> The actual act of writing is no easier than it was. You can have all the awards and sales and reviews you want, it doesn't get any easier the next day. On the other hand, I feel a deeper confidence in myself. It doesn't come from [his best-selling book] *Snow Falling on Cedars*. It comes from the years going by. I feel more confident because I've practiced more.

When you hear the voice of The Critic telling you your idea is stupid, your writing dull and pedestrian, tell the voice to wait. He may, indeed, be right. And he will have his turn, you promise, but it's not his turn now. The early draft is not the place for The Critic. If he insists on interfering, try not to fight him directly. Instead, observe the voice, name it The Critic, and let it go. Continue writing despite the distraction, just as you've learned to write when your kids have the television cranked and are fighting brutally over the remote control.

Listening and letting go is the process used in meditation to let go of your Thinking Mind. The meditator knows that thoughts will intrude. When they do, she simply tells herself, "Thinking," and lets the thoughts go, without labeling them good or bad, without labeling herself weak or scattered. Don't turn The Critic into that bifocaled, bun-haired termagant with a red pen; don't turn The Critic into that insidious editor with a blue pen. The Critic is a necessary voice, at times. As you grow as a writer, you cultivate an aesthetic, a criteria for recognizing strong writing and weak. With this growth, you become a more useful reader, of your own work and the work of others.

But in the early stages of a piece, send The Critic to a movie or on a nature hike or into the other room where he might at least fold laundry. He'll probably pop his head in from time to time, asking, "Ready for me yet?" In as kind a voice as you can muster, simply say, "Not yet."

THE JUDGE

This guy is your conscience. I see him as Judge Kenesaw Mountain Landis, the first commissioner of baseball. You've probably seen a picture of Landis in history books—a grim-faced, fierce-eyed gent, an old-time moralist, a hard-line arbiter of right and wrong. He appears when we feel guilty about spending time writing. Would our families be better served if we were with them instead of shut behind doors with "Do not disturb" signs warning intruders to stay away? Would our spouses be grateful if we didn't head off to bed early to get up and write in the morning? Shouldn't we, for heaven's sake, be

- raking the yard?
- playing with the kids?
- cleaning the furnace filters?
- making money?
- paying bills?

How selfish of us to demand this time to indulge pointless fantasies of publication. How silly to be working through yet another draft of the memoir, dredging through events that took place twenty years go. This is the voice of The Judge. His weapon: Writer's Guilt.

Women, especially, seem to have a wrangle on their hands with this guy. In our society, women, more so than men, have been raised to ignore their needs, to put themselves at the service of their families. And families, therefore, expect this behavior. Ask your family for an hour alone in the evenings, then watch their need to bond erupt. You'll field more questions and solve more dilemmas than if you'd plopped down in front of the television with them. Or, if you do get the quiet you ask for, the voice of The Judge might start speaking in your head.

In an interview with *Publishers Weekly,* fiction writer Gish Jen spoke of fighting The Judge, even after publishing three successful books:

> Even today, I think my family would be more relieved than dismayed if I were to stop writing. I still struggle with the question, Is it selfish? It's hard on the people around me, it's hard on the children. Is it worth it? I was programmed to be selfless, and I go through periods where I wonder.

Men, too, suffer from Writer's Guilt. We feel we should be out there winning some bread, bringing home some bacon or, at the least, spending time with our spouse and kids. Our own fathers, by God, wouldn't be nursing along some narcissistic novel project when the grass could be cut or the garage painted. What a damp-souled, ineffectual man to have this need to create art at the expense of our dearest loved ones.

Of course, times have changed, and, I hope, things are not quite so regimented and old-fashioned in your world, but there's no denying that Writer's Guilt strikes often, and is tough to beat. The Judge would seem to have bivouacked himself on the moral high ground with a phalanx of rocket launchers and barbed wire. To take back that ground, ask yourself why you're spending time writing rather than with family and friends and your ever-beckoning "To do" list. Is it because of your undying hope of fame and fortune? Are you seeking revenge on high school teachers who said you'd never be a writer? Are you intentionally hiding from responsibilities by using writing as a shield?

Probably not.

If you're writing out of a need to communicate, to hear your own voice on the page, then you owe it to yourself—and to your family—to write. You have a moral imperative to do it. Try to ignore this imperative and you will unleash The Victim, the woeful sod who would write if only the world were a more understanding place. To be the best mother/father, husband/wife, son/daughter, brother/sister, friend or lover you can be, you need to have an outlet for your creativity. Even if those around you don't understand what you're doing, they should be able to understand that.

Of course, stealing creative time may require some sacrifices—getting up earlier, scheduling your time more tightly, delegating some responsibilities to family members. Can you do this and keep writing with a clear conscience? For most people, it's possible. But those blessed or cursed with an especially guilty conscience may have some trouble with The Judge. I may be one of that group. I've always admired people who put their writing first and live their lives accordingly. I remember reading John Gardner's *On Becoming a Novelist,* in which he says, in effect, use the people around you. Live off a spouse. Accept money from parents. Don't get a job. Write, write, write.

For some, this works. Books do get written that way. Take Gardner's advice at face value and make your own choices. My advice leans more toward striking a balance between the needs of others and the needs of your creative life. As much as possible, meld them. Work to see them not as warring factions but as two key elements that make you a unique individual. If The Judge rears his tyrannical head, don't trust what he says. Insist upon your need for writing time. In fact, write about it.

PROMPT: Write about your need for a creative life or simply your need to write. Why do you do it? What needs are fulfilled through it? Call your essay "Why I Write." For examples, you can find an anthology of such essays—titled *Why I Write*, edited by Will Blythe—in which big-name authors explore their need to write. In your essay, be honest and be thorough. Try to achieve a better understanding of your impulse to write. Use this understanding to explain to The Judge, and to all the enemies, why you must write, despite blocks or guilt or a hundred other really cool things to do.

The following excerpt is taken from Lee Smith's essay, title "Everything Else Falls Away," which appeared in *Why I Write.* Throughout the essay, she gives a number of reasons for writing, but this reason stands at the core:

For me, writing is a physical joy. It is almost sexual—not the moment of fulfillment, but the moment when you open the door to the room where your lover is waiting, and everything else falls away.

It does fall away, too. For the time of the writing, I am nobody. Nobody at all. I am a conduit, nothing but a way for the story to come to the page. Oh, but I am terribly alive then, too, though I say I am no one at all; my every sense is keen and quivering.

PROMPT: Write a character description or a poem about a person based on you, one struggling to create some type of art but who is bound by family obligations. When you finish, ask yourself how you feel about this person. Are you sympathetic to his struggle? Then ask yourself if you extend such sympathy to yourself.

THE AUTHOR

Last year, in one of my idea workshops at a writers conference, I guided the conferees through a few prompts to help them generate ideas for essays and articles. When the session was nearly over, a woman in the back shot a vehement arm into the air and asked with barely contained frustration, "So now what do I do with it?" Of course, I hated her on the spot.

But that's beside the point. The true point is that she missed the purpose of the workshop. We were gathered to tap into our creative selves, to generate ideas for pieces that could be developed and completed later. Instead, she was under the spell of The Author, who sees every moment of writing as important and valid only if it leads to publication. Instead of following our own desires to write, we write with the marketplace in mind. We write about what's hot. At nearly every writers conference I attend, I sit on an editor-agent panel, fielding questions about publication. Inevitably, many people want to know what's selling. It's good for any serious writer to understand the marketplace, but writing for the marketplace is usually a bad idea. If you don't feel passionately about a subject, you won't write well about it. If you're writing for a byline or simply to see your name in print, you're probably going to find yourself blocked on a regular basis. This is the curse of The Author.

We all like to be published. It's fun to see our words in print; it's satisfying to reach an audience of readers; it's nice to make a little money for our literary efforts. We feel validated in some way. Publication makes us feel not simply like someone who writes but like A Real Writer. All of these desires are fine. They can help keep us motivated and focused. But in the early stages of a work, you'll be more creative and successful if you send The Author away. Allow her to return at the end of the session to embrace your great work and indulge you in daydreams of glory.

When you've finished a project, put The Author to work zipping off your stories to magazines and websites.

But when you're writing, write. Enjoy the work for its own sake. Relish the process itself. If you don't, The Author will become a voracious, nagging mate who is never satisfied. Publishing is a tough business, full of frustrations for even the most successful writers. If you write primarily to be published and to be An Author, you will never be a happy writer. I swear it. Nothing will be good enough. Publications will take far too long to respond; agents and editors will be hated enemies, fickle in their tastes, cryptic in their responses; less talented writers will get ahead because of their despicably sycophantic sucking up to every well-known writer who comes to town; your work won't receive the praise it deserves; your books will have terrible covers and the publishers will be out to cheat you on your royalties; and no one, no one, no one will ever have the human decency to call you back. In short, no matter how much success you achieve, everything will suck.

As Pema Chödrön says throughout her book *When Things Fall Apart,* give yourself a break. Be kind and compassionate to yourself. Give your creative side the love and respect it deserves. There will be time, if you want, to confront the business of publication. Publication can be a great motivator and is not a bad ambition. But when you're trying to get words on paper, to generate ideas that interest you and fill you with that feeling of elation that making art can inspire, push The Author away.

THE CAPRICIOUS GUEST

The composer Peter Ilyich Tchaikovsky called inspiration The Capricious Guest. Wait for him to arrive and you may be waiting for a long time. Write regularly and you will find ideas flowing through you. In his book *The Craft of Fiction,* William Knott makes the point that The Capricious Guest usually arrives when you no longer need him, when you're doing just fine on your own. He makes the point, too, that when you compare pages you've written in moments of inspiration to those you've written when simply doing your daily work, you won't notice much difference.

The key to beating all of the enemies of creativity is to do your daily work. The experience of writing, as you already know, varies greatly, from times of exquisite, nearly sybaritic delight to spirit-pummeling slogs not unlike the Bataan Death March. Realize that both are part of the process. Some days, the ideas will pour forth. Other days, they won't. Enemies like those we've discussed in this chapter will appear. Know who they are, know where they come from, and keep going.

THE WRITER'S IDEA BOOK

CHAPTER THREE

LEADING A CREATIVE LIFE

The voyage of discovery lies not in finding new land-scapes, but in having new eyes.

—MARCEL PROUST

You are a creative person. You have the power to transform the raw stuff of daily life into something beautiful. Trust yourself. When you are trying to begin a new piece of writing, you needn't strive for some gravity-defying idea. The strain will show. A new idea may appear in something you've already written, a detail that was not explored, a topic that was a small part of a larger one. When you feel blocked on a project, read what you've written so far and focus on what is working well. Push deeper into those ideas. "Creativity often consists of merely turning up what is already there," wrote author Bernice Fitz-Gibbon, adding that, "Right and left shoes were thought up only a little more than a century ago."

We've discussed the need for balancing discipline and joy in your writing, and we've looked at ways to silence the inner voices that hinder creativity. Now let's explore ways to accomplish those goals by getting to know your creative life more completely.

PROMPT: Write about the most creative person you've ever known. Explain why you feel she is so creative, offering examples of her creative accomplishments.

PROMPT: Write about a creative person you admire but don't know personally, such as a famous painter or musician or writer, living or dead. As in the previous prompt, explain why you feel this person is or was so creative. If necessary, do a little research to find out more about this person's creative gifts and habits. When you finish this piece, compare the people you wrote about in these two prompts. What qualities do they share? What qualities do you most admire in them?

PROMPT: Repeat the process one more time, putting yourself at center stage. What qualities in your creative self do you most admire? List your own accomplishments. Be direct and honest—no humility here, please. If necessary, describe your creative life through someone else's eyes. Perhaps this person can be more objective.

WHERE YOU WRITE

Let's begin evaluating your habits by giving you something else to worry about: where you write. This can be an important question or an irrelevant one. You decide how well it applies to you. I know writers who can plop down anywhere and start scribbling. Others need special spots and more lucky talismans gathered around their computers than a bingo player. One person I knew was obsessed with her work space—a desk in her spare bedroom. This was her sanctified altar of creation, and woe be unto him who sat at the desk to sign a birthday card or write a check. Such a violation was catastrophic.

Think about where you write. There is no right or wrong place to do it. Legend has it that Thomas Wolfe wrote standing in his kitchen. And since Wolfe stood 6'6", he usually wrote on top of his refrigerator. The only wrong place is a place you don't like. To write well and often, it must be a pleasure, and finding a place you love to be can be part of that pleasure.

PROMPT: Fantasy time. Describe your ideal writing setting. Fill it in to the last detail. Perch yourself on a balcony overlooking the Pacific. Snuggle yourself next to a fire in a richly paneled study. When you finish the description, read it with an eye toward patterns and details. Do you prefer an open or a closed place? Light or dark colors? A sense of freedom or safety? Again, no right answers here.

PROMPT: As a way to help you notice your surroundings and work space (and, perhaps, improve them), write a detailed description of your work space. Pan your eyes all around you. Look out the window and describe the view. Again: details, details. To this writing, add a few paragraphs describing your feelings about the space. Is it a haven? Does it offer enough privacy? Do family and friends respect the boundaries of this space? If you write in more than one place, do this exercise for each one.

THE WRITER'S IDEA BOOK

Whatever space you use, fill it with things you love, things that make you feel happy, confident, and creative. It's important to like the space. On the other hand, don't use the lack of a space as an excuse not to write. Many are the wannabe writers who are waiting—probably still waiting—for an ideal space to write. When such a space is found or built, the making of literature will commence. Trust me. It won't happen. Waiting for a space is a reason to wait to write. And those who wait are not generating ideas, nor are they getting ideas on paper. The best writing room I ever had was in a house where I lived when I was married. A wonderful shelf ran along every wall, so that I was literally surrounded by books. I had an overstuffed reading chair, a reading lamp, and two windows. I wrote there hardly at all. On the other hand, for a year I worked in a back room of an old house, a room that was added on, and had no heat and little light. I wrote five hours a day, every day. If you deeply want to write, you will write—no matter what type of space you have at your disposal. But, if possible, be good to yourself. Give yourself, as best you can, a space that is yours and that you like. It will make "showing up" that much easier.

PROMPT: Design the ideal writing space. Fill it with all the things you want and love. Take your time and really develop your descriptions. Ladle on the details. Now step back and look at your description. Does it tell you anything about your writing goals and dreams? Does it say anything about your vision of what a writer is? Does it tell you anything about how you see yourself as a writer? Consider these questions. They will help you design a good place for you to write and will help you understand better your own writing impulse.

So now you've imagined a great space for writing. Maybe you already have such a space or one you like very much. If so, congratulations. If you don't, or even if you do, but you still feel stale sometimes, consider writing in other places—the library, the park, a bus. The strange surroundings can infuse your writing with new energy. New ideas pop up and a new zest enters the prose. I'm not, however, a big believer in coffeehouse writing. When you write where others can see you writing, a certain self-consciousness can enter the prose. You are a deep, dark, mysterious writer. For me, writing, in its generative stage, needs to be a private act, even a secret one. The secrecy adds power to the words. But that's my bias. Maybe you have found such a place that, in the company of strangers, you can create a keen sense of aloneness. If that works for you, by all means keep doing it. Each of us finds his own process, his own rituals that spark creativity.

PROMPT: In one week, write for at least a half hour in three different places. After the week is over, if not before, reread what you wrote. Look for variances in tone and voice. Are these differences the result of your moods at those times, or do they stem from the nature of what you were writing? Was one place more productive, more free than the others? If so, revisit that place, especially when you're feeling blocked or stale.

WHEN YOU WRITE

Some of us are morning writers. We are sharpest then, perhaps still fresh from the night's sleep, or with our minds still partly in the world of dreams. We like morning light, the silence of the house before others awake. We enjoy the freedom from the noise of the day, the demands of family and work. We've yet to plug into our to-do self, who scurries about with a head full of errands. Our "monkey minds," as the Buddhists would call them, have not yet turned on.

Some of us prefer writing at night. The day's activities are behind us, our to-do list is completed (or, more likely, abandoned) for the day. This is our time. We can focus. The night brings with it mysteries and dreams of its own. Our imaginations are set free. Some of us find afternoons most productive. Certainly late afternoon, when the shadows grow long and sunlight takes on a golden hue, we feel drawn into ourselves. This feeling can coax ideas to the surface.

I know a few writers who find evenings great for first drafts, in which they make riskier moves, and they revise in the morning, when they feel better able to evaluate the quality of their ideas. One writer I know will not consider a short story finished until she has revised it at various times of day. She needs to see the story from all perspectives—"all her selves," as she says—to be sure she's found all the story's possibilities.

When do you prefer to write? When are you feeling most creative? Not many of us work well at all times. But by cultivating other sides of your creative self—the morning side if you're an evening writer, and vice versa—you can expand the range of your ideas and the tonalities of your world. If you're waking up feeling stale, try waiting until the evening. If you're stuck on a piece of writing, not sure where to go or just tired of it, try looking at it during a time of day when you normally don't write.

PROMPT: Begin a piece of writing in the evening. If you need an idea, flip to the prompts in the next section. Write at least a page. Put away the page. Then, in a few days, write on the same subject, as if starting it from scratch, during a morning session. Put away the page. After a few more days, pull out both pages and compare them. Which do you like better? Try this exercise a few times to help you gauge your best time for being creative.

PROMPT: Write a scene that is set at night. It should possess an element of intrigue or mystery. Write this scene at night. Push yourself to take risks with the language or the images or simply with the events in the scene. Allow the scene to end without resolution so that at least one more scene will be needed to provide some sort of closure. Write that scene in the morning. Put the scenes away for a few days, then take them out and read them. Do they connect? Do the actions and the tone match?

Nicholson Baker, who I mentioned earlier, takes the process a step further. As he begins writing a novel, he develops a new process that he hopes will shape the story as well as the tone. In his novel *A Box of Matches*, the protagonist wakes early every morning and ruminates about his life while gazing into a fire he builds in his hearth. Baker woke very early to write that book. He even turned down the "brightness" on his computer screen to increase his sense of dark mornings. For his novel *The Anthologist*, he videotaped himself talking—even teaching to an imaginary class—to capture a clearer sense of the protagonist's voice. Each approach, he says, affects the sound of the novel.

HOW YOU WRITE

You'll be more creative if you approach writing in a healthy state of mind, one conducive to letting go of inhibitions. Some writers meditate to achieve this state; others drink a glass of wine. We'll explore specific ways to get started in the next chapter, but let's spend a few minutes examining the state of mind we're trying to achieve. I believe that we want to achieve an alert passivity, a state of mind that allows us to trust our instincts and frees us to take risks.

YIELD

Ideas don't respond to the force of our wills—damn them. We can't make them appear. That's why, when we're feeling blocked, it does little good to try to pound our way through. It won't work. We'll grow even more frustrated and further away from where we need to be to find ideas (though I'll admit a good hard slam of fist onto table feels pretty good at those times).

Getting ideas requires allowing our minds to yield. The ideas are there, but we have to wait for them quietly. Poet William Stafford compared the creative process to fishing. We cast a line into the water, then wait silently, patiently, for a nibble. If we make a lot of noise, the fish won't bite. With experience, we learn how to read a nibble, how to wait for the right moment to pull the fish in.

The process also can be compared to yoga. We learn to resist the temptation to force a stretch or a twist. Our impulse is to push ourselves, to stretch or twist farther than we have before. But the teacher will tell us to yield to the stretch, to "breathe into it." Then we can go deeper because our bodies are not straining. We're relaxing into what we are able to do naturally.

Maintaining this mind-set is not easy. We live in a results-oriented society. We learn to be productive, to have something to show for our efforts. We want proof we are making progress, getting better. As writers, we want finished pieces, and each piece should be better than the one before it. If we're going to the trouble of rising at the crack of dawn, we'd better get something out of it.

To be more creative, you need to resist these impulses. Some days will be effortless. Some days will be impossible, just as some days, the fish bite and other days, they don't. Your job is to show up, to write and enjoy, not to evaluate.

PROMPT: I used two metaphors for yielding—fishing and yoga. Think of a few of your own. What activities do you do that require this approach? Describe the process. Teach it to someone who has never done it.

GET IN YOUR BELLY

In her book *Awakening the Warrior Within,* Dawn Callan speaks of a warrior's ability to "get in the belly." By this, she means the practice of trusting your instincts and depending upon them to avoid the distractions of thought and emotion. If you've seen experienced martial artists spar, you've noticed that their bodies are loose and relaxed until the moment they strike. They breathe gently. They trust their training to defend them against an attack and disable the attacker. If they think too much, their bodies won't respond naturally. If they feel too much—anger, fear, aggression—they lose their balance, missing opportunities to strike and making themselves vulnerable to attack. As writers, we can take a similar approach. Get in your belly. Trust your instincts. Don't listen to the voices we discussed in the last chapter. When an idea rises to the surface, be ready to seize it. If you practice your writing, read good work, build your vocabulary, study the craft, remain aware of the world around you, and keep your imagination fresh and fertile, the ideas will come and you'll recognize them.

PROMPT: Open this book to any page and do one of the prompts. Don't consider if it interests you or is appropriate to your background. As you do it, try to move past distracting thoughts and feelings. Focus on the prompt and let yourself go.

THE WRITER'S IDEA BOOK

TAKE RISKS

Winston Churchill once said that the key to success for the beginning artist is audacity. I think that's the key to success of an artist at any level of experience. When you find an idea, push it to its limits. Explore all of its possibilities. Too often, we decide what type of idea we want, knowing what will work for us. We reject other ideas before really digging around in them, especially if they demand that we go beyond where we normally go—in length, in depth, in emotional connection. An idea can seem "too crazy" or "impossible to pull off."

Compare this reaction to learning to doing a somersault when you're a kid. Yeah, yeah, you were a plucky four-year-old and just flipped right over. But for the rest of us, that first trip over the top was a little scary. After we put our heads on the ground and kicked our legs up a bit, we let them fall back to the ground. Sometimes it takes someone to pull our legs over the first time. We felt sort of dizzy, but the movement was fun. Before we knew it, we were flipping backward off diving boards.

Many ideas never develop because we grow bored with them. We aren't blocked as much as we're just not interested anymore. This boredom could signal a weak idea not worth developing. But before abandoning it, try adding a new element. Take a risk. Up the stakes a bit. Surprise yourself. Risk embarrassment. When you hear yourself say, "I can't let anybody read this," or, "This is too weird," you've probably hit a vein worth mining a little deeper.

Sometimes you'll finish a piece and not like it. For some reason, it just doesn't shimmer. Perhaps the problem is that it's too safe, too pat. As an editor and contest judge, I've read hundreds of stories that were done well but weren't interesting. Of course, in some cases, it's a matter of taste. But sometimes the stories simply lacked the energy that comes from a writer's true and total engagement. My advice is to try to find the spark in the piece. Pull it out and pour some time into that place. If you widen your imaginative net, you'll catch more ideas. Follow Winnie's dictum: Risk audacity.

CHAPTER FOUR

READING IS FUNDAMENTAL

A good style simply doesn't form unless you absorb half a dozen topflight authors every year.

—F. SCOTT FITZGERALD

The author W.P. Kinsella *(Shoeless Joe, Box Socials)* tells his students that they have to write forty stories before they can write one about the death of a family member. His reason for this rule: He reads too many dead grandparent stories in his classes.

Allow me to augment his dictum a bit. Don't try to write a short story until you've read fifty of them, preferably a hundred. Don't try to write a novel until you've read fifty of them, preferably a hundred. The same is true for scripts, essays, poems, and so on.

I'm only being partly serious. If you feel compelled to write, I won't recommend delaying the urge. But when you begin that short story, begin your process of reading fifty stories. I cannot stress enough that reading is fundamental to learning how to write. In fact, if there's a *secret* to learning to write well—other than, of course, writing and writing and writing—it's reading, reading, reading. Nearly all of the good writers I've ever known love to read. Many writers who continue to struggle with the craft do not read a lot. A personal observation. If you are serious in your desire to improve as a writer, and I could limit my advice to a single word, it would be *read*.

WHY READ

Reading adds richness to your language and imagination. By reading *good* work, we learn the sound of good writing. We learn how to handle the elements of craft. We cultivate an aesthetic, developing and honing our opinions about what works and why. We learn about—and thereby more truly inherit—the tradition in which we're working. We even can steal techniques, ideas, and phrases from the masters.

I've noticed that apprentices who don't progress as writers haven't read much. The language of their work lacks richness. They have not cultivated a critical aesthetic that would make them good editors of their own work. They make the same mistakes time and again. They don't know the sound of good writing.

Yes, there are those blessed with exceptionally rich material—life experience that supplies their work with a power that makes for compelling stories all by itself. Or they have a natural sense of voice that connects with readers in an almost primal way. You probably know some writers of this type. They haven't read much, but their work transcends the limitations of their ability. Most of us, however, must work to unearth our material and to discover our voices. Part of that work, of learning the craft, involves reading.

Reading feeds your imagination. It puts you in touch with the language part of your brain. It develops your vocabulary. It teaches you the names of things. It shows you how successful writers work, the techniques they use to develop characters and structure stories. It places you within the ongoing literary discussion of the times in which you live. In fact, I feel safe in saying that if you don't read widely and well, you won't be as good a writer as you can be. Amass, if you will, evidence to the contrary, and I'll still believe that reading is a fundamental element of writing.

Through the years, I've heard a number of apprentice writers claim they're as good as this or that much more accomplished writer. They'll decry the "crap being published today" while their own work is ignored. It's not tough, I'll admit, to find plenty of examples of published work that was better left unpublished, but usually when I hear these writers make such claims, I'm much more painfully aware of what they are missing, the undetected differences between what they're doing and what the more successful writer is doing. They lack the critical faculties to notice those differences, and the lack of those critical faculties makes improvement a very slow process.

If you believe that most of what you read is crap (and you're reading well published books and magazines), perhaps you simply don't like to read, which could mean you really don't like to write all that much. You're pursuing a craft for which you have no genuine passion. You may be writing, therefore, for the wrong reasons. I hear writers, for example, say that they don't read literary magazines because "they're so boring," and yet those writers are trying to publish in those magazines.

If you want to be a good writer, you have to read a lot, and you have to learn to read like a writer. It's that simple. If you want to be able to assess and develop your writing ideas more effectively, you have to read widely and well. By reading, you develop your critical aesthetic. You learn what works and what doesn't. You learn what's been done and what's been done to death. You learn the techniques that work and those that don't. You learn the techniques that may have worked in the past but no longer work.

In *On Writing*, Stephen King sums up the point very well:

> The real importance of reading is that it creates an ease and intimacy with the process of writing; one comes to the country of the writer with one's papers and identification pretty much in order. Constant reading will pull you into a place (a mind-set, if you like the phrase) where you can write eagerly and without self-consciousness. It also offers you a constantly growing knowledge of what has been done and what hasn't, what is trite and what is fresh, what works and what just lies there dying (or dead) on the page. The more you read, the less apt you are to make a fool of yourself with your pen or word processor.

In short: If you want to be a good judge of your ideas and understand why they're working or why they're not working, you have to read.

PROMPT: Make a list of your five all-time favorite pieces of writing—the poems, stories, novels, or whatever that you find yourself returning to again and again. Re-read those five pieces, this time from the perspective of one writer learning from another. Make notes in the margins of the book or in your notebook. Focus on the ideas that drive the piece and how the writer was able to execute those ideas on the page. What obstacles were overcome? How did the writer complicate and develop the ideas? What words and phrases affect you most powerfully?

PROMPT: Make a list of the books you've read in the past year, writing a sentence or two about each one. Then choose your favorites and write about how the writer moved you or impressed you. What qualities about their work did you particularly enjoy?

WHAT YOU READ

If you're going to learn how good writing sounds and how it works, and if you're going to learn how to assess your ideas, you'll have to read good writing. Inferior work is not going to teach you a lot. Read the great stylists and the great storytellers. Read classic as well as contemporary writers. Read writers who work in various forms. If you write fiction, don't limit yourself to reading only fiction.

Do read, however, the masters of the form in which you write. If you are working on a mystery novel, you should know the masters of the genre. Without a clear sense of the tradition in which you're working, it's tough to write well. You'll spend a great deal of time making discoveries that have been made many times before you. Sometimes, of course, we have to discover something for ourselves to understand it fully, but learning the basic lessons of the craft can involve much more time in trial and error if you don't bother to read what's been done before.

Some apprentices worry that they'll be tempted to imitate the masters if they spend time reading them: the old "anxiety of influence." They fear they won't find their own unique voice. They fear their ideas will lack originality. This concern, I think, is vastly overrated. Most apprentices can benefit much more from that type of influence than by trying to avoid it. In the early stages of your development as a writer, you might sound like an imitation of your favorite writer, but as you continue your progress, your own voice will emerge. The stylistic tendencies of the influential writer will drop away because they'll sound false. They won't sound like you. Your own ideas will break away from the master's ideas. In the meantime, you'll be learning the craft and learning how good writing works.

No less a writer than the late great John Updike admitted in an interview in *Guernica* magazine, published around the time of his death, that as he reads, he keeps an eye peeled for words, images, and rhythms he can, well, steal. He says:

> Yeah, you're always looking for something . . . . I have stolen images, I think, in the course of my work, when I thought nobody would notice. Sure. At first, I think trying to form an approach to writing you look for a model. But after you're formed, then basically you kind of read for things so admirable that you wish you had done them and you're not above maybe stealing them, if you can find a good place to hide them.

Updike sounds a bit glib here and self-effacing, but he also is stating a truth about writers that is worth noting and is one of the values of reading. From other writers, we can discover and adapt strategies. None of us writes in a vacuum. We can—and must—draw on our literary heritage. In a famous—and often misquoted—statement, T.S. Eliot says it well:

> Immature poets imitate; mature poets steal; bad poets deface what they take, and good poets make it into something better, or at least something different. The good poet welds his theft into a whole of feeling which is

unique, utterly different from that from which it was torn; the bad poet throws it into something which has no cohesion.

We often hear writers and even teachers of writing use the opening of this statement, and often they use it without a firm grasp on the point. They use it in a facile rationalization of a theft rather than to suggest that they have made whatever they have stolen into something else, have given it their own singular stamp. And that's the point Eliot is making: If a poet does not weave the theft organically into his own work, the theft is obvious, calling attention to itself as something that doesn't belong.

PROMPT: Steal an idea from something you've read. And not just a little idea. Steal the premise of a piece, its main conflict or situation. Write at least a page, shamelessly lifting this premise but changing names of characters, location, whatever. Then, after a page, add a complication of your own, one different from the first major complication in the piece. Write at least one more page.

PROMPT: Think about a specific area of writing that is particularly challenging to you—perhaps you struggle with suggesting the passage of time or have a propensity to insert too many explanations into your scenes. Then look for a model in which a writer handles this stylistic challenge in a way you admire. Now write a passage in which you use whatever techniques that writer uses. Just lift the device or language or whatever it is and flow it into your own piece.

PROMPT: Extend the story of a minor character or person in a piece you've read. Is there a character in a novel who intrigues you, who you wish played a larger role? Spend a session exploring that character's life, circumstances, or situation. James B. Hall took this approach in a story he wrote about Friday, the sidekick in Daniel Defoe's *Robinson Crusoe*. The title character does not appear in the story at all. It takes place after Crusoe has been rescued.

PROMPT: Steal a line from something you've read. It might only be a phrase, but grab that sucker and plunk it into a piece of your own. If you don't have a piece in progress, spend a session exploring an idea in which that line or phrase can appear.

HOW YOU READ

Reading as a writer requires that you slow down and pay attention to the story as a story. It requires reading a passage, even an entire piece, more than once. The first time through, you can allow yourself to be caught up in the story (though the more you read as a writer, the tougher it becomes to let go completely of your consciousness of the piece

THE WRITER'S IDEA BOOK

as a piece, as something created by a writer). After you finish a piece that strikes you as successful in some way, go back and find out how the writer achieved that success.

During the time I was an editor at *Story* magazine, I read thousands of stories. This job helped me improve tremendously as a writer. It introduced me to the work of many wonderful writers, of course, but it was particularly helpful because it required that I read many times the stories we selected for publication. The staff would read those stories a few times before deciding to accept it. Then we would read it again with an eye toward editing, working with the writer to make any final changes. Then I would read it another couple of times while copyediting and fact-checking the story. Then it would be typeset and I would proofread the story a few more times. In all, I probably read those stories more than a dozen times. The repetition helped me realize how the stories worked. I learned how the stories were structured and how the writers achieved certain effects.

To read as a writer, try to put yourself in the writer's place. What ideas drive the piece? What possibilities exist within those ideas? Given those possibilities, what choices did the writer make? Why? What difficulties are overcome and how did the writer succeed?

The more you read as a writer, the better you'll become. *Elements of the Writing Craft,* by Robert Olmstead, is a very good book on this subject, and I recommend it highly. Olmstead breaks storytelling down to its smallest moves and provides examples from great writing to show those moves in action. If you want to learn how to read better as a writer, get a copy of this book.

Get copies of a lot of books. Begin reading them. Make time in your weekly schedule for reading. You'll find yourself improving more quickly as a writer, and you'll find yourself a much more insightful critic of your own work. If an idea isn't working, you'll know it—and why—more quickly than before.

PROMPT: From your list of five all-time favorites, choose one piece and spend at least a week reading it a number of times. If it's a long piece, such as a novel, read a few chapters or a section. Each time you read it, make more notes. Again, practice reading as a writer. Assess what's working. Assess what you'd have done differently. Concentrate on discovering how the writer brought the main ideas to life.

PROMPT: Dig through your archives of writing and read something you wrote a long time ago. It might be a school report or a diary entry or a creative piece. After you recover from the glow (or the horror) of nostalgia, try to read it objectively. What ideas drive the piece? Can you read it objectively? If, at the time, you thought it was a fabulous piece, what do you think now? Can it be saved?

PROMPT: Write a brief report about a piece you've written, but write the report from the point of view of an objective reader. Refer to "the writer" rather than to yourself. Assess what's working with the piece and what needs help. Consider what you, "the reviewer," would have done differently.

PROMPT: Keep an ongoing list of new words you learn while reading. Make this list a key part of your writer's notebook.

PROMPT: Keep an ongoing list of phrases and sentences that strike you as particularly good in what you read. Get into the habit of writing them down.

PROMPT: Read something in a form you usually don't read, and spend a session adding elements of that form to an ongoing project—or you might try beginning a new project. For example, if you usually limit your reading to literary fiction, spend a couple of hours with a thriller or romance novel. As we've discussed, read as a writer, noting how stories in the form are told. What assumptions do they make of their readers? How are conflicts established? How are the characters presented?

MOVING FORWARD

Keeping in mind the ideas about the nature and craft of writing we covered in this first section of the book, let's move ahead and begin exploring subjects for actual pieces—fiction, nonfiction, poetry, or whatever form and genre you prefer. I hesitate to say that this is the "fun part" because every stage of writing can be—and should be—fun. But in section two, we do get to talk (and write) quite a bit about ourselves, which, let's be honest, is a whole lot of fun. We get to tell stories and explore our tastes and hobbies, our memories and our thoughts on a wide rage of subjects. Again: fun stuff. Just keep in mind as we move on that you'll hear from "The Enemies of Creativity" and that you must continue to read and to be willing to explore subjects that might not always be comfortable. If you find yourself distracted or unable to focus on a prompt that really grabs you, just breathe, remember that you're not being graded on any of this writing and that you are doing it, ultimately, because writing is something you want to do, even need to do. Nothing else is at stake. No gold stars will be given out at the end, and if your first attempts fizzle, it doesn't mean you are a failure. The process is a way of discovering and accessing new parts of ourselves—and thereby enlarging ourselves. It's about understanding ourselves in new ways and understanding the world around us. It's about discovering empathy. Put your emphasis there and the rest will take care of itself.

Part II

EXPLORING
ideas

CHAPTER FIVE

I YAM WHAT I YAM AND OTHER LIES

The writer can only explore the inner space of his characters by perceptively navigating his own.

—PETER DE VRIES

I love Popeye. I used to love him because someone I once loved collected Popeye memorabilia, and together we'd scour antique shops in search of Popeye stuff. We built a fine collection. During that time, the old sailor sort of grew on me. Who, for heaven's sake, doesn't like Popeye? An even larger question: Why do we like Popeye, a sketchy, quirky refugee from a long-forgotten comic strip? Most of his contemporaries have faded to obscurity or, in the case of superheroes, have been updated for today's audience. Not Popeye. He's still drawn in those primitive lines, still follows the single flimsy plotline of nabbing the fickle Olive Oyl from the hairy clutches of Bluto by glugging down a thatch of spinach.

His appeal, I think, is in his simplicity. He yis what he yis. That's comforting. We all would like to be that sure of who we are, but noncartoon characters like us are a lot more complicated. Getting at who we are is tough to do, and who we are changes depending on day, time, location, and circumstance. We are parent, boss, motorist, son/daughter, employee, mate, shortstop, tourist, reader, writer, expert, novice, and many other identities. As writers, we suffer from even more elusive identities. We are "the chameleon poet" and we "contain multitudes." There is a famous anecdote about the poet James Dickey nervously waiting backstage before a national television appearance. Someone told him, "Relax, just be yourself," and he answered, "Which one?"

So it's a bit troubling when books on writing and creativity urge us to write from our true self, as if there exists inside us a single *real* person, that the other selves are merely cranks and imposters who can be dismissed, leaving only the authentic person, from whom a tidal wave of words and ideas will rush forth. Truth is, that won't happen.

But getting to know who you are as a person is indeed helpful—and it's probably one of the reasons that you write. It's also helpful to get to know yourself better to find the sources of your creativity.

PROMPT: List the top ten experiences of your life—*top* meaning significant. Wondrous. Glorious. Terrible. Illuminating. Demoralizing. Jubilant. Ten, of course, is an arbitrary number. But start there. Think about it for a moment, letting your mind roam free, keeping your pen on the page. There's no penalty for going beyond ten, but if you do, cut to ten when you review the list. Stop reading now and make your list.

How did you do? Did you stop at ten? Did you find yourself listing the *big* events—births of children, marriage, divorce, relocations, career moves? I did. Now take time to make another list of ten. We've cleared the monuments from the field and can now look at smaller ones.

PROMPT: Brainstorm a new list of ten events.

PROMPT: From your lists, pick one event. Don't think about it for long. Choose the first one that pops into your head. Or, if you want, discard the first one and choose another. The second one is often better. Explore it in a piece of writing by recounting the event in a narrative—first this happened, then this, then this, etc. Take your time and put yourself back in that place and time. Relax and allow the memories to trickle into your mind. You'll be surprised by what you remember. The act of writing pulls memories from the depths of our subconscious minds, which is one of the great aspects of the process. I've been told by students more times than I can count that they remembered far more details about the event than they expected to recall when they started writing. After you've finished telling the story, write a few paragraphs about why this was a significant moment, or better, how it was significant. What did it mean to you? How did it change you? What does its significance say about you?

PROMPT: Spend a writing session making top ten lists of events in your life. Top ten happy times or enlightening times or whatever you want. Then look at these lists for patterns—recurring themes and images. Try to view them objectively, as if they happened to someone else. Who is this person? What do you like about her? What motivates this person? What mistakes does she continue to make? What demons dog her? What qualities does this person possess and how would you, as the objective writer, express these qualities?

PROMPT: Write about your first experience with death. Who died? When? What did you know about death before the event, and what did you come to learn after the event?

PROMPT: Write about your first experience with birth (not your own, of course). Who was born? What did you know about birth before the event, and what did you come to learn about it after the event?

PROMPT: Describe yourself from the perspective of someone you know, in a first-person monologue, as if the person were describing you to someone else. (To ensure your friend's candor, let's say you're not around when this description takes place.) Try this exercise a few times, choosing several people to describe you. Be faithful to the people you've chosen in all of these descriptions. Describe yourself in their voices, from their true perspectives.

PROMPT: Keep a grocery receipt—a long one. When you get home, put it away and then pull it out a few weeks from now. What does this person buy, and what can you tell about this person from what she buys?

PROMPT: Spend a few minutes looking in the mirror. Just stare back at your reflection. Then write a self-portrait, describing yourself in detail. Try to imagine that you're looking at a stranger. What assumptions would you make from this person's appearance?

PROMPT: While we're looking in the mirror, what is your best physical feature? Write a physical description of yourself emphasizing that feature. Explore its history, so to speak. Do people compliment you on it? Has it led to any romantic encounters (or romantic turmoil)? Tell those stories.

PROMPT: At the risk of blatant narcissism, keep looking in that mirror. What physical quality do you like least about yourself? Has it led to self-consciousness or attempts to hide it? As you did in the previous prompt, explore its history. When did you become aware of it? How has it affected your life?

PROMPT: Brainstorm a list, beginning each entry with the words "I am a ..." Don't stop yourself during this brainstorm, even if you feel the word or phrase that comes to mind seems silly or just plain wrong. In a number of my workshops, this prompt has yielded some surprising results.

PROMPT: Make a list of the things in your home that are yours: furnishings, pictures on the walls, souvenirs. Go from room to room and write down what you find. Write about what these things say about the person. If you could pick one item from your list as emblematic of you, which one would you choose? Write about why you chose this item. Choose another item and try again.

PROMPT: Remember the old question that goes something like, "If you could be any kind of tree, what would you be?" Dumb, I know. But let's use it, changing it to, "If you *were* a tree, what kind would you be?" How would you answer, and why do you think so? If you want, try it with car, animal, bird, food, color, or era in history.

PROMPT: Personal blogs are all the rage, so maybe you've already given this medium some thought, maybe you are blogging already. If not, or even if you are, brainstorm at least five ideas for personal blogs you could create, ones that focus on personal interests—gardening or motherhood or whatever. Now review your list. Which subjects seem most appealing to you? They offer insight into your passions, the subjects ripest for exploration in your writing.

PROMPT: Mona Simpson begins her story "Lawns" with the sentence "I steal." Begin a story or essay or poem or journal entry with the line "I _____." Push forward from there. If you can think of one action that speaks to who you are, what would it be? Write at least a few paragraphs. Try this experiment a few times, using different actions.

PROMPT: Keep a dream journal for at least a week, preferably longer, waking up every morning and writing down what you can remember. Write about a character who appears in one of your dreams, someone who lingers in your mind or has appeared in past dreams. Who is this character? What can you learn about yourself from him or her?

PROMPT: Do you have a five-year plan? If not, take time to make one. Write down how you want your life to be in five years. When you finish, read what you've written and think about *why* you want to achieve these goals. What do the goals imply about your life as it is now? What do they suggest about you as a person?

PROMPT: Cast yourself five years into the future. You have achieved all the goals you wrote about in the previous prompt. In the persona of you-five-years-from-now, write a letter to the current you. Having achieved the goals, what advice would you impart to yourself? Explain how it feels to be living the life that you now hope to achieve.

THE MANY FACES OF YOU

All of these prompts should help you begin exploring yourself. The other chapters in this section will help, too, by focusing on specific facets of your background, your experiences and your personality. In working through these chapters, allow yourself to have fun and to take risks. Enjoy the process. Be daring. Don't worry about sounding literary or angry or weak or whatever tag you're tempted to stick on yourself. In fact, avoid tags of any kind. The key is candor. You need only bring the courage to dig deep inside yourself.

And learn the lesson of Popeye: Don't worry about consistency. He is what he is, but you have many facets and dimensions. Need proof? Read your journal. Not only will you find yourself in many moods, your handwriting will change from day to day. Remember Emerson's line about consistency being "the hobgoblin of little minds."

PROMPT: You are afflicted with a rare (and getting rarer) disease in which you can only tell the truth, the whole truth. No holding back. Now, introduce yourself to someone you don't know—on the page, of course. Explain to the stranger who you are. Go into detail. Tell your life story if you have to. The stranger is fictitious and, unlike a real person, will listen intently for hours.

PROMPT: Create two or three characters from facets of your personality. Put them in a car, driving to the coast (whichever coast is farthest from where you live). Who takes the wheel? Who navigates? Give them a topic of conversation, such as the best route to take or what they should do when they arrive.

PROMPT: Prepare questions for an interview with someone you admire. Try to get at what makes that person tick. Ask her probing, personal questions, no matter how inappropriate they might seem. When you've finished your script, ask these questions of yourself. And answer them.

PROMPT: Transport yourself back to when you were twelve years of age. Close your eyes and really try to put yourself into your own twelve-year-old mind. Have that child prepare a list of questions for you—questions about life and what to expect, questions about love, questions seeking advice on the trials of a twelve-year-old. Now bring yourself back and respond to those questions. Explain why you've lived as you have, why you made the decisions you've made, and how you feel about those decisions.

Try the same experiment again, this time imagining yourself much older than your current age. What observations and advice does Old You have to offer?

PROMPT: Write an alternate story of your life, like an alternate history book, in which the author changes one key fact of history, then explores the possible changes that would occur as a result. Change one key fact of your life, one decision that you made, and explore how your life would be different. If you hadn't committed to your mate, for example, or moved to a new city or passed up a certain opportunity, how would things change? You can do this in a serious way, striving for the most plausible possibilities, or you can go wild, concocting crazy scenarios. Better yet: Do it both ways.

PROMPT: You need a reference, someone to say what a wonderful person you are. Perhaps you're at the gates of heaven and there's some question about letting you in. Pick the person you would ask for this reference and write what he'd say.

PROMPT: Wait a second. You're not past the pearly gates yet. A second reference has been found, someone you know who will not say good things about you. Write her rebuttal to the previous prompt.

PROMPT: Write a monologue in which a character describes herself—her nature rather than her appearance. As her description develops, begin to make clear that her self-portrait is not accurate. She might, for example, speak in a self-congratulatory tone about her humility, or she might mention events in her life to prove she is a terrible person, when in fact they show she was justified in her actions. Remember Huck Finn's self-accusatory description of himself as a bad person for hiding his friend Jim, the slave. This character is not self-effacing or a liar; he simply has no insight into his true nature. Let's face it: We all have blind spots, a lack of awareness about ourselves. This person, however, is pretty much one big blind spot.

PROMPT: Recall a time when someone told you something about yourself that surprised you—an observation about some trait the person believes you possess, one that, even now, you're not quite convinced is true. Put yourself in that moment and then put it on the page. How did you react at the time? Did the person's observation make you see yourself in a different light?

PROMPT: Write about a time when you acted in a way you consider out of character. For example, if you think of yourself as shy in social gatherings, recall a time when you were the life of the party. If you think of yourself as calm and diplomatic, recall a time when you, uh, weren't.

PROMPT: Another classic question to shed insight on yourself: If you were a superhero, what power would you possess? And what would you do with that power? How would you use it? If it sounds fun, spend a writing session focusing on this superhero—putting him or her into action. Or, if it sounds more fun, cast yourself as a supervillain. What power do you possess and what would you do with it? Base these supercharacters on aspects of yourself. In other words, have them embody qualities and flaws you recognize in yourself.

PROMPT: Begin a story with a character based closely on you. Put the character in a place you've never been and write about what happens.

PROMPT: Begin a story with a character based closely on you, who is told he or she has a very negative quality or trait. At first she dismisses this observation but awakens to the fact that it's true.

PROMPT: For the last prompt in the chapter, let's return to where we started, with a comic strip character. Cast yourself in the starring role of a comic strip. It's called "Your Name." Describe this character, the supporting characters, and the tone and focus of the comic strip. Would it offer trenchant political commentary? The foibles and frolics of family life? Whimsical wit about the single life? Daily life as viewed by a group of cats? A world of children coming of age? Okay, I'm out of descriptions. You take it from here.

CHAPTER SIX

SCHNITZEL WITH NOODLES

If there's a book you really want to read but it hasn't been written yet, then you must write it.

—TONI MORRISON

Knowing what to write, as we've discussed, involves knowing yourself. You will write with passion if you write about topics and people close to your heart.

I learned this truth again when a friend told me he wanted to be a writer but was struggling. He'd been a cop for more than fifteen years but was tired of the job. In a few more years, he could retire with a full pension, which he planned to use to support himself while he knocked out novels. Crime novels. He had the experience, we agreed. He should give it a try. But the pages of what I read were dull, larded with technical jargon and the accoutrements of police work. They were weak on plot and character. He clearly was not engaged by the stories.

One night while we were talking about how to make his stories more interesting, we drifted to the subject of his collection of beer memorabilia. As he discussed the old beer bottles and vintage advertisements that filled his house, his eyes lit up. He was clearly engaged. We agreed that maybe he was writing about something he didn't really like—police work—and the novels reflected his disinterest. He should try, instead, to write about beer stuff. He did, and he has since published several excellent articles in trade magazines. He also was a big Elvis fan and eventually wrote a book of trivia about The King.

The point is that the truism about writing what you know isn't exactly true. Instead, write about what you *like*. If you're afraid to write about what you know because you think readers will be bored, don't be so sure. If you're afraid to write about what you know because *you're* bored, trust your instincts. Avoid that subject. Too often, we choose to write about what we think other people will like, or about what's hot in the marketplace. If writing about something feels like a guilty pleasure, you're on the right track.

PROMPT: I picked a corny title to this chapter, so let's use it. Write a list of a few of your favorite things. If possible, don't stop at a few. Write a list of a lot of your favorite things—foods, activities, possessions, seasons, settings, whatever comes to mind. Brainstorm your list and add to it later as more things occur to you. An artful example of this process occurs in Woody Allen's *Manhattan* when the protagonist is lying on a couch, speaking into a handheld recorder, rattling off the things he loves best, from Cézanne's still lifes to Willie Mays. With the list, he slowly builds to whom he loves most of all, a woman he left earlier in the film for another woman. Pick an item from your list and explore it, giving your reasons for liking the item or developing a history, perhaps, of how long you've liked it, what associations it holds for you, particular memories of enjoying the item.

PROMPT: In *Manhattan*, another character builds a list of overrated people and things, popular favorites the character feels receive unwarranted praise. Compile your own list of overrated things. As with the previous prompt, look for patterns in the list, trends that say something about you as the compiler. Then choose an item and write about it as you did with the one above.

PROMPT: Pick an item from each list and write a piece comparing them in some way. Avoid simply making it "This is good; this is bad." What qualities do they share? How might someone dislike the thing you like and like the thing you don't? Try hard to make a fair, detailed assessment. Develop a convincing case, perhaps in a light, humorous way.

PROMPT: Let's play the old "If you could take five things to a desert island, what would they be?" game. This will help narrow your list of favorites. Write about why you would choose these five things. Then imagine yourself on that island for six months or a year. Which items have grown dull in your eyes? Which ones continue to shine?

PROMPT: Write about a favorite thing from your childhood. A doll you carried everywhere? A prized baseball card? If you want, explore what your attachment to

THE WRITER'S IDEA BOOK

this object suggests about you as a child. Why do you think it was such an important thing in your life?

PROMPT: Write about a desired thing in your childhood that you didn't own, something you wanted—such as a toy or a trip to Disneyland—that you didn't get. Give us the details. How long did you covet this thing? What does your desire for it tell you about yourself as a child? If this focus interests you, do it again but explore your teens. What did you want during that time? If you want, push into your adulthood.

PROMPT: Write about a favorite activity in your childhood, something you enjoyed and did as often as possible. As with the previous prompt, look for insights into yourself as a child through this examination of the activity. In his poem "The Hummer," William Matthews writes of a boy who plays countless baseball games in his mind while pitching a wet tennis ball against a toolshed door:

> Some days he pitched
> six games, the last in dusk,
> in tears, in rage, in the blue
> blackening joy of obsession.

PROMPT: The previous few prompts about favorite things from childhood probably brought back many memories. So let's go back there and write about your beloved thing from your perspective at the time—the child who cherishes the thing. You could present a memory as a present-tense event or you could fictionalize it, whichever is more interesting to you.

PROMPT: Now render the action from the previous prompt from your perspective as an adult, looking back with the wisdom and insight you can offer now but lacked as a child.

PROMPT: Has anything ever been too much of a "favorite thing" in your life? An addiction? If so, write about the addiction and your experience with it. If you've never struggled with addiction, create a fictional character who is addicted to something and have him describe his feelings about his compulsion. In her memoir, *Drinking: A Love Story*, Caroline Knapp chronicles her battle with alcoholism. In the following excerpt, she explores her love for alcohol:

> I loved the way drink made me feel, and I loved its special power of deflection, its ability to shift my focus away from my own awareness of self onto something else, something less painful than my own feelings. I loved the sounds of drink: the slide of a cork as it eased out of a wine bottle, the distinct glug-glug of booze pouring into a glass, the clatter of ice cubes in

a tumbler. I loved the rituals, the camaraderie of drinking with others, the warming, melting feelings of ease and courage it gave me.

PROMPT: In the previous prompt, Caroline Knapp gives us specific details about the sound of her addiction. These sounds suggest her feelings about the subject. Use her example to write about a favorite activity by focusing on the sounds of it. No need to focus on an addiction. The activity can be something positive and beautiful in your life. The key is concentrating your imagination on the sounds.

PROMPT: Repeat the previous prompt, this time focusing on the smells involved in a favorite activity.

PROMPT: Repeat the previous prompt, this time focusing on the tastes involved in a favorite activity.

PROMPT: One more time, though now focus on the sense of touch.

PROMPT: And once again, this time pulling your favorite sensory details from each of the previous pieces, mixing them in surprising ways. Can you build on this fully developed description, bringing in action and character?

YOU ARE WHAT YOU LIKE

Writing about favorites can be a way to characterize yourself as a writer to your audience and can be a way to see yourself from an oblique angle, or through the filter of an objective thing, so that you might better understand yourself. Anna Quindlen, for example, begins an essay with the sentence "I was a Paul girl," meaning that, as a young girl, her favorite Beatle was Paul McCartney. Girls who liked Paul were different from the ones who liked John, George, or Ringo. Each musician, apparently, attracted a different type of girl. The essay establishes her childhood identity as a Paul type, a bit conventional and romantic, and explores the changes she's undergone since those days.

On the other hand, David Foster Wallace, in his essay "Shipping Out," writes a blistering and hilarious account of taking a Caribbean cruise, definitely not one of his favorite things. We learn much about him by what he notices and the attitude he expresses about these things. Through tone and selection of detail, rather than through direct statement, the narrative persona comes to life.

> I now know every conceivable rationale for somebody spending more than
> $3,000 to go on a Caribbean cruise. To be specific; voluntarily and for pay,
> I underwent a 7-Night Caribbean (7NC) Cruise on board the m.v. Zenith

(which no wag could resist immediately rechristening the m.v. Nadir), a 47,255-ton ship owned by Celebrity Cruises, Inc., one of the twenty-odd cruise lines that operate out of south Florida and specialize in "Megaships," the floating wedding cakes with occupancies in four figures and engines the size of branch banks.

The narrator clearly does not consider cruises one of his favorite things. His tone characterizes him, and we learn about him from what he doesn't like. (Author's note: "Shipping Out" is one of the funniest essays ever written.) Writing about things we don't like can be a delightful exercise, allowing us to indulge our dark sides without compunction.

PROMPT: Write about something you deeply dislike. Here's your chance to blast it. Go for the jugular on this one.

PROMPT: Write about yourself by writing in detail about one of your favorite things. Begin by only mentioning and describing the thing. Don't mention yourself at all. Then review these paragraphs. Make a general statement about the type of people who love this thing. Sophisticated and discerning? Simple and practical? We're dealing in stereotypes here, of course, but these could lead us to more sophisticated and discerning conclusions.

PROMPT: Follow Quindlen's lead. Describe yourself as a child or teen by filling in the blank of this sentence: "I was a _____ boy/girl." From there, write about your view of yourself as a child by refracting your view through the prism of this favorite person or object. If you want, keep going, exploring your childhood personality. If you want, continue the exploration by comparing your view of yourself today. What changes have occurred and why?

PROMPT: Continuing the theme of change in the previous prompt, pick something you used to like, but now don't like nearly as much. A subject that has grown tiresome, perhaps. An activity that once consumed you and that now holds little interest. Explore the changes in you that may have caused this change in attitude toward the thing. You can take the opposite approach, too, if this topic engages you. Pick something that you once disliked and now enjoy quite a bit.

PROMPT: Follow the process of the previous prompt, but this time focus on a person. Is there someone you cared about or admired very much five or ten years ago who now does not appeal to you? How did this disillusionment occur? If possible, avoid choosing someone with whom you were involved in a romantic relationship. Choose a friend or, perhaps, someone you had a crush on but nothing came of it. What does this change in attitude suggest about changes you've undergone?

LITERARY LIKES

In stories, we can use favorite things to develop and show character. Laura Wingfield, in Tennessee Williams's play *The Glass Menagerie,* for example, loves her collection of glass animals. We cannot think of this character without thinking of her hobby. Williams uses the hobby to say much about Laura. She has no romantic interests, so her deep wells of love are spent on the glass figurines. The collection, therefore, reinforces our sense of her loneliness. The fragility and innocence of the figurines also mirrors Laura's fragility and innocence, giving the audience a sharper sense of these qualities without the playwright stating them directly.

When using favorite things—hobbies, activities, possessions—in your work, consider what these things suggest and how they amplify your characters. If you're struggling with a character, give him a favorite song or a favorite food. Show him enjoying it. Without having to explain the character, you've shown your reader something significant about him. Avoid, of course, stereotypes: Construction guy loves guzzling six-packs while watching ESPN; soccer mom loves shopping at the mall and buying expensive clothes. Nor should you play too obviously against type: Construction guy loves making dried flower arrangements; soccer mom relishes weekend fly-fishing. Instead, get to know your character. Find out what works for that person.

PROMPT: Use the prompts above in a piece of fiction or a poem. Show the change in a character by showing how a once-loved hobby or object or activity now holds no interest. You may want to speculate in your mind upon the reasons for this change, but don't include these thoughts on the page. Show the character's change in attitude. The character might not even notice the change. For example, in Frank Norris's novel *McTeague*, the eponymous main character is a shy, oafish man, a not-very-good dentist with a taste for simple pleasures. Early in the novel, we learn that he delights in a Sunday afternoon ritual of eating a big lunch, buying a pitcher of steam beer at a saloon, and returning to his office to nap and play "some half dozen very mournful airs" on his concertina:

> McTeague looked forward to these Sunday afternoons as a period of relaxation and enjoyment. These were his only pleasures—to eat, to smoke, to sleep, and to play upon his concertina.

THE WRITER'S IDEA BOOK

Later in the novel, McTeague's fortunes change, which causes a change in him. He falls victim to his own avarice, a change shown through his growing dislike for steam beer and his other simple pleasures. As he changes, his tastes and preferences change.

PROMPT: Let's follow the Wallace example again. Write about a character who clearly does not like a place or activity, but don't let the character speculate on what this dislike says about him. Allow the readers to draw their own conclusions. Indulge yourself. Take this thing to task. Excoriate it.

PROMPT: Review your list of things you like. How many of these items have you written about or used somewhere in your writing? With luck, quite a few. If not, keep this list handy so you can refer to it the next time you're feeling blocked or stale. Maybe you're feeling stale because the material does not engage you. Add some spice by bringing in something you enjoy or care more deeply about, something that, to you, is fun and interesting.

PROMPT: To help you write more about the things you like, write at least a paragraph about every item on your "favorites" list. If you want, add to the list, and write about those items, too. You might simply sketch a description of the thing or explain briefly why it's a favorite. You could cluster around the thing, generating details that could lead to further explorations. You could begin a poem or essay, attach the thing to a character and see where that leads you. You could put the thing in the middle of a room and begin a scene.

CHAPTER SEVEN

NELLIE MALONE FROM FIFTH AND STONE

They are passing, posthaste, the gliding years … The years are passing, my dear presently no one will know what you and I know.

—VLADIMIR NABOKOV

My grandmother grew up in the Irish ghetto of Cincinnati's West End at the turn of the twentieth century. She was poor, Catholic, and she dropped out of school in the seventh grade to go to work. Though her name was Helen, kids in the neighborhood called her Nellie and the name stuck. She was probably more a Nellie than a Helen. For a while, the kids called her Nellie Malone from Fifth and Stone, chanted it sometimes, like a jump-rope singsong. My grandmother, from what I could discern, didn't really care much for the name, but bore it without complaint. She was Nellie or Nel to the people who knew her, right up until her death at the age of ninety-four.

If I were to write about her, I might begin with those names, then characterize her as a woman who aspired to be a Helen but always was seen as a Nellie. Through those names, I could talk about her work ethic, her sense of humility and sacrifice, her eagerness and inability to dance, her desire to pull herself up from humble beginnings to be, as she constantly coaxed us to be, "refined."

A few years before Grandma was born, her mother had come to the United States from Ireland, traveling with a brother named Tom. Great-Grandma settled in Boston, working as a maid, then later moved to Cincinnati. Tom didn't settle at all. He left when the pair reached America, said he was heading for Australia and would write soon. No one in the family knows what happened to him. He was never heard from again.

There are a number of other family stories I could tell you. No doubt, you could tell me many stories of your own family and heritage. These stories offer great sources of ideas. In this chapter, we'll look at those stories, exploring and developing them. Your goal is to use heritage—ethnic and familial—as material for your writing. It's probably the richest source you possess.

FAMILY

You might think your family is deadly dull: Mr. and Mrs. Americana, two point five kiddies, a station wagon with wood-grain side panels, a house in the trim-lawn suburbs, a shaggy dog named Rex. Okay, maybe not that dull. Probably not dull at all. Look closer. Dig deeper.

Or, you might have come to the opposite conclusion. You might think your family so strange, the relationships so convoluted and dysfunctional, the myriad battles so exhaustingly bitter and complicated, the interactions so fraught with shattered dreams, unfulfilled needs, grudges, rituals, secrets, lies, internecine feuds, and chronic disappointments that you couldn't possibly cover it all in your lifetime. Hooray! Now you're thinking like a writer.

PROMPT: Tell a family story, one that gets passed around at holiday dinners more often than the gravy boat. Tell as many as you can recall. If you want, brainstorm for a while, tagging the stories with just a word or a phrase to help you remember them. Then pick a few and develop the narrative and the details.

PROMPT: Pick one family event that is emblematic of your family, something that happened once that sums up your family's general behavior and outlook. A trip? An emergency? Or perhaps something smaller, less significant to an outsider but freighted with meaning to those involved. If the event doesn't do your family justice, if it shows one side but ignores other sides, pick a second event, even a third one, and follow the same process. Can you combine these stories into a single story, a portrait of your family in its myriad guises?

PROMPT: Talk to family members in search of a mysterious relative from the past: someone who struck out on his own and was never heard from again; someone who lived modestly and died with a surprising amount of money; someone who abruptly left a marriage; someone who lived alone and rarely visited anyone in the family. Imagine a life for this person, the details, based on what you know but, if possible, pushing beyond into the realm of imagination.

PROMPT: Write about a family ritual, something your family members do only with each other. How did it start? Why has it continued? Do your family members have nicknames for each other? Write about them. How did they start? Why did they stick? What do the nicknames suggest about the roles people play in your family?

PROMPT: Write short biographies of family members, living or dead, close or distant. Who is the black sheep? Who is the success story?

PROMPT: Write about a family secret. I'd give you an example from my own family, but they're secrets. If your family has no shared secrets, write about a family shame, something that simply isn't discussed, such as Aunt Alice's two-week affair in Atlantic City with the dashing cable guy.

PROMPT: Find some family photos and use them as sources for writing ideas. Describe the people in the photos—what they're wearing and what they're doing. If you know the circumstances, write about where the photo was taken and why and what it suggests about your family. Impromptu photos probably will work better than studio portraits, but use whatever you can find. If the photos are very old, find out about the people. Photos are a great way to get older family members talking about the past, and surely you will hear fascinating stories that you've never heard before. Write them down.

PROMPT: Describe your family to a future family member, an unborn or recently born child. Tell her about the legacy she inherits. What qualities do members of your family usually possess—industry, creativity, good teeth? What qualities bear close awareness—fiery tempers, moodiness, large appetites? If you want, read your piece onto a digital recorder. Share it with other family members, and use their thoughts to help you revise.

PROMPT: Write a eulogy for a family member who has passed away. Be honest, bringing up flaws as well as good qualities. Tell a story that is emblematic of the person's nature.

PROMPT: Create a family crest, if you don't have one. What animal—or charge, as it's known in heraldry—best represents your family? What color?

THE WRITER'S IDEA BOOK

PROMPT: Write about your family, making them the First Family, plopping them into the White House. How well do they represent the country? Which member becomes the media darling? Which member causes no end of embarrassment?

PROMPT: Write about your family, making them the very first family, living in a cave, killing the occasional mastodon. How long could your family survive? Have fun with this one. Stretch your imagination.

PROMPT: Begin a story with a statement about the nature of family. The most famous one (so famous I'm loath to use it for fear of appearing ponderous and ill-read) opens Tolstoy's great novel *Anna Karenina*: "All happy families are alike, but each unhappy family is unhappy in its own way." Your statement could be more upbeat, but it should be broad and sweeping in this way. You could follow the statement with an essay-istic investigation of families, or you could glide into fiction, introducing characters in a family, perhaps in a scene.

PROMPT: Make a general statement about motherhood or fatherhood, and follow the same process you used above. You could write an essay or poem, taking a more direct approach, or you could follow the statement with a fictional story using a mother or father as the central character.

PROMPT: Write a description of your family focusing on the most prominent quality they share. Recall and evoke an episode in your family's history that dramatizes that quality.

PROMPT: Write about your family by comparing them to a well-known family—real or fictional. For example, compare your family to the Kennedys or the Brady Bunch, even the Royal Family. You might want to do this by focusing on how your family is the same as that family or how your family is very different.

ETHNICITY

If your family has lived in America for more than a few generations, you probably feel about as ethnic as hot dogs and apple pie. But if you look closely, you may notice that a few ethnic traits and traditions still linger. Explore them. If you want, do a little genealogical research.

PROMPT: Find out about an ancestor's arrival in America. Dig up as many details as possible, then write a piece—true or fictionalized—based on the ancestor's experience. To develop this piece, research a bit of social history. Find out what people wore and ate during the time when your ancestor arrived.

PROMPT: Read a book by someone from a culture far different from your own, a book that explores that culture. Write about the differences between the cultures. Or, if you prefer, begin a piece similar to the book, but focus on your own culture.

PROMPT: In a single sentence, declare who you are—your ethnic and regional background, your social class, your religion or whatever is appropriate to you. For example: "I am a third-generation American of Irish-German heritage, raised Catholic in the middle-class suburbs of the Midwest." Follow this sentence with an autobiographical paragraph or two, perhaps shifting back to the time you were born, or perhaps showing how your background influences your beliefs and actions today. If this interests you, keep going. You may have begun your life story.

PROMPT: Substitute a character for yourself and do the prompt above, this time embellishing it, allowing the character to declare who he is beyond ethnicity. If you want a model, read the opening of *The Adventures of Augie March*, by Saul Bellow. (In fact, read the whole book. It's a masterpiece.)

PROMPT: Give a tour of your childhood home, focusing on details that portray your ethnic background or family history. You can do this as a narrative or simply in lists or in freewriting. If you want, draw a blueprint of the house, noting in the floor plan where objects were placed, or where old photographs were hung.

PROMPT: Give the tour again, this time focusing on your family's more recent history: events, social class and background, tastes. And be honest. Admit to that avocado fridge with the goofy magnets from all the states you visited on vacations. Draw a blueprint or floor plan of your house, noting where things occurred and how rooms were furnished and decorated. Take your time with this one. Allow it to spark memories and stories. Write them down.

PROMPT: Write a bigoted diatribe against your ethnic heritage. Use all the common myths and stereotypes. Then write a defense. If you want, create a dialogue between two characters, each one giving voice to one of the viewpoints.

PROMPT: Explain your heritage and upbringing to someone from a decidedly different one. You might write to someone from a different country or different part of the United States, someone from a different planet, someone interviewing you on television. If you want, use a script format or a question-and-answer approach. Turn it into a scene.

PROMPT: Write a scene in which an American family is visited by a relative from a different country. If you want, base the family on your own. Quickly establish a conflict: The relative plans to live with the family; the relative is of a higher or lower social class; the family is in a state of crisis and has no time or energy for visitors.

THE WRITER'S IDEA BOOK

CHAPTER EIGHT

WITH A BANJO ON MY KNEE

Whatever our theme in writing, it is old and tired, Whatever our place, it has been visited by the stranger, it will never be new again. It is only the vision that can be new; but that is enough.

—EUDORA WELTY

Mining the places you have lived can be a great way to unearth ideas. Too often, we feel that the places we were born and raised lack the sort of exoticism that will attract readers. We think this because the places are not exotic to us. We take them for granted. Believe me, I share this feeling. I was born and raised in Ohio, which is synonymous with, even symbolic of, bland America.

Of course, what is ordinary to us can be exotic to someone else. The key is being able to truly see the world around you, finding the details that evoke it. A world that is keenly evoked will be exotic to those who don't know it well and will allow those who do know it well to see it with fresh eyes. So don't dismiss the place where you live or where you grew up as bereft of idea possibilities. In fact, it's probably full of them. If you aren't seeing them, look harder. If you hear yourself say, "Nothing happened where I grew up," or, "It was just a normal, typical place," you're missing something. In my creative writing classes, I always stopped students who wrote of—or even spoke of—something as "normal" or "typical." These words are a writer's enemies. They tell us you're not seeing beneath the surface, and readers come to writers for help in seeing beneath the surface.

When evoking a sense of place, writers today, unfortunately, must look harder than writers of fifty to one hundred years ago. They must peer deeply through the filter of what writer Max Apple called "the oranging of America." By this he meant the disappearance of regional and ethnic nuance. The melting pot of the world is melting into one giant franchise. His story with that title chronicles the quest of Howard Johnson, restaurant owner and hotelier, to erect his orange-roofed establishments from coast to coast as beacons of reassuring sameness to comfort weary, hungry travelers. This trend is truer now than when Apple wrote of it in the 1970s. In your own travels, you've surely noticed that towns from Maine to California all have the same Burger King, Walmart, Starbuck's, and, of course, the ubiquitous Golden Arches.

The proliferation of this franchise mentality, strip-mall America, makes it more difficult than ever for writers to see and to evoke a particular sense of place in their work. And yet our jobs as writers—whether poets or playwrights, novelists, or essayists—is to make the world new again for our readers, to allow for fresh insights and discoveries. Avoid the shorthand, brand-name approach, which too easily characterizes a place. Instead, look for ways to follow Ezra Pound's artistic commandment to "make it new."

PROMPT: (This one is borrowed from Bill Roorbach's *Writing Life Stories*.) Draw a map of the neighborhood where you grew up. If you grew up in several neighborhoods, draw maps for each or choose one from among them. On the map, write who lived where, note places where events, large or small, took place. The process of detailing your map will spark memories of time and place that can lead to ideas for writing.

PROMPT: Continuing the map theme, find your city and state in a road atlas. Look at the place through the eyes of a traveler, someone who has never been there before. Note the names of highways and counties, rivers, and places of interest. Write these down as though they are unfamiliar to you. Which ones would you like to see? Continue your investigation of this place by thumbing through a travel guide or go online and read the sites that give information about the area—its history, geography, economy. Note places of interest, and note details that you didn't know about or had forgotten. If you want, send for state or local tourism brochures. These brochures can lead to article ideas that you might have overlooked or story settings and details that, again, were right in front of your nose.

PROMPT: Research the history of the places you lived. Find out how they were settled, which tribes of Native American lived there. What events in the past helped to shape the identity of this place? What cultural forces helped shape it? Of course, take notes. Use your writer's instincts for story ideas. You may find an interesting historical character upon whom to base a fictional one. Or you can enrich a character's background by linking her to a particular ethnic movement that occurred in real life. By linking the particulars of your characters to the context of place, you anchor the reader more firmly in the world of your story. You create a sharper sense of texture and immediacy.

PROMPT: What is the public perception of your city, state, or region? In other words, what do people who don't live there think about—or think they know about—where you live? For example, those of us not from the South believe it to be a backward, slow-paced world of politically conservative views. We think of southern California as a place of glamour and hedonism. How is your area perceived? Start big, with a region or state, and move to the small. For example, I live on the west side of Cincinnati, which is seen as less sophisticated and interesting by snobby east siders.

THE EYES OF A NATIVE

Of course, most of these prompts will offer a broad historical, geographical, or sociological perspective. This can give a strong context to your character, but you'll now need to push deeper, looking for the particular details and rhythms of life that make a place truly unique. Otherwise, your writing can sound like travelogue—researched rather than lived. Elsewhere in this book, I mention Richard Russo's essay "Location, Location, Location: Depicting Character Through Place," in which he praises John Cheever's ability to evoke the world of Shady Hill, his fictional commuter town. In the same essay, however, Russo takes Cheever to task for his less compelling evocations of Italy, where the Cheevers spent time later in the author's life:

> The later Cheever stories, many of which take place in Italy, are much more descriptive, but there's a touristy feel to them, as if the author feels compelled to give us what filmmakers call "establishing shots." The film takes place in New Orleans? Then you open with a shot of the bridge over Lake Pontchartrain, Cajun music in the background, then obligatory shots of the French Quarter.

We do need, at times, an "establishing shot" or two in our stories, a detail to quickly place the reader. But Russo makes an important point. Too often, we reach for the easy description, the "touristy" detail that simply tells the reader what she already knows rather than evoking a vivid world where the reader can settle in and view the people and events of the story you're telling.

PROMPT: Cruise around your city or neighborhood, keeping a sharp eye for interesting details. If you can, have someone drive you. Even better, ride a bus, especially if you rarely ride buses. The novelty of the experience will freshen your view. Note details—storefronts, faces, places where things have happened, in your life or in the news. And really try to see. Note patterns of architecture and dress; note the types of cars people drive. Imagine yourself, if you can, a stranger to the place, just arriving to take residence here. If you're focusing on your neighborhood, walk it, especially if you don't normally do that. If you do walk your neighborhood, you know that it's amazing how you're able to notice things that, while driving, escape your attention.

PROMPT: Tour the area by using Google Earth. Begin high above it and then drill down to street level. Write about how this view offers a different perspective than the one you recall or that you see every day.

PROMPT: Write a letter describing your place to someone who has never been there. "What is Idaho like?" they've asked. They think of mountains and potatoes. Fill in the blanks. Give them an insider's view of the place, while keeping in mind they know nothing about it. Take time to linger, elaborate. You will avoid the clichés of the place because you know the particulars. In fact, take time to explode the clichés. If you're from Georgia, explain how the myths of the South, or Georgia, or your city, just don't apply anymore. Is Nebraska really the breadbasket of Bible-beating boredom, or does some pretty interesting stuff occur there?

PROMPT: Write a letter describing your neighborhood, town, city, state, or region from the point of view of someone who has just arrived. Though this persona will lack your insider's knowledge, he will be wide-eyed at the world he's discovering. And he will notice different things from what you notice, if you can push yourself deeply enough into the persona. To him, this place is exotic.

PROMPT: Write about how you are an ideal representative of the place where you were raised—your ethnicity, ideas, values, likes, and dislikes. Then write about how you are an anomaly to your place of origin, utterly unlike the other people who live there. Put these pieces away for a few days, then return to them and look for ways to fuse them into a piece about how you are both like and unlike the stereotype of people in your place.

PROMPT: If you need more distance, move your town to a different state in a different part of the country, but be true to the smaller details. Use it as a setting for fictional events. How easily does it move? What changes—such as accents or weather—need to be made to fit the new part of the country? Or, move a troubled story to a new place, one based on a place where you've lived, one you know well.

PROMPT: Sometimes it's easier to write about a place where you no longer live. If you grew up in one place and now live in another, write from memory about the place where you grew up. Don't look at old pictures or use an atlas. Rely solely on what you remember. Feel free to exaggerate.

PROMPT: Characterize a place by focusing on its predominant industry or business. Try to use the industry to suggest the nature of the place. For example, I live in Cincinnati, where one of the major businesses is Procter and Gamble, maker of soap, detergent, and toothpaste, an interesting fit in a city that prides itself on cleanliness—physical and moral. For an example of how to do this in fiction, in his novel *The Nephew*, James Purdy places a ketchup factory in his small town. The industry helps characterize the town as a bland place—the factory isn't, after all, churning out spicy mustard. The blandness and conformity of the town oppress its citizens, making them emotionally ill, just as the pervasive odor of brewing tomatoes from the ketchup factory makes them physically ill.

PROMPT: Write a scene in which a character returns home after an extended absence. Tour the character through the streets. What has changed and what has stayed the same? If you want, heighten the tension by creating a disparity between the descriptive details as seen by the character and the character's reaction to them. The character, for example, could view sad, shabby storefronts as quaint and cozy or look-alike suburban streets as unique and distinctive.

PROMPT: Tour the area with someone from another era in its history. That someone might be you, circa twenty years ago. Explain what has changed, pointing out things like cell phone towers and electronic billboards that were not there twenty years before.

PROMPT: Create a fictional hometown. Draw a map of it, creating the streets and noting the stores and the homes where people live. If you want, base this fictional place on your own hometown—or part of town if you live in a city. Write a description of the town. Give it a history. Give it landmarks, noting where certain fictional events took place.

PROMPT: If you had fun with the previous prompt, put some people in that fictional hometown. Write some character sketches of these people. If you catch a spark, begin a story. You may want to collect the stories into a single work. A famous example of this type of book is Sherwood Anderson's *Winesburg, Ohio*. A more recent example is Laura Hendrie's *Stygo*.

PROMPT: Write about a place you haven't seen for many years, preferably not since you were a child. Then, if possible, visit that place. How close does your description from memory match the reality? You may be surprised how your memory has changed it. Writer Wright Morris wrote of a favorite childhood place he remembered well, a cool, dark spot under the porch of his boyhood home in Nebraska. He remembered hiding in this spot, and even in his middle age still could see the flat sweep of land fanning out in front of the house. When he returned to the house for a visit, his family long since moved away, he was shocked to find the space beneath the porch far too small to accommodate even a child. He had made it up. Over time, his imagination had created a place that didn't exist.

CHAPTER NINE

THOUGHTS OF A SUN-DRENCHED ELSEWHERE

Go slowly, breathe and smile.

—THICH NHAT HANH

In the previous chapter, we examined places you know well, places you've lived for an extended period of time. In this chapter, we'll continue investigating ideas of place by focusing on where you *want* to go and on places you've been and would like to see again. As we saw in Wright Morris's anecdote, places exist in our minds as much as they exist in the corporeal world. We can tell much about ourselves by how we relate to place. Can't stand that one-horse town where you grew up? Perhaps this suggests feelings of inadequacy about your background. Dreaming of a move to Montana? Does this dream embody your hope of embracing a more adventuresome life?

I won't dispense any nickel psychology about your relation to place. You must discover the relationships for yourself. For myself, I find great insight in Isabelle Eberhardt's line from *The Passionate Nomad*: "I shall always be haunted by thoughts of a sundrenched elsewhere." Does this speak to my desire to go to the Caribbean, lie on the beach, and stick my toes in the warm sand? Yes. Does this desire also speak to my romantic nature, ever wistful for a place that is not where I am, one that holds the promise of unfulfillable fulfillment? Yep. Let's start there.

PROMPT: Write about the best place you've ever been. "Best" can have a few meanings: most exciting, most fulfilling, most interesting. It could mean the place where you felt most in sync with the world, where you had the keenest sense of belonging, coming home to a place you've never been. Or it could mean the most exciting place, or the one where you had a great time. You choose. Take time to describe it in detail, beginning with those details that first come to mind. Avoid, at first, explaining why you liked the place. Just describe it. After you have a few pages of description, you can begin to explain and speculate upon why this place had such a profound impact on you.

PROMPT: Write about the place you most want to go—for a visit or to live. It must be a place you've never been before. As with the previous prompt, open with details and without explanation. Describe what you know of the place, what you've seen in photographs or on television. Then move to exploring why this place appeals to you so much. Which elements of your personality are hooked into this place?

PROMPT: Sometimes places hold more appeal when they remain in our minds. The reality doesn't match our romantic notions of the places. Has this disillusioning experience ever happened to you? Write about it. Begin with what you believed the place would be, then move to the reality you found. How were they different? Were the people less charming? Was the weather too hot? The streets too dirty? Or maybe your expectations were simply too high. In his travel memoir, *Chasing Oliver Hazzard Perry*, Craig Heimbuch, who grew up on the southern shore of Lake Erie, writes about always having wondered who is looking back from the other side of the lake. In his thirties, he finally makes the trip, which ends up being both fulfilling and disappointing.

HIGHS AND LOWS

High expectations can lead to disappointment. They also can tell us about ourselves by shedding light on what we seek, what we feel is missing in our lives and in ourselves. I knew a woman who, for many years, wanted to see the Taj Mahal in India. When she finally visited this great Wonder of the World, she found it not so wonderful. I remember her telling me, "It was great, but not really great like you'd think it would be." I thought this was a great line, a telling statement that exemplified the woman's romantic nature, which, by the time I met her, was beginning to sour into cynicism and disillusionment. I used the line verbatim in a short story, placing it in the mouth of a character who possessed a similar mix of romantic notions and cynicism.

Maybe all places we visit are a bit disillusioning if we have wanted to see them for a long time. Like the Tom Waits song says of wanderlust, "The obsession's in the chasing, and not the apprehending, the pursuit, you see, and never the arrest." Of course, he is comparing wanderlust to romantic love, and maybe, at some level, they are not so different. Is there often not a fantasy person tucked away in your fantasy destination? Or, perhaps, the fantasy person is you, the worldly you who has been to myriad exotic spots and thus can move with the grace of royalty through any place or situation.

Pico Iyer investigates the nature of our love for travel and its associations with romance in his essay "Why We Travel: A Love Affair With the World":

> We travel, initially, to lose ourselves; and we travel, next, to find ourselves. We travel to open our hearts and eyes and learn more about the world than our newspapers will accommodate . . . . And we travel, in essence, to become young fools again—to slow time down and get taken in, and fall in love once more.

PROMPT: Write about your desire for travel, be it great or small. Perhaps you have traveled extensively in your life and are a little jaded. If so, write about that. If not, pour forth on where you want to go and why.

PROMPT: Write a scene in which a character arrives in a new place, one where she has longed to be but now finds disappointing. Suggest the reasons for her disappointment through descriptive detail—what she sees, the people she meets. Or, if her problem is that she's dragging more emotional baggage than physical luggage, intimate this situation. What is she running from?

PROMPT: Put a character in a place where he doesn't speak the native language. Explore the problems this barrier creates.

PROMPT: Write about a character who goes to a place she's never been in order to find something or someone. She is on a quest. In William Trevor's novel *Felicia's Journey*, a young Irish woman named Felicia travels to a small town in England to find a British soldier whose child she is carrying. With a deft touch, Trevor slowly lets us know that her search is in vain. If you're feeling adventurous, create your own quest, such as "In search of the best barbecued ribs in [your town]." This could lead to a fun essay or article for a local publication. You could even build a blog around this quest, along the lines of Julie Powell's blog about cooking her way through Julia Child's book, which is not focused on travel, but does have a goal in mind that centers the quest.

The way characters relate to place can be an avenue of development. A character who is yearning constantly for "a sundrenched elsewhere" is different from one who has never been out of the state where she was born and doesn't feel much need to go. A person who carries a clear sense of self wherever she goes is different from one too anxious to fit into new cultures by taking on all the trappings of that culture—suffering from "when in Rome" syndrome.

YOUNG FOOLS

Experiencing a new place can be a wonderful experience for a writer, because everything is so fresh and new. Your soul is wide open to notice all that's around you. If you're feeling stale in your writing, take time for a trip, even if just a day-trip, to a place you've never been. It doesn't matter where you go. Take a notebook to write down your impressions, and use these in your current project or to start new ones. They need not lead to a nonfiction piece about the trip itself. As with all excursions of this kind, use it to load your arsenal of impressions and details, people and dialogue and scenes. When you need them, they will be there. They may end up in something completely different from where you found them.

PROMPT: Write about a public gathering you attended in a place you visited. A baseball game or street fair, an outdoor concert or historical reenactment. Put yourself there by freewriting or clustering, allowing your mind to wander back. Write about the people you saw, the smells in the air. You'll be amazed by how much you remember once you begin writing about it. To help you develop this description into something richer, look for similar descriptions in books you've read. The one that comes first to mind is the Pamplona street celebration in Ernest Hemingway's *The Sun Also Rises*, at which Jake Barnes and his crew of lost generationers dance and drink in exquisitely rendered moments of color and exoticism. Of course, many such moments are captured in books. Which ones are your favorites?

PROMPT: Use the description above as a backdrop for fiction, writing at least one scene in which characters deal with some sort of conflict while attending the event. Or, you could use it in nonfiction if you've had an experience while in such a place. Weave your personal conflict into the swirl of the event going on around you.

PROMPT: Write about a private moment you've experienced in a distant place. Perhaps a solitary walk along a beach or a glass of wine in a restaurant far from home. Your goal, first, is to transport yourself back to this moment, then to put your reader there. If you want, use this moment in time and place for a fictional story, creating a character who experiences the same moment for reasons different from yours.

THE WRITER'S IDEA BOOK

PROMPT: Write about someone you met while traveling. Pick someone strange and eccentric, if you've met such a person, or pick someone with whom there was an undercurrent or confusion. Perhaps a language barrier made communication difficult. Perhaps you were looked on with suspicion as a visitor. Or, pick someone who made a strong impression on you, someone who, perhaps, taught you something or who filters back into your memory now and then. Write down as much of the meeting as you can remember, taking time to set the scene in all its details.

PROMPT: Practice describing places by doing a sketch of each of the following: a place next to an ocean or some large body of water; a place in or very near mountains; a large city; a small town. Try to avoid the clichés of these places. Also, try to avoid explanations. Instead, focus on using specific, particular details. Let these details evoke your tone and your notions of the place.

PROMPT: Choose one of the places you described in a previous prompt as a background for a scene. In the scene, one character lives in the place; the other character has just arrived, for reasons I'll leave to your imagination.

PROMPT: Write about a character who visits a place for a practical reason, such as a business meeting or conference, but allows the trip to become something more (in a positive or negative way). At least for the length of his stay, the character's life changes significantly. He is transformed. In the essay mentioned on page 63, Pico Iyer writes that our desire for transformation lies at the heart of our desire to travel:

> For me the first great joy of traveling is simply the luxury of leaving all my beliefs and certainties at home, and seeing everything I thought I knew in a different light, and from a crooked angle . ... And if travel is like love, it is in the end, mostly because it's a heightened state of awareness, in which we are mindful, receptive, undimmed by familiarity and ready to be transformed.

CHAPTER TEN

9 TO 5

You'll never plow a field by turning it over in your mind.

—IRISH PROVERB

When searching for ideas to write about, many of us ignore our jobs and careers. The reason, perhaps, is because many of us think of our jobs as a necessary evil, the thing we do in order to support ourselves and our loved ones, to pay our bills, to survive. But most of us spend more of our time working than doing anything else in our waking lives. We meet people who we date and love through work. We meet many of our closest friends there. Often, we define ourselves by what we do, and even more often, we define others by what they do. When we meet someone, one of our first questions is invariably, "So what do you do?" In his essay "In Search of Novels About Working Life," British writer D.J. Taylor makes an insightful point when he writes, "Work ought to occupy the literary imagination as much as sex, money, or power, and yet for the most part the Anglo-American novel has spent at least half of the first two or three centuries of its development resolutely denying its existence." I would venture that the same is true of other literary forms. Mainstream film and television frequently offer workplace settings, but the dramatic focus rarely has much to do with what people actually do in that workplace.

Why don't we spend more time writing about our jobs and careers, mining them for scripts, stories, and poems? Well, in this chapter, that's exactly what we're going to do. Even if we say we hate our jobs and that they have nothing to do with our true selves or the inner lives we want to explore through writing, it's still ground more fertile than we realize. For example, Richard Yates's classic novel *Revolutionary Road*, more recently made into a feature film, explores the lack of fulfillment of the main character's position in the advertising department at a business machine company. The conflict between that career and his sense of his true self drives the narrative.

In fact, I'll wager that more literary pieces in whatever form are written about disliking one's work than celebrating it. So even if you aren't crazy about the work you do, it still can provide ideas for writing. What's important is that you view the considerable amount of time you spend working as worth exploring for literary gold. Your tales of a tyrannical boss could lead you to write the next *The Devil Wears Prada*, Lauren Weisberger's novel about the fashion industry. Your search for meaning in the world of business could be the next *The Man in the Gray Flannel Suit*, Sloan Wilson's classic novel about a World War II vet trying to balance family and career while maintaining his personal values.

PROMPT: Let's begin with a question people asked when you were a child: "What do you want to be when you grow up?" Can you remember how you responded? Personally, I was torn between being a cowboy or the pope. In college, I wrote a wacky and not very successful little tale about a character who managed to combine these lofty, if disparate, vocations. But you can do better. Write a short piece about a character who wants to be what you wanted to be and tries hard to achieve your dream jobs.

PROMPT: List all the "things you have wanted to be when you grow up." When you finish your list, try to write a short piece about it, the common themes you discover. What do these choices reflect upon the person who aspires to these jobs?

PROMPT: Reflect a bit on the road not taken, the career choices you considered but for whatever reason didn't pursue. How would your life be different if you had taken that road? If you're engaged by the idea, create a fictional character who regrets (or is relieved by) not having taken that road.

PROMPT: Make a list of all the jobs you've ever held, even ones as informal as cutting a neighbor's lawn or babysitting. When you finish your list, arrange the jobs chronologically, from the first one to your current one. Then write at least a few paragraphs about each one, fleshing out the particulars—how long you held the job, the name of your boss and, if applicable, your colleagues.

PROMPT: Put together a résumé and a cover letter to apply for your ideal job. Really sell yourself, detailing your professional skills and accomplishments. On a separate page, write your work history, listing jobs, places of employment, reasons why you left each job, how well you performed at each job. Unlike the less formal list you created in the previous prompt, style this one as you would for a résumé.

PROMPT: From the previous list, choose one job for further exploration. Brainstorm a list of dramatic experiences at the job—any moments of anxiety or tension or joy. Pick one from the list and flesh it out on the page. What happened? Try to focus on the dramatic action and details rather than explanations. Allow the reader to arrive at conclusions about the people in the drama without your overt guidance.

PROMPT: From your list, pick your "favorite" and "least favorite" job, and write a short piece comparing the two. Explore the qualities that made one job a joy and the other a trial. Try to provide insights into how the jobs fit—or didn't fit—your personality or the stage of life in which you held the job.

PROMPT: Write about your most memorable job interview, one in which your star shined brightly or, well, didn't. Brainstorm and freewrite to gather as many details as possible about the place, the interviewer, the questions, and your responses. Include, of course, whether or not you got the job and how you felt about the result.

PROMPT: Write about a time you lost a job, when you were fired or were laid off in a more general downsizing. What happened? Who told you? Was there a confrontation? How did you feel? And how do you feel about it now? If you've never had this experience, or even if you have, write about a time when you had to fire someone. Again, focus on the details and the action. In your first run, you can explain how you felt, but if you want to refine the piece, limit the explanations, instead trying to evoke how you felt through detail and action.

PROMPT: Create a character or persona who holds the job you'd most like to have. Take that character through a single day, performing the duties that you'd love to be doing. If possible, be realistic, including in that day the bad as well as the good. Can you dive deeper into this imagined world, creating colleagues, bosses, and clients who interact with your character? If so, keep going. Your emotional connection to the ideal job could fuel a longer piece.

PROMPT: Write about a favorite colleague, someone you enjoyed working with. What made them special? What qualities did you admire? What was the nature of your relationship with that person? If this sketch interests you, write about a specific event involving this person. Tell it as a story, inserting physical descriptions into the narrative or as a poem or maybe as a scene in a play.

PROMPT: Write about a colleague you didn't like. What qualities about the person turned you off? Did you have overt conflicts with this person? As in the previous prompt, explore the emotional connection, be it ever so disagreeable. Writing about people who spark strong emotions within us, positive or negative, can be an effective way of infusing our writing with those emotions. One of my favorite descriptions of the hated colleague appears in Frederick Exley's *A Fan's Notes*. Here's a taste: "Harold imagined himself a bright, ambitious, clean-cut and rising young executive. Harold sweated and picked his nose. He was neither ambitious nor bright. On the one hand he was the worst kind of sycophant, a whimpering two-faced Stinky Pete whose toadying bordered on the obscene; on the other hand, he was a man of, at first perplexing, then benumbing, and finally, a horrifyingly vast stupidity . . . ." Exley then tells an on-the-job anecdote about Harold so we can see that these observations are true. He finally concludes "without feeling any remorse whatever, I could kill him, destroy him, remove him from the race of men."

PROMPT: Bosses tend to engender strong emotions within us. Something about the dominant-subservient nature of the relationship, our need to withhold our true feelings about them personally or about the work, can be fertile ground for writing. I'm reminded of the song "Frankly, Mr. Shankly," by the Smiths, in which the speaker finally musters a moment of candor to tell his boss, apologetically, that he's "a flatulent pain in the ass." Write a short piece in which you speak directly to a boss—former or current—and articulate your true feelings about the person.

PROMPT: Continuing the theme of the previous prompt, have you ever had a boss who was a mentor, who helped develop your skills and confidence, boosting you toward achieving your career goals? If so, take time to put that person on the page. You might want to write a descriptive piece about the person or, as in the previous prompt, directly address the person, articulating your feelings of admiration and gratitude.

THE GRIND

In her poem "The Secretary Chant," Marge Piercy turns her body literally into the work itself with such lines as "My hips are a desk,/ From my ears hang/ chains of paper clips./ Rubber bands form my hair." Piercy pushes her metaphor to show the dehumanizing nature of the work, a daily grind of repeated duties. Most literary writing tends to take this approach, focusing on how work is dull and stultifying while rarely fulfilling. Two classics that you likely read in school are Herman Melville's "Bartleby, the Scrivener" (whose answer to corporate directives usually is "I'd prefer not to") and George Orwell's *Animal Farm*, in which the nonporcine animals work for very little reward.

PROMPT: Let's steal . . . ahem . . . I mean, let's pay homage to these classic literary gems by employing their strategies: job as metaphor for self; character in conflict with job; workplace as social satire. Pick the approach of greatest interest to you and match it to your own experience. For example, you could write a poem turning yourself into the trappings of your job. You could recall a situation (or create a fictive one) in which someone engages in a show of civil disobedience, rejecting the orders of a boss. What happened? Was the person fired? Did the employee regret taking a stand? What was your role in the situation?

PROMPT: What would happen if employees staged a revolt, refusing to follow management's directives, and just walked out? At gatherings of disgruntled employees, someone invariably pipes up, "We should all just refuse." Imagine a situation based on your own job experience in which this suggestion actually leads to an uprising. What happens?

A more recent book, Joshua Ferris's very funny novel *Then We Came to the End*, takes a comic look at a failing ad agency. Ferris uses first-person plural point of view to characterize the collective mind-set of his characters in the following passage:

"We were fractious and overpaid. Our mornings lacked promise. At least those of us who smoked had something to look forward to at ten-fifteen. Most of us liked most everyone, a few of us hated specific individuals, one or two people loved everyone and everything. Those who loved everyone were unanimously reviled."

PROMPT: Write a few paragraphs using Ferris's first-person plural approach to give voice to a staff of employees you worked with. Try to be as specific as possible about the functions of the staff as well as the objections they commonly raised.

PROMPT: Of course, work doesn't have to be a grind, though in literature that tends to be the case. An exception is Nicholson Baker's short first novel, *The Mezzanine*, which celebrates the typical workplace by describing it in what seems to be microscopic detail. Rather than feeling mistreated, his narrator claims that he and his colleagues are "treated like popes." Spend a writing session celebrating the things you like most about your current or a previous job. Following Baker's lead, describe the work in sharp and intricate detail.

PROMPT: One reason for writing about your work is that, if you've done it long enough, you know the terrain. You know how to perform the tasks, the equipment that is used, the pace and rhythm of a typical day, the types of challenges that commonly arise. Use this information to lend specificity and authority to your writing. Put a fictional character into your job and write about a single morning, presenting in detail what the character does. Halfway through that morning, things begin to go very wrong. What happens?

PROMPT: One of the classic books on work is Studs Terkel's *Working*, in which the journalist interviewed many people about their jobs and presented the subject as sort of an oral history. Spend a session or two interviewing friends and family about their jobs, finding out their feelings about what they do. When you've completed a few, try to find common themes that run through them and write about what you've learned, or, like Terkel, you could present them as an oral history.

PROMPT: Another reason to use our jobs in our writing is that we know how to do them very well. Most of us don't have the time to practice playing golf or the piano as often as we'd like and therefore don't play as well as we'd like. But our jobs give us plenty of reps to perfect job performance. And it's engaging for readers to watch someone work at a high level of expertise, whether she's an artisan blowing a beautiful glass sculpture or a receptionist putting through five hundred calls per day. Describe a character performing a work process that you know how to do well. Make clear that the character is gifted at the process and describe the steps involved, taking time to show how it's done as specifically as possible.

CHAPTER 11

WHAT'S YOUR ROAD, MAN?

In many ways writing is the act of saying I, of imposing oneself upon other people, of saying listen to me, see it my way, change your mind.

—JOAN DIDION

The characters in Jack Kerouac's novel *On the Road* ask each other this chapter title's question while on their coast-to-coast trips. They want to know, of course, each other's philosophy of life, primary set of beliefs, path to enlightenment. If you want to get to know someone, find out what he believes in. If you want to get to know yourself better, explore your own beliefs. That's our focus in this chapter. Through a clearer understanding of your own beliefs—be they ever so vague and contradictory or so deeply held—you can generate writing ideas.

Let's run through a series of prompts that offer a variety of ways to ask yourself, "What's your road, man?" In fact, we'll begin with that question, but ask it in whatever language is most natural for you. You don't have to use the word *road* or call yourself *man*, but it feels kind of cool if you do.

PROMPT: Explain your philosophy of life, your personal set of beliefs. You can do this as an essay or simply in a long journal entry. This is not an easy exercise, but give it a try. We all have beliefs, and yet rarely do we think of them with such cool objectivity. Now's your chance. It may be easier to begin by making a list or a cluster, writing down things you believe, then putting them into cogent sentences and paragraphs.

PROMPT: List as many clichéd truths—truisms, rather than truths—as you can. For example, "time heals everything" (and "all wounds"); "you can't fight city hall"; "what goes around comes around." Then choose one entry from your list and write about it, defending it or exploding it or, perhaps, a bit of both. If you sometimes use one of these clichés in your day-to-day life, take it to task. Argue passionately against its validity. Then rise to its defense. (As the old saying goes, clichés are clichés because there's an element of truth in them. Of course, that sentiment is, in itself, a cliché.)

PROMPT: Create a character who speaks—and therefore thinks—about life in clichés and truisms. Develop the voice, perhaps in a monologue. If the voice interests you, place the character in a situation that challenges and eventually shatters those clichés.

PROMPT: Write about how you came to hold a particular belief, beginning with the event or the person who led you to your conclusion. Move from the specific to the general. After you finish the explanation, review it, asking questions of yourself to lead you to deeper explorations. Does the logic of your conclusion hold up? Does it require a leap of faith? Do you believe this truth more strongly than ever? Have you been too hasty in your conclusion?

PROMPT: Is the glass half empty or half full? Without thinking, write your response. Fast. Now take some time and explore in writing why you hold this belief. Then write a brief essay in which you try to convince someone who sees it the other way that you are right. If you want, write a rebuttal to your own argument. Or you can write a short poem, using images to make the same point.

PROMPT: Building on the previous prompt, put a glass-half-full character in a setting with a glass-half-empty character, then have them interact. You might make them strangers seated in a waiting room or at a bar. Or you could make them a romantic couple or perhaps parent and child. Try this out in a few ways to find which ones clicks for you.

PROMPT: As a sentient adult, you've been well aware for some time that life, indeed, is not just a bowl of cherries. Nor is it only a paper moon. So what is it? Pick a metaphor for life and explore it in a piece of writing. Begin with "Life is just a …" And you must use a noun, a specific, concrete thing. From that opening metaphor you can move in a number of directions: Write new lyrics to the melody of "Life Is Just a Bowl of Cherries"; write a poem, perhaps using the same meter as the song lyrics; write an essay supporting and exploring your metaphor; begin a scene with a character's statement that "Life is just a …"

PROMPT: Find a religious or philosophical quotation that makes a statement about the human condition. Consider looking in the Bible, a book of quotations, the Koran or Torah, or a book of philosophy. Use that statement as the first sentence in a piece of writing (or as an epigraph to a piece). In the piece, refute or demonstrate the efficacy of the statement.

PROMPT: What favorite line from a movie speaks to your view of the world? Write it down. Begin a piece of writing by explaining the context of the line in the movie: Who says it? To whom? Why? Where? What is its significance? Then explain your affinity for the line, detailing why you believe it is true.

PROMPT: Write a letter to someone whose worldview you strongly oppose. Explain why the person is wrong, making a strong case for your own view of things. Choose a well-known person if you want—a political or religious leader, someone from the media, the local shock jock. Or you can write to someone you know well, preferably someone around whom you've been forced to endure in silence—your sweet but wrong-headed father-in-law, perhaps.

PROMPT: You're very old. You're on your deathbed. (Sorry.) Family and friends gather around you. What do you tell them about life? What advice about living do you offer them? Spill a few pearls of wisdom from your experience.

PHILOSOPHICAL CHARACTERS

Some literary works ponder the big questions of life. Think of Yann Martel's novel *Life of Pi* or the plays and novels of Ayn Rand or Samuel Beckett's plays or many of Saul Bellow's novels. The novels *Infinite Jest* and *The Pale King* by David Foster Wallace also come to mind. The characters work largely as devices to explore philosophical issues. If this approach interests you, take some time to check out some of these works and see if they inspire you to give it a try.

PROMPT: Explore your own philosophical questions and conflicts by creating a small group of characters who represent each view of the questions you're mulling. Put them all at a dinner party or on an island and start an argument. Allow them to state their views. It needn't be an obvious or mechanical process. Just allow them to speak as characters and allow the narrative thread to go where it will.

The themes that run through your writing reflect your beliefs, even if unintentionally. In fact, a good way to gain a clearer understanding of what you believe is to read your fiction with an eye toward theme. What are you saying to your reader? What contradictions and struggles for understanding lie at the foundation of your art? What

THE WRITER'S IDEA BOOK

themes surface in story after story? Some writers and critics feel we tell the same story over and over, in different ways, using different sets of characters. I don't know that this is true or false, but it's fun to think about. What is your story?

You also can use beliefs and philosophies in your fiction to develop characters. Ask yourself: What does this character believe about life and the way the world works? Put the answer on the page and find out what happens. One of the best-known examples of a character stating his philosophy occurs in *The Great Gatsby,* when Jay Gatsby, the stupendously romantic gangster, tells an incredulous Nick Carraway, "Can't repeat the past? Why of course you can, old sport." In that statement of belief, we see Gatsby in all his deluded splendor. Wham. He's right there before our eyes. The line speaks to the heart of the novel's themes, foreshadows Gatsby's ultimate failure, and eventually wakes Nick from his moral torpor.

Though I'm loath to place a humble creation of my own right next to Fitzgerald's shimmering masterpiece, let me offer another example, one in which a character's statement of belief not only placed him more clearly on the page but led me to understand him better. While working on a novel, I was troubled by the protagonist, whom I couldn't fully understand and whom readers didn't find sympathetic enough. I could sense within him a certain strength that I couldn't quite express on the page because I didn't understand it fully myself. After completing a draft of the novel, I abandoned it, but the protagonist, Mitch, popped up later in a short story titled "Touchdown Jesus." In a scene near the end of the story, Mitch, who is in his thirties and down on his luck, speaks to a freckle-faced college freshman named Tom and tries to impart a bit of hard-earned wisdom about the shootings on the campus of Kent State University in 1970. Mitch had been a student there at the time. While writing the story, I read James Michener's *Kent State* and learned that many of the students were shocked when the guards opened fire. The students hadn't realized the guns were loaded. A lot of sixties idealism died that day. And the sentiment seemed perfect for Mitch:

"The gun is always loaded, Tom," Mitch told the boy. "Make no mistake."

With that line, I suddenly understood Mitch as I never had during the writing of the novel. The story was published and even nominated for a Pushcart, but I never went back to the novel, which, sadly, is a product of another time and place, another me. My point here, however, is that discovering what a character believes can lead to your understanding him better and can help the reader understand him, too.

PROMPT: Choose a character from a project you're working on or planning to begin. Ask him to explain his beliefs, even if only in a scattered elliptical way. Try to dig into the character's mind and let him talk to you, without forcing it. Put the page away for a few days, then return to it. Any surprises? Does it make sense? Does it fit the character as you knew him?

PROMPT: Create a character who states a belief with which a second character disagrees. Have them work through their differences or simply accept them. A classic example of this situation occurs in Robert Frost's poem "Mending Wall," in which one character states the belief "good fences make good neighbors," meaning that people can get along with each other if they don't try to connect. The narrator does not share this belief. He feels, as Frost clearly feels, that it's much more natural, even inevitable, for people to share their lives with others. Ironically, the neighbor's sentiment has gained wider usage than the narrator's, is even quoted by people: "As Robert Frost said, 'good fences make good neighbors'."

PROMPT: Have a character espouse a viewpoint on life with which you very much disagree, but have the character argue it well, citing examples from her life to buttress her stance. Resist the temptation to make her sound foolish or harsh. If you can, relate the character's view in third person, as if it's coming from the narrative rather than directly from her mouth. The narrative should be sympathetic in its approach.

PROMPT: Okay, now you can make it sound foolish. In fact, exaggerate the view. Show it in all its stupidity. For models, look to the great satirists, such as Sinclair Lewis, James Thurber, and Dorothy Parker.

Another great model to use for the previous prompt appears in John Kennedy Toole's novel *A Confederacy of Dunces,* in which the protagonist, Ignatius J. Reilly, is quick to explain his view of life, usually in wildly pompous, hypocritical language. Here is a bit of Ignatius, who is writing (in Big Boy tablets) a preposterously inflated document on the decline of Western civilization:

> After a period in which the western world had enjoyed order, tranquility, Unity, and oneness with its True God and Trinity, there appeared winds of change which spelled evil days ahead. An ill wind blows no one good. The luminous years of Abelard, Thomas à Becket, and Everyman dimmed into dross; Fortuna's wheel had turned on humanity, crushing its collarbone, smashing its skull, twisting its torso, puncturing its pelvis, sorrowing its soul. Having once been so high, humanity fell so low. What had once been dedicated to the soul was now dedicated to the sale.

THE WRITER'S IDEA BOOK

Not that Ignatius doesn't have a couple of points worth considering. But his grand style and linguistic ineptitude undercut any point he might make. Toole is having fun with the voice here, as he does throughout the novel. If you want, try the previous prompt again, and strive for the wild absurdity Toole manages to create.

CONTROL

Now that you've had some fun, let's get a bit more serious. There is danger in allowing a character to step up on a soapbox: You can lose control of the narrative. If the character's viewpoint agrees with yours and lies near the story's themes, the character could become simply a mouthpiece and the story could descend into didacticism. Resist this temptation. Especially in early drafts, we sometimes feel overly eager to pump a few bright red thematic flares into the sky above our narrative landscapes. In early drafts, this compulsion is not a problem. It can help us understand the story's themes more clearly and understand the character better. But then we must remove it, relying on drama and indirection to carry forward the themes.

But if you can manage to control the voice—which is especially difficult in a first-person story—you can create some powerful moments in your fiction. One such moment that I like occurs in Alan Sillitoe's "The Loneliness of the Long-Distance Runner." The speaker is a lower-class boy of seventeen, doing time in a juvenile detention center (called a Borstal, in England) for robbing a bakery. The boy's view of the world is tough and unsentimental, and yet Sillitoe manages to make him sympathetic, even when he's violent. In one scene, the nameless narrator and some friends break up a picnic, scaring away a group of upper-class teens and taking their food. In explaining his actions, the narrator offers a glimpse into his view of how life works:

> Well, I'll always feel during every day of my life like those daft kids should have felt before we broke them up. But they never dreamed that what happened was going to happen, just like the governor of this Borstal who spouts to us about honesty and all that wappy stuff don't know a bloody thing while I know every minute of my life that a big boot is always likely to smash any nice picnic I might be barmy and dishonest enough to make for myself.

A very dark sentiment from a seventeen-year-old narrator, but it is one that speaks to the sense of hopelessness that surrounds his life. By understanding this view, the reader can more clearly understand why the boy acts as he does and can sympathize more fully with his plight. Note, too, that the narrator is far different from the writer. He is not a mouthpiece. His revelation does not sound didactic.

PROMPT: Begin a story in the voice of a character who espouses some viewpoint or belief about life. Have the character explain why she feels this way. The character should be different from you in some significant way, and her belief should be clearly not your own. If you want, introduce a second character who does not share this belief, as you did in the earlier prompt.

PROMPT: Place two characters in a room. They have vastly different views of life. Create a dialogue in which these differences become clear to the reader, but don't allow the characters to confront these differences directly. Instead, they might argue or talk about an innocuous subject. For example, a father and son watch a football game and speak mostly about what they're watching. Two sisters meet for dinner in a trendy restaurant. A boss and employee work together in a sales booth at a convention. The different worldviews, again, should not be stated directly.

CHAPTER TWELVE

THE LOVE YOU MAKE

*Writing about people helps us to understand them,
and understanding them helps us to accept them as part
of ourselves.*

—ALICE WALKER

The comedian Lenny Bruce once got into trouble for what the media perceived as an insult to Jackie Kennedy. This incident occurred not long after the president's assassination, after the famous Zapruder tape was released. In his comedy routine, Bruce noted that after the president was shot, while the car was still moving, the First Lady climbed across the trunk in an effort, Bruce thought, to get away. A Secret Service man was running along behind the car and helped Mrs. Kennedy back into the car, which then sped away. Pictures of the First Lady on the trunk of the car were presented in the newspapers and on television as her attempt to help the Secret Service man into the car. Bruce's assessment: "The First Lady was hauling ass."

His point in bringing this up was that the media makes heroes from people who are not heroic, who suffer from the weaknesses of human nature from which everyone suffers. This sort of lie, he felt, makes people feel terrible when they cannot reach what is, in fact, an unachievable standard. "Nobody stays," Bruce told his audience. And though he was speaking of Jackie Kennedy, I believe he was also speaking about love. Bruce never fully recovered from his wife's leaving him after their tempestuous marriage. He had grown cynical—or realistic, depending upon your view of love. Love, said Bruce, does not conquer all, and when times get tough, people leave. Even the First Lady ditches the president when the bullets start flying.

ROMANTIC LOVE

What do you think? Is love really a capricious emotion, subject to the winds of fortune? Or are people capable of staying—not out of fear or comfort or inertia but out of a selfless concern for someone to whom they feel deeply devoted? We're speaking now of the love between mates, between couples, rather than the love we feel for our families and friends.

PROMPT: Write about your beliefs about love, following some of the questions raised above. Is it a powerful emotion? What is the nature of love? How long can it last? Does it inevitably fade? Begin an essay titled "On Love," or write a poem about love. Or, if you prefer, write a scene that dramatizes your beliefs about the nature of love.

I won't tell you what I think, but consider that Bruce's story has stuck with me for a long time. But another line has stuck with me, too. It appears in Woody Allen's *Manhattan*. In fact, it's the last line of the film and thus has a strong thematic resonance. After realizing he has made a stupid mistake in leaving the young woman he'd been seeing, Allen's character rushes to her apartment to beg her forgiveness and win her back. He finds her leaving for a three-month stay in London. Though he begs her not to go, she insists on leaving but promises to return. When he pleads that she'll meet someone new while there, she tells him, "Sometimes you've got to have a little faith in people."

A wonderful and sentimental line. Let's use it for the next prompt.

PROMPT: Make a case for our capacity for love, for our right to deserve "a little faith." Even if you're the most hardened cynic about affairs of the heart, give it a try. If you're a true believer, this one should be easy, but imagine that hardened cynic reading your piece. Anticipate objections and arguments and rebut them.

PROMPT: Write about a couple you know that embody the view of having "a little faith in people." Describe them and show them in action, relating an anecdote that portrays the depth of their love and commitment.

PROMPT: Reverse the previous prompt. Write about a couple whose commitment was not lasting, that broke when things got tough. Again, use an anecdote to show us the situation rather than explaining it.

PROMPT: Let's have a little fun with the couples in the two previous prompts and send them on a double date together. What happens?

PROMPT: Write about your first love as an adult or, at least, after the age of sixteen. Give all the details—when, where, why, etc. How long did the relationship last? Why did it end? What did you learn about love from this first experience?

PROMPT: Write about your current love. If you haven't got one at the moment, write about your most recent one. Again, give us the when and why. Describe your mate. What is unique about that person? Which of your partner's qualities do you love most?

PROMPT: Write about your experience with—or desire for—an illicit love. Of course, each of us must define for ourselves what is "illicit," but let's take the view of conventional society: Write about a relationship or encounter you experienced with someone who was off-limits. If you've never had or desired this experience, create a fictional character and recount a fictional illicit love.

PROMPT: Write about "the one who got away," a past love for whom you still yearn, perhaps, or who you feel would have been a good mate. If you don't have such a person in your past, create a fictional character or focus on someone you know who has had this experience.

PROMPT: Maybe the one who got away is largely imaginary for you. Write about what might happen if you actually meet this person. We're in the realm of fantasy now, so let yourself go and really do it right!

PROMPT: You're Dr. Frankenstein: Build your ideal lover. List all of the qualities he or she would possess. You may even want to throw in a flaw or two, shortcomings that you'll find endearing. When you've finished your list, create a character sketch of this person, a detailed description.

PROMPT: Write about life with the ideal lover you created in the previous prompt. Where do you live? What do you do? Take time to develop the "happily ever after."

PROMPT: Describe the nature and feeling of love to someone who has never had the experience—a young person, perhaps, or someone who simply has never been smitten. What insights and advice can you offer?

PROMPT: Write about a time when you suffered a broken heart. Explain what happened, how you felt, how you handled it and how you mended yourself. Then write a letter to that person, expressing your feelings—how you felt at the time and how you feel now. Write freely, assuming you won't send the letter.

PROMPT: Write a scene from the point of view of a character being left by another character. If possible, avoid all the clichés of soap operas and televisions and bad books and movies. Unfortunately, that doesn't give you much room to work. It seems that everything on this topic has been said to death. You'll need to reach down into your characters to find something fresh, something particular to them. If you want, keep dialogue to a minimum. Work with action and gesture.

PROMPT: Write about a time when you broke someone else's heart. Again, explain what happened and how you felt. Then write a letter to the person, expressing your feelings. Again, assume you won't send the letter.

PROMPT: Write a scene from the point of view of someone breaking someone else's heart. If you want, recast the scene you wrote above, this time showing it from the other character's point of view. Again, do your best to keep things from veering into melodrama and cliché. Rely on action and gesture. Rely on indirection. The couple could talk about something completely off the subject, making little mention of what's taking place.

PROMPT: Write a scene in which two former lovers meet after many years. What happens? If you've had this experience, base your scene on what happened to you, or change it in whatever way feels right.

PROMPT: What song or songs best capture the nature of love? Defend your choices. Or, if you'd prefer, what song or songs are outrageous lies?

PROMPT: What's the most romantic book you've ever read? What's the most romantic movie you've ever seen? Or, again, what book or movie got it all wrong?

PROMPT: At the end of his short story "The Sensible Thing," F. Scott Fitzgerald writes, "There are many kinds of love in the world, but never the same love twice." Though the statement seems sentimental, it's worth a close look. First, do you feel that it's true? Explain your feelings. Second, write about the kinds of romantic love you've experienced—passionate, blissful, quietly assuring, erratic and unpredictable. Use Fitzgerald's sentence to begin a piece about your own experiences with love.

PROMPT: You have a blog or a print column offering advice to the lovelorn. What advice do you give about love's most common issues? You might cast your advice as an instructional article—the top ten truths about romantic relationships.

PROMPT: Back when you were younger, you pretty much had this romance thing all figured out, right? Well, odds are you've learned a few things since then. Sit down with your younger self and explain what life and experience have taught you.

If you want, fictionalize the situation, having a younger person and an older one discuss the vicissitudes of romance and love.

SEX

We love to write about sex. We love to read about it. It's a universal subject that, even if we live to be a hundred years old, retains its power. If you were flipping through this book in a store, you'd have passed through dozens of pages with barely a glance, but I'll bet if you saw this subhead, you'd stop for at least a skim.

Which is why I included it. In truth, sex is tough to write about. We can write about passion and desire and the first stirrings of sex, but the actual sex act, and most of what leads up to it, has been exhaustively well charted and, with some exceptions, doesn't quite work on the page. The act is so primal and focused and is more than the sum total of the physical mechanics. To do it well, you must get into the minds of the characters—make it mean something. If not love, then some sort of connection. As Elizabeth Benedict writes in her book *The Joy of Writing Sex:*

> In the best fiction writing about sex, even if it is a brief paragraph, we come to the end knowing not just "what happened" but something about the characters, their sensibilities, circumstances or inner lives, about the narrator who is relating the events, the concerns of the author—or all of the above. A well-written sex scene engages us on many levels: erotic, aesthetic, psychological, metaphorical, even philosophical.

Her insights apply to nonfiction as well. Beyond the gymnastics—or, as Cathleen Schine put it in *The New York Review of Books,* "tab A being fitted breathlessly into slot B"—we need to provide details on how the sex affects the characters involved. In that way, the scene becomes particular and interesting.

PROMPT: Write about what arouses you sexually. Take time to consider what popular media tells you arouses you sexually, and then dismiss it. I don't know about you, but to me, seeing a lover in a setting of candlelight, soft music, and flowers through the rosy glow of a glass of wine always feels like a cardboard cutout of romance, someone else's idea of intimacy. To create a scene more your own, spend a little time recalling the specifics of that last really blazing encounter. Who were you with? What triggered your reaction? Where were you? What time of day was it? How did that person make you feel? Randy, yes, but exactly how? Where did you specifically like to be touched? How did that make you feel? Write a few of these scenes, and then give yourself a break. You may need it.

PROMPT: Mine the rich ore of your sexual fantasies. Write about your favorites, the ones you depend upon when you're dead tired and your partner is desperately in the mood.

PROMPT: In her nonfiction book *Aphrodite*, Isabel Allende writes that she grows amorous watching her husband cook. She especially admires his hands and the economy of motion with which he chops and mixes and sautés. She playfully imagines him slowly undressing, as he continues to cook, as a prelude to spontaneous lovemaking. What unlikely settings or circumstances trigger the same response in you? Write a description of what you feel, taking time to linger over the sensual details. Can you speculate on what arouses your desire? How would that desire play itself out?

PROMPT: Write a sex scene in which conflict simmers beneath the surface. What happens next? Do the characters address the issue or continue to bury it beneath the motions of lovemaking? If you want, try both ways. Which one better fits the characters? Which one makes for more compelling drama? Can you recall a similar experience in your own life? If so, write a narrative explaining what happened.

PROMPT: In an interview, Carol Shields said, "The most erotic scene I've ever witnessed was my uncle, bending over at the dining room table to kiss the back of my aunt's neck. It was summertime and she was wearing a sundress and just lifting a spoonful of sherbet to her lips. They were middle-aged then. I was child of nine or ten but I recognized 'it.'" Write about the most erotic scene you've ever witnessed. Like Shields's scene, it can be subtle and understated. Or it could be passionately sexual.

PROMPT: Whom in your past would you most like to make love to again? Set the scene. How would this happen? Detail the seduction. Or, if you prefer, whom in your present life would you most like to make love to? Again, plot the story of the seduction from start to finish.

PROMPT: Create a scene in which two people desperately want to connect but can't seem to pull the trigger. As they move toward intimacy, throw roadblocks in their path, keeping them on edge, almost succeeding but not quite. It will take some doing on your part to keep these two apart, but use your imagination and boil the water without letting it froth over the top of the pan.

PROMPT: Sex scenes can be dull if they maintain a single emotional tone, as they often do on television and in movies. The scene is humorous or ardent or romantic or edgy from start to finish. In real life, they tend to move among a variety of emotional textures. Write a scene in which the tone does just that—a romantic start leads to a funny moment or two and then things maybe get a bit rough and then tender.

THE WRITER'S IDEA BOOK

FAMILY AND FRIENDS

The final type of love we'll look at in this chapter is the love we have for family and friends. We discussed your family in an earlier chapter, so we won't explore the topic in detail here, but a chapter on love could not be without mention of family. Though I've been a parent for more than twenty years, I continue to be amazed at the depth of love I feel for my two sons. They have stirred in me feelings I didn't know were possible before they were born. Dive in front of a bullet for them? No problem. If you're a parent, you know what I mean.

If you're not a parent, these feelings can come from other sources, perhaps your family or a very close friend. For many years, I was very close to my brothers and felt a strong bond with them. Perhaps you've enjoyed a similar relationship with siblings. In this section, let's explore your feelings for family and friends.

PROMPT: Write about your relationship with your parents by describing an event from your childhood, an event from your teen years, one from your early adulthood and, depending on your age and the ages of your parents, one from later adulthood. Each event should suggest the nature of your relationship with your parents at the time it occurred.

PROMPT: Write about parents and their children struggling with an empty nest. The kids are ready to fly off on their own while the parents are not ready for that to happen. There is love on all sides of the conflict, and yet nature must take its course.

PROMPT: Make a list of the good friends you've had in your life. Briefly describe each person and the nature of the friendship. Choose one to explore in greater detail. Then write in a more general way about the nature of the friendships you've enjoyed. Do they usually last a long time? What sorts of needs are satisfied by your friendships? Do you consider yourself a good friend? Why or why not?

PROMPT: I once dated a woman whose brother told me, "Friends are just people who borrow things." I remember thinking how lonely the guy must feel or how friends in his past must have disappointed him. Begin a piece of writing with a sweeping assertion about the nature of friendship, then develop your statement or refute it, or just go where it leads you.

PROMPT: Write a scene in which a group of friends get together—to watch a football game, to attend a baby shower. Imagine they share a secret or bad experience of some kind from their past that no one ever discusses. Keep that secret—a robbery in which they all took part, a trip to Florida that went out of control—on the fringe of the discussion, bringing it up slowly until finally it's out in the open.

PROMPT: Some friendships last beyond their natural life spans. By that I mean that many of us have a few friendships that are relics from a different, often much earlier, time in our lives. Though we still like the old friends, we share nothing in common and find we have very little to talk about when we get together. Falling quickly into reminiscence when you do get together is a good indicator that a friendship is well past its prime. Do you have a friendship of this type? If so, write about it. What factors keep it alive? How would you feel if it ended?

PROMPT: A family, perhaps one based loosely on your own family, heads off in the car for vacation or for a day-trip. Describe what happens. The scenario is a classic one in American literature and movies. Two examples that come quickly to mind are John Barth's short story "Lost in the Funhouse" and Flannery O'Connor's short story "A Good Man Is Hard to Find." Read these stories as models for handling this situation. Unfortunately, neither of these trips turns out well for the family. If you have a cheerier trip in mind, you'll want to look elsewhere.

PROMPT: I used "The Love You Make" for this chapter's title, so let's end with that, a quote you no doubt recognize from a Beatles song titled "The End." The line goes, "And in the end, the love you take is equal to the love you make." Do you believe that love works in this way—the more we love, the more we are loved? I ask that question, which seems valid, even important, knowing well that the late Chris Farley asked Paul McCartney the same question in a classic moment of *Saturday Night Live*. But I'll ask it anyway. What do you think?

CHAPTER THIRTEEN

DON'T GET ME STARTED

I write to find out what I'm talking about.

—EDWARD ALBEE

What ticks you off? Poor service in a restaurant? Traffic jams? Incompetence where you work? The injustice of untalented people—far less talented than you, for example—enjoying unwarranted success? We all have our flash points, the buttons that people had better not push. Let's spend some time looking at what makes you good and mad, and search there for ideas.

WHAT MAKES YOU ANGRY?

We like to talk about what makes us angry. We like to write about it. Years ago, we conducted focus groups at Writer's Digest Books as part of researching a new line of guided journals. As moderator, I threw out a half dozen topics for the group's consideration. A few sparked interest; a few sparked yawns. I asked when the members of the group felt most like writing in their journals. "When I'm mad," a woman declared. "I write it down and get it off my chest." Others in the group nearly shouted their agreement. At the next focus group, I offered this topic and the members jumped all over it. We had touched a nerve.

So if you enjoy grumbling in your journal about what ticks you off, as most people do, don't feel ashamed. Enjoy it. Get your feelings out there on paper. If you have a short-fused character, indulge her for a while. Try to find out what is behind the anger.

PROMPT: Let's start with a list. Write down the things that have made you angry in the past week—or the past month, if your week has been mild. Take some time and try to remember all of them, from stubbing your toe on a chair leg to your child's adamant refusal to do what you asked to your senator's cowardly vote on a bill you strongly support. Keep a running tally for a few days, if necessary. Pick one item from your list and freewrite about it, telling in a rush of words (don't sweat punctuation and style at this stage) how you felt and why you felt that way. Can you fashion this into a more considered essay or poem? If you want, pick other items from the list and follow the same process.

PROMPT: Place the items from your list above into categories, such as "home," "the office," "family," "friends," "the news," "social injustice," or whatever categories are appropriate for you. Then add to each list by moving farther back in time—a month, even a year. Write down what you can remember, then pick a category and look for patterns. Is there something at work that angers you on a regular basis?

PROMPT: Make a list of chronic anger sparkers. Pet peeves, if you will. When you finish your list, choose one and freewrite about it. Include examples of times this peeve has made you angry. Did you express your feelings or did you try to suppress them? Ruminate and write about why this peeve is a sore spot with you. Is there a way to resolve this problem? Write about some possibilities.

PROMPT: Review the list from the previous prompt and look for patterns. What *types* of things tend to make you angry? People who are chronically late? Machines that break down? Kids with attitudes? Parents with attitudes? You will probably spot a few patterns. Choose one and write about it. Explore the reasons behind the pattern, offering some theories about why this is a vulnerable spot for you. Use examples.

PROMPT: Write about your relationship with anger. Are you an angry person? Do you hold in your anger or let it out? Do you let it out in what could be considered appropriate ways? Do you express anger at the true sources, or do you find other people and things at which to vent? Road rage, for example, is usually the result of anger at something else. The guy who cut us off in traffic is simply an easy target for you to vent upon. That's why, on some days, we could care less if someone cuts us off in traffic while, on other days, we wish we had a handy flamethrower to scorch that rude so-and-so.

PROMPT: Choose someone you know who handles anger well and describe how she does it. If you tend to hold in your anger, you might admire someone who speaks her mind. If you tend to unleash your anger too quickly, you might admire

THE WRITER'S IDEA BOOK

someone who exercises more self-control. Either way, write about why you wish you could handle your anger as this other person does.

PROMPT: If you could embody your anger with an animal, what one would be the most appropriate. Tiger? Vulture? Write about why you chose that animal.

PROMPT: Write a letter to someone at whom you are angry or once felt anger. Really blast him. Then write a letter to that person in a calmer tone, explaining how you feel or felt. This letter can be particularly effective if you didn't show your anger at the time.

PROMPT: Write a letter to someone who is or was angry with you. Apologize, if necessary, or explain your reasons for doing whatever made her angry.

PROMPT: Psychologists tell us that beneath anger lies fear. Think about how this theory applies to you or, if you're writing a story, to one of your characters. In a free-write, try to dig beneath the anger and find what fears might be causing the anger.

PROMPT: Write an essay titled "On Anger," in which you begin with your own feelings about anger—such as what makes you mad, how you and other people handle anger—and move to some conclusions about the nature of this complicated emotion.

PROMPT: Write about a time in which anger caused you to make some public display, one that no doubt sparks more embarrassment than anger in you now. What did you do? How was the situation resolved? If you're interested, cast a fictional character into this same situation, one who reacts as you did, and let the situation resolve itself in a different way.

PROMPT: Because it's easier to watch someone else embarrass themselves than to think about ourselves doing it, recall a time when someone let loose with anger in a public place, attracting the attention of the people around him. If you know the circumstances that caused the display, explain them, but if not, feel free to focus only on the specifics of what happened. Brainstorm to recall as many details as possible.

ANGRY STORIES

Now that you've explored your own anger for a while, let's move to using anger in stories. Anger can be a great motivator for writing and can keep you going when the story lags. Some writers nurse anger for years against teachers who told them they couldn't write, using this anger to keep them going when times are tough. Writers also use stories as a place to express anger that they cannot express in their lives. Some of these writers get sued for it, so beware of what you say in print.

Writers use the anger they feel for people they know as the basis for stories. Eugene O'Neill's great play *Long Day's Journey Into Night,* published posthumously but written years before his death, seems to explore the anger he felt toward his father. Anger at social injustice has led to great novels, such as John Steinbeck's *The Grapes of Wrath,* Upton Sinclair's *The Jungle,* and Richard Wright's *Native Son.* Great characters have been developed who are motivated primarily by anger. Think of Captain Ahab in *Moby Dick* or Allie in Paul Theroux's *The Mosquito Coast,* or Mira in Marilyn French's *The Women's Room.*

If you want an example of an angry character in action, consider the following bit of vitriol from Robert Penn Warren's *All the King's Men.* Throughout much of the novel, Willie "The Boss" Stark rages against anything that stands in the way of his ambitions. In this scene, in a pique of paranoia, he blasts an underling who he feels has betrayed him:

> As soon as I opened the door, I ran right into the Boss's eyes like running into the business end of a double-barreled 10-gauge shotgun at three paces, and halted. "Look!" he commanded, heaving his bulk up erect on the big leather couch where he had been propped, "Look."
>
> And he swung the double-barrel around to cover Tiny, who stood at the hearthrug before and seemed to be melting the tallow down faster than even the log fire on the bricks would have warranted.
>
> "Look," he said to me, "this bastard tried to trick me, tried to smuggle that Gummy Larson in here to talk to me, gets him all the way up here from Duboisville and thinks I'll be polite. But the hell I was polite." He swung to Tiny again. "Was I, was I polite?"
>
> Tiny did not manage to utter a sound . . . .
>
> "You thought you'd trick me—trick me into buying him. Well, I'm not buying him. I'm going to bust him . . . . I made a mistake not busting you. But I figured you'd stay bought. You're scared not to."
>
> "Now, Boss," Tiny said, "now Boss, that ain't fair. You know how all us boys feel about you. And all. It ain't being scared, it's—"
>
> "You damned well better be scared," the Boss said, and his voice was suddenly sweet and low. Like a mother whispering to her child in the crib.

Notice that the author modulates the tone of Stark's voice at the end, which paradoxically makes him even more menacing. Characters who are angry do not have to shout. By varying your approach to presenting their anger, you can produce more chilling effects.

PROMPT: Place anger at the center of a scene between two characters, but keep it below the surface. Allow the tension to build slowly. You can end with a blowup, in which the anger finally boils over, or you can resolve the anger, allowing the emotion to dissipate.

PROMPT: Write a monologue in which a character vents his rage. As the monologue develops, add clues that suggest the character is more fearful than angry, or is angry as a result of fear.

PROMPT: Write a monologue in which a character vents her rage, but this time vary the tone. Instead of one long howl, soften the voice, or add a touch of humor. Perhaps the entire monologue can be delivered quietly, the rage burbling just below the surface. This technique will deliver a greater tension to the scene than an outburst.

PROMPT: Write a scene, based on a real experience in your life, in which two characters are angry with each other. Do not base the viewpoint character on yourself. Instead, give the viewpoint to the person with whom you argued.

PROMPT: Begin a story with a character in the middle of a rage. The character's anger seems completely inappropriate to its source. For example, a character can be cursing in great anger about a minor inconvenience or disappointment—the local baseball team lost an unimportant game, the cookie jar is empty. As readers watch this character explain—and bellow—his frustration at the characters around him, it becomes clear that the character is angry about something else, which you could name or not.

PROMPT: Write about a social injustice, some issue that makes your blood boil. Begin with an essay, titled "On [issue of social injustice]," and try to get your ideas on the page in an expository way. Then try to move to a less direct approach—fiction or a poem or a script.

PROMPT: Write about something that happened to you that made you very angry at the time but now seems funny. Recall the event in as much detail as possible, writing it down exactly as it happened. Then try to fictionalize the event, adding a few details, sharpening the situation, exploring the dramatic possibilities. Don't feel tied to the story as it happened.

PROMPT: Write a scene in which someone (real or imagined) who rarely ever expresses anger really lets loose. The tension has been building inside him for a long while, and he's finally unable to suppress it. You could handle this explosion with humor or show the shock of those around him who are stunned by this uncharacteristic behavior.

CHAPTER FOURTEEN

YOUR FIFTEEN MINUTES

Let us not be too scornful of fame; nothing is lovelier,
unless it be virtue.

—CHATEAUBRIAND

Andy Warhol promised all of us fifteen minutes of fame. He *promised*. I don't know about you, but I'm still waiting for mine. But all of us, in fairness, have had times in our lives when we were in the spotlight, if only in a small way. There have been times, too, when we have met someone famous or been involved in some event that made a stir. In this chapter, we'll look at such times, in hopes of moving our experiences from the private to the public arena.

A friend of my father taught English for many years at a local high school. He was a smart man who, in his youth, aspired to be a writer, but gave up, for reasons I never knew. He also was a fine baseball player and spent a couple of springs with minor-league clubs. One spring, while playing against the Dodgers' farm team, he faced the great Sandy Koufax, albeit before Koufax learned how to control his fastball. This showdown must have occurred in the late 1950s. With two strikes on him and Koufax blazing the ball into the strike zone that day, my father's friend smashed a single into the outfield. After a drink or two, he would tell that story—his brush with fame.

The husband of a woman who works with my brother was in the armed service in 1963, stationed in Washington, DC. He was one of the guards assigned to Jackie Kennedy on the day the president was assassinated. He remembers that throughout the evening and into the next day, Mrs. Kennedy wore the dress stained with her husband's blood.

Though neither of these men is at all famous, each experienced a brush with fame and has an interesting story to tell as a result. My family and friends are by no means famous, and yet I know at least a half dozen stories of this kind—a second cousin who starred on a 1950s TV sitcom, a friend's father who landed at Normandy Beach on D-Day, a friend's sister who invented an important synthetic heart valve. In my workshops at writers conferences, I often ask students to write about such moments in their own lives. Some have told fascinating stories. One I remember very well involved a young woman's meetings—two of them, a few years apart—with Indira Gandhi. Both meetings left the woman frustrated. She wanted to express her deeply felt admiration for her hero and yet couldn't seem to find the right words when she needed them. Though she was disappointed at the meetings, they led to a short piece of writing that moved a roomful of writers. I hope she developed the piece further when she returned home from the conference.

PROMPT: Write about meeting a famous person. Even if it was only a handshake in a crowd, put the event on the page. Freewrite or cluster to stir your memory of the meeting. Tell it as a narrative, step by step, including as many details as you can recall. If you want, take time to do a little research on the famous person. Expand your piece by adding this information to it. When you finish the account of the meeting, speculate on its significance. What did it mean to you, if anything? How did the person measure up to your expectations?

PROMPT: Write about a news event to which you have some connection. Did an important event occur in your hometown? Were you ever involved, even as a bystander, in an event that the general public will remember? Follow the process you used in the previous prompt. Freewrite everything you can remember about the event, form the details and the actions into a narrative, research the event to add relevant background, speculate on its significance to you.

PROMPT: Ask family and friends and colleagues about their own fifteen minutes of fame. Most people have some story to tell. Write down these stories as best you can. Research the people and events mentioned in the stories you find interesting. Is there an article idea here? Do you detect any patterns within the stories? Do you believe all the stories, or have some clearly been embellished in retellings?

PROMPT: Many famous people have appeared in works of fiction. Try this yourself. Write a fictive scene involving a well-known person—historical or contemporary. Try to be true to what you know about the person. If you want, relate the scene from the famous person's point of view. Or, if you want, add a few more famous people to the scene. In the following excerpt from a long scene in Mark Winegardner's *The Veracruz Blues*, the narrator attends a party at Ernest Hemingway's house. Guests at the party include Babe Ruth and former heavyweight boxing champion Gene Tunney. Notice how the author shows the celebrities in actions we recognize from reading about them—Ruth and Hemingway full of bluff and bluster. Notice, too, that he adds specific details to humanize these larger-than-life folks, to make them seem like believable story people rather than like animated monuments:

> Throughout dinner no one spoke to me. Babe Ruth and Ernest Hemingway, both drunk, at a single dinner table, swapping suspiciously exciting tales of manly prowess (here a dead beast, there a pair of friendly twin redheads, everywhere a sweaty triumph), provided little chance for others to talk.
>
> Above the sideboard were framed photos of Hemingway with famous men and dead animals. I was in none of them. I had taken one of the ones from Paris, a blurry shot of Hemingway and Scott Fitzgerald (in for a brief visit), each in a brand-new beret.

PROMPT: Write a fictive scene in which a character meets someone famous. Perhaps the character could be based on you or someone you know, and the famous person could be someone you admire. Develop the scene as fully as possible. In the following scene from Kim Herzinger's short story "The Day I Met Buddy Holly," the narrator meets a man who he believes is the famous rock-and-roll star. The story does not reveal if the character is really Buddy Holly. Instead, it investigates the nature of celebrity and the light they can bring into ordinary lives:

> The sun was shining down onto the top of Buddy's head; like most rock and roll stars Buddy had sort of short hair, with a just a tiny curl coming down in the front. I had to squint to see him.
>
> "Well, usually the trains are here on time," I said.
>
> He lit a cigarette. "Not today."
>
> "No. Not today. There might be something wrong. Maybe a log problem or something. Sometimes we get a log problem in town because of all the lumber companies here. You've probably smelled some of them. Maybe some logs have fallen off and hurt the tracks. That's lumber for you . . . ."
>
> "You're Buddy Holly aren't you?" I was surprised at myself, and I thought for a minute that Buddy was going to turn and walk away from me. But he didn't. He took it in stride.
>
> "I wish," he said finally. "My name is Tom Truehaft. I'm from Lake Oswego. I'm a barber."

I looked at his shoes. They were not the shoes of a barber. No barber would have ever known that they have shoes like that.

PROMPT: What famous person do you physically resemble? In other words, who do people say you look like? Write about that resemblance, perhaps in a nonfiction piece in which you could compare yourself to the famous person. For example, many people tell me I look like the actor Chuck Norris—same beard, same build, same coloring. Though Chuck is probably fifteen years older than I am, I try not to be insulted by the comparison. In fact, while in Aspen (a place where people expect to spot celebrities), a young family pointed at me and smiled excitedly. I figured out the error but gave them a hale-and-hearty Chuck Norris wave. Or you could write a fiction in which you *are* the famous person. Or, using the example in Kim Herzinger's story, the tale could involve a character who is mistaken for a celebrity. Perhaps the character does little to correct the mistake, perhaps even tries to exploit it. I'm reminded of the song by the late Kirsty MacColl titled "There's a Guy Works Down the Chip Shop Swears He's Elvis." The "guy" very much tries to exploit the resemblance, while the speaker holds him up as a classic liar.

Two of my favorite books concern meetings with famous people, though in neither case was the meeting the primary focus of the book. The celebrities are used as metaphors, as ways for the writers to explore aspects of their own personalities. In *A Fan's Notes,* Frederick Exley uses football-player-turned-commentator Frank Gifford, whom, before the book was written, Exley met only once, very briefly, when both were students at the University of Southern California. In the novel, which is called a fictional memoir, Exley uses Gifford as a symbol of fame and celebrity, both of which elude the narrator, who is called Fred Exley. Much of the book is a true account of Exley's life. After the novel was published (Exley's first novel), he met Gifford and the two remained friends until the author's death a few years ago.

The other book is Nicholson Baker's *U and I,* a nonfiction account of Baker's adoration of writer John Updike. In the book, and in real life, Baker meets Updike, twice, very briefly. The book investigates a number of literary themes, including the trials of developing one's unique voice and viewpoint while under the influence of another writer's work. Both books take a thin relationship to a celebrity and develop it in powerful ways.

PROMPT: Write about a moment you experienced in which you were celebrated, if only on a small scale. Did you star in a high school play or on a sports team? Have you won a contest? Have you sat on a float in a parade? Have you performed before an audience in any way? Take yourself back to that moment and write it down. After you've finished the narrative part, speculate on what that moment meant to you then and what it means now.

PROMPT: Let's look at your fifteen minutes of infamy. Warhol never said they'd be *good* minutes, did he? Have you ever had a publicly embarrassing moment? If so, write about it. As with the others, the event need not be of grand import. It simply needs to involve more than family and friends. Did you, for example, fall off that float you were riding on in the previous prompt? The one such moment that comes to my mind is the day in second grade when I forgot to wear a shirt. My family overslept (the only time I remember this happening), and I got dressed in a hurry and rushed off to school with my brother. When we arrived, a few minutes late, my classmates had already trooped off to morning Mass. I found them and breathed a sigh of relief as I settled into the pew with as little commotion as possible. Then I took off my heavy winter coat to find only an undershirt. No shirt. No Catholic-school-issue tie. The kids around me noticed, though I was quick to slink back into my coat and dart to the teacher, telling her I needed to run home right away. But word spread, as it will in grade school, and for weeks I was "the kid who forgot his shirt," even to older kids who didn't know me. Alas. But after years of therapy, I've worked through this traumatic episode, and I can now use it here in this book to put you at your ease to explore your own moment or two of crushing humiliation before a deriding crowd of onlookers. I also used it as the center of a short piece published in an online magazine. One of the good things about a writer's life is that the most traumatic events can be grist for the literary mill. In fact, they make the best grist.

PROMPT: Write down your dream of a moment in the spotlight. Do you see yourself accepting an Oscar for a screenplay? Catching a Super Bowl-winning touchdown? Saving the lives of millions by developing a cure for a disease? Winning a big legal case for an embattled underdog? Put yourself in that moment and write about what happens. Indulge the details. Write about what this dream means, what it says about you. We can tell a lot about ourselves and about each other by what we dream of attaining.

PROMPT: Give yourself an award, one, perhaps, that you dream of winning. Write your acceptance speech, thanking those who helped you and offering advice on the nature of the achievement. If you're interested, find copies of Nobel Prize acceptance speeches, and read what the winners say about the nature of writing.

PROMPT: Take time to reflect on your characters' moments of glory or dreams of glory. Explore their moments in the sun and the way these moments influenced their lives. A character's dream or memory of glory can be a good place to begin

THE WRITER'S IDEA BOOK

a story. An example that comes quickly to mind is Irwin Shaw's classic short story "The Eighty-Yard Run," in which a man sees his life ambitions fading, his one great moment being a long run for a touchdown while playing for his college team. That moment, which Shaw renders in extensive detail to open the story, haunts him, casting every other event in his life in its fearsome shadow. Another well-known example is Arthur Miller's play *Death of a Salesman*. After Biff Loman's big day in the city championship game, neither he nor his father, Willy, ever achieves such a moment of glory again. The cheers of the crowd, their chants for "Lo-man, Lo-man," echo in Willy's mind years later, as his own dreams of success slowly evaporate.

PROMPT: Begin a story with a scene in which a character enjoys—or suffers—a public moment. Take time to fully develop the scene, and, if possible, avoid narrative explanation. Don't tell the reader of the moment's significance; show it. If you want, in the next scene, you can provide a bit of background to establish the moment's particular significance to the character. *Revolutionary Road* by Richard Yates begins with a community theater group performance starring one of the main characters, April Wheeler. The play is a complete disaster. Yates loads his description with specific details, lingering over the painfully bad performance. April believes she is more talented and sophisticated than her neighbors, who watch the play, and she is devastated by her public failure:

> She was working alone, and visibly weakening with every line. Before the end of the first act the audience could tell as well as the Players that she'd lost her grip, and soon they were all embarrassed for her. She had begun to alternate between false theatrical gestures and a white-knuckled immobility; she was carrying her shoulders high and square, and despite her heavy make-up you could see the warmth of humiliation rising in her face and neck.

PROMPT: End a story with a character's public moment. The story should build to this moment, in which the character's dream of glory is either achieved or denied. A model for this approach is Beth Henley's play *The Miss Firecracker Contest*, which was adapted as the film *Miss Firecracker*. Throughout the play, the protagonist, Carnelle, has worked toward appearing in the Miss Firecracker beauty contest. Though she doesn't achieve her goal of winning the contest, she performs well and enjoys her moment in the spotlight.

CHAPTER FIFTEEN

ALL OUR SECRETS ARE THE SAME

Look, then, into thine heart and write.

—HENRY WADSWORTH LONGFELLOW

I took this title from a collection of *Esquire* fiction, edited by Gordon Lish, and published many years ago. Aside from the smooth and beguiling alliteration of *secrets* and *same,* I've always liked the statement's declarative quality, its confidence in the face of unknowable truth. How can we know if our secrets are the same? Fact is, some of our secrets aren't the same. In this chapter, you'll explore your secrets, and your hopes and fears, your goals and regrets and dreams. We'll focus on the *you* that doesn't meet the eye.

Writing about this side of yourself can be fun and can be a great source of creativity. If creativity ignites from the spark of conflict and tension, then the tension of concealment serves a writer well. Use it. Write as if you must burn the pages as soon as you finish them. Expose yourself to the white of the page. Some of what you write, of course, may be too personal to show others. We all try to appear calm and capable, in control, masters of our lives. Talk of secrets and lies, guilt and regret, longing, hopes, and dreams shoves into the light a more vulnerable part of ourselves. But, with luck, it will be a source of insight, even revelation, for you.

SECRETS AND LIES

PROMPT: Write about a secret you've held for a long time, which you have told no one. What would happen if you did reveal it? Write a scene or a poem supposing that you do reveal the secret. What would happen? What consequences would be suffered?

PROMPT: Write about a time that you revealed a secret, and detail the consequences. Why did you reveal it?

PROMPT: Write about your ability (or lack of ability) to keep a secret. If you had a secret, for example, would you tell someone like you about it? Why or why not? If you did have a secret, what person in your life would you tell? Why? If you're not good at keeping secrets, don't be hard on yourself. As writers, we are eager to know the secret lives of others, but we're also just as eager to fashion those secrets into stories. It's our nature. People who know us well enough to trust us with secrets should know us well enough to not tell us those secrets. At least, that's my take on the issue.

PROMPT: Write about a time when you told a secret and found out the person you told revealed it to someone else. How did you feel? Did you confront the person? Describe the circumstances and consequences of this experience.

PROMPT: Write a monologue in which a fictional character reveals a secret. Make it a significant one. Give urgency to the telling of the secret. This situation can add urgency to whatever you write. If you're feeling stale on a piece, imagine it as a secret being revealed.

PROMPT: Write a scene that leads up to the revelation of a secret. If you want, write the revelation first, then go back to the start of the scene and move toward the revelation.

PROMPT: Write a scene in which a character reveals a secret that is actually a lie. What happens next? In a wonderfully human anecdote, Tobias Wolff told of a time in which he shared a close friendship with fellow writer Raymond Carver. The two met often late at night and told the stories of their lives to pass the time—both were insomniacs. Carver's revelations were frequently much more powerful and painful than Wolff's, so one night Wolff revealed the story of his heroin addiction—an outrageous lie. He soon noticed colleagues asking him about heroin or seeming especially sympathetic to him in a general way. Carver, obviously, had found this secret too juicy to keep to himself. Wolff was faced with admitting he had fabricated the story to make his past seem darker and more interesting, or accepting his new reputation as an ex-heroin addict. One night Carver admitted he'd told the secret and Wolff admitted that the secret was a lie. The pair had a long laugh at their writerly penchant for making up stories and for revealing the secrets of others.

PROMPT: Write about a lie you've told—a whopper, as they say in old movies. Did you fess up later? Were you caught in the lie? What were the consequences? Depending upon how honest a life you've led, you can feel free to do this prompt more than once.

PROMPT: Write about a time when someone significant in your life lied to you and you found out the truth. How did you feel? What did you do?

PROMPT: Write an essay titled "On Lying," exploring the nature of lies and lying. Mix personal experience with a philosophical stance.

PROMPT: Write about the worst liar you've ever known—worst in the sense of most ready to lie and then worst in the sense of least convincing. If you want, fictionalize these people and begin a story about one of them, or both of them. Perhaps put them in the same story.

PROMPT: I have a friend who is an excellent liar. His secret: Believe the lie yourself when you're telling it. (He has made a lot of money in sales.) Begin a story in first-person point of view in which a character reveals his secret of being a good liar. In the story, make clear that, at times, he is not telling the truth, but keep this implicit. Let the reader enjoy making the discovery.

PROMPT: Surely you've known people who tell white lies about themselves and their personal accomplishments due to feelings of inadequacy. Write about one of those people—or create a fictional one—whose lies make us feel more sympathy for them than disdain. Try to make the reader feel the same way.

PROMPT: Write a scene in which a character lies to another character. Then write a second scene in which a second lie must be told to cover up for the first one. Continue in this way, weaving a tangled web for your character.

PROMPT: Write about a character whose very identity is based on a lie. The classic example would be Jay Gatsby, whose name and past are fabricated. For a recent example, Don Draper, the protagonist in the popular TV show *Mad Men* has built his current life on a lie. What happens when your character's dark secret is revealed?

THE WRITER'S IDEA BOOK

GUILT AND REGRET

Feelings of guilt and regret can be devastating, and they can be tenacious. As much as we are aware of them, try as we might to exorcise them, they can persist. And because we feel them so deeply, they can be a good source of ideas for writing. Sometimes writing about them can be a way to dispel their hold on us. However you approach them, don't ignore them as a source for ideas. In the opening pages of his novel *The Sportswriter,* Richard Ford establishes regret as a major theme by addressing it directly in the voice of his narrator, Frank Bascombe. Bascombe leads a lonely life of failed ambition and a failed marriage, and he copes, too, with the loss of a child. Through most of the novel, he battles regret:

> For now let me say only this: if sportswriting teaches you anything, and there is much truth to it as well as plenty of lies, it is that for your life to be worth anything you must sooner or later face the possibility of terrible, searing regret. Though you must also manage to avoid it as your life will be ruined.

PROMPT: Write about a regret you feel or that you struggled for some time to put to rest. What did you do or not do that led to the regret? How did you manage to put it to rest? How does it affect your life now?

PROMPT: What would your life be like now if you had done or not done something that you regret? Indulge the feeling for a while and write about this different life. Then try to look objectively at this other life. How much would be different from the way things turned out?

PROMPT: Write a letter to someone explaining a regret you feel that involves this other person in some way. Explain your feelings. You needn't send the letter, of course.

PROMPT: Write about a character who feels deep regret about some part of his life. Put the character in a scene so readers can see his regret in action. If possible, don't address the regret directly. Allow it to inform his behavior, but don't try to explain it.

PROMPT: Create a metaphor for regret, a physical object that embodies the feeling or allows you to explore the feeling in a fresh way. Begin with a metaphorical statement: "Regret is . . ." and move from there. If you prefer to write fiction, use the line in a scene, perhaps to begin a scene.

PROMPT: Write about something that makes you feel guilty—a memory that still has the power to create this emotion inside you. Describe the source of the guilt and how you cope with the feeling.

PROMPT: Like regret, guilt can be a destructive force in anyone's life. Create a character who, unlike Ford's narrator in *The Sportswriter*, has not managed to avoid regret or guilt. Develop a story in which a character's life is nearly ruined by one of these emotions. Though Frank Bascombe is not quite the master of his emotion that he pretends to be, he does manage to persevere (though Ford fans know that in his more recent novels *Independence Day* and *The Lay of the Land*, Bascombe is still struggling). In Graham Greene's novel *The Heart of the Matter*, the protagonist is ruined by guilt. He has an affair with a young widow, and after early feelings of elation and renewal, his conscience begins to hector him. When his wife returns from her extended vacation, the protagonist, Scobie, becomes ravaged by guilt, which Greene dramatizes in a number of powerful scenes, some of which are set in church. In the following scene, Scobie, a Catholic, feels he is in a state of mortal sin and therefore cannot take the sacrament of Communion. And yet, if he refuses the sacrament, his wife will grow suspicious and find out his guilty secret. He can see no way out:

> Father Rank came down the steps from the altar bearing the Host. The saliva had dried in Scobie's mouth: it was as though his veins had dried. He couldn't look up; he saw only the priest's skirt, like the skirt of the medieval war-horse bearing down on him: the flapping of feet: the charge of God. If only the archers would let fly from ambush, and for a moment he dreamed that the priest's steps had indeed faltered; perhaps, after all something may yet happen before he reaches me: some incredible interposition . . . But with open mouth (the time had come) he made one last attempt at prayer, "O God, I offer up my damnation to you. Take it. Use it for them," and he was aware of the pale papery taste of an external sentence on his tongue.

PROMPT: Write about a time when you did something hurtful but did not feel guilty. Explore the emotional complexities of the situation and your reaction to it.

PROMPT: Write a scene in which a character professes feelings of guilt but clearly does not feel that way. Use action, gesture, and voice to signal her true feelings.

PROMPT: Try the opposite approach to the previous prompt. Write a scene or a monologue in which a character professes to be free of guilt or regret and yet clearly is still struggling with these feelings, perhaps without even being aware of the struggle. Ford uses this approach throughout *The Sportswriter*, as Bascombe continually professes to be free of the past and to enjoy the simplicity of his life, and yet we detect that the issue is more complex, that the narrator has not worked through his regrets.

PROMPT: What are the clichés of guilt and regret, the gestures, actions, statements that typically are used to suggest these emotions? Show these emotions in a character, but find fresh ways to do it. Avoid the bowed head, the angry outbursts, the expressions of self-hatred. In the film *The Apostle*, the protagonist, a hypocritical minister, literally baptizes himself in a river and begins to lead a more honest life, understanding and accepting the sins of others far better than he did before admitting his guilt and regret to himself. Perhaps your character can find a new sense of purpose and direction through these feelings.

LONGING, HOPES, AND DREAMS

In her book *Creating Character Emotions*, Ann Hood writes that "even the word 'longing' gives me an ache in my chest." If you've ever experienced longing, you know what she means. By longing, we don't mean an occasional bout of wistfulness—for the past, for a simpler time—but heartfelt yearning for someone or something. Like all powerful emotions, longing can be a great source of ideas.

PROMPT: Write about someone you long for or have longed for in your past. Perhaps a lost love or a family member who has passed away. Try to describe the feeling and how you respond to this feeling. How long does it last? What usually triggers it? For example, I lost a brother with whom I'd been very close all of my life. He died suddenly at the age of thirty-two. He used to call on Sunday nights, just to talk about the week or whatever. Even though he's been gone for five years now, I still feel a strong sense of longing for him, especially on Sunday nights. When the phone rings, part of me still expects to hear his voice on the other end.

PROMPT: Write about longing by comparing it to a place. What place seems to embody longing or to evoke it? What does longing look like? I think of some of Edward Hopper's paintings, those empty streets with the long shadows. For me, they manifest longing. The key to making your reader feel a sense of yearning is to make it tangible on the page. Simply saying that someone feels it doesn't convey the emotion. Search for physical details that express this emotion.

PROMPT: Write about the physical sensations of longing. What does it literally feel like? Give these sensations to a character, adding movement to suggest this emotional state without using the word directly.

PROMPT: (This one is borrowed from Ann Hood) What is the time or person or thing you most long for right now? Write about it as clearly as you can. Describe it with concrete details. Try to evoke the essence of that time or person through sensory triggers. (How did it taste? Look? Smell?)

PROMPT: Longings usually are associated with the past, the desire to reunite with a time or place or person who is no longer around. Create a character who longs for someone or something in her past, but show the reader (rather than telling her) that the character's longing never will be fulfilled because they never existed in the way the character remembers them.

Hope is a complex emotion. It's tied to longing, in some ways, but it's more focused and directed, even energetic. While longing suggests a certain enervation, even malaise, hope can suggest positive thoughts, as if we can *do* something to achieve the subject of our hopes. I opened this book by saying that writing is an act of hope, meaning that hope embodies determination in the face of adversity, a belief, despite evidence to the contrary, of a positive outcome. The Buddhists, however, feel that hope leads to illusion, to a grasping after solutions that don't exist. To find our true selves, we must abandon hope, accept that hope leads only to confusion. Psychologists believe that hope slows the grieving process. When we suffer a loss, we tend to deny, to hold onto the hope that the loss we've suffered is not permanent. Until we give up hope and accept the loss, healing cannot begin. So hope has many facets, and for that reason, hope can lead us to interesting ideas for writing.

PROMPT: Write about a time in which you remained hopeful in the midst of anguish or adversity. What was the source of your hope? How did you manage to sustain it? In retrospect, was the hope beneficial or was it a delusion that delayed your recovery?

PROMPT: Write about a character who remains hopeful, partly through denial, and uses that hope as a source of strength. For example, in *Death of a Salesman*, Linda Loman remains hopeful of the family's success despite the turmoil in which they stew. She expresses her hope by exclaiming, at two moments in the play, how "the whole house smells of shaving lotion." She associates that smell with good times and with her sons preparing to conquer the world. Try to find a gesture or line that expresses your character's hope.

PROMPT: Write about a character whose hope is clearly an aspect of denial. Use first-person point of view, allowing the character to express her hope directly while showing through action and detail that the hope is illusory. To sustain our hopes, we sometimes hear and see selectively, focusing on evidence to support our hopes and ignoring evidence to the contrary. Show your character choosing to hear and see only what supports her unrealistic hopes.

PROMPT: Write about a character struggling with hope, trying to be realistic while keeping a positive outlook. In Beth Henley's play The *Miss Firecracker Contest*, the protagonist hopes to win the eponymous contest, though she's not especially pretty or talented, nor is she well respected in the town. When she loses the contest, she feels that she's suffered a broken heart, an overwhelming disappointment, but then doesn't allow herself to dwell in self-pity. She does give credence, however, to the validity of her desire to win the contest, saying, "How much is it reasonable to hope for?"

PROMPT: Let's end on an upbeat note. Write about a time in your life in which you achieved the subject of your hopes, when, in a sense, your dream came true. Or, if you prefer, write a fictional scene or story in which a character's hopes, which at first seem unrealistic, are achieved.

CHAPTER SIXTEEN

TROUBLE WITH A CAPITAL T

I made mistakes in drama. I thought drama was when actors cried. But drama is when the audience cries.

—FRANK CAPRA

Fact of life: Conflict is a fact of life. There is just no avoiding it. Even if you avoid the daily drama of everyday living by hiding in a cave under a rock, you still face problems. First of all, you live under a rock. That can't be much fun. You are plagued with feelings of isolation. And where do you find food to eat? Lack of sunlight brings feelings of depression. You struggle to give meaning to such an isolated, futile existence. The days and nights are endless.

You get my point. Conflict is unavoidable. Turmoil, tragedy, and loss are woven into the fabric of human existence. And for writers, this situation isn't a bad thing. You could argue that the suffering inherent in the human condition is a key reason why we write, even why art exists. In this chapter, we'll explore the Trouble with a capital T in your own life and how to use those experiences and those thoughts and feelings as grist for your literary mill. The title of the chapter comes, of course, from the song "Ya Got Trouble" from Meredith Willson's classic musical *The Music Man*. You'll recall that the show's protagonist, huckster Harold Hill, largely fabricated the trouble in order to con the good folk of River City into buying musical instruments from him. But River City, for all its innocence, was not without real troubles. The town clung fearfully to a mythic notion of an innocent past as the world around them pushed into the modern age. Hill taps into those fears, into the town's narrow view of morality and the emotionally arid life and colorful existence that cowers behind what they refer to as their "Iowa Stubborn" attitude. It is their hunger for richer lives—ones full of music—that allows them to be hoodwinked, just as much as it is their fear of dark forces invading their town. Seen in this way, though Hill largely fabricates the "trouble" indicated by the opening of a pool hall in River City, the town is indeed rife with troubles of other kinds.

And troubles always lay at the heart of good storytelling—in whatever form or genre you want to use. As in the example from *The Music Man*, the trouble can exist on a variety of levels. In mining your own troubles for writing ideas, you needn't focus on the most obviously dramatic situations. When writers tell me that their lives have been predominantly pleasant and free of loss and are therefore not fertile ground for exploration in their work, my first thought is that they are not exploring deeply enough. When I hear these statements, I'm reminded of Mark Twain's well-known observation: "There was never yet an uninteresting life. Such a thing is an impossibility. Inside the dullest exterior there is a drama, a comedy, and a tragedy."

PROMPT: As in the other chapters in this section, let's start with a list. This time make a list of the major upheavals in your life, beginning with deaths or significant illnesses and injuries among family members and friends. These losses are the biggest ones we face. They're the ones from which we never fully recover. Include in your list any significant illnesses or injuries in your own life, ones that altered your life in some way.

PROMPT: Make a list of significant upheaval in your professional and financial life—such as losing a job, being forced to change your career or your main career goals, bankruptcy, and so on.

PROMPT: Make a list of significant upheaval in your personal and romantic life, such as the breakup of a cherished relationship, a divorce, the end of an important friendship, the fracture of a relationship with your child, even being left behind in an empty nest.

PROMPT: Make a list of significant upheaval caused by moving to a new place, whether it be to a new city and state or moving to a new part of town when you were young.

PROMPT: Make a list of important losses in your life. In the prompts above you listed some, but put them on this list too. Add to that list losses and upheavals that you didn't include on the previous ones—the death of a pet, perhaps, the loss of a career position you wanted, the rejection of a writing project by an agent or publishers, and so on. Here we're drilling down to significant losses that perhaps weren't life altering but were felt deeply nonetheless.

PROMPT: Review the lists you've made in response to the previous prompts. From them, choose the two or three situations that draw you most and spend a writing session on each one. If one beckons you back to it, keep going.

PROMPT: Write about an experience of crisis in your past that ended with a sigh of relief. Take the reader step-by-step through the experience.

PROMPT: Write about a time of grief in your past. Focus on the nature of the loss, trying to focus on the actions and details that will evoke your feeling rather than simply explaining those feelings. Take the reader through the process of coming to terms with the loss that caused your grief and, if possible, show how you got through that time and found a way to move forward with your life.

PROMPT: Write about a significant problem that you faced in your life that you handled poorly, perhaps as a result of being young or too emotionally involved to see a better course of action. After you finish that draft, write an alternative history—telling the story but changing your actions to give it a new (and more positive) resolution.

PROMPT: Write about a brush with death—a time when you weren't sure you would survive. What happened that allowed you to live through the experience?

PROMPT: Write about a situation in which plans went astray, leading to some sort of disastrous consequences. Did you go off to college with grand visions of success only to flunk out or retreat home feeling lost and confused? Did you fall in love with the wrong person, leading to a painful breakup?

SWEATING THE SMALL STUFF

Another fact of life: Most of us do sweat the small stuff. If we didn't, Richard Carlson's best-selling series of books would not have sold nearly so well. The small stuff plagues us every day. And sometimes the small stuff can provide the trouble with a capital T for our writing—because, very often, the small stuff doesn't seem all that small when we're sweating it. Most of the time, the small stuff—exasperation with a loved one, a pile of bills to pay, an annoying boss, a fickle car—is connected to larger issues and patterns in our lives. We get angry, for example, when a careless driver cuts us off in traffic. But does our anger concern only that driver? Or does it arise from more general feelings of frustration in our lives or from our feelings that society as a whole has grown more careless?

THE WRITER'S IDEA BOOK

The small stuff sometimes can provide even sweeter grist for the literary mill than the larger stuff so do not ignore it. The key to good storytelling is conflict, yes, but that conflict must be keenly observed and well presented. I have read—and surely you have too—memoirs of Cold War operatives that put me to sleep. Any number of people during my many years in publishing have approached me with manuscripts about their fascinating lives in the military or in the entertainment world or in Big Business. They have met famous people, accomplished amazing feats, and they tell me that people always say they should write a book. And so they do. And most of the time it's really not at all a good book. Yes, the tales of derring-do provide a certain amount of visceral interest, but the story lacks insight and observation, lacks focus, lacks engagement and strong writing. Their manuscripts are little more than loosely collected anecdotes with little dramatic tension and even less observation. Therefore, even a story about rescuing political prisoners in Communist Russia requires effort just to get through.

My point is not to bash these folks. In fact, I admire their perseverance in being able to complete a manuscript. My point is to convince you from my personal experience that you needn't have led a life of international intrigue or hung out with celebrities or hit a home run in a World Series game to have powerful stories to tell. As we've discussed in earlier chapters and as we'll explore more deeply in the next sections, the power of the story is very much in the telling. Anecdotes that rivet listeners at parties often remain flat on the page unless the writer truly is a writer.

I've also worked with writers who created powerful stories from trouble that would seem to require only a lowercase t. One that comes to mind was a long essay by a writer who explored her lifelong battle with weight. She was not obese, and so the problem did not have serious impact on her health, but for her it was a significant issue, one that she thought about almost every day. Her level of observation, her use of both humorous and serious insights, and her ability to connect with her reader made for a powerful piece of writing that I've not forgotten through the years. Her struggles with her weight may not have affected the course of world history, but it was important to her and she was able to make the reader feel that importance.

PROMPT: Write about a conflict—trouble with a capital T—that you dealt with at the age of ten that might seem like "small stuff" now but at the time seemed quite large. Take yourself back to that time and place. Did an unrequited crush fill your nights with anguish? Were you cut from the grade-school basketball team? Were there no other kids your age living in your neighborhood, forcing you to fill long summer afternoons alone? Brainstorm details that surround the conflict and that filled your life at the time.

PROMPT: Use the same approach as in the previous prompt but focus on a different age. If this exercise interests you, pick any age from your childhood and teen years and write about it, focusing on that one primary trouble. You could spend a few weeks of writing sessions focusing each day on a different year in your life. You'll be surprised at how much you can recall when you start brainstorming. Pick a year, brainstorm about it, settle on a conflict, put it at the center of a story, and tell that story in any form that interests you.

PROMPT: What conflicts exist in your life at this moment? List them as quickly as possible. Then take some time to add to the list. At any one time, the average adult deals with multiple conflicts in various stages of resolution. Some of those conflicts will disappear; others might never be resolved. Remember that you needn't include only major conflicts on your list. The conflict simply must be meaningful to you, even if it might seem small to others.

PROMPT: Write about a spiritual or intellectual conflict that you've gone through or that still exists in your life. A good friend of mine, for example, struggles mightily with his religious faith, which was a cornerstone of his childhood and teen years but for most of his adult life has been difficult to sustain. This conflict would not be apparent to people who meet him socially or professionally but is on his mind almost every day in some way.

PROMPT: Taking a cue from the writer who explored her struggles with being overweight, write about a physical issue that you have dealt with during your life. Perhaps you have always had poor eyesight or you lost your hair at an early age or led a more sedentary life due to asthma—whatever. I probably don't need to offer more explanation. You already have chosen your subject. Get started.

PROMPT: Write about a habit that you have that's "not good for you," such as overeating or smoking or a penchant for tanning. How have you tried to "kick the habit" and how well have you succeeded?

THE NEED FOR DISTANCE

I think we've shown that the problems in our lives—large and small—can be fertile fields for literary projects. But to handle them effectively on the page, we need to have a certain emotional and intellectual distance from these problems. We might feel compelled to write about them when we're feeling them most acutely, and that's fine from a healing perspective but probably won't be as successful from a literary one. We lack the distance that lets us use the techniques we've learned in order to connect with the reader.

I've witnessed this situation many times as a writing teacher and coach. The writer produces work that is simply overwhelmed by the writer's still-raw emotion about the subject itself: a death or divorce or career misfortune, whatever it is. That raw emotion brings energy to the page, but the energy is uncontrolled. It might possess visceral impact, but the reader cannot connect with it. Our emotional response often is sympathy for the writer but not much more. The writer is unable to make us feel the emotions she's feeling. It's as if she's so locked into her own emotional state that she's unable to reach us.

At one of our Writing It Real conferences, I worked with a writer who recently had lost his teenage son. He hoped that he could get through his profound grief through writing, and I believe that writing was helping him deal with his feelings. But the work itself was of little worth in a literary way. The members of the workshop offered him sympathy and compassion but had little to say in terms of literary critique. And it's unlikely that he'd have been able to hear such a critique anyway. He needed time to work far enough through the grief to approach poems and essays about his feelings with at least a certain amount of emotional distance.

My good friend and Writing It Real colleague Sheila Bender faced the same situation when her son was killed in a skiing accident during the holidays in 2000. Overwhelmed with grief, she wrote some poems about the tragedy and read them at the conference the following summer. Given her level of artistic skill, the poems did resonate with the audience, but they lacked the mastery of her other work. She began writing a memoir about her son's death and her own efforts to work through the grief of that tragic loss. That book took her years to write. With each year, she gained a bit more distance that allowed her to recast scenes and make the manuscript resonate far beyond its basic story. Published in 2009 as *A New Theology: Turning to Poetry in a Time of Grief*, the book is an amazing achievement in a variety of ways. If you are struggling to write about a deep loss, I highly recommend reading Sheila's book. I had the good fortune of hearing her read from it every year during the decade between her son's death and the book's publication. Each incarnation of the manuscript showed improvements, enlarging in its intellectual and emotional range far beyond her first attempts when she was most deeply buried in grief.

A better-known example is Joan Didion's memoir *The Year of Magical Thinking*, which chronicles her year of grief after losing her husband, writer John Gregory Dunne, to a sudden heart attack. During that year, Didion also had to deal with her daughter's very serious health issues. The emotional weight of these struggles easily could have sunk the memoir into a discursive—and eventually dull—recitation of her feelings. Instead, Didion, a gifted journalist, leavens the emotional material with keenly observed scenes as well as with fascinating research about the nature of grief. In all, the book is a triumph of the spirit but also of a writer who directly faces her anguish while letting the reader into the story.

If you're writing while in the midst of your trouble with a capital T, keep going. And keep what you've written. When you've moved further through the grief, you can come back and look for ways to fashion that raw emotion into work that connects with readers.

PROMPT: If you have written in journals through the years, pull them out and read them. We tend to write most zealously in our journals when we are dealing with some type of trouble—trying to figure out what to do or how to deal with our emotions. Look for subjects and themes that you want to explore now with a cooler head and heart.

PROMPT: Write about a significant problem you faced at least a decade ago. Tell that story as best you can from your perspective today. Then write about it in present tense, as if you are dealing with the problem today.

PROMPT: Write about a problem that you're dealing with in your life right now, but tell the story from the perspective of looking back on the problem—using your future self to relate the events.

Some writers have told me that they fear if they wait to begin writing about the significant upheavals in their lives that they'll lose interest or will lose the emotional energy they're feeling at the moment. As I mentioned earlier, there's no harm in writing while deep in the throes of the emotion, but you then want to go back after you've gained some distance on the subject.

Other writers tell me that they avoid writing about the problems in their lives because they feel such material is of no interest to other people. They fear they'll sound dull or whiny. There's no question that we won't attract a lot of readers by simply crabbing about the problems in our lives. We need to remember that the reader is concerned primarily with herself. The story of your problems and losses and grief will help the reader understand and resolve her own problems, especially if they are similar.

Actor and singer Judy Garland said, "I try to bring an audience's own drama—tears and laughter they know about—to them." Having experienced a good bit of pain herself, Garland was able to convey those emotions in her performances with authority. You can do the same.

THE WRITER'S IDEA BOOK

CHAPTER SEVENTEEN

MINDING OTHER PEOPLE'S BUSINESS

I don't see how a writer can operate without going out as a reporter. Think of the feast that's out there.

—THOMAS WOLFE

Getting ideas is sometimes simply a matter of paying attention. A writer must keep in mind Henry James's famous advice about being "someone on whom nothing is lost." Notice what is going on around you—the people and situations, the places and objects. These can be fodder for your writing and can spark ideas for stories and characters, articles and essays, poems and scripts. Sometimes, as writers, we live a bit too much in our heads, blind to what's going on around us.

We must practice mindfulness, and by practicing, we grow better at it. We are more aware of what we're doing and what other people are doing. That awareness becomes our normal state of mind. True, when we're deeply involved in projects, we live in the worlds of the projects. (Let's be honest; part of our interest in the projects is to escape the world around us.) This absorption can make us forgetful, absentminded, and unseeing. A couple of favorite examples of this state of mind:

- According to A. Scott Berg's biography of editor Maxwell Perkins, Thomas Wolfe once took Perkins home to Wolfe's apartment, breaking into the place after the key didn't work, then was surprised to find other people living there. Absorbed in his novel, Wolfe forgot he had moved.

- Thomas Edison once went to a government office to apply for something but was forced to leave without the document because he couldn't remember his name.

These are great stories, and if you're the writer in your family, you probably have a reputation for being dreamy and impractical. That's okay. But let's try some prompts that will help open your eyes to what's going on in your world.

PROMPT: Perform a household chore that you do on a regular basis—cut the grass, wash dishes, load laundry in the washer. As you do this chore, remain keenly aware of every step in the process. Feel the texture of the towels as you place them in the washer, listen to the hiss of water as it fills the cylinder, smell the detergent. Be there, in the moment. If you catch yourself drifting into reverie or thinking of what else you could be doing, stop these thoughts and gently guide yourself back to the task at hand.

PROMPT: Read everything in today's newspaper, from the front-page news to the comics to the ads. Don't use the newspaper's website; buy a copy of the paper. Make a list of the stories you find interesting or amusing and cut them from the paper. Also list any ideas for your writing that you find. Do this for a week. Begin a folder in which to place article clippings that interest you. Keep this folder active and current. When you're feeling stale or uninspired, a quick shuffle through your folder can help spark some ideas.

PROMPT: Choose three of the articles that offered ideas and try to put them together into a single piece.

PROMPT: Go to a public place you frequent—the grocery store, church, fitness center. Try to see the place as if for the first time, noticing people and how they behave, the way they speak and relate to each other. Go to a second place and compare the modes of behavior. Do people act differently in church than at the grocery store? Are they less or more guarded? Notice details. Are postures similar or different? Body language? Style of clothing?

PROMPT: Go to a public place and eavesdrop. That's right: Invade people's privacy. Of course, don't get caught. But if you feel comfortable with this, try to overhear some conversations. Write down what you hear. Try to record it exactly as it's said. Restaurants are great places to do this. You can be anonymously scribbling in your notebook, not even looking at the people, and writing down what they say. Another great eavesdropping place, according to writer and friend Tom Chiarella, is the airport. You can get pretty close to conversations and yet seem a disinterested bystander. Also, at airports people often are parting. They're trying to sum up, to put everything in order before leaving.

PROMPT: This one I stole from comedian George Carlin. He called it "spy at the airport." He would try to pick from the bustling crowd the person who was an international spy. As a writer, it would be better if *you* played the spy. Give yourself a spy persona and watch people. Something about pretending to be a spy or some type of security person will make you much more aware (not that I've, ahem, done this myself). Write brief observations in a notebook, and keep your eyes and ears open. Of course, Carlin played this game before our era of zealous airport security. This option is more limited now. But you can play "spy" in a lot of places, from a park to a shopping mall.

PROMPT: Break out of your routine. Wake up at least an hour earlier than usual and go for a walk or a drive. If you're up very early in the morning, go to an all-night grocery or gas station. Take notes on what you observe, and develop these details into a sketch when you get home. Or, if you prefer, do it the opposite way, staying up an extra couple of hours and venturing out into the world. You'll find that your senses are much more sensitive to the world around you.

PROMPT: Go to a type of place you don't normally visit. For example, if you tend to shop in quaint boutiques, spend a couple of hours at a big-box store. If you're an outdoorsy kind of person, hang around in an art museum. The sensory information and the type of people you see will be far less familiar to you.

PROMPT: Head out on a short road trip to a place in your area where you've never been, spending some time not only driving but actually walking around in a new locale. Write down your impressions, the things you notice, the conversations you hear.

LISTENING FOR IDEAS

Eavesdropping requires sharp listening skills. All of us can become better listeners, and writers need to be especially good. Listen to how people say things, and listen to what they say. The quick aside, the tossed-off anecdote, the boring trudge of a life story can hold ideas for writing. For example, I spoke at a writers conference a couple of years ago and heard a story that turned into a published article. At breakfast, a woman told a funny story about driving across the country with her mother and daughter. Three generations of women in one car for thousands of miles, from California to Pennsylvania. In the middle of the story, she mentioned stopping in a small Louisiana town at the Bonnie and Clyde museum, noting that the place was tiny and uninteresting and was run by a ninety-year-old man who claimed to have witnessed the famous ambush of the gangsters. The story continued as the three women headed northeast, but that museum and that guide stuck in my mind. The writer did not see an article idea there; it simply wasn't of interest to her. But it was to me. I scribbled the idea in a notebook later in the day and began poking around on the Web, finding out more about the museum. The passing remark became an article that was a lot of fun to write and later was honored in *The Best American Travel Writing*.

PROMPT: Every day for a week, write down something you've learned in a conversation. Impossible for you because your friends and colleagues are boring and uninformed? Fine. Go to an expert. Chat with the manager of a store about the product she sells. Go to the library armed with a dumb question or two. (Librarians love dumb questions. They really do.) Write down what you learn. You can choose to learn about subjects that especially interest you, or you can make your quest for knowledge random.

PROMPT: Begin a scene with a line you've overheard someone say recently. It needn't be a catchy or powerful line. Something mundane will work: "How much are these pants?" "If you're good, I'll let you pick out some candy at the counter." "Is he ever on time for a meeting?" Begin there, and move forward, providing a completely different setting and context for the line.

PROMPT: Fill up dead time with observations. Notice the people around you at the grocery checkout. Make mental notes about them, and write down these observations when you leave. Look around you while waiting in traffic. What are people doing in their cars? Car observations are great because, for some reason, we all feel invisible in our cars, as if we're in protective bubbles. People sing to themselves, check out their faces in their rearview mirrors, make out with each other, angrily bang their steering wheels in frustration. Try to pull away a few details each time you sit in traffic. Get a small recorder and place it in the seat next to you so you can record your observations while driving. (Trying to write them down could be dangerous.)

PROMPT: Spend some time on an elevator, especially if you don't normally ride one. Here you'll find people who have nothing to do or to distract them. Watch body language. If you're feeling bold, strike up a conversation. One way to do this is to ask a question. Watch the person's reaction. Of course, you don't want to seem intimidating in any way. Respect the person's space. But try to get the person talking.

Sometimes we simply find an idea already formed and neatly packaged, there for the taking. A poem in a letter to a friend. A story in an anecdote told to us at a party. A perfect line of dialogue on a soup can. The opening for an essay on a sign in a store window. When such good fortune befalls you, grab it and go. A well-known example of this type of "found" idea is the John Lennon song "Being for the Benefit of Mr. Kite." He found the lyrics to the song on an old poster announcing the attractions at an upcoming fair. He wrote them down and used them verbatim. By pushing them into a more artistic context, the words took on resonance. They gained a new meaning.

These accidents, of course, require that you discover them, that your eyes and ears and writer mind are open to chance. Surely hundreds of people saw that poster, but only Lennon was able to turn it into something bigger, a piece of art. Debra Spark speaks to this awareness, this keeping one's eyes open for ideas, in her essay "The Trigger: What Gives Rise to a Story?" She recounts going to the Cave of the Mounds, "a rather tacky tourist spot in Wisconsin," with several women, including fellow writer Lorrie Moore. All the women in the group endured a dull tour of the place, except Moore, who, Spark realized, was taking notes. Then,

> Two years later, I opened up *The New Yorker* and read Lorrie Moore's funny, sorrowful story "The Jewish Hunter," which takes place partially at the fictitious Cave of the Many Mounds in Minneapolis. I felt excited, the way one does when one's a party to another's romance or sees a setup working at a dinner. Why, I had been there! Had seen the initial sparks! And I felt something else, too: jealousy. Sure, we'd all met the guy, but only one of us had the skill to fall in love.

While in graduate school, I had a similar experience. The renowned author Wright Morris held the visiting professor chair for a semester, though outside of class he was rarely seen. He stayed in the little cottage on campus reserved for the person who held the chair that semester, seeming to live there like a hermit. But a year after he left, he, too, published a story in *The New Yorker* about an eccentric, impoverished, middle-aged couple who walked frequently along the main drag of the college town. Though there were at least thirty or forty apprentice writers in our MFA program, not one of us had seen the potential of that couple for use in a story. Morris did. For me, at least, that story was a wake-up call to begin noticing the rich details available in my daily life.

PROMPT: Make a list of all the people you see on a daily (or very frequent) basis, from the barista at the coffeehouse where you stop in the morning to regulars at your gym to the neighbor down the street who waters his roses in the evening. Describe each of them in as much detail as possible. Write down any interactions you've had with them. Try to use at least one of these people to begin a story or a poem or whatever form seems suited to them.

SEEING BEYOND THE SURFACE

Before leaving this subject, let's pause a minute to discuss the writer's need to see. In this chapter, we've focused on seeing the world around you, taking time to notice details, striving to become someone "upon whom nothing is lost." With that phrase, James means more than simply noticing the surface of things and reaching for a conclusion. As writers, we must see beneath the surface and beyond it. Tempting as it is, we can't settle for the certainty that some people possess—people who, in fact, are incapable or unwilling to push beyond appearance. Limiting yourself to the appearance of things leads to cynicism or intellectual and emotional blindness. Again, we must see deeper.

This approach involves risk. We must accept ambiguity, knowing that we can't know all there is to know. In his theory of negative capability, John Keats explores this need of the writer to remain open and fluid in his thoughts and feelings. As a creative person, you must accept this challenge, must find a way to balance the practical reality before you with the awareness of the mystery beneath the surface. In his memoir, *Nola,* Robin Hemley explores this point with beauty and insight. He objects to the facile wisdom of people who tell you to "see things as they are":

> Beware of people, I think, who tell you this, because they are invariably hiding something. They mean you harm, or harm you, by putting a mask on their uncertainty and calling it certainty. (Like those searchers for Noah's Ark, who are missing the point completely; even if they found the ark miraculously intact, sitting on top of Mt. Ararat, that would show us nothing. It's the story, not the artifact, that's important.)

If you want to be creative, you must seek the reality behind the appearance, the story, to use Hemley's example, not the ark. Anyone can see the ark. Anyone can say that if an ark is found, the story is true; if an ark isn't found, the story is false. As a writer and creative person, you must seek the truth in the story even if there never was an ark.

PROMPT: Pick one of the people on the list you made in the previous prompt and dive in more deeply, creating for them an interior life as well as a life beyond the context in which you usually see them. Is the barista, for example, working two jobs to achieve her dream of finishing college and working in a different field? Does she have a family or does she live alone? What plans and dreams and disappointments does she hide behind her smile? What does your neighbor think about as he waters his roses? Why do they mean so much to him? What does he do when he turns off the hose and goes back into his house?

PROMPT: Think of little ways to break your routine. If you're right-handed, for example, spend a day favoring your left hand. If you drive to work, take public transportation. If you always listen to music while you exercise, pull out the ear buds and listen to the world around you. Make notes of the new details you notice.

CHAPTER EIGHTEEN

A DAY IN THE LIFE OF A WRITER

The boundaries of our world shift under our feet and we tremble while waiting to see whether any new form will take the place of the lost boundary or whether we can create out of this chaos some new order.

—ROLLO MAY

Short chapter here. You're going to do most of the work yourself. I'll contain my penchant for verbosity and try to get out of your way and let you get to it. This chapter, which is essentially one long prompt, guides you through the process of writing down everything that happens to you in a single day. The thinking behind the prompt is easy enough to understand: In a single day, you can find enough ideas to write about for a good long while. Details, images, dialogue, events—in your life, in the news, in the lives of those around you. We have hundreds, maybe thousands of thoughts, ideas, impressions, and reactions that often are forgotten minutes later.

We notice that the roof on the garage takes on a golden hue in the morning sun; our mate always puts milk and sugar in the coffee cup before pouring the coffee; the woman in accounting who usually looks so enervated is suddenly dressing up a bit and has a new spring in her step; drive-time disc jockeys are the most annoying creatures on the face of the earth; the water in the shower is never quite hot enough; the guy in front of us at the grocery checkout is buying enough hamburger to feed Ecuador; we feel a touch of melancholy around seven o'clock every evening. Many, many more.

This exercise is also an exercise in what the Buddhists call "mindfulness." As we discussed in the previous chapter, writers must pay attention; they must cultivate this mindfulness. Again, as Henry James told us, we must "be someone upon whom nothing is lost." An entire day of journalizing everything surely will push us in that direction. Doing this prompt more than once will help, too. The first time you do it, you may be very self-conscious and, perhaps, too aware of your writer's apparatus: the notebook and pen or the tape recorder that you use to record what's going on. Doing it a few times will diminish your concern about the equipment and will allow you to focus more on what you're doing and observing. Also, it helps to try this experiment on various days—a workday and an off day, for example, or a weekday and weekend day.

Your goal here is not to develop material for a single piece but to plump your notebooks with ideas and details. It could lead, of course, to a day-in-the-life piece, perhaps a story or an essay. If you want a model for this form, read F. Scott Fitzgerald's essay "Afternoon of an Author." You'll notice that nothing much happens in it. The events and observations are not pulled tightly together. Observation mingles with reverie. But Fitzgerald does create unifying elements and themes, and the accretion of detail creates a quiet, somber essay about a man moving on the fringe of his own existence, dispirited and yet obviously quite aware of the subtle nuances of his life and the world around him:

> He went into the kitchen and said good-bye to the maid as if he were going to Little America. Once in the war he had commandeered an engine on sheer bluff and had it driven from New York to Washington to keep from being A.W.O.L. Now he stood carefully on the street corner waiting for the light to change, while young people hurried past him with a fine disregard for traffic. On the bus corner under the trees it was green and cool and he thought of Stonewall Jackson's last words. . . .
>
> The bus was all he expected—only one other man on the roof and the green branches ticking against each window through whole blocks. . . . Somewhere church bells were playing "Venite Adoremus" and he wondered why, because Christmas was eight months off. He didn't like bells but it had been very moving when they played "Maryland, My Maryland" at the governor's funeral.

A DAY IN YOUR LIFE

Let's get started. Tonight before you go to bed, spend a few minutes setting up your tools. It doesn't matter if you use a notebook or a digital recorder. You could use, I guess, a video recorder if you want, though that will be a big distraction—to you and to those you meet throughout the day. The point is, use what makes you feel comfortable. Place your notebook—we'll call it a notebook for the sake of convenience and consistency—on the nightstand next to your bed. Set your alarm, perhaps a little earlier than normal, to give you time to get this exercise underway. You'll be writing a lot, so you'll need to adjust your schedule to allow for the added activity.

Decide, too, how you're going to do the writing. You can't scribble a conversation while you're having it, obviously. You could do hourly reports, checking to note what's happened, or, if it works better for you, jump in whenever you get a minute. But don't let more than an hour pass without writing. Too much will be lost. Remember, you're trying to get *everything* on paper. So even if you're thinking that absolutely positively nothing is going to happen, structure your day for writing it down.

When you wake up, grab your notebook and record what you can remember from your dreams. Quickly. They can slip away even as you're writing them down. Scribble everything you can recall.

Get out of bed and start your day, taking your notebook with you. As you go through your morning routine, jot down what you're doing and what you're thinking. It may look like this:

> Eating a bagel and a banana, coffee. Coffee is too weak again. need to set up time for oil change in Jeep. In newspaper—county commissioners still fighting about where to put the new stadium. Morning sunlight looks warm and yellow on the countertop, pours in through the east window. Packing lunches for kids. Remember when I was in grade school, racing through my lunch to get to the playground where we played big games of catchers, sometimes using the whole parking lot, coming in after lunch our hair damp from running....

And on and on, moving through the day: Shower and dress, drive to work, talk to people, do your job, eat your lunch. And as you experience your day, keep your notes short and simple. They shouldn't be long asides, unless you have a lot of time for writing today and won't miss out on the day by writing about it. Try to keep your notes short, impressionistic, capturing details, thoughts, memories. Write only what is necessary to help you remember the thought or event or detail later.

Whatever you do, don't stop. Trust me on this. Keep pushing ahead. Halfway through the day, you may begin to feel that nothing much is happening and you'll try again tomorrow. Fight this urge to give up. Try again tomorrow if you want, but finish this day. If the day grows too hectic to write about it as you go along, shorten your notes to a few words. You will take tomorrow—and the next day and the next day—to flesh out the notes.

Continue taking notes throughout the evening, making the final note as you get into bed and turn off the light. The next day, examine what you've done. Highlight details or events that interest you. If you find nothing of interest, put away your notes for a few days, even a week. When you return to them, you will see them more clearly. Highlight the details of particular interest. You will be amazed at how much is there and how much, even after only a few days, that you've forgotten.

Write a piece narrating your day, selectively using what seems to be most interesting. From the distance of a few days or a week, offer insights and observations about the day as you write, enlarging the scope of the piece. If you want, create a fictional character and allow him to experience your day.

CHAPTER NINETEEN

A LIFE OF THE SPIRIT

Everything that I have written has the closest possible connection with what I have lived through inwardly.

—HENRIK IBSEN

Let's close this section by investigating your spiritual life and religious background. Ignore the cliché about avoiding talk of "religion and politics." Use your writing to focus on subjects people tell you *not* to talk about. Question the prevailing Truths. Dig beneath the surface of things to find out what's really happening. This approach confers a deliciously secret, sneaky, cut-through-the-bull quality to your writing, which makes it more fun and more meaningful. It also is what makes writers dangerous folks to be around.

I'm not suggesting that you betray those you love and who love you. I don't share Faulkner's much-quoted belief about a good story being "worth any number of old ladies." But I do believe a writer's job is to seek to find and to represent in writing the truth as she sees it. To question. To risk seeming too negative or too positive or just too nosy. To attempt to say what has not been said, perhaps because no one had the power or the insight to say it right. In her essay "Your Mother's Passions, Your Sister's Woes," Bonnie Friedman articulates the writer's role very well:

> The force of the forbidden draws us. We want its power. We want to use it for our work. We also long to understand the unarticulated, our own most potent reality not yet structured by words. For in fact the secrets we most want

to understand are not secrets at all; they are nothing hidden so much as not yet discovered. They are what has been there all along, not furtively denied so much as never consciously noticed.

Sometimes there have been furtive denials, and each writer must decide what can be revealed and what must remain hidden to protect the lives of others. And always we must leaven our honesty with kindness. Pema Chödrön addresses this point in her book *When Things Fall Apart,* and though the following quote focuses on looking inward, the same consideration applies when we view the world around us:

> The challenge is how to develop compassion right along with clear seeing. Otherwise, all that happens is that we cut everybody else down, and we also cut ourselves down. Nothing ever measures up. Nothing is ever good enough. Honesty without kindness, humor, and goodheartedness can be just mean. From the very beginning to the very end, pointing to our own hearts to discover what is true isn't just a matter of honesty but also of compassion and respect for what we see.

HAIRY THUNDERER OR COSMIC MUFFIN

Let's talk about your vision of a supreme power, an order in the universe, a spiritual center. We explored some of your beliefs in an earlier chapter, but let's take a more spiritual slant in this chapter. Your spiritual beliefs can shed insight into who you are and can lead to powerful writing. Though our spiritual beliefs are important, even, at times, life sustaining, we needn't approach them timidly. As with the prompts in other chapters, take risks here, and have fun.

PROMPT: Write your own spiritual creed, following the form of creeds, beginning each sentence with "I believe ..."

PROMPT: Take some time to explore your beliefs—or lack of them— regarding a supreme power. How do you perceive this power? What evidence do you find of it in your life, in the world?

PROMPT: Write about your spiritual upbringing. In what religious faith were you raised? How did this faith shape your early life? What values and sense of morality did it give you? Did your family possess a strong sense of religion, attending regular services, or was religion not an important part of family life?

PROMPT: Write about your spiritual history, picking up where you left off in the previous prompt. Did you fall away from your early faith? If so, when? Have you returned to it? What beliefs have you retained? What spiritual beliefs do you now hold? If you retained your faith throughout your life, what forces helped you along the way?

PROMPT: Explain your beliefs to someone who does not share them. Be as clear and specific as possible, and try to intuit her objections or disagreements. Respond to them, not as a way to convince the person of the correctness of your faith so much as to help her understand your beliefs better.

PROMPT: Write about a representative of an organized religion—a minister or priest or member of a clergy. Choose someone you admire, explaining why you feel this way. Try it again with someone you never especially liked. If you want, try it with someone who is a spiritual leader but does not speak for an organized faith.

PROMPT: Write about your spiritual practices. Do you attend church or belong to a spiritual organization? Meditate? Take long walks in nature? How do you feel during these times? How have these practices changed and evolved in your life?

PROMPT: Write about a spiritual breakthrough or revelation you've experienced, a moment of epiphany or understanding that renewed, restored, or changed your spiritual beliefs in some way. This need not be a moment in which the clouds parted and celestial trumpets blared. Your experience might have been subtle, its full significance not even apparent until some time later.

PROMPT: Write about the first time you questioned or were shown a new side of your faith. For example, I was raised in a strict Catholic family and attended Catholic school for twelve years. I remember as a boy hearing with something near awe—and indeed with revelatory shock equal to St. Paul's blinding by the sun—an album on which comedian George Carlin skewered certain institutional hypocrisies of the Catholic religion, making insights that I knew were true but had never heard anyone actually come right out and *say*. Of course, the institutions of organized religion and living a life of the spirit are not the same thing, but at the time I didn't know this. No one else I knew seemed to separate them. It was a small but powerful breakthrough that led all of us good Catholic boys to begin cracking wise about the Church, though, in truth, it sort of frightened me for a while. Wasn't it heretical to joke about the sometimes oppressive and arbitrary rules of the local parish community (such as the one that a woman could not enter church without something on her head—a hat or a scarf or, amazingly, a hankie bobby-pinned to her hair)? Wasn't it commensurate to making fun of, well, God? Carlin's comedy didn't launch me down the road to spiritual ruin or turn me toward Krishna. But hearing that album allowed me to articulate questions I had not dared ask before.

PROMPT: Write about a difficult time in your life during which your spiritual beliefs sustained you—or didn't sustain you. Did that experience increase your devotion? Or, if you did not feel sustained, cause you to question your beliefs? Write about the long-term effects of this experience on your spiritual life.

PROMPT: Write about your vision of the afterlife, if you believe in one. If you don't believe in one, write about what happens after we die or, if you prefer, write about your vision of what the afterlife *should* be.

PROMPT: Consider a conventional view of heaven—pearly gates, clouds, angels, harps, etc. Put yourself there. What happens? Have fun with it. While you're in heaven you meet a fictional character who seems in no way heavenly. You wonder why he ended up here. What happens between the two of you as you discover heaven together? If you want, give yourself the opposite fate. You end up in hell—devils, fire, pitchforks, the works. What happens? While you're there, you meet someone who surely should have made St. Peter's cut. Try to find out why he didn't. For a model of fictional heaven, check out Daniel Wallace's hilarious short story "In Heaven These Days."

NATURAL AND SUPERNATURAL

Thus far, we've talked about spiritual faith mostly within the context of an organized religion. But for many people, spirituality spills beyond those boundaries. If that is true for you, explore the sources of your faith or lack of faith. Do you find spiritual fulfillment and connection in the natural world? Of course, many writers through the centuries have explored the natural world for higher meaning. The Romantic poets come first to mind, though many others have done the same. Time spent in reflection surrounded by the beauty of nature can revitalize our spirits. If you spend important time in the outdoors—hiking, biking, paddling, camping—then you need to make this a topic for writing.

PROMPT: Write about moments spent in nature that led to spiritual reflection and connection. It might be easiest to begin with the moments you remember most, whether they occurred recently or in the distant past. If none come to mind, write about your most recent experiences in nature. Again, they needn't include a burning bush or a soaring eagle. The key is to capture these moments on the page.

PROMPT: Now let's write about that burning bush or soaring eagle. What is the most profound experience you've ever had in nature? Maybe the bush wasn't actually burning, but it did lead you to some type of personal revelation or epiphany. For me, the first experience that comes to mind occurred during a stroll along the

THE WRITER'S IDEA BOOK

Roaring Fork River near Aspen, Colorado, where I'd gone to speak at a writers conference. I stopped for a bit to watch the river when, not more than a foot or two from me, a hummingbird buzzed into a flower, hovering there for what seemed like minutes. It was as if the world telescoped into that one moment when the bird and I somehow connected. Now, I don't know what spiritual truth I took away from that moment, but even after fifteen years, I recall it very clearly. You surely have had a similar experience.

PROMPT: Spend a morning or afternoon walking in nature—be it a state park or preserve located near where you live—without pen in hand. On the drive back home, avoid turning on the radio or making calls on your cell phone. Instead, stay in the dreamy, ruminative state of mind that walks in nature usually inspire. When you get back home, write down your thoughts—not necessarily the details you noticed on your walk so much as the feelings and ideas floating around in your mind. If those thoughts lead to a poem or the first stirrings of a story, explore them.

PROMPT: Write about what nature means to you. Does the natural world embody the spiritual world? Does it possess restorative power? Or, if you're not a person who enjoys nature, explore those feelings. Woody Allen, for example, joked in one of his movies that it seemed like "one big restaurant."

PROMPT: Write about a personal experience with a strong and even destructive force of nature—a blizzard or tornado or flood. Focus first on the details of the event. If necessary, search for information about the event online, the news coverage. Then explore your own role, what happened to you during this event. Finally, explore its meaning in a spiritual sense. Do you see it as the work of God? Or do you see nature as fundamentally amoral, a force that can offer humankind pleasure or pain?

Okay, let's move from the natural to the supernatural. It seems that we all have had an otherworldly experience or two in our lives, some weird moment that we just can't explain. For several years, I worked for a publisher that specialized in books about haunted locations. These books were some of our top sellers, and the authors spoke frequently at stores, libraries, and on the radio. Though their explorations had netted quite a few fascinating stories, when they shared them at public gatherings, they found that many people simply wanted to tell their own stories. There was no dearth of stories about ghosts among the people in the audience. Whether you've seen a ghost or strange lights in the sky or some mythical creature, these events are worth exploring in your writing.

PROMPT: Write about an unexplainable event that you've experienced—an apparition or ghostly sounds or whatever. Flesh out your description of the event with as many details as you can recall. In refining your draft, avoid explaining how you felt as this event took place, focusing instead on the specifics of what happened. Then you can explore how this event made you feel and how you tried to find an explanation.

PROMPT: Write a "ghost story," whether based on personal experience or something you've heard or simply something you make up.

PROMPT: Write about your beliefs regarding the paranormal. Do you believe in ghosts? Do you believe in earthly visitations by creatures from other planets? Why or why not? How did you reach this conclusion? Or are you skeptical but open to the possibility? Whatever your beliefs, explore them on the page.

THE SPIRIT OF YOUR STORIES

God, belief, and the spiritual life appear in many works of fiction and in film. In the work of William Kennedy and Toni Morrison, for example, the corporeal world and the spirit world are interwoven so that the narratives easily move between them.

Other novels explore the religious facet of our lives, trying to reconcile personal morality and spiritual belief within the structures and codifications of religious institutions, from classic works, such as Nathaniel Hawthorne's *The Scarlet Letter,* to lesser-known ones, such as Harold Frederic's *The Damnation of Theron Ware.* Of course, in most serious novels and stories, characters face moral dilemmas of some sort that call upon their spiritual beliefs or challenge their lack of them.

PROMPT: Write about a time when you were "on the horns" of a moral dilemma, one that challenged or called up your spiritual beliefs to help you make a decision. How did you handle the situation? Would you handle it the same way again? Was your moral compass helpful in providing direction?

PROMPT: Place a character in a situation similar to the one you detailed in the previous prompt, but have the character choose a different course of action. What happens next? Perhaps the character doesn't share your spiritual beliefs. If not, how does this change her actions?

PROMPT: Take a risk and mix the spirit world with the corporeal world. Create a scene in which a character speaks to spirits or spirits speak to each other. This is

THE WRITER'S IDEA BOOK

not an easy task, I know. How to avoid making the spirits sound silly? I can't say for sure. But give it a try.

PROMPT: How large a role do religion and spiritual faith play in your writing? Review some old short stories, essays, poems, or whatever you've written in the past, looking for how spiritual faith or the lack of it figures into your work. Look for patterns and write about them.

PROMPT: Write a scene in which a character experiences a vocational calling to be some type of spiritual leader. How does she determine what to do next? Does she follow the call?

Part III

FINDING
FORM FOR
ideas

CHAPTER TWENTY

OF SONNETS AND TOASTERS

Get a girl in trouble, then get her out again.

—KATHLEEN NORRIS

Author Michael Martone once proposed an instructional book to me at Story Press about what he called "appliance fiction." Martone is a brilliant guy with a lot of great ideas. But this one gave us pause: appliance fiction? He explained that technology supplies our lives with many wonderful devices, new ones all the time. When we think we've put ourselves on the very cutting edge of gadgetry, new ones arrive. He felt that these appliances, for lack of a better word, could be a great source of stories, ones that could never have been written in the past. We didn't feel confident we could publish the book, but the idea stayed in my mind. A few months later, I decided to write a story about some type of everyday technology. I would start there and push forward, setting up the story as an exercise, allowing the "appliance" to work as a formal device, something to render form and unity. A few months later, I completed a story titled "Redial," about a woman who, by punching the redial button on the telephone every night when she comes home from her late-shift job, discovers her husband is having an affair.

Sometimes finding an idea is as simple as that. Martone later gave the AWP (Associated Writing Programs) fiction-instruction anthology, titled *Creating Fiction* (and published by Story Press, I'm proud to say), a variation on his appliance idea, and I'll begin this chapter on finding form by offering that prompt here.

PROMPT: (This one borrowed from Michael Martone) Research the history of a common device or gadget, paying particular attention to the compelling social and historical elements that motivated its invention. Have a character use this trivial knowledge, perhaps as an anecdote that informs an activity the character is performing while speaking of or thinking about the device. A character, say, narrates the history of the zipper while making love.

PROMPT: This prompt is from me, but it's based on Martone's ideas from that long-ago meeting. Write a piece using an appliance or technological process or product as the central element in the plot. Use my own story as an example. Another story that comes to mind is John Cheever's "The Enormous Radio." In that story, the radio has magical powers, allowing the young couple to eavesdrop on the lives of their neighbors. If you want to go in a more fantastic direction, following Cheever's example, don't stop yourself.

Our focus in this chapter is on choosing a form to shape your ideas, and it also explores using form to generate ideas. In the example above, the appliance gives your story a focus, if not necessarily a shape. And it works, in part, because it sets up a task: Find a way to use an appliance. This type of task can free our imaginations by, paradoxically, providing a distraction. You won't worry so much about granting your character an epiphany if you're trying to work a toaster into the story.

IDEAS FROM FORM

I'm not a poet. I enjoy reading poetry, but I've never felt the impulse to write it. So I wasn't crazy about having to take poetry workshops in graduate school. I was taking the fiction track in an M.F.A. program, but in order to graduate, fiction students had to take two poetry workshops. But it really wasn't so bad. I had a great teacher, Chase Twichell, who was smart and dedicated and kept things interesting. Her assignments always involved form. Rather than assigning a topic like Write a Descriptive Poem About Your Family, for example, she told us to find a poem we like and write a poem using exactly the same meter. By concentrating on getting the damn meter right (it was never easy) I lost my self-consciousness and came up with a few nearly mediocre poems, far better than I thought I'd do. The prompts in this section of the chapter are designed to help you get ideas by focusing on form rather than on subject.

PROMPT: Choose a topic you wrote about in an earlier prompt. Now write a sonnet about the same topic. Not sure about the rules of a sonnet? Look them up. After the sonnet, write a sestina, a haiku, and a rondeau. The formal requirements for each type are readily available on the Internet.

THE WRITER'S IDEA BOOK

PROMPT: Write a piece of flash fiction—a short story less than five hundred words long—in less than a half hour. Set a timer. Need a topic? Use a prompt from an earlier chapter. Don't spend too much time looking for one. In fact, you may do better by simply flipping to a page and choosing the first one that catches your eye.

PROMPT: Find an essay or story or poem that you like. Outline it, noting turns in plot or shift in topic or approach. Write a piece of your own using the outline, simply changing the topic.

PROMPT: In some of the prompts in the previous section, you created lists. Find two. Don't worry if they're related in any way. It's better if they're unrelated. For example, use the list of five things you'd bring to a deserted island and the list of truisms. Pick an item from each list and begin writing about them, looking for connections. Try to bring them together in a single piece of writing.

PROMPT: Write a story based on a myth or a fairy tale, setting it in contemporary times. For example, you might retell the Hansel and Gretel story using two children you know. If this works for you, pick another myth or fairy tale and try again.

PROMPT: Retell a myth or fairy tale, changing what happens or exploring character more deeply than the original does. For a model, read John Gardner's *Grendel*.

PROMPT: Write a piece of historical nonfiction, recounting a historical event, such as Lincoln's assassination or the stock market crash on Wall Street. But relate the event through the eyes of a fictional character, someone you invent who was an eyewitness.

PROMPT: Write a piece based on a classic story. Jane Smiley used Shakespeare's *King Lear* as a source, known as a metatext, for her novel *A Thousand Acres*. The film *Clueless* was based on Jane Austen's novel *Emma*. The metatext need not be one you deeply admire. In fact, your reason for retelling the story may be because aspects of it bother you. In an interview, Smiley explained her choice of *King Lear*:

> What came first was a long-standing dissatisfaction with an interpretation
> of *King Lear* that privileged the father's needs over the daughters'. I felt a
> growing sense of a link between a habit of mind that perceives daughters
> and children as owned things.

PROMPT: In several interviews, Smiley mentions her bringing together several ideas in order to write short stories, comparing the process to placing three or four objects on a desk and moving them around "until you can see some relationship among them." Try this process yourself, but let's, for the moment, take her literally.

Gather three or four items from your house and place them on your writing desk. Don't think much about your choices. Just grab three things—a potato, a candle, a jacket. Freewrite about them, looking for connections. Your piece begins with the first object, a scene involving a potato. The plot turns or is complicated by the second object, the candle. The third and, if you want, final scene, involves the jacket.

PROMPT: Write a short story, essay, or poem using the form of an instructional article, employing a step-by-step method, such as "How to Know If You're Enlightened" or "Ten Steps to Losing Your Mind." Or try to weave two topics into an instructional piece. In her book *Sugartime*, for example, Susan Carol Hauser explains the steps involved in gathering maple syrup while weaving in meditations on life and nature.

PROMPT: Try your hand at ekphrasis—using another art form as the focus of your own art. For writers, it means, put simply, creating a piece of writing about, say, a photograph or painting or song. Don't worry the source for long, just pick a photograph or painting that hangs in your home. Start there. Describe it—the implicit drama, its meaning to you, and so on.

PROMPT: Open a piece with a line of graffiti that you've seen somewhere. Jeff Mock wrote a poem based on a line he read in a men's room in a bar, which, apparently, drew a somewhat philosophical crowd. The line, which he used as the title, was "I Feel More Like I Did When I Came in Here Than I Do Now."

PROMPT: Relate a dream you remember clearly. Write it down exactly as you recall it, presenting the narrative as though the weird dream logic were completely normal. In other words, don't call attention to crazy jumps in time and space or when one character morphs into another. This is a good exercise for breaking down expectations, of allowing your mind to move in unusual directions.

PROMPT: Begin a piece with a speaker making an audacious claim. Here's an example from Diane Lefer's short story "Man, Wife, and Deity," which opens "My hobby is gathering evidence that Shakespeare was Jewish, or maybe black. My wife's thesis is that Homer was a woman."

PROMPT: Richard Ford opens his novel *The Lay of the Land* with his narrator reading in the newspaper of a senseless murder that took place in Texas, far from his home in New Jersey. The narrator knew none of the people involved and yet is greatly disturbed by the story. Begin a piece by opening with a news story that is not related to the speaker or protagonist but look for broader thematic connections. Ford's speaker, for example, experiences a sudden fear of his own death after reading the news story.

PROMPT: In his book *Exercises in Style*, Raymond Queneau tells the same anecdote ninety-nine times. A man gets on a crowded bus and sees a man accusing another man of deliberately bumping into him. Queneau uses his exercise to explore writing style, but you can use it to explore form. Pick an event, a small one, that you witnessed recently: a car stalled on the highway and another car stopping to help; a man holding a door for a woman and the woman refusing to accept the gesture, insisting that the man go first. Write it as it happened, as you would if recounting the event in a journal or letter. Then write it as it happened but focus only on sounds and smells. Then fictionalize it, adding a few details or a bit of drama. Then write it as a structured poem, a haiku, perhaps, or a villanelle. Then write it as a fiction again, this time changing the characters in some significant way, such as their ages, dress, or appearances. Then write it in reverse order, beginning with the final action and moving to the first. Then write it in first-person point of view using one character, then first-person point of view using another character. Then write it by setting it in another place—maybe the front door to Bloomingdale's in New York rather than the front door of your office building. If any of these approaches sparks your interest, keep writing. Freewrite or cluster the possibilities of where to go from here.

PROMPT: Think of a situation, perhaps one you created in an earlier prompt. Outline or sketch the story, deciding how you would tell it. Now create at least two other outlines or sketches, telling the story in a different way—different order, different scenes.

PROMPT: Recount a somewhat serious anecdote—a real or a fictional one—in the form of a joke. Use the rhythms and the voice you use when telling a joke, such as premise, setup, and punch line.

CHOOSING FORM

You've no doubt had the experience of beginning a piece of writing without knowing what form the idea should take. The idea might spring from real life, but should it be developed as a memoir? Should it be fictionalized? Should you focus on a key moment and turn it into a poem? Maybe you've got a novel on your hands. Of course, your choice of form will influence how you develop the idea. It also will lead to more ideas on the subject.

The answers to these questions are sometimes tough to find, and there are no formulas to apply. The key is working with the idea until you know it well enough to decide which form to use, to allow it, in a way, to choose the form by itself. Sometimes, for example, a personal essay simply grows into a book-length memoir, a short story into a novel. Other times, we decide by experimenting with forms and finding which one works best. Some of the prompts in the previous section can help you play around with form to find the most appropriate one for an idea, but consider a few more to help you explore your options.

PROMPT: Write about an idea in a few forms, experimenting with ones you wouldn't normally choose. For example, if you usually write short stories, try to render the idea in a play. If you write essays, see what you gain by developing the idea in a poem.

PROMPT: Write about an idea by imposing upon it the conventions of a genre you don't normally try. For example, if you're a mystery writer, place your story in the context of a romance. If you're a literary writer, take a stab, so to speak, at a horror story. An example that comes to mind is Thomas Berger's novel *Who Is Teddy Villanova?*, which explores the conventions of the hard-boiled mystery while examining sophisticated philosophical themes.

PROMPT: Write your story as a play or film script, focusing only on dialogue. Do you find that you need the benefits of description and summary? If so, you may need to render your story as a narrative.

PROMPT: If your story is based on a real experience, write it down exactly as it occurred. How closely can you stick to the truth? Will feelings be hurt or secrets revealed if you use a nonfiction approach? Do you feel limited, even frustrated, by sticking to the actual events? Does the story suggest greater dramatic possibilities than what really happened? If so, move to fiction.

PROMPT: Fictionalize an idea based on a real event but stick to the facts as they took place, simply changing minor details, such as names and the characters' appearances. Is the event believable? Does it seem logical? Do characters act in ways that seem motivated and understandable given what we know of them? Truth is often stranger than fiction, but beware that this fact benefits only the writer of nonfiction. The fiction writer must create a sense of believability and logic within the context of the story. Sometimes a true story just doesn't hold water as a fictional piece. The reader won't believe it, even though "it really happened" and even though you're presenting it as fiction, which would seem to eliminate the need for believability. If, for example, your real-life experience involves striking coincidences and unaccounted-for behavior, better make it an essay. This may not seem fair or logical, but as writers we strive to satisfy our readers. In his book *Writing Life Stories*, Bill Roorbach, who writes fiction and memoir, notes with humor that some readers have questioned the truthfulness of his nonfiction, accusing him of exaggeration, while other readers have believed that the fiction is true.

THE WRITER'S IDEA BOOK

PROMPT: Think of a wild coincidence that has occurred in your life. If a few have occurred, write down all of them in a paragraph or two. Now develop the incident, giving us the necessary background information and specific details. Use this incident in a piece, striving to make it believable, credible. Use the coincidence in an opening scene of a piece, fictionalizing it if you want, and moving forward from there.

PROMPT: Write about an event from your somewhat distant past, capturing the details as well as you can recall them. After you've got the anecdote on paper, read what you've written, noting, perhaps, which details or actions might be exaggerated or misremembered. If you find a number of them, you've more than likely begun fictionalizing the event in your mind. But rather than "correct" the errors, push deeper into them, using them as portals into a more deeply imagined piece. In his posthumously published novel *Chinaberry*, author James Still presents a richly detailed story about a strange episode involving a thirteen-year-old boy. When the novel was published in 2011, Still's friends recalled him telling them a very similar story about his own childhood. Was the book, therefore, a novel or a thinly disguised memoir? Well, probably both.

PROMPT: Write a piece as a series of questions, such as in an interview—or interrogation. For a model, read Stephen Dunn's poem titled "Questions." Every sentence in the poem is a question, but Dunn is able to capture the essence of a relationship.

Creative writers today are mixing and bending forms in all kinds of exciting ways. Think about, for example, the film *Adaptation*, in which screenwriter Charlie Kaufman writes a story about a screenwriter named Charlie Kaufman who is struggling to write a screenplay adaptation a real nonfiction book by real-life writer Susan Orlean. In the early stages of developing your piece, don't allow yourself to be too bogged down by questions of form. Instead, play with form as part of the creative process. Use it as a source of ideas and development.

CHAPTER TWENTY-ONE

FOLKS LIKE YOU

I let my characters do the talking, simple as that.

—TERRY MCMILLAN

There's an old rule about writing that says readers won't care what happens in a story if they don't care who it happens to. If we agree with this statement, then we put character before all other considerations in a piece of writing. In this chapter, we'll focus on getting ideas for characters and on shaping the characters you've developed in earlier prompts. If you're feeling blocked on a character in an ongoing project, perhaps some of the prompts in this chapter can help you break through.

OBSERVING

Developing characters demands a variety of skills—observational as well as writing skills. The first step is choosing a character or group of characters who interest you. Finding such a character may mean hearing a voice in your head, one that compels you to write. Or it may mean seeing a person in your life who intrigues you. The key to creating a great character is something of a paradox: The character should begin as a mystery, and you must work to know as much as possible about the character. Terry McMillan addresses the need for mystery:

> I don't write about characters unless I don't fully understand why they do
> what they do. And it's sort of like the only way, even if that person is confused
> and flawed, like most of us are, you get a chance to connect with them.

If you know too much about a character before writing about him, you might grow bored very quickly. The character will offer no surprises, and the piece will lack tension. Compare this situation to having a guest in your home who is unpredictable, volatile. At any moment, the most innocuous topic or comment could set off an emotional outburst. Even an offer of cheese dip becomes fraught with tension. Your character, of course, needn't be so volatile, but he should offer your piece a level of tension. The reader isn't sure what to expect.

But we're getting ahead of ourselves. The first step in evoking people on the page is being observant. Noticing how people act, talk, and look— catchphrases, gestures, dress, patterns of behavior. A good writer is always a good observer. You may be way behind on what's in the news and on keeping up with home repairs. And your checkbook balance—forget about it. The roof could cave in and you'd barely notice. But in observing the idiosyncrasies of human behavior, you must be sharp, noticing subtle shifts in mood, intuiting thoughts that people attempt to conceal. In an interview, Marge Piercy attributes her sources of characters to talking to people, listening to what they say, and being interested in their lives. To sum up, she admits, "I'm a nosy person."

PROMPT: Choose a character who intrigues you, perhaps one from an earlier prompt. Put that character in a brief scene, where you can observe her. Let her interact with other characters while you watch. There needn't be tension in the scene. The character needn't talk about herself. You are trying to see the character in action and to note some observations about her.

PROMPT: Think of a person you know whom, in fact, you've felt that you really don't know at all. Something about the person's behavior simply mystifies you. Write about this person, in descriptions and in recollected scenes. Try to find out more about this person in your writing.

PROMPT: List at least a half dozen people you know who interest you enough to write about them. Describe why you find them interesting. If you want, re-create them as fictional characters, making up new names and changing some aspects of their personalities, but leaving the real people pretty much as they are.

PROMPT: Combine aspects of two of the people or characters on the list you made in the previous prompt, turning them into a single character, one who embodies elements of both characters. For example, you could combine your brother's appearance and conservative politics with your landlord's *joie de vivre* and love of vintage sitcoms. If you want, place that character in a scene or a situation.

PROMPT: Combine aspects of four of the people or characters on your list, turning them into a single character. Try to pick aspects that are in some way related, making the character complex but not too fractured.

PROMPT: Practice your powers of observation. Go to a party or some group gathering and be very aware of what's happening around you. Who taps his foot? Who flounces her hair? Who brags and who mumbles? Who is the liar? Who is trying out a new look? Who fidgets? Who laughs loudly? And listen to what people are telling you and how they speak. Try to pick up on unusual rhythms of speech. When you get home from the gathering, write down your observations. Keep the notebook handy. When you're stuck for a detail or description for a character, your notebook can supply what you need.

PROMPT: Flip through some magazines or surf online, looking for a picture of a person who looks interesting. Don't choose a celebrity or someone about whom you know anything. Don't read the caption. Cut out the picture and put it on your desk or download and print it. Now, freewrite about the person, creating a character sketch. Write about the person's life, her problems and her goals, her background, whatever comes to mind. Move toward some conflict in which the character can be involved. Then write a scene to explore that conflict. If it interests you, keep going. Try this prompt every day for a week, choosing a new picture for each writing day. Keep these characters and pictures in a file and begin building a stable of characters.

PROMPT: Use at least two of the characters from your stable, putting them together in a scene. Force them to talk to each other. If you want, make the scene a first meeting. Put these strangers in a waiting room or on a bus or in an elevator—some place where they will have to talk. Force the proximity.

PROMPT: Spend some time on Facebook, typing in a few made-up names and seeing where the search function sends you. Don't invade these random people's privacy—in fact, you don't want to learn much about the real person at all. Instead, use them as the basis for fictional characters.

GETTING TO KNOW YOUR CHARACTERS

In the next few prompts, we'll focus on ways to get to know your characters better as you begin working with them on the page. The old saw about knowing what's in your characters' drawers is valid (unlike many old saws). You should know much more about the characters than meets the page. If you're writing narrative nonfiction, the same rule applies, though you may not know what's in their drawers. The prompts that fol-

THE WRITER'S IDEA BOOK

low can be used on any character. I've kept them generic so you can use them whenever you need them. Also, you can use many of the prompts in section two for characterization. Rather than responding about your own family or favorite things, respond for your character. To avoid repetition, I haven't covered some of these topics again here. In getting to know your character, you will need to know these things, too.

PROMPT: Describe your character's physical appearance in minute detail: height and weight, hairstyle, body type, gait, posture, hair color, eye color, nose type, and all the extras. Mention, too, the plantar wart on the ball of his foot, and the tiny scar on the left knee where he got stitches when he was seven. What aspects of his personal appearance does he especially like? What aspects are sources of self-doubt or frustration?

PROMPT: Describe your character's facial expressions and body language. Describe any tics, repeated gestures, or physical habits, such as clearing his throat when he's irritated or stroking his chin when he watches television.

PROMPT: Describe your character's wardrobe. Know everything he wears, but pay particular attention to favorite clothes. What image does this character try to project through clothes, and what does that desired image say about the character?

PROMPT: Describe your character's large possessions: car, home, furnishings, boat. Note what he especially likes among these things. What are sources of pride?

PROMPT: Describe your character's small possessions, including souvenirs and keepsakes. As in the previous prompt, identify what objects the character likes best. What memories do the favorite objects hold?

PROMPT: Describe your character's interests and hobbies. How active is he in each of the areas? Which hobbies has he abandoned through the years? What is the hot interest of the moment?

PROMPT: Describe your character's interests that, in fact, he doesn't actively pursue. For example, does your character see himself as an adventurer but does little more than subscribe to adventure magazines?

PROMPT: Describe your character's personality. Outgoing? Shy? Both? The life of the party but given to melancholy when alone? Give this description some depth. Here's where you begin to go deeper toward the heart of the character.

PROMPT: Write your character's life story in a few pages, focusing on the key moments in his life, the turning points—a career shift, a divorce, a first child.

RENDERING CHARACTER

Now that you've gotten to know your character better, inside and out, you have to put him on the page. In his book *The Art of Compelling Fiction*, Christopher Leland creates the 7-Ds approach to evoking character: description, declaration, dressing, dialogue, demeanor, dramatics, and deeds. Through this method, you show the readers your character, rather than simply telling about him, and it can work for narrative nonfiction as well as fiction. Let's try the 7-Ds through prompts.

PROMPT: Describe your character. Try to avoid a bland recitation of facts. Instead, show the character doing something and put the description in motion. Allow the details of body type, complexion, and such to filter through the action, giving the reader a chance to participate in the narrative rather than passively receive a fact sheet. In the following description from Truman Capote's *In Cold Blood*, we get our first look at Perry, one of the murderers. As we learn throughout the book, Perry is a paradoxical person, a sentimental songwriter and vicious killer. Capote suggests this paradox in this early description, by focusing on Perry's strangely proportioned body:

> Perry folded the map. He paid for the root beer and stood up. Sitting, he had seemed a more than normal-sized man, a powerful man, with the shoulders, the arms, the thick, crouching torso of a weight lifter. But some sections of him were not in proportion to others. His tiny feet, encased in short black boots with steel buckles, would have neatly fitted into a delicate lady's dancing slippers; when he stood up, he was no taller than a twelve-year-old child, and suddenly looked, strutting on stunted legs that seemed grotesquely inadequate to the grown-up bulk they supported, not like a well-built truck driver but like a retired jockey, overblown and muscle-bound.

PROMPT: Make a few statements about your character. This approach, of course, is more telling than showing, but it can be effective if used judiciously. But be aware that you must support these statements with the actions in your story. As a writing teacher told me many years ago, if you tell us that "Joe was the funniest guy in my graduating class," Joe better damn well be funny. Here is a statement about a character from *The Stone Diaries* by Carol Shields:

> Barker Flett at thirty-three is stooped of shoulder and sad of expression, but women who set their eyes on him think: now here is a man who might easily be made happy.

PROMPT: Show us your character through clothing styles and dress, through his possessions, the things he buys. As with the first prompt in this section, put your

THE WRITER'S IDEA BOOK

description in motion. Allow the reader to make discoveries and reach conclusions about the character. You control the reader's conclusions by selecting the right details, not by directly telling her what to think. In the following description from Nicholson Baker's *The Mezzanine*, we see a character in action and possessions that help to characterize her quickly:

> "Have you signed the poster for Ray?" said Tina, rolling out in her chair. Tina has lots of hair, moussed out impressively around a small smart face; she was probably at her most alert just then, because she was watching the phones for Deanne and Julie, the other secretaries in my department, until they returned from lunch after one. In the more private area of her cube, in the shadow of the shelf under the unused fluorescent light, she had pinned up shots of a stripe-shirted husband, some nephews and nieces, Barbra Streisand, and a multiply xeroxed sentiment in Gothic type that read, "If you can't get out of it, get into it."

PROMPT: Think of a character you want to write about. Write down her name and her job, such as "Fiona Ferguson, graphic designer." In the next three sentences, describe her so that she fits commonly held beliefs or stereotypes about people who do this type of work. In the next three sentences, tell us something about your character that goes against the stereotypes.

PROMPT: Try this variation on the previous prompt. In the game of Taboo, a player tries to describe something without using certain related words. He tries to describe it well enough so that his partner can guess the thing. For example, if the key word is "lipstick," the player can't use words such as "lips" or "mouth" or "make-up" or "kiss." Let's use that approach in describing characters. Choose a character and a job—such as "Fiona Ferguson, graphic designer." List all the clichés and stereotypes of someone who does that job. Now write a few paragraphs about the character, but don't use any of the words or phrases on your list.

PROMPT: Place your character in a scene and present him through action and dialogue. Create a situation in which your character is involved, or simply place him in a room with another character or two and focus on bringing him to life for the reader. Try not to move into the character's head, which may be a tempting way to present his feelings. For this experiment, allow us to interpret what he's thinking and feeling through his actions and through what he says and how he says it. In the following scene from Don DeLillo's *White Noise*, the protagonist, Jack Gladney, undergoes a diagnostic interview following exposure to hazardous material. He is nervous, eager for the technician to give him a clean bill of health. But DeLillo gives us no direct statement of Jack's emotional state and gives us few telling descriptions. He relies on the pace of the dialogue and the tone of Jack's statements:

"Here's where we ask about smoking."

"That's easy. The answer is no. And it's not a matter of having stopped five or ten years ago. I've never smoked. Even when I was a teenager. Never tried it. Never saw the need."

"That's always a plus."

I felt tremendously reassured and grateful.

"We're moving right along, aren't we?"

"Some people like to drag it out," he said. "They get interested in their own condition. It becomes almost like a hobby."

"Who needs nicotine? Not only that, I rarely drink coffee and certainly never with caffeine. Can't understand what people see in all this artificial stimulation. I get high just walking in the woods."

PROMPT: Stay in the scene you wrote in the previous prompt. This time, add details that are more subtle, presenting the way your character does what he does. Try to suggest his level of comfort with the other characters. Is he distracted? Bored? Nervous? Relaxed? Does he have a hearty laugh or a tight one? How does he sit and stand? In the following scene from Anton Chekhov's "The Lady With the Toy Dog," we see the first meeting between two characters who soon will fall in love. Through gesture and dialogue, Chekhov shows us their feelings of nervousness and attraction:

> He snapped his fingers at the Pomeranian and, when it trotted up to him, shook his forefinger at it. The Pomeranian growled. Gurov shook his finger again.
>
> The lady glanced at him and instantly lowered her eyes.
>
> "He doesn't bite," she said, and blushed.
>
> "May I give him a bone?" he asked, and on her nod of consent added in friendly tones: "Have you been long in Yalta?"
>
> "About five days."
>
> "And I am dragging out my second week here."
>
> Neither spoke for a few minutes.
>
> "The days pass quickly, and yet one is so bored here," she said.
>
> "It's the thing to say it's boring here. People never complain of boredom in godforsaken holes like Belyev or Zhizdra, but when they get here it's: 'Oh, the dullness! Oh, the dust!' You'd think they'd come from Granada to say the least."
>
> She laughed.

PROMPT: Use the same scene again, this time focusing on what Leland calls dramatics, how the character carries himself. This mode of presentation is similar to the previous one, but here we're concerned a bit more with tone of voice, the way a character acts and speaks in general terms, rather than in reaction to the other characters around her. In short, we're more concerned with typical behavior rather than

THE WRITER'S IDEA BOOK

the mood of the moment. In the following scene from Flannery O'Connor's "A Good Man Is Hard to Find," the protagonist, known only as "the grandmother," is shown as manipulative and hypocritical. Blind to her own faults, she believes she is a good person who is misunderstood and unappreciated in a changing world that has lost a sense of traditional values. In the following excerpt, we see her sentimentality and racism in action as the family drives down a highway. Her one gesture—"folding her thin veined fingers"—suggests her age and her self-satisfaction:

> "In my time," said the grandmother, folding her thin veined fingers, "children were more respectful of their native states and their parents and everything else. People did right then. Oh look at the cute pickaninny!" she said and pointed to a Negro child standing in the door of a shack. "Wouldn't that make a picture now?" she asked, and they all turned and looked at the little Negro out of the back window. He waved.
>
> "He didn't have any britches on," June Star said.
>
> "He probably didn't have any," the grandmother explained. "Little niggers in the country don't have things like we do. If I could paint, I'd paint that picture," she said.

PROMPT: As F. Scott Fitzgerald once wrote, "action is character." As we've seen, character is more than just action, but action is the primary mode writers use. Put your character in a scene involving some sort of conflict. If the scene you've been developing in the previous prompts does not contain much conflict, try a new one. Give your character an obstacle and test his mettle. In the following excerpt from Lorrie Moore's "People Like That Are the Only People Here," a mother is made aware that her son has cancer. Notice that Moore manages to show the mother's fear without stating it directly. The mother uses sarcasm to mask her feelings, a trait we will see in action throughout the story:

> "The surgeon will speak to you," says the Radiologist.
>
> "Are you finding something?"
>
> "The surgeon will speak to you," the Radiologist says again. "There seems to be something there, but the surgeon will talk to you about it."
>
> "My uncle had something on his kidney," says the Mother. "So they removed the kidney and it turned out the something was benign."
>
> The Radiologist smiles a broad, ominous smile. "That's always the way it is," he says. "You don't know exactly what it is until it's in the bucket."
>
> " 'In the bucket,' " the Mother repeats.
>
> The Radiologist's grin grows scarily wider—is that even possible? "That's doctor talk," he says.
>
> "It's very appealing," says the Mother. "It's a very appealing way to talk." Swirls of bile and blood, mustard and maroon in a pail, the colors of an African flag or some exuberant salad bar: in the bucket—she imagines it all.

PROMPT: Write about a character whose appearance and actions are far different from her interior self. Place the character in a scene, showing her actions, but occasionally move into her head to show what she's thinking and feeling. A cynical, sophisticated woman, for example, can hold the floor at a party with her wit, but in her mind, readers learn of her boredom and loneliness. In her novel *Remember Me*, Laura Hendrie's protagonist, Rose, is known as a fiery, stubborn, independent person, and her behavior around the people of the town where she lives gives credence to this reputation. But Hendrie lets us know that sometimes Rose is on the verge of tears while confronting other characters, that her gruff behavior is a defense against the isolation and powerlessness she feels in a community that has never accepted her.

PROMPT: Write a scene in which your character does not appear. Instead, other characters talk about him, giving the reader a sense of the character through how these characters portray him to each other. If you want to add an extra element of tension, have the characters discuss your absent character unfairly, making him seem better or worse a person than he actually is. Beauty may be in the eye of the beholder, but some characters can be just plain wrong about another character. For example, the title of this chapter, "Folks Like You," is taken from a poem inscribed on Bonnie Parker's gravestone. As you probably know, Bonnie and Clyde were responsible for the murder of more than a dozen people. Here is how her family remembers her: "As the flowers are all made sweeter by / the sunshine and the dew / so this old world is made brighter by / the lives of folks like you."

MORE THOUGHTS ON CHARACTER

As should be clear to you by now, I'm a believer in learning to write by reading. Study the masters. This belief holds true for characterization, maybe even more so than for the other elements of narrative. It's difficult to teach someone how to create compelling characters. This skill requires observing people, knowing your character, and mastering the modes of dramatic presentation. We've covered these aspects of the subject. But having the ingredients of a character is not the same as creating a great character. Two cooks can use the same ingredients and have vastly different results.

By studying the masters, you can learn the subtle strategies. Begin by making a list of the characters you like most, the ones you find most memorable. If you read a lot, your list probably will be very long. If you want, include film favorites on your list, but be sure it's the character rather than the actor that you like. My own favorites that come quickly to mind: R.P. McMurphy from Ken Kesey's *One Flew Over the Cuckoo's Nest*, Benna Carpenter from Lorrie Moore's *Anagrams*, George

Babbitt from Sinclair Lewis's *Babbitt*, Frank Bascombe from Richard Ford's *The Sportswriter*, *Independence Day*, and *The Lay of the Land*.

After you finish your list, read the story or essay or novel or memoir closely. If you can, read it a few times. Rereading can teach you much about writing. Each time you notice something new. As I mentioned earlier, I learned a lot about writing short stories while I was an editor at *Story* magazine. In editing, copyediting, and proofreading stories, I'd read them close to a dozen times. Hidden structures would emerge, and I could determine how characters were coming to life or remaining flat on the page.

If a character is not yet working for you, perhaps you need to know him better. If he's not interesting enough, find a strong quality and amplify it. If readers don't find your character sympathetic, find out why. Amplify a few likable traits. In a novel I wrote years ago, my protagonist was too mild to hold the novel together. The secondary characters, who were much more plucky and interesting, stole every scene. In revising some of the early chapters, I realized that the character was always playing the straight man. He was losing the spotlight because I was unconsciously setting him up to do that. I changed his name and made him bigger. With those two simple changes, he became clearer in my mind and more active, more assertive.

PROMPT: If a character is not working on the page, change some aspect of her personality or behavior. If the character is based closely on you, change more than one aspect. We are always a little ambivalent about characters who are based closely on ourselves. It's tough to get the necessary distance.

PROMPT: If a character is not doing what you'd like him to do, assess your decision to have the character perform the action. Perhaps the action doesn't feel right for the character because it isn't right. If he must do the action for the sake of the plot, rethink the plot. Try to find another way to accomplish the plot goal. The problem lies there, not in the character.

PROMPT: Write a scene in which you let loose of your characters. Allow them to do whatever they want. Write down whatever actions occur to you first, without worrying if the action fits the scene or the character as readers know her. This experiment will help you practice letting go of your characters. Some writers have an easy time letting go, especially if they've spent some time with the characters and know them well. Other writers never let go. Vladimir Nabokov once referred to his characters as "galley slaves."

PROMPT: Write a scene in which a character takes a surprising action. Then, on a separate piece of paper, explain the character's motivation. Why is she doing what she's doing? Be as specific as you can be. Go back to the womb if you must. When you feel you have a pretty good understanding (as much as you can ever understand human motivation), move forward with your story. Resist the urge to explain the motivation in the story.

PROMPT: Grab a few characters from your list of favorites. Place them all in a scene. Maybe they're all up in character heaven. Sorry. To evoke these characters, use the strategies you picked up from reading the stories in which the characters appear. Feel free to steal entire paragraphs of description from the originals, if you want. Add to them, echoing the original authors' voices. Have fun with this one.

PROMPT: If you're writing memoir or biography or a historical narrative, you can use many of the same strategies as in an imagined story. Of course, you need to stick to the reality, but observation, insight, physical details, hobbies, actions, and so on can still develop this person on the page. For great examples, read the work of Erik Larson or David McCullough, or any of the many great nonfiction storytellers. Their use of the techniques and strategies of what we normally consider fictive devices can be very instructive.

CHAPTER TWENTY-TWO

THE SHAPE OF THINGS TO COME

When the plot flags, bring in a man with a gun.

—RAYMOND CHANDLER

Sure, easy for Chandler to say. He wrote hard-boiled mysteries. What if you're trying to structure a memoir? Do you even know anybody who owns a gun? Or how's a gun going to fit into that meditative poem you're trying to shape? Or maybe you're working on a whimsical children's tale. Which of the bunnies in the downy meadow pulls a pistol? Oh, well. Ray was doing his best.

Advice: All advice on structure and plot (and on writing) must be taken at face value. Learn the craft, use what applies to you, and be aware that every piece is a new challenge, a start from scratch. What worked last time may not work this time. In fact, regard with suspicion any plot that comes too easily. True, sometimes a story will just write itself, all the twists and turns, the scenes and summaries just falling into place. But most times, finding the best shape for your story requires some shuffling around. That's our focus in this chapter.

Though structure is a key element in any kind of storytelling, and would seem as fundamental to writing stories as, say, the alphabet, it's a controversial topic. Does one outline or not? How much should one know when beginning? Writers can't even agree on what to call structure. Some writers revile the word *plot* and would never dare to include anything as barbaric as a sequence of connected events in their work. These writers prefer the word *shape*. Other writers feel that *shape* is a pretentious bit of foppery. They feel that any story in which the events can't be followed like shampoo directions isn't really a story. Most writers fall somewhere in between. Some of us tell stories in impressionistic, associative moves, shifting between past and present, between action and reflection. Others think in chronological terms, seeing a story as a grand inevitable sweep. Director John Huston once was asked how he managed to create such unique structures for his films. He replied that he couldn't imagine telling his stories in any other way. He did what came naturally for him. John Irving, in a disarming bit of open-mindedness, feels the writer needs to know the plot before beginning:

> If you don't know the story before you begin the story, what kind of story-teller are you? Just an ordinary kind, just a mediocre kind—making it up as you go along, like a common liar.

John Updike, on the other hand, prefers the common liar approach:

> I really begin with some kind of solid, coherent image, some notion of the shape of the book and even of its texture. *The Poorhouse Fair* was meant to have a sort of wide shape. *Rabbit, Run* was kind of zigzag, *The Centaur* was sort of a sandwich.

So there's no right answer on how to structure your stories. If you want to outline, outline. You won't be a conventional, uncreative lout nor will you be a clear-eyed, commonsense professional for doing it. If you prefer to write until the story finds its own shape, write until the story finds its own shape. You won't be a true artist nor will you be a hopeless fool for doing it. Instead, keep in mind Eudora Welty's observation about the craft: "Every story teaches you how to write that story but not the next story."

Because this book focuses on getting ideas, we'll concentrate on structuring before beginning, but many of the prompts can be used if you've already begun and are still looking for a shape or if you're stuck in the middle and need to rethink how you've told your story.

PROMPT: Write or outline your story in chronological order, noting each event on a separate index (3" x 5") card. Then shuffle the cards and read the story in a new order. Do this a few times, looking for interesting juxtapositions and for possibilities for creating conflict and dramatic tension. If you prefer, try the cut-and-paste approach. Cut your story into pieces and rearrange it. This latter approach might work better if you've completed a draft of your story.

PROMPT: Begin a story with a moment of decision or insight, an epiphany that more commonly appears at the end of a story. Then jump backward, allowing the reader to find out what led to the decision. Avoid simply summarizing the events in a narrative flashback. Take readers dramatically up to the moment of decision. Frederick Exley's *A Fan's Notes* begins with the narrator having "what appeared to be a heart attack." When told he's simply been drinking too much, he realizes he has reached a turning point in his life and must begin finding out why he drinks and why he is so troubled. Much of the novel concerns his investigation of how he got to the point where he collapsed.

PROMPT: Build on the previous prompt. After you've led the reader to the decision, push beyond it. What happens next, as a result of the decision?

PROMPT: Combine the two previous prompts. Begin with the decision or insight, then allow the character to push forward while filtering past events into the narrative. Lisa Dale Norton uses this structure in her memoir, *Hawk Flies Above*. In the memoir, she confronts the emptiness of her peripatetic life by returning to her childhood home and confronting the demons of her past.

PROMPT: Rather than a decision or epiphany, open with an action scene: Something happens. You can move forward for another scene or two if you want, then jump backward and show what happened that led to that moment. The film *Mildred Pierce* uses this structure. A character is murdered in the opening, Mildred is arrested as a suspect, and then she tells the story of her life to the detectives investigating the murder to help explain what happened. Most of the film focuses on her story, returning to the police station only at the end.

PROMPT: Build a story by bringing together two distant—either geographically or socially—characters. Begin by focusing on one character, using her in a scene or two, then switch to a second character. Your story will gain structure and tension as you move these characters closer and closer toward their inevitable meeting. For a tour de force example of this approach, read *Continental Drift* by Russell Banks. He brings together two very different story lines: a blue-collar man living in New Hampshire and the geological formation of the Earth's crust.

PROMPT: Read a story or essay or poem, or watch a film at least five times. You can use a book-length work if you're feeling particularly ambitious. After the fifth time, write what you've been able to discover about the structure of the piece. Through numerous viewings and readings, you'll be able to pick up on how the piece was put together.

PROMPT: Write an opening scene for a story. You could use a scene you've written in response to a prompt or simply explore a story idea you've had for a while. Next, write a scene in which the key character from the earlier scene is in a different place or in different circumstances from the first scene. Then out-line—or write about—how he moved from one situation to the next. If the second scene does not close the story, push on. If you want, repeat the process, jumping forward to another place or circumstance and moving the character slowly to that point.

PROMPT: Use a framing device. Write a story in which a character tells a different story, one with a different setting and characters. Of course, the stories need to have some connection. An example: *The Wizard of Oz.* The scenes in Kansas act as a frame for the vast majority of the story set in Oz.

SHAPE IN SPACE AND TIME

Many writers use movement in space and time to structure and unify their stories. They focus on specific periods in time or on journeys from one place to another. This method may seem obvious, but writers often overlook the benefits of this approach. The benefits of a ticking clock—find the villain in forty-eight hours or the world blows up!—are easy to understand and are common in suspense films and novels. Dramatic tension is immediately evoked. But even if your characters aren't racing against time, you can use time to give your stories a frame.

If you use this approach, find some models to study how the writers suggest time's passage. If you use a spatial structure, using movement from one place to another, find models to study how the writers suggest this movement. In the prompts that follow, explore the possibilities of shaping your stories by focusing them in this way.

PROMPT: Structure your story by using a specific period of time. Set it in a single day, opening in the morning, ending at night. For a model, read *Ulysses* by James Joyce. Okay, not exactly an easy read. Find an easier model.

PROMPT: Structure your story by setting it in a weekend. For this one, you can use *Saturday Night and Sunday Morning*, by Alan Sillitoe.

PROMPT: Structure your story by using a season. In a famous example, *The Great Gatsby* begins at the onset of summer and ends as the leaves begin to fall.

PROMPT: Structure your story using a year. The novel *Bridget Jones's Diary* by Helen Fielding uses this structure as does the film *The Four Seasons.*

THE WRITER'S IDEA BOOK

Let's shift the focus to spatial structures. A number of films use coast-to-coast journeys—*Midnight Run* comes quickly to mind. *Dumb and Dumber* provides another example (I know, dumb example. Give me a break. My, um, kids like to watch it ...). *Rain Man* covers much of the country. The reader is subconsciously anchored in the story as he locates where he is in relation to the journey's end. For example, if we're headed to Los Angeles, we can plot our course from New York, knowing where we are in the story's arc by knowing where we are geographically. Older films amplified this arc by visually showing the lines on the map—where the characters began, where they are, and how far they have to go. *The Adventures of Huckleberry Finn* uses a journey structure, the rafting trip down the Mississippi River providing structure for the picaresque story. The river itself also provides unity, a constant amid the various adventures. Bill Bryson's *The Lost Continent* involves an extended trip through most of the states. *Blue Highways* by William Least Heat-Moon uses a series of trips.

PROMPT: Structure your story by using a trip or journey. Let your reader know the destination early in the story. Note the examples above.

PROMPT: Write a story based on a family vacation. Use a personal experience or simply make up the trip. Vacations can force family members to interact much more than they do when at home and going about their daily lives. Conflicts can burble to the surface.

PROMPT: Write about a birthday party. It could be for a child, especially these days, when a kid's birthday bash seems to require more planning and gimmicks than halftime at the Super Bowl. Or, you could focus on the birthday of the family's oldest member. Or, maybe the party is for someone who is unhappy to be reaching the milestone—turning thirty or fifty or whatever. Remember that you can focus mostly on the buildup to the event, if you prefer.

PROMPT: Use a framing device, place your journey within a larger story. *The Wizard of Oz*, as mentioned earlier, uses this structure. We know that when the group arrives in Emerald City, Dorothy still must find a way back to Kansas and the story's original setting.

PROMPT: The physical journey provides structure and movement to your story and is often used to show changes in a character. The character is in a different place emotionally at the end of the journey. Something has been lost or gained. A friendship has been forged through the events of the trip, as in the film *Thelma & Louise*, or has broken apart, as in Jack Kerouac's *On the Road*. Write a story, or plan one, using the journey to show narrative progression as well as progression within your characters.

An event also can structure your story—a wedding, a funeral, a high school reunion, a family party. Readers are familiar with these events and will have an implicit sense of each stage of the event (the rehearsal dinner, the wedding ceremony, the reception afterward, etc.), so you can use their knowledge of the stages to keep your reader anchored in the story as each stage unfolds. Try some of the following prompts to experiment with this approach.

PROMPT: Structure a story around a holiday. Readers will know how these holidays work and the various stages of preparation and celebration, and will have that structure in their minds as they move through the story. The holiday needn't be the story's primary concern. It can provide a background for the main story, simply working as a unifying device.

PROMPT: Write a story involving a wedding or a funeral or a birth. As in the previous prompt, this activity need not be the story's primary focus. The event can be used as a subplot or background device, providing a silent structure.

PROMPT: Write about a family reunion, either one from your personal experience or one you create. Such occasions are full of possibilities for drama, as family members have long-standing and complex relationships.

PROMPT: Write about a class reunion—a fully imagined one or one from personal experience. At these events, relationships are complex and usually based on events and attitudes from some years ago. They can be arenas for settling old scores.

PROMPT: Write a story involving a blizzard or a drought or some other type of weather event. The same conditions apply here as in the previous prompts. You could tell the story of a family's unraveling, concentrating on the interrelationships of the characters while using the heavy snow as a counterpoint to the main story, allowing it to provide unity and structure.

PROMPT: Write a story that builds to—rather than focuses upon—any of the above times, events, or activities. For example, begin a story that ends with a big Fourth of July celebration (and showdown). Or, begin with a chilly day or two and build slowly to a blizzard.

THE WRITER'S IDEA BOOK

CHAPTER TWENTY-THREE

IT ALL DEPENDS ON YOUR POINT OF VIEW

I'm about to write a novel. The only problem is I don't know if I am an I or a she.

—ELIZABETH HARDWICK

The title of this chapter is not an overstatement, especially when turning your ideas into fiction, poetry, a script, even nonfiction. Your choice of who tells the story and from what perspective may be the most important decision you make. A good idea can become a great one if presented from the right point of view. Conversely, I've seen many a good idea botched by the point of view.

Having taught at writers conferences for many years, I've learned that many writers aren't especially interested in discussing point of view. They want characterization. They want plot. Point of view? Yawn, well, okay, if we must. But it's a key subject, some might say the most important one when telling a story in whatever form. It involves so many questions: How do I know which one to choose? How can I dramatize scenes that the narrator can't possibly have witnessed? Many others.

In the next two chapters, we'll explore this subject in detail, trying to find ideas, shape material you've begun writing already, and solve problems that have arisen in your work by helping you see it in a new way. In this chapter, we'll focus on first-person point of view, perhaps the most troublesome of them all, because it's the most tempting to use and it's the most misunderstood.

FIRST PERSON

A quick review: In first-person point of view, a character in the story tells the story, using the first-person pronoun. A few examples:

> I read about it in the paper, in the subway, on my way to work.
>
> > —JAMES BALDWIN, "SONNY'S BLUES"

> I will wait for her in the yard that Maggie and I made so clean and wavy yesterday afternoon.
>
> > —ALICE WALKER, "EVERYDAY USE"

> I am Gimpel the fool.
>
> > — ISAAC SINGER, "GIMPEL THE FOOL"

> I steal.
>
> > —MONA SIMPSON, "LAWNS"

The events of this type of story are related to the readers through the narrative *I*. The readers see, hear, think, and feel right along with this character. They are told only what he thinks, knows, and does.

PROMPT: Find four pieces of writing that open with the word *I*. (First-person pieces that don't begin with *I* are off-limits for this prompt.) Copy the first few sentences. Then write four of your own openings, all beginning with the word *I*. At least one must follow the Singer example, a statement of identity: "I am _____." Another must follow the Mona Simpson example: "I [action verb]." Push on for at least three paragraphs, if you're writing narrative, or at least a dozen lines if you're writing poetry.

In response to this prompt, here's one I wrote. We'll use this sample throughout the point-of-view chapters to discuss the qualities of each viewpoint:

> I saw Alice walk into the club, radiant in an orchid dress, her hair drawn back in a French braid, just the way I like it. It'd been two weeks since I'd seen her, three weeks since our getaway trip to the shore. But she looked different. Thinner maybe, her skin paler, her dark eyes tense, like she had something on her mind.
>
> But her chin was tilted back in this way she had, like she was some kind of queen. You had to look close to see it was all an act. Like always, she

looked around the smoky room, pretending that she was trying to decide where to sit or that maybe she was meeting some people there. Then, like always, she headed for the one empty bar stool at the far end, by the waitress station. I'd put a glass of water there an hour ago to save the seat.

"This seat taken?" she asked, like it was the first time I ever saw her in my life.

Sweeping away the glass and bar nap, I said, "They left," solemn as a judge.

FIRST PERSON—THE GOOD STUFF

In this example, we can see some of the positive aspects of point of view. First, it supplies an immediate *focus*, a central consciousness: the bartender. He provides the story with boundaries, a frame to use for shaping the narrative world. This point of view also allows us to establish *conflict and tension* very quickly. Alice looks different, is apparently troubled by something. What gives? This question is then complicated by the game the two play, pretending not to know each other.

First person also gives the narrative *immediacy,* since readers receive the events directly from the bartender, let's call him Jim. With first person, there's no narrative middleman diluting the impact of the drama. Readers feel and think right along with the narrator, and the narrator is taking part in the drama. If they're rooting for him, the narrative stakes are raised for them: To put it simply, if he wins, they win; if he loses, they lose.

First person gives your story a strong *voice.* The voice characterizes Jim and creates a tone for the story. Note that Jim uses slang and that his grammar is not perfect: He uses *like* to render the subjunctive case rather than the correct *as if* or *as though.* Through a unique and vivid first-person voice, you can captivate, charm, and seduce your reader.

PROMPT: Push forward with the openings you wrote above, writing at least one page for each one. By the end of the first page, your "I" should establish conflict and tension, and the reader should gain a sense of the character through voice. Tip: Don't go overboard on the voice, especially in using slang and dialect. A little goes a long way.

PROMPT: Begin a story in which the first-person narrator is at work. She'll use jargon and slang to describe what she's doing. To make it easier, give the narrator a job you've done, one that you can speak of in the shorthand style we use in our jobs.

FIRST PERSON—THE BAD STUFF

The good news is that some of the bad stuff isn't really bad. You can use it to your advantage if you're clever. But do be aware of the limitations of this point of view. You can avoid roadblocks in your stories by knowing in advance that trouble awaits, and you can be more successful with your ideas if you've found the right perspective from which to tell the story.

The first problem is *limitation*. You're limited to what your narrator can reasonably see and know and feel. If key action occurs elsewhere, you can't render that action dramatically. Perhaps Alice has just been fired from her job in an explosive confrontation with her boss. More than twenty thousand dollars has been discovered missing and all the evidence points to Alice. She declared, but could not prove, her innocence. Since the readers know Jim was working behind the bar, they know he couldn't have witnessed this scene. Alice can tell him about it, but that loses the immediacy, even if Jim imaginatively re-creates the scene and relates it directly. He wasn't there.

And then there's the problem of *distance*—your own and the narrator's. If the story is autobiographical and the narrator is a slightly altered version of you, first person is a risky choice. (Of course, if you're writing an essay or memoir, there's no way around this dilemma, but still you should be aware of the pitfalls.) A big, deep, hairy-looking pitfall is the temptation to explain everything rather than showing it. Let's face it, we like the sound of our own voices. And who better than we to tell the readers what they should think about the stories we're telling? Even if you create a voice completely different from your own, you'll grow to like that voice and might be less stingy than you should be with how much that voice gets to talk.

If the story is autobiographical, you also might tend to stick too closely to *what really happened*. In nonfiction, you'd better stick to what happened; in fiction, that's a danger. You're limiting your material and assuming that, because the events took place, they possess logic and believability.

For these reasons, I'd advise not using first person if you are too close to the voice or character of your story. Successful first-person point of view *exists* in the distance between the writer and the voice. From that gap blooms the story's conflict and tension, along with a great deal of useful irony. The voice is not only your guiding light through the jungle of plot, it is a device you consciously manipulate. You need to hear it clearly, objectively, from a distance.

PROMPT: Create a narrative voice that is distinctly different from your own by changing a key element of the character. If you're a woman, write in a man's voice.

THE WRITER'S IDEA BOOK

If you're under thirty, create the voice of a character over sixty. Make a change in appearance or education or background. Put that character at an event or in a scene from your own recent experience—at a friend's wedding, at a restaurant with your mate—and retell the story through this new voice.

PROMPT: Put yourself in the previous scene, but narrate it again through the voice of the new character. For example, if you placed someone else in the restaurant where you argued with your mate about his family's continuing interference with your lives, allow this new person to observe, perhaps as a waiter or as a nosy patron at a nearby table.

PROMPT: Write about an event from your childhood through your adult eyes, adding perceptions that you could not have known at the time.

PROMPT: Write about that event from your childhood through your eyes at the time, even casting the episode in present tense.

PROMPT: Write about that childhood event through the eyes of someone who witnessed it—a parent or a friend or a sibling or whomever. Allow him to comment on your actions.

PROMPT: Take some time to read the three versions of the one event that you've written for the previous three prompts. What qualities do they share? How are they different? Can you see ways of pulling material from all three into one piece?

This series of prompts speaks to the next concern in using first person: the problem of *perception*. In our story, the readers will see and know what Jim knows—and what he feels obliged to tell them. This can create difficulties in telling the story. For example, if Jim has worked at the nightclub for a long time, why would he describe it? He's known Alice for a while, so why would he describe her? We avoided this problem by having him describe her because she looks different than normal when she enters the bar. He notices changes and through them we can slip in a few details about her general appearance.

Another aspect of the perception problem concerns the narrator's observational powers. Can the writer, on the one hand, characterize Jim as a self-absorbed dolt and on the other hand have him supply all the specific and particular details necessary to bring his world to life? Possibly, but not easily.

Our narrator Jim seems to be observant, but can readers trust his perceptions? First person always brings up the question of *reliability*. Whenever we tell stories, we have our own best interests at heart, especially when telling stories of some significance to us. As readers and listeners, we automatically reserve judgment. For example, when someone tells you about his divorce, citing all the reasons his wife is to blame, do you believe him, or do you believe you're only getting half of the truth? Conversely, if the speaker, obviously pained by guilt and regret, puts all the blame on himself, do you believe you're getting the full story?

A bit of advice: If your story requires a speaker of absolute truth, first person is not the right choice. The reader can take Jim's word that Alice walks into the bar and peers around the room. The reader can accept that her dress is orchid and that her hair is styled in a French braid. If we establish him as somewhat perceptive, we can even believe that the objective observer would perceive her as self-confident, though this poise masks the doubts she's feeling.

But because Jim is romantically involved with Alice, readers must question his perception of her as "radiant." Is she merely attractive, no more radiant than the last five women who walked in the place? And does she really look like she has "something on her mind," or is this the result of Jim's feeling insecure? Perhaps he's a bit concerned that they haven't been together in two weeks and is seeing everything as significant and potentially negative.

You can take great pains to establish the speaker's validity—choosing the pope or Mother Teresa to tell your story. But the intelligent reader will still question. This is not a bad thing in itself. Again, choose first person when you want to use the reader's doubt, when the story truly lives within the disparity between what the voice says and what the reader can determine is true. Use that doubt, that disparity, to create and sustain tension in your narrative. In *The Great Gatsby,* when Nick Carraway proclaims, "I am the most honest person I have ever known," Fitzgerald wants us to think, *Yeah, right.* Nick is, in many ways, honest. And he's very observant. He is perceptive and he's selfless enough to empathize with other characters. Good qualities for a narrator. But he's also a bit blind to his own priggishness and to his inability to commit himself to any one side. He tries too hard, in short, to be fair. In some ways, he doesn't quite get the point of what happened in that strange summer of 1922 among the rich and decadent of East and West Egg.

PROMPT: Write a monologue from the point of view of a character who insists he's "telling the truth" about something that happened. Try to show that he doesn't grasp the full story or is fudging that truth a bit.

PROMPT: View a scene from the perspective of someone who is clearly biased in her perceptions. If you want, base the scene on a real event in your own life. Perhaps this character is jealous of the bride at the friend's wedding. She finds fault with everything she sees. Or perhaps she's trying so hard to "take the high road" that she characterizes the event in a better light than it deserves. Allow the biases to be revealed slowly.

PROMPT: Use the same character and event as in the previous prompt, but don't mention the biases. Try to be more subtle this time, allowing the narrator to appear coolly objective and observant while tainting ever so slightly the details and events.

PROMPT: Watch and take notes (or record) as a political pundit speaks on a current issue. More than likely, he or she will be quite confident and rattle off no end of statistics. Now find a political pundit who has a decidedly different perspective, and take notes. How does each bend the "truth" to fit his or her opinion? What concepts are largely a matter of perspective? If you want, create a fictional pundit and write a speech in which an issue is presented in a biased manner.

WHOSE STORY IS IT?

You've decided the story needs to be handled in first person. Now you must choose which narrator to use. In short, whose story is it? Our story, for example, doesn't have to be rendered through Jim. Let's switch to Alice:

> I walked into Jim's club—loud and busy, as always—and looked around for a minute before heading for the last open stool. Though I was happy to see Jim, this was about the last place I wanted to be. The trouble at work was all I could think about, and taking the time to explain it to Jim would require more effort and energy than I could manage.

Same bar. Same action. Different story. It's no longer about a man worried about keeping a budding relationship alive with a woman who might lift him from the tawdry world in which he lives. It's now a story of a woman's struggle after being fired for a crime she didn't commit. In fact, Jim's role might be small, a peripheral relationship for Alice as she attempts to prove her innocence.

We have other options, too. Our scene could be seen through the eyes of a different character, describing Jim and Alice briefly before launching into his own tale of love. He might idealize the young couple, setting them up as a comparison to his own meager love life. Or, that character could tell the story of Jim and Alice, working as a peripheral narrator, perhaps a regular customer at the bar or someone who socializes with one of the characters. A peripheral narrator is an excellent choice when dealing with unperceptive characters or ones who are potentially unsympathetic. The narrator's interest in these characters can be used to foster the reader's interest.

Consider, again, *The Great Gatsby,* perhaps the most famous use of this approach. Nick tells the tragic story of Jay Gatsby and Daisy Buchanan, neither of whom is perceptive enough or likable enough to tell the story him- or herself. Nick's fascination with them leads us to care about them. However, the story, in its larger sense, is not about Jay and Daisy. It's about Nick. When choosing a peripheral narrator, know that you're changing the story and its larger implications. The story is always about the person who is telling it. Allow me to repeat that statement for emphasis: The story is always about the person who is telling it—no matter how far they seem to be from the central action. Nick is peripheral to the events he relates, but he is, in fact, the center of the story, which is less about the love affair than about Nick's disillusionment and, ultimately, his moment of awakening. Seen from a thematic perspective, Gatsby and Daisy are merely the vehicles of Nick's transformation.

PROMPT: Pick one of the pieces you wrote for one of the prompts in this chapter. Change the narrator but keep the piece in first person. The events of the drama can remain the same, but their implications should change now that the narrator has changed. Push forward with this new story.

PROMPT: Write a scene as observed by a peripheral character, someone on the fringe of the action. If you want, choose an event from an earlier prompt and retell it from this new perspective.

A FINAL WORD ON FIRST PERSON

In my experience as an editor, I feel that first person is used too often and for the wrong reasons. Too many writers use it without fully understanding it. Nevertheless, as we've discussed, this viewpoint offers many advantages to your story. There is more to learn about first person than we can explore here. We didn't cover first-person plural, the use of past and present tense, the use of various distances, the use of first person in nonfiction, but there are many good books that offer advice on these subjects. Find them and read them. And when reading a first-person piece, don't believe everything you hear.

CHAPTER TWENTY-FOUR

OTHER ROOMS, OTHER VOICES

Everyone is in the best seat.

—JOHN CAGE

Now let's look at a few other point-of-view options. As I said in the previous chapter, we don't have the space here to cover them all in the necessary detail. Our goal, instead, is to know enough about point of view to find the full potential in our ideas and, with luck, to generate new ideas.

SECOND PERSON

A risky venture, this second-person viewpoint. In it, instead of *I*, the writer uses *you*, as if talking to someone:

> You walk down the street and turn left into Sam's deli, where the smell of cured meats and Sam's delicious salads causes you nearly to swoon with hunger. Sam waves a bustling hello at you and turns to wait on the man standing at the counter.

The "you" seems to be the reader. Instead, it's an aspect of the narrator, as if the narrator is speaking to herself. The problem with this approach is that it's too apparent, too vehicular. The reader is aware that she's not actually in Sam's deli, and the reader questions if anyone would talk to herself in this way. In short, readers see the wires holding Superman aloft, making his heroic deeds seem like so much back-lot farce.

Can this point of view work? Absolutely. The most commonly cited example— so common I hate to repeat it here—is Jay McInerney's novel *Bright Lights, Big City*. His great feat is that he sustains this point of view for an entire novel, making it, after a while, almost invisible. In the novel, a bright and sensitive young man with lofty aspirations surrenders to his self-destructive impulses while recovering from a divorce and the death of his mother. He abuses drugs and alcohol in all-night forays through the trendy world of New York nightlife, a drastic departure from his normal life. He is living, in a way, outside himself. Through second person, the better angels of his nature attempt to drag him back to safer ground. So the novel becomes a monologue in which one level of the character's consciousness addresses another.

For other examples, see the short story "Lord Short Shoe Wants the Monkey" in Bob Shacochis's collection titled *Easy in the Islands,* or Tess Slesinger's "On Being Told That Her Second Husband Has Taken His First Lover," or Lorrie Moore's brilliant collection of stories titled *Self-Help.* Moore's stories use the conventions of instructional writing, directly addressing the reader but offering advice on subjects such as "How to Be an Other Woman."

Use second person if it feels the most natural way to tell your story, but be aware of its limitations. Even McInerney doubted if this was the best choice as he was writing his novel, which grew out of a short story told in second person. In an interview he reflected:

> I thought, what the hell, I can pull this off for ten or fifteen pages. It just seemed to work, and in the best sense the story seemed, on the momentum of that voice, to write itself. When I went back to the story with the idea of writing a novel, I thought, "I have to change this to first or third." But when I did, the prose went flat. Something drained out of the narrative—a certain distance and a certain intimacy as well. And somehow it wasn't as funny. [The editor] said to me, "Don't even think about trying to write a novel in the second person." I was almost fatally discouraged by that comment, but since I was already halfway there I just kept going. The moral would seem to be—trust our instincts.

PROMPT: Shift one of your first-person writings from the previous chapters to second person, substituting *you* for *I*. Note how the piece changes. Assess what you lose and what you gain. If you're taken with the new point of view, push forward with the piece.

THE WRITER'S IDEA BOOK

PROMPT: Use second person to write a few pages of a personal essay recounting a difficult moment in your life. Does it supply a pleasing distance? Do you find yourself being more candid? Again, if it works, push forward.

PROMPT: Let's steal Moore's idea and write a piece using second-person imperative, as if we were writing an instructional piece. But choose a topic that offers narrative possibilities, one you've thought about writing as a story or an essay, and, if you want, choose a subject that the reader really will not want to learn. For example, "How to Wreck Your Car With Style"; "How to Speak to Your Mother-in-Law at Christmas Dinner"; "How to Spend Your Birthday Alone." Have fun with this one.

PROMPT: Write a poem or narrative piece addressed to a specific reader, as if you were writing a letter to the person.

THIRD PERSON

In third person, the most commonly used point of view, the writer refers to the characters by name or uses the pronoun *he* or *she* to tell the story. A few examples:

> Her doctor had told Julian's mother that she must lose twenty pounds on account of her blood pressure, so on Wednesday nights Julian had to take her downtown on the bus for a reducing class at the Y.
>
> —FLANNERY O'CONNOR,
> "EVERYTHING THAT RISES MUST CONVERGE"

> He came from the twenty-third floor down to the lobby on the mezzanine to collect his mail before breakfast, and he believed—he hoped—that he looked passably well: doing all right.
>
> —SAUL BELLOW, *SEIZE THE DAY*

> To begin at the beginning, the airplane from Minneapolis in which Francis Weed was traveling East ran into heavy weather.
>
> —JOHN CHEEVER, "THE COUNTRY HUSBAND"

These characters and situations are presented by a narrative voice that exists outside them, and yet the voice can move inside their minds to show their thoughts. The voice in Cheever, for example, is distant, using phrases such as "To begin at the beginning," which make clear that the story is being told by an outside voice. In Bellow, the perspective, still in third person, is much closer to the character, presenting his thoughts and doubts. Let's look at a few of the types of third-person viewpoints.

OMNISCIENT

In the omniscient approach, the voice of the story knows all. It can be in all places and know every character's thoughts. The main advantage of this choice is *flexibility*. We are not limited to the thoughts of a single character. The disadvantage is that the narrative can lack a sharp focus as the voice moves from character to character, from a godlike distance to a detailed close-up. Contemporary writers tend to avoid the omniscient, for technical and philosophical reasons too complex to enumerate here. Omniscience does appear now and again in all its glory, but not often.

PROMPT: Write a scene using the omniscient point of view, moving into and out of the characters' minds, drawing back to make general observations. If you want, create a party scene that includes at least four or five characters. Dip into the minds of at least three of the characters. Also, make a few general observations about the place where the party is held and even make a pronouncement or two about the nature of parties.

PROMPT: You are a supreme being. From your all-seeing, all-knowing vantage point, render a scene based on an experience you've had recently. Make yourself one of the characters and tell what you thought and did, but move into the other characters' minds, imagining their thoughts during the experience. The experience can be something very small—tossing a Frisbee at the park, a trip to the mall. The key is the all-knowing voice.

PROMPT: Use the omniscient, all-knowing voice to present a scene, but allow the voice to be, in fact, less than godlike. Allow it to show biases and to make mistakes in its descriptions or statements.

OBJECTIVE

Sometimes known as "fly on the wall," this viewpoint does not venture into the minds of any characters. It stands apart, observing the events, describing the details. It reports. That's all. You can move in space and time, report scenes that occur simultaneously, but you cannot enter anyone's thoughts. For an example, let's return to Alice and Jim from the previous chapter:

> The young woman in the orchid dress walked into the bar, scanned the crowded tables with one eyebrow cocked. She strolled past the tables and found a stool at the bar. The bartender, a dark-haired man wearing a too-tight black vest slapped a bar napkin in front of her.
>
> The woman said, "Margarita," in a soft voice.
> "Sorry, we're all out," the bartender said.

"Out?"

"All out." He looked at her closely, his elbows propped on the bar. "Something else instead?"

No thoughts or interpretations are included in this exchange. The writer simply observes and reports. This viewpoint is attractive for several reasons. The action of the story dictates and supplies a natural focus and gives immediacy to the narrative. Tension arises quickly as the reader tries to understand what is happening, why it's happening, and what it means.

The difficulties of this viewpoint should be obvious. You must *suggest* the meaning of actions and details rather than explain them or have characters supply the meaning. If Jim begins wiping shot glasses when Alice arrives, you cannot explain that he always does this when he's nervous. You must suggest his nervousness by describing how he wipes.

This viewpoint is rarely sustained for an entire story and is not used often anymore. It enjoyed a certain vogue in the late 1970s as part of the minimalist era. Raymond Carver, the godfather of minimalism, uses the objective viewpoint with amazing results in some of his early stories. Read his "Why Don't You Dance?" for a great example of this viewpoint at work. The classic example of the objective approach is Hemingway's story "Hills Like White Elephants," in which a couple debates whether or not the woman should have an abortion. We enter neither character's mind. In fact, they don't even directly state what they're discussing.

PROMPT: Describe a room using the objective viewpoint. Simply state the details. Don't speculate on who lives there or on the person's traits or tastes. But do select details that will show what the person is like by what is in her room.

PROMPT: Create a scene that includes at least three characters. They don't like each other or some sort of disagreement exists among them. Demonstrate the emotions rife beneath the surface, but stay outside all of the characters' heads. You cannot explain what any of the three is thinking.

PROMPT: Place a character in a location where he feels uncomfortable, a hotel lobby, perhaps, where he knows no one. Or, if you prefer, a dinner party at which he knows everyone but still feels out of place. Describe the character from an objective viewpoint, showing his discomfort without mentioning it.

LIMITED

Much more common in fiction and poetry written today is the third-person limited approach. In this one, we use the pronouns *he* and *she,* but we enter the mind of only one character at a time. As writers, we enjoy the tight focus of first person but can drift back to a more objective perspective, as in this version of our story:

> The bar at the Marriott hotel was exactly like all the business bars in all the airport hotels in America—sterile, graceless, a little sleazy. Not the kind of place a woman especially enjoys entering alone, unless she's powerfully assertive or trained in the martial arts.
>
> Alice Downy was neither. When she entered the bar, she kept her eyes trained on Jim, the bartender, with whom she was having what she sometimes allowed herself to call "a relationship." After the day she'd had, it was a relief to see him. He was, in a way, such a wonderful man.

In this description we shift the narrative distance, moving from a general assertion about the bars in airport hotels, which is not necessarily Alice's perception, to the statement that Jim is "a wonderful man," which definitely is Alice's perception. We cannot, however, now jump to Jim's point of view unless we're using an omniscient viewpoint. In the limited approach, we are limited to Alice.

PROMPT: Retell your story from the previous prompt, this time in limited third person, from a character who is not you. Pick someone else. Then, if you want, try it again from the character who is you.

SHIFTING PERSPECTIVE

In contemporary novels, it's common for the author to use third person limited but shift the focus from one character to another, a shift usually signaled by a chapter or section break. We could open our story with Jim as our narrative eye, then, in chapter two, switch to Alice. This approach allows us to enjoy the focus of a single character without creating a claustrophobic narrative, one too tightly absorbed with a single character.

You may want to limit yourself, however, to a few characters or you risk muddling your focus. Readers often want a character or two to root for and identify with. If you switch back and forth between a number of characters, this pleasure is tougher to achieve. Of course, if your story needs more shifts, make them. Some writers use quite a few third-person viewpoint characters. Robert Stone's *Damascus Gate,* for example, employs at least a half dozen. But he relies on plot and setting to keep the reader anchored, and he's not especially concerned with the reader's rooting for someone. He is using a broad canvas to paint a picture of the sociopolitical forces at work in the Middle East. Again, know your goals in your story to make the best choice in point of view.

PROMPT: Write a scene in which a store is robbed. The cast: the robber, the store employee, a shopper. Relate the event three times, each from a third-person limited perspective of a different character. This approach is know as the Rashomon Effect, taken from *Rashomon*, the famous film by Akira Kurosawa, in which the same story is told from various characters' perspectives.

Some writers even shift between third person and first person. In *The Barracks Thief*, Tobias Wolff shifts from third to first person even while focusing on the same character. He also shifts between past and present tense. It's a very short novel and technically brilliant and ambitious. To get some ideas on how you can manipulate point of view, it's worth reading. These shifts between first and third person are growing more common in fiction, but be aware of what you're doing and know why you're doing it.

That advice applies to all point-of-view choices. Like Jay McInerney, you must trust your instincts. You also must know your goals for your piece and know whose story you want to tell. These are not simple decisions but can be great fun to make.

CHAPTER TWENTY-FIVE

VAST IS THE POWER OF CITIES

Setting exists so that the character has some place to stand, something that can help define him, something he can pick up and throw, if necessary, or eat, or give to his girlfriend.

—JOHN GARDNER

In two earlier chapters, we explored writing about places—places you've lived, places you want to go. Now we'll look at ways to use place and descriptions of places and things in your writing. Let's begin with a question: How large a role does place play in your writing? Think for a moment before you answer.

Next, a few more questions. Do you base your fiction in your hometown or, perhaps, a fictionalized version of your hometown? Is your novel or screenplay set in your ideal hometown, a place you've never been and that probably doesn't even exist? Do you usually use natural settings, or are you drawn, instead, to describing people packed onto dirty sidewalks? Are your stories set in the present time or in an earlier historical era? Do you tend to move around in place and time?

No matter what you're writing, remember that readers want to feel anchored in a place and time. Think about your own favorite stories, novels, movies, poems. Odds are that you immediately recall images of the place where the story is set:

the hardscrabble farmland in Robert Frost's poems, the grimy New York docks and streets in the essays of Joseph Mitchell, the golden fields of Nebraska wheat in Willa Cather's *My Antonia*. The details of time and place are the stuff of storytelling—whether your writing fiction, nonfiction, poetry, or plays. We'll discuss quality vs. quantity later in this chapter, but keep in mind that your job as a writer is to transport the reader. A sharp sense of place makes the process more powerful and pleasing.

PROMPT: List all the places you've written about or as many as you can recall. After making the list, review it, looking for patterns, types of places to which you're especially drawn. Think about, or write about, the nature of these places and your connections to them. Note, too, which places played a large role in the pieces and which ones were nearly invisible.

PROMPT: List all the places where you've spent at least a little bit of time—say, more than a day or two. Note which of these places have appeared in a piece of your writing, comparing this list to the one from the previous prompt. Then note which places on your list haven't made it into a piece of your writing. Ask yourself why you haven't written about them. Are they not interesting to you? Do you feel that you don't know them well enough? Pick one of these places and write a short piece either set in or about that place.

PROMPT: Describe the place where you are sitting now. Freewrite the details you observe—and push yourself to observe a lot of details. Describe the people you can see, the architecture and the furnishings. Use your senses. After you've written down what you see, close your eyes and focus on sounds and smells. Now open your eyes and pull the description into a few paragraphs.

PROMPT: Write about a place you've been in the past week—think fast, write down the first place that comes into your mind.

PROMPT: Choose two characters you have written about or two people you know in real life, and put them in the place you just described. If possible, pick two people who would feel out of place here. Give them a reason for being here, and record what they say to each other. One has coerced the other into coming here. From your freewrite in the previous prompt, select details to use in your drama. Use the place as part of the drama.

PROMPT: Buy some old postcards at an antique store or secondhand shop. (They're usually very cheap.) Choose ones that have writing on the back. Begin a story, set in the time the postcard was sent, about a person or group of people going to that place. Or, if you prefer, begin with a description of the place pictured on the postcard. Your character is looking at this place as your story begins.

PROMPT: Let's try the ekphrastic approach we discussed a few chapters back: Set a piece in a place used in an artistic photograph. If the photo includes people, turn them into characters and write about the moment in which they are forever frozen by the camera. Then write about what happened leading up to that moment. How did they come to be where they are?

SETTING AS CHARACTER

One of my favorite novels is Sinclair Lewis's *Babbitt,* set in the mythical town of Zenith, a midsize Midwestern city based, in part, on my hometown of Cincinnati. (Though the novel is a broad satire that pokes no end of fun at Zenith the Zip City, our city paper mentions this connection with pride every few years in some feature story on "literary Cincinnati.") George Babbitt, the boorish, boosterish protagonist of the novel, loves his city, as does, in his own way, Lewis. Consider this description, which opens the novel:

> The towers of Zenith aspired above the morning mist; austere towers of steel and cement and limestone, sturdy as cliffs and delicate as silver rods. They were neither citadels nor churches, but frankly and beautifully office buildings.

And, later in the chapter:

> Cues of men with lunchboxes clumped toward the immensity of new factories, sheets of glass and hollow tile, glittering shops where five thousand men worked beneath one roof, pouring out the honest wares that would be sold up the Euphrates and across the veldt. The whistles rolled out in greeting a chorus cheerful as the April dawn; the song of labor in a city built—it seemed—for giants.

Notice the many functions of this description. It establishes clearly, if indirectly, the setting of the novel. It establishes that setting will play a large role. It also establishes the novel's tone—arch, satirical, romantic. The ordinariness of Zenith is heightened by the hyperbole in the description. Mundane products are destined for exotic locales; the shops are "glittering." And yet specific details abound: "sheets of glass and hollow tile," "steel and cement and limestone." Lewis takes time to anchor that arch tone, which gives it weight rather than an airy smugness.

PROMPT: Follow Lewis's lead. Describe a mundane setting in an exaggerated tone. Make a backyard birdbath a hallowed sanctuary; turn a suburban street of look-alike houses into a place of exotic intrigue. Tip: Choose a place you know well so your tone will be anchored with specific details.

PROMPT: Reverse the previous prompt. This time, describe an extraordinary place in mundane terms. Reduce the Grand Canyon to a big hole in the ground.

PROMPT: Describe a place from a first-person perspective of someone who has strong opinions about the place. Try to show that the person is coloring the readers' view of the place. For example, a man who was jilted returns to the home he shared with his ex-wife. A woman who owns a restaurant that she loves views it from the kitchen on a busy Saturday night.

PROMPT: Try the previous prompt again, but this time don't let the reader know why the view is colored. The character simply describes the place in a particular tone of voice. For example, consider the following, borrowed from John Gardner's *The Art of Fiction*:

> Describe a building as seen by a man whose son has just been killed in a war. Do not mention the son, war, death, or the old man doing the seeing; then describe the same building, in the same weather and at the same time of day, as seen by a happy lover. Do not mention love or the loved one.

THE IMPORTANCE OF DESCRIPTION

We can see in these prompts how description provides a rich backdrop for drama and how it characterizes the observer and influences the reader. Good description of place can—and should—perform a variety of narrative functions. Beginning writers too often ignore this fact. Many of the short stories I read while at *Story* magazine or continue to read in writing contests lack the richness of place. Today's writers, fearful of losing the reader, don't include the details that, in fact, are crucial to their stories. They hold to their hearts Elmore Leonard's advice to "leave out the parts readers skip."

Or perhaps the problem is that the writer hasn't imagined herself fully into the place. She doesn't truly see it herself and is therefore unable to render it for the reader. This flaw often occurs in stories we are too anxious to complete. We want them out there, making the rounds, getting published. I've spoken to numerous editors who complain about reading skeletal early drafts submitted as completed stories and novels. Fiction lies in the details. Don't make the mistake of sparing them. Throughout this book, you've plumped your store of details and images. Use them.

And push yourself deeper into the places you're writing about. If you're writing a memoir, be sure that what you're seeing is on the page.

The key to good descriptions lies in selectivity. Today's reader is, without question, less patient than ever before. Rhapsodic passages glorifying setting for its own sake won't work anymore. Descriptions that are little more than weather reports will be skipped. But ignoring everything but drama isn't the answer either, because the drama has no scenic context, no frame. The voices call out from a void. As the writer, you must construct a stage from which your characters can speak, a stage that adds dimension to what your characters say, that affirms or contradicts their lines, that provides an extra nub or two of meaning.

In his nonfiction book *U and I,* Nicholson Baker takes exception to the argument that descriptions merely clog the narrative:

> The only thing I *like* are the clogs. ... I wanted my first novel to be a veritable infarct of cloggers; the trick being to feel your way through each clog by blowing it up until its obstructiveness finally revealed not blank mass but unlooked-for seepage-points of passage.

Baker, admittedly, is a special case, an exceptionally talented novelist who can do what few of us could even attempt. The first novel he mentions is *The Mezzanine,* a tour de force of description. In it, readers' normal expectations for drama are frustrated over and over as very little happens. A man who works in an office goes to a drugstore during his lunch break to buy shoelaces. He buys them and returns to his office. That's it. But Baker's powers of observation are so amazing that the novel works on a variety of levels. I am not suggesting that you must pause the action in your current novel or memoir or story for a detailed review of office supplies, but if you feel your descriptive powers need improvement, read Baker's novel.

PROMPT: Describe in great detail some object of seemingly minor importance—the rust-eaten basketball hoop on your garage, for example; a curling iron; a stick shift. Get up close and really eyeball the thing, noting every tiny nuance of detail. Try this experiment on a few objects. After you have at least a few paragraphs, allow yourself to move from the object into free associations. What does that plant stand remind you of? How is it emblematic of plant stands everywhere? This prompt will help you practice your powers of observation and will help you move from the specific to the general. It also will allow you to linger, at times, on a description that is important to your story.

THE WRITER'S IDEA BOOK

PROMPT: Begin with the image you described in the previous prompt. A character is looking at the thing, as if it has some great significance. Decide why it is important to the character and move forward. For example, your character might find the curling iron in her boyfriend's apartment, but it is not *her* curling iron.

PROMPT: Find a short description in a piece you've written. Now, as backyard quarterbacks used to say, go long. Expand it to at least twice the length. Add details or describe more intricately those you've included.

PROMPT: Describe the outside of the place where you live—your home or apartment building. Use a lot of details. If you want, research the building, finding out when it was built and by whom. Find out, if you don't know, its style of architecture. Take time to fully develop this portrait of a place.

PROMPT: Describe a building in your city that you have not noticed before—this prompt requires you to do some scouting around. Again, really take time to observe its details. If you want, use a public building that you can research. When was it built? How has it changed through the years?

SELECTIVITY

Despite Baker's defense of descriptive "clogs," you do need to handle them deftly. The key, again, is selectivity. In workshops, students are sometimes amazed that the rest of the class doesn't "get" their stories. Very often, the problem lies in selection of detail. The writer either shows us nothing, having a clear view of the place in his own mind, or shows us so much that we don't know what's important. Selectivity means showing just the right details that bring a place to life and rooting those details deeply into the lives of the people in the story. Richard Russo makes this point brilliantly in his essay "Location, Location, Location: Depicting Character Through Place." At one point he discusses the sense of place in John Cheever's Shady Hill stories. Shady Hill is based in part on Cheever's town of Oneida in the Hudson Valley. He knows it well. Russo remembers wonderful descriptions of the place and recommends the stories to a student who is having problems with description. The student reads the stories but finds little description. Russo rereads them himself and is shocked that the student is right:

> The deep sense of place that emerges from the Shady Hill stories has more to
> do with life's rhythms, where things are in relation to other things, whether
> the characters can walk there and how long that will take, whether they'll

drive or take the train. We won't be told that the cocktail shaker is pure silver; we'll be told that it's sweating in the lazy Sunday mid-morning sun.

The point here is that Cheever's descriptions evoke a strong sense of place and yet are nearly invisible. The pace of the stories is not slowed, and yet the reader perceives the story world clearly. The world of the story is clear in Cheever's mind, so clear that he can evoke it with a few deft strokes. True, the setting is based on a town he knows well, which, I guess, argues for writing about places you know. But if you spend enough time in an imagined world, you will come to know it well enough to write about it.

PROMPT: Revise the long descriptions of the building where you live and of the short description taken from a piece of earlier writing, this time selecting only a few details, the most telling ones. Then review both descriptions of each subject. Which one works better?

PROMPT: Review pieces of your writing, looking for ways to sharpen the sense of place. Are there too many details? Too few? Do the details suggest "life's rhythms" Russo mentions in his essay? Choose at least three details that could be improved, either through better placement or greater specificity. Choose at least three details that could be deleted.

PROMPT: Describe your neighborhood. Freewrite a list of descriptive details about it, then choose two or three details from your list, searching for those that are most emblematic of the place, the ones that best characterize it. If this is difficult, push deeper and add details to your list. Try again. If this is simple, you're not doing it right.

PROMPT: Take us on a trip through your neighborhood or on a trip you make frequently, such as to the grocery store or your commute to work. Give us a detailed description, taking time to include those details that you probably know so well you don't even think about them anymore.

AUTHORITATIVE DESCRIPTION OF PLACE

When you know a place, or a type of place, very well, you cannot only find the specific details, you can speak in broad terms about it. In an earlier prompt, we moved from the specific to the general. Now let's try it the other way, moving from general to specific. In this passage from *Babbitt,* Lewis speaks not specifically about Zenith but generally about cities:

THE WRITER'S IDEA BOOK

Vast is the power of cities to reclaim the wanderer. More than mountains or the shore-devouring sea, a city retains its character, imperturbable, cynical, holding behind apparent changes its essential purpose.

PROMPT: Previously, you wrote a specific sensory description of the place where you're sitting now. This time, make a few general observations about the type of place you're sitting in now. Address the nature of coffee shops or libraries or even living rooms—wherever you're sitting. You don't need to use Lewis's high-blown language, but do speak with a declarative authority. Tell us what we need to know about such places, what we may not have considered before. If you want, adopt Lewis's tone and try again. This may seem silly, but give it a try. Have fun with it. Write at least a paragraph or two in this way. Then, if you want, and if you're sitting in the same place you described in your earlier writing, shift to the more specific details you generated in the other prompt.

PROMPT: Describe two places and compare them to each other. Choose places that are very different. For example, compare the Vatican to a laundromat, the Oregon Coast to a strip mall. You may find this impossible to do, but keep trying. Look for ways to connect these places, if only in the most peripheral ways. The point is to see beyond the surface, to avoid the easy detail, the most obvious modifiers. Anyone can talk about the awesome splendor of the Grand Canyon; only you will find it as eternal as an all-night gas station.

The goal in describing place is to give your story a dramatic context. The goal also is to make that place a player in the drama. It needs to move beyond mere scenery. Your descriptions of the place should give us insights into the characters themselves. For an excellent example, read Erik Larson's *The Devil in the White City*, which tells the story of the 1893 World's Fair held in Chicago. The two main characters—the architect who designed the fabulous fairgrounds and the serial killer who exploited the fair to murder a number of people in a makeshift hotel full of secret rooms—are linked closely to the places they create to achieve their ambitions.

CHAPTER TWENTY-SIX

DOT THE DRAGON'S EYE

Caress the detail, the divine detail.

—VLADIMIR NABOKOV

Hualong dianjing is a phrase used in Chinese painting and roughly translates to "Dot the dragon's eye, and it comes to life." It refers to the need for including the key detail in a painting. When the painter takes time to dot the center of the dragon's eye with the tip of the brush, the dragon seems to gain the ability to see. It comes alive on the canvas. The admonition also speaks to the need for including the right details. A painter can brocade the dragon's tale with intricate scales of many sizes and hues, but without the dot in the eye, the dragon will remain dead on the canvas.

The applicability of this statement to writing isn't difficult to see. When we take time to present the details, our writing comes to life. If we focus only on big strokes, the writing remains generic, abstract, and lifeless. Henri Troyat makes this point (with a well-chosen detail of his own) when he writes:

> No detail must be neglected in art, for a button half-undone may explain a whole side of a person's character. It is absolutely essential to mention that person's button. But it has to be described in terms of the person's inner life, and attention must not be diverted from the important things to focus on accessories and trivia.

In my experience as an editor and teacher, no other aspect of craft leads to unsuccessful stories more than the lack of specific details and poorly chosen details. Most apprentice writers have seen enough movies—if they haven't yet read enough books—to have a basic understanding of structure. Though they fret about whether to use past tense or present tense, the question of point of view, while important, often doesn't speak to the core trouble in the project. Most often, the writer hasn't evoked the world of the piece, its people and the place, and the situation. Through the details we select, we guide our readers, showing them what they need to see. Through the details, we present the characters, as in Troyat's "button half-undone."

Too often apprentice writers perceive details as merely lending atmosphere to a piece, describing what the walls look like, the scent of a budding meadow. The details of the place need to do more than create atmosphere. Each should be chosen for its effect on the piece. It should be there for a reason.

Moreover, the details should be specific. Most apprentice writers know this law of narrative. We learn the need to write *tulip* rather than *flower*, *BMW* rather than *car*. But the lesson doesn't end there. The fact that the flower is a tulip directs the reader in some way, reflects on the character admiring or holding the tulip, brings in the varied connotations of a tulip in the reader's mind. The tulip evokes the physical world of the piece and speaks to its inner world. If "tulip" is an arbitrary choice, it doesn't have much meaning within the context of the piece and doesn't give the reader anything more than a visual marker.

The lack of specific, telling details creates a sense of emptiness and confusion. Inexperienced readers complain that it's boring or that "I didn't *get* it." Often a writer will conclude that the premise is dull or that the ideas aren't good, but that's not necessarily the case. It may be a matter of finding the key details that will bring the story to life. It may be a matter of emphasizing certain details and subordinating or cutting others. It may be a matter of examining the details in an early draft and looking for patterns that hold the key to the essence of the piece. By focusing efforts in this area, the writer can find a new understanding and feel a renewed interest. The piece then can move forward.

You probably will find yourself in this situation, if you haven't already, in your writing career: You show a story to your writers' group and receive wildly different interpretations of it or hear a whole lot of confusion going on. This response shows you that the story isn't fully formed yet, but it doesn't mean the ideas are weak. It may be a matter of guiding the reader by selecting and presenting details more effectively. Every writer has suffered through this situation. Often, it's a matter of assuming a piece is finished too soon. Time to go back and reinvestigate it, to bring those key details to the fore.

Even if you don't show it to other writers, you might find yourself feeling that the piece lacks a certain wallop. You're satisfied with the structure and feel your characters are working. What's missing? Why is the piece just sort of *okay* but really not riveting or moving in the way you'd intended? Put it away for a little while, and then read it with an eye for the details. Is there a way of using a detail to embody a certain theme that you've spoken to directly and thereby lost the juice of it? Is there a detail in the story that you can develop into a motif or pattern, recalling it throughout the piece in an affecting way? Is there a key detail mentioned early in the piece that you might mention again at the end, giving the detail, and the ending, an extra bit of resonance while giving the piece a stronger sense of unity and closure?

In my work as an editor, I've guided many writers through revisions, and often the focus is on using more details. One example I recall was on a book titled *Frozen in Time*, by Nikki Nichols. An accomplished ice skater as well as a journalist, Nikki was working on a book about the tragic airplane crash in 1961 that killed the U.S. ice-skating team, along with their coaches and some parents, on the way to the world championship in Prague. Nikki had done an amazing job with the research, conducting many interviews and reading everything she could find on the subject. The manuscript worked pretty well, but the people who died in the crash were not yet on the page. For the most part, they remained names—and, sadly, names the average reader today would not even recognize. The reader could not fully experience the emotional impact of the tragedy because we didn't yet really know these people.

We needed personal details to bring them to life on the page. Nikki went back to many people she had interviewed previously, but instead of asking about skating performances, she asked very specific questions about the skaters—what did their voices sound like? How did they walk? What gestures and expressions did they often use? Who was a sloppy dresser and who played the piano in her spare time? Those kinds of details would help the reader fully experience the tragic loss. Again, Nikki worked hard to gather these details, and her book achieved a whole new level of dramatic power. The people she wrote about were no longer "frozen in time." They were alive on the page. She had taken the time and made the effort to dot the dragon's eye.

PROMPT: Think about a piece you've read recently by another writer. Make a list of the details that stick out in your mind—not your favorite scenes or stunning twists of plot, just the small details that you recall. When you've made your list, look for themes or patterns. How do these details connect to the piece as a whole? How do they amplify the story and its people?

PROMPT: Let's practice those powers of observation. Pick a few people who you know well and write a short descriptive piece about each of them. You might want to start by brainstorming all the details you can recall and then select from that list the ones that are most evocative of them.

PROMPT: Do the previous prompt but this time focus on a few places that you know well. We described places in the previous chapter, I know, but this time we're sharpening the focus—selecting a few details and exploring them rather than amassing broader descriptions of the entire place. For example, rather than describing at length your favorite restaurant, hammer in on the chronically dismissive air of the hostess or the photograph above the cash register at the bar of the owner standing arm in arm with a local sports star.

PROMPT: If you're stuck on a piece or disappointed with its results, read it with an eye for the details. You might want to choose a piece you've written in response to an earlier prompt in this book. Make a list of the key details and find ways to amplify them, perhaps by repeating them or by describing them more fully.

PROMPT: While working on a story, create a specific detail for each of your characters—or for characters you plan to use in a future piece. Freewrite about each character, noting as many details as possible. Choose one or two that evoke the essence of the character. For example, a character who is very neat and well organized (and perhaps a bit controlling) could be evoked by precise descriptions of her clothing—not a thread out of place.

PROMPT: To make a character surprising and complex, add a contradictory detail. Does your neat-as-a-pin, control-freak character from the previous prompt decorate his bedroom with posters of heavy metal bands? This detail suggests another layer to the character. Is his neatness a way to project a certain image, one that is not entirely accurate? Suddenly, these details begin to create new levels of conflict and tension.

PROMPT: Review a piece in progress with an eye for seemingly insignificant details—a character's brown hair, a piece of leftover birthday cake, a neighbor's dog. Freewrite about a detail, expanding its role and importance, perhaps making it the center of its own piece. Then decide if it can take a more important role in the piece in progress.

PUTTING IN AND TAKING OUT

So how do you know which details bring the dragon to life and which ones just make the dragon's tail longer? Unfortunately, there's no easy answer and no answer that applies to every situation. You must find the answer with every piece you write. However, there are ways to improve your odds of finding it. First, you have to understand your habits and tendencies as a writer. Does your style tend to include many details or few? Do you often write long, lush descriptions that serve mostly to create atmosphere and show off your language skills? Or perhaps your descriptions serve your stories well but simply tend to run long. Do you fear seeming too obvious in using details as signposts and therefore obscure them whenever possible? Do you tend to have an instinctive sense of where to place and repeat certain details?

In a famous exchange of letters, F. Scott Fitzgerald and Thomas Wolfe debated their approaches to narrative. Though they were discussing issues beyond details, encompassing all the elements of storytelling, their views are appropriate to our discussion in this chapter. Responding to Fitzgerald's claim that highly selective writers were the real geniuses, Wolfe wrote:

> You say that the great writer like Flaubert has consciously left out the stuff that Bill or Joe will come along presently and put in. Well, don't forget, Scott, that a great writer is not only a leaver-outer but also a putter-inner, and that Shakespeare and Cervantes and Dostoevsky were great putter-inners—greater putter-inners, in fact, than taker-outers . . . .

While reading this passage, I'm comforted by the realization that discussions of craft between literary giants feature no more erudition than what I find in similar discussions with my friends. "Putter-inners"? Not exactly the type of phrase you'll want to tape to your computer or to drop oh-so-casually into conversations at the next literary fête. Wolfe liked to conceal his erudition behind a big-old-country-boy persona. He's well aware of what he's talking about. It's interesting to note that Wolfe was very much *a putter-inner,* while Fitzgerald was a *taker-outer,* and so their views reflect their own approaches to writing.

Consider your approach. Are you a taker-outer or a putter-inner? How does this approach help your work, and how does it hinder your work? Are you putting in the right elements—a telling detail or two rather than hunks of exposition and explanation? Are you taking out the right elements—unnecessary and redundant passages and scenes—and allowing the reader to make discoveries? As writers, we need to know what to put in and what to take out. In fact, that process is the essence of storytelling. Anyone can simply spill the facts of "what happened" onto a page. It takes a writer to organize those facts into a compelling story, to select the most important details and discard others, to emphasize certain elements and subordinate others.

After we have a draft, we examine the details that bring the piece to life. We look for patterns of details and ask ourselves how these patterns shape the story. We ask ourselves why, for example, that eucalyptus tree in the front yard keeps inching into every scene? Why do we note three times that the protagonist carries a sharpened crayon in her purse wherever she goes? We note, also, where details are missing: Where characters are standing in relation to each other during a pivotal conversation, the look on a character's face, the length of the metal pipe the character hides under the driver's seat.

These details bring the piece to life and help you guide the reader to certain themes, but they also ensure that your reader is not distracted by questions sparked by the lack of specific details. If the length of the metal pipe is not important, you tell the reader it's not important by not bothering to describe it. On the other hand, if the pipe plays a key role, you tell that to your reader by providing a more specific description. If it does play a key role and you *don't* describe it, your reader may wonder about it, leading to questions that disturb the tension you're trying to create in the piece.

PROMPT: Brainstorm a list of at least a dozen details about your character. From that list, select only one or two images to include in the piece, choosing the ones that are most telling. I once interviewed the principal of a local boys high school. The school's colors were purple and white. The principal's office was full of purple-and-white banners and such, suggesting his lifelong dedication to the school. During the interview I wrote down as many details about the office as possible in hopes of evoking the principal in the article. From my list I chose a detail that I thought was the most telling—purple and white gravel in a small aquarium in a cluttered corner of the office. For me—and, I hoped, for the reader—that gravel showed this man was truly devoted to the school, down to the most insignificant items in his life.

PROMPT: While working on a draft, try to find which detail "dots the dragon's eye." Which one brings the piece to life—or could bring it to life if it were more prominently or more effectively placed. If you can't find that dot, ask yourself which detail definitely could not be cut. If you had to keep only one, which would it be?

DETAIL IDEAS

In your writer's notebook, create a place for jotting down details that occur to you or that you observe as you go about your day. They can spark ideas for a new piece, and they can spark ideas for work that's ongoing. When you're feeling stale or blocked, flip through your notebook and read the details you've collected there—a smashed pumpkin in the middle of a street, the smell of old books unearthed from a box in the attic, the way a friend's mouth crooks whenever she's trying to be clever, the smell of earthworms after a spring rain, and so on. You might find one that's a good fit for the piece in progress. Or a detail might spark a new idea for the piece.

As we discussed, writers need to be observant. If you keep your eyes open, you'll fill your notebook in a month. As you fill your notebook, you'll see that you notice certain types of things more than others. Your cache of details, for example, will include a lot of faces or gestures or cars or natural images. You might be particularly aware of smells or sounds. Or you might notice details that suggest a certain mood. As you review the details in your notebook, you'll learn about yourself as a writer. You may want to review pieces you've written to find out if the tendency you noticed in the notebook carries over to your stories. For example, do your stories rely heavily on one sense? Are the details mostly suggestive of a certain mood? Can you vary your pattern a bit, adding sounds and smells, for example, to a piece that's largely visual?

For some reason, I write down interesting signs that I see—billboards in front of churches, on streets, and along highways. Recently, a store near my house closed. It had sold jewelry and fabric and statuary from India and was called Divine Miracles. One day, while out for a jog, I noticed the store was empty, leaving behind only the message: "Divine Miracles—Out of Business." That one went into the notebook.

PROMPT: Go on a detail hunt. Take a walk in your neighborhood and jot down all the interesting details you observe. If you feel the neighborhood is too familiar for you, go to a different one. Focus on sensory impressions, and while looking for the extraordinary, don't ignore the ordinary.

PROMPT: Go on a detail theft. Read a piece of fiction or nonfiction or a poem and steal a detail you like. Use it to begin a piece of your own or add it to an ongoing piece. Don't feel guilty. Details take on their significance mostly through the context of the piece itself. Therefore, if you steal a cold bucket of chicken from Raymond Carver or a hunk of rope from Katherine Anne Porter, it quickly will become your own.

PROMPT: Freewrite about a place, either one in a piece you're writing or one you may write someday. Load on the details. Then step back and choose three or four of the most telling ones, the ones that evoke the essence of the place. Cut most of the others and subordinate those you do decide to keep while giving prominence to those few details that are most important.

PROMPT: Write a scene in which characters are not confronting an issue between them. They're discussing something else. For example, a married couple has a running feud about moving to a new city. She wants to go; he wants to stay. But rather than argue about it, they talk about plans for this year's garden. Use a detail to suggest the undercurrent. For our couple's scene, you could use a gardening catalog that has arrived in the mail.

PROMPT: Read a piece you've written and cut five details from it, ones you feel aren't essential to the piece. Then add five details to it. How has it changed? To extend the exercise, choose two details that are mentioned only once or twice and find ways to mention them at least two more times. How has their meaning changed within the piece?

In his tour de force article titled "The Things That Carried Him," Chris Jones offers a fine example of dotting the dragon's eye. The article chronicles the death of a soldier in Iraq and the return of the body to the soldier's home in a small town in Indiana. (What makes the article such an achievement is that Jones tells the story in reverse order, beginning with the soldier's funeral and then taking us step-by-step backward in time through the body's journey until we end with the soldier's death.) The soldier grew up in a hard-luck working-class family with few financial and educational resources. In writing the piece, Jones interviewed the soldier's mother, a sad woman on meager means. They sit at the small kitchen table where the mother smokes "brandless cigarettes" and drinks from "cans of Bud Light." Despite her grief and the hard life she has led, the mother takes pains to maintain her dignity. She wants no pity from the town. As she drinks and smokes throughout the interview, Jones captures her personality through a single detail:

> She has a kit—a little black leather bag to hide the warnings on the cardboard pack, linked by a brass chain to another little black leather bag that holds her lighter. There was something touchingly ladylike about the kit, and there was something touchingly ladylike about her whenever she pulled it out . ... She had thought a lot about quitting, but whenever she had built up enough nerve, something happened that made it impossible for her to put the kit in a drawer and close it.

Without going into great detail about how she handles her grief or her attempts at refinement in an unrefined place, Jones beautifully captures these ideas within that single detail—a little cigarette case with a brass chain that holds a lighter. With that detail, the mother comes to life for the reader. We understand her and feel her pain, admire her dignity and strength. With that detail, Jones dots the dragon's eye.

CHAPTER TWENTY-SEVEN

WESTERN UNION

The role of a writer is not to say what we all can say, but what we are unable to say.

—ANAÏS NIN

Books about writing tend to avoid the subject of theme. It's a slippery rascal and is so much in the purview of literature courses and so misunderstood as it applies to the writing of narrative, that we usually don't confront it directly. We say that theme is organic, that it grows naturally out of the story itself and to be conscious of it is to risk flagrant didacticism. And there is a lot of truth in those statements. If pressed, we fall back on the famous, if perhaps apocryphal, statement by movie mogul Samuel Goldwyn, who, in discussing themes in films reportedly said that if you want to send a message, you should use Western Union. The statement bristles with the reductive fury that is so simple and reassuring to embrace. Right on, Sammy boy. Damn straight. None of that self-conscious message sending for us.

But let's you and me take a little time to talk about theme as a source of ideas for writing and as a technical element of the craft. First, a word about what theme *isn't*. It's not the "moral of the story." It can't be wrapped up in a quick sentence imparting some truth like "cheaters never prosper" or "what goes around comes around." It is not The Main Point, as discussed in literature courses. English teachers use the term frequently, often on final exams, asking questions like "What is the theme of William Faulkner's *Light in August*?" Using the word *theme* in that way is perfectly acceptable when studying literature. But we're going to talk about theme as it relates to us as the makers of stories and poems and plays and so on.

Theme, as we're discussing it, also is not one of those *man vs. nature, man vs. man, man vs. himself* phrases. You know the ones. They're a critical shorthand that can lead us into the study of a work of art, and they serve their purpose in that regard. But we're not particularly interested in a lot of versus-ing at the moment. For us, theme means the abstract, unifying ideas that drive a story, that give it resonance and, for lack of a better word, meaning beyond the specifics of the story's characters and actions. Often that resonance is difficult, even impossible, to articulate in a way that does it justice. It's a conceptual matter, one that, as writers, we struggle to capture on the page, though we realize that if we were able to capture it completely, it would be destroyed. It would be, to quote T.S. Eliot "not what I meant at all." Or, if you prefer a pop cultural reference, it's what the rock group Pink Floyd pointed to in the lines "The time is gone/ the song is over/ thought I'd something more to say." Theme is the something more we have to say.

Critics and writers point to theme by saying a story's theme is "loneliness" or "passing youth" or "family" or "romantic love." It's the concept imbedded in human experience that the story in some way investigates. Your story about a family's struggle to move beyond old grudges and rituals can be said to investigate the theme of "family." Very often, these themes rise organically from the story, as mentioned earlier. Nevertheless, it's worthwhile for a writer, as she writes, to gain a sense of the theme that is rising organically from what she's writing. Through her awareness, she can hone and amplify the theme as the story progresses, using it as a guiding light to discover the story's essence and direction. In short, it can be a source of ideas for developing a piece of writing or for getting a stalled piece moving again.

PROMPT: What themes permeate the writing you've done in the past? How have you explored these themes? Were you conscious of them as you wrote? Spend a writing session exploring your answers to these questions.

PROMPT: Are there themes you've tried to avoid in your writing, ones that are too close to you emotionally? Are you ready to tackle them yet? If so, let's get started with an essay about that theme and why you've avoided it. Use examples from your personal experience to illustrate your feelings of avoidance. You might have avoided the theme of parenthood due to feelings that you failed somehow in raising your children. You might have avoided writing about loneliness due to your experience as an only child.

PROMPT: If you followed the previous prompt, you've done some writing in a discursive, exploratory format. Let's now move to something more consciously creative—fiction or poetry or a script. Create a character in a situation that forces you to confront the theme you've avoided. You might, for example, write a poem about a moment in your childhood when you felt sharp pangs of loneliness.

PROMPT: What themes are you exploring in an ongoing piece? Read what you've written so far with an eye toward recurring details that point toward an underlying theme. Spend a writing session focused on those details.

IDEAS FROM THEME

If I were coaching a writer on a blocked or unsuccessful story, I wouldn't suggest investigating the theme as the first place to start the revival process. As we discussed earlier, it's important to look at structure, character, point of view, and details. However, don't ignore the possibility of using theme. Writers often miss this option and thereby limit their possibilities for success.

Exploring the themes of past writing also can be helpful. You'll learn about who you are as a writer and how your themes tend to imbed themselves in your work. Our stories often investigate the same theme or themes time and again. Something in our psychological makeup draws us back to a theme or two, even if we're trying consciously to avoid that theme. If you read pieces you've written one after the next, you'll find that a particular theme asserts itself throughout them, even if the pieces explore vastly different material. It's quite likely that your funny essay about your first love, your short story about a supernatural grocery clerk, and your poem about a serial killer all share a similar theme—disillusioned idealism, perhaps, or the search for personal identity.

In using theme to build your pieces, to add ideas to the generative idea, it's helpful to reach a point at which you're aware of the themes you're investigating. You'll find them in recurring images, in patterns of character and event. They'll spring from your imagination, your unconscious. I'm not saying you should force them out. I'm saying that after you've written your way into a piece, maybe the point of a completed draft, be mindful of what's appearing on the page and look for ways to amplify those patterns.

For example, let's explore the following scenario.

You have an idea for a story and have begun writing it, unsure exactly where you're headed but engaged nonetheless. You've written a few pages, a couple of scenes, descriptions of the characters. The story involves a woman who breeds collies. A childless widow, retired from her job, she dedicates her life to her dogs. She has built elab-

THE WRITER'S IDEA BOOK

orate kennels in her backyard, where she keeps a half-dozen dogs from various litters. Her neighbors have begun complaining to her about the constant barking. They want something done about it.

As you develop the story, you are engaged by this character. You've described her in detail, written a history about her in your notebook, sprinkled key moments from that history into the story. You want to write more, but after a couple of scenes in which the neighbors confront her about the noise, you're not sure where to go. What would she do? What are her options? What should happen next? You try a few ideas but nothing seems right. The new scenes don't ring true.

One way to move the story forward is to look at the theme or themes emerging from what you've written so far. What abstract idea drives you to write this story? Who is this character and why does she appeal to you? Do you admire her? Pity her? Which details recur in the pages you've written? The woman's mud-spattered boots, in which she trudges around her yard and cleans the kennels? Or perhaps you've spent several paragraphs describing the kennels themselves, how they're connected by chicken wire, how each dog has a favorite toy on the floor of the kennel. From these details, and the tone in which they're presented, you'll be able to perceive the themes you're exploring. Is this a story about loneliness? A story about the ways we survive loss? Maybe it's a story about the connection between humans and animals, how we help each other to persevere.

With a sense of your theme, even if you can't articulate it, you'll gain a sense of direction, and you can use that direction to build new ideas into the story. Again, I'm not suggesting you reduce your story to a one-sentence capsule. I am suggesting that you be mindful of the patterns emerging from the story and use those patterns to direct you as the story unfolds. For example, you've noticed that the woman's muddy boots are mentioned three or four times. They seem to be linked to the nature of the character. When you see the character in your mind, she's always wearing those boots. You see the boots in your mind when she's not wearing them, when they're standing by the door that leads to the backyard.

Brainstorm new ideas about those boots. Were they a present from her dead husband? Were they a gift to herself upon the husband's death? How do they feel on her feet? Do they pinch the bunion on her left foot, or do they slide on easily, a reassuring element of her daily routine? How can they play a greater role in the story? Do they figure in the ending of the story? If they took a more prominent role, how would the story change?

As we've discussed, writing stories requires a balance between control and letting go, the conscious and the unconscious. This is true especially in regard to theme.

We must be aware of our theme and yet not force it. We can use it to foster new ideas, gently guiding the piece forward. Look for theme in your characters—their goals and attitudes, the situations that confront them. Look for theme in the conflicts. Look for theme in the details, the tone, the point of view. Question each of these elements, separately and as they work with each other.

Though some writing teachers might advise against it, you can begin a piece with a theme in mind. This approach is more often taken with nonfiction, particularly the essay, but it can be used in fiction, plays, and screenplays, too. For example, you could say, "I'm going to write something about ambition. It's a subject I think about a lot. I'm fascinated by the power of ambition to shape a person's life." Begin brainstorming about ambition and see where you go. If you're feeling stuck on a piece, or if you're fiddling around with what to write next, choosing a theme can fire your imagination. Try it.

When taking this approach, however, be sure you're exploring a theme rather than dramatizing a conclusion you've already reached. For example, if you want to investigate the nature of ambition, you could move in many directions and generate a lot of great ideas. But if you've already decided what you think about ambition and are using the story simply to present your conclusions, your story will be limited, your characters mere pawns to those conclusions. For example, if you've already decided that ambition leads to greed and narcissism, all that's left is for you to create a character who enacts that conclusion. The story will seem self-conscious and manipulative. There will be no room for give and take with your reader and no room for your imagination to roam. It will be little more than propaganda for whatever point you've already decided you want to make.

It's far better to explore a concept and allow yourself to be surprised and enlightened by the results on the page. In fact, as writers, we often discover what we think about something through the act of writing. I know a number of talented writers of journalism who avoid more creative forms because they tell me they "have nothing to say." What they don't realize—or admit—is that writing creatively is a means of finding out what you have to say. If you already know exactly what you have to say, there's little point in writing the story.

PROMPT: Pick a dark theme to explore, such as death, despair, or a loss of some type. In a few pages, write a dramatic scene to explore this theme, but use a light, even humorous, tone.

PROMPT: Write about three pet peeves—things that really get your blood boiling—and explore them one at a time. After you finish the three, look for patterns and similarities, themes that connect all three peeves, even if they don't seem to be related on the surface. With this theme in mind, connect all three into a single piece.

PROMPT: Follow the directions in the previous prompt, but this time focus on things that make you feel good, that touch your heart or make you believe in the essential goodness of life.

PROMPT: Staying with this approach, this time focus on three moments in your life when you laughed yourself silly—tears rolling down your cheeks. Again, after completing the three vignettes, read them in search of patterns, a thematic tissue that will guide you to bring the three pieces into a single piece.

PROMPT: Pluck a character from your notebook, someone you've been itching to write about. Write a few pages—a character sketch, biography, a scene or two. Then read what you've written with an eye toward theme. What do you discover about the character, his significance to you in a thematic sense? Can you keep going?

PROMPT: Use an object in your house as the focus of a couple of pages of writing. You might want to place the object on your writing table and describe it, or you could begin a piece with a description of the object. Push on for as long as you can. Don't think about theme or "the point." Don't analyze what you're doing at all. Be content to freewrite, allowing the object to guide you. When you finish, put the piece away for a week and then read it. What patterns emerge—words, images, tone, whatever. What theme does the pattern suggest?

BREAKING BLOCKS WITH THEME

As we've discussed, starting a piece by focusing mainly on theme can be challenging. Focusing on theme, however, can be a great way to jump-start a stalled piece. In the "lady with the pet dogs" example earlier in this chapter, we touched on how theme can supply direction and get your story moving, but let's explore this idea a bit further. If you're blocked on a piece, perhaps the reason is that you're being untrue to the essential theme. Therefore, the story rings false to you. You need to go through what you've written and try to discern what theme you're investigating.

One reason you may be off track is because you're pushing the piece in a direction it doesn't want to go. In the dog-breeder story, we might be forcing the conflict with the neighbors. We've developed a compelling character and don't know what to do with her. Sometimes putting a piece away for a while can help give you fresh insights into its essence. We can pull it out of the file later and see clearly that the neighbors have nothing to do with the real story. We'd trucked them in to supply conflict;

they are merely a device, a way of pushing the story forward dramatically. If we conclude—perhaps through our investigation of the boots as a dominant detail—that the woman is coping with her own sense of mortality, heightened by the death of her husband, we can shift direction away from the neighbors and focus on other possibilities. Perhaps the conflict should involve the impending death of one of the dogs. Or perhaps the birth of a new litter. Or perhaps a family with young children that arrives to check on the impending birth of a puppy they've bought. Or, well, lots of things. Now, instead of feeling dry and blocked, we have a number of options to explore. By discovering the story's theme, new doors have opened.

PROMPT: As we discussed, theme usually is embedded in patterns—of event, detail, character, tone, setting. Read a piece of writing from your dead-end file or one that appears to be stalled, and focus on patterns, on elements that recur. It may be as simple as the lady's boots in our example of the dog breeder. Write a few pages expanding on this pattern. For something like the boots, I could tell their history from the day she bought them.

In the past few weeks I've been thumbing through some story files, ancient ones from years ago. I found one that contained drafts of a story I'd forgotten I'd written—or attempted to write. It concerned a man who frequents an all-night gas station. The station sat on a corner of a busy street in a small town and featured a rather large, concrete fountain. The man enjoyed ambling to the station at midnight, buying a soda or a candy bar, and sitting next to the fountain. And that's what he did. Unfortunately, that's *all* he did. The station was based on a place near where I was living at the time, and I liked going there. I wanted to write about it. The man in the story wasn't based on me. He was much older, alone, with few prospects in his life. I must have tried a dozen different ways to get a story from him. Never happened. In reading the story recently. I realized that I wanted to explore his loneliness and feelings of uncertainty. The station, open all night, provided a small sense of permanence and comfort, something to count on in the dark night of the soul. With those ideas in mind, I hope to return to that story, if it's not too late, and focus on those themes.

Sometimes it takes awhile for the themes to emerge. And sometimes we need to complete a draft of a piece to discover its theme. That discovery, and the opportunities for new ideas that it offers, become part of the revision process. In the first draft, we may be focused on getting the story's basic elements in place, developing the characters, moving the plot toward its conclusion, keeping the details sharp and interesting. When the draft is finished, we can investigate what our unconscious minds are trying to tell us through the story. When we discover that essential unifying element, we can revise to bring it to greater prominence. It can inspire no end of new ideas for taking a solid draft and making it into something wonderful.

PROMPT: Read a piece of writing that's been in your dead-end file for a while. Read with an eye toward theme. What themes run through it? Locate where that theme is strongest—a scene, a paragraph of description, even just a phrase or sentence. Using that moment as your core, write a few pages to expand upon it.

PROMPT: Are you blocked on a piece at the moment? Have you investigated the theme? What might the theme be trying to tell you about the direction of the piece? After reading the piece again—probably several times—decide on what theme you want to push forward and use it to guide you.

PROMPT: Spend some time reading work you've completed, at least three pieces. Look for recurring themes. Choose one and begin a new piece with that theme in mind, writing at least a few pages. Explore it in a way you've never tried before. For example, if you've written some short stories with the theme of unrequited love, begin an essay on that subject. Or, if you've dealt with that theme in stories with a somber tone, set out to write a funny story about it.

PROMPT: Pick a theme that interests you and write a page or two of an essay titled "On [your theme]." Now write a page or two in which you explore the theme dramatically in fiction, memoir, or a script. If you want, decide which of the two approaches interests you more, then keep writing.

PROMPT: If you're blocked on a piece, read only the first page. If the piece ended there, what would you say is its theme? Then read the next page and state the theme to that point. Work your way through the piece reading one page at a time. Is the theme consistent? Is it elaborated on? Does it shift and grow muddled? Try to determine what the theme should be and begin writing from there.

PROMPT: Read the jacket of a book you haven't read. You may want to go to your bookstore and pick some at random from the shelves. Back jackets often state the themes of the book. A quick browse of my own shelves led to "a personal journey of the nature of miracles," "reaches for a deeper understanding of fatherhood," "an uplifting story of community," "a story of fearsome sadness." Of course, these phrases are the stuff of sales copy, but the copywriter, with the help of the editor and sometimes also the author, tries to find the essence of the book. Pick one phrase that interests you, that suggests a theme of some type, and write a few pages. You might begin, for example, your own "story of fearsome sadness" or your own essay on "fatherhood."

PROMPT: Try the previous prompt on a book you *have* read. How do the themes stated in the copy match your own view of the book's theme? Does the copy provide insight into the book's themes and goals? If you've finished a draft of a piece but are struggling to improve it, write your own jacket copy for the piece. How would you describe it to someone browsing a bookstore? If that jacket copy provides insight you didn't have before, begin revising with those insights in mind.

PROMPT: Make a short list of your favorite pieces of writing. Freewrite about the themes of these pieces. Do they share similar themes? Are these the themes you tend to explore in your own work?

There will be writers, I'm sure, who will take exception with some of the advice in this chapter, believing that such abstractions and classroom notions will undermine the fragile workings of the imagination. And thinking too much about theme does have the potential of making a writer overly conscious of what he's trying to do. Susan Sontag once said, "Interpretation is the revenge of the intellect upon art," and there's validity in that point. At the same time, it seems shortsighted, when revising a piece or trying to revive a piece, not to use theme as one way of trying to understand it. Just as there is danger in thinking too much about a creative project, there also is danger in thinking too little. We've all heard the famous line by E.M. Forster, who wrote "How do I know what I think until I see what I say," meaning that the act of writing about a subject provided insight into his ideas and feelings on that subject. Very true. And I think we can trust that after Mr. Forster saw what he said, he went back to the page looking for ways to say it better.

CHAPTER TWENTY-EIGHT

IT WAS THE BEST OF TIMES

It's appropriate to pause and say that the writer is one who, embarking upon a task, does not know what to do.

—DONALD BARTHELME

Quick—what novel begins with the words in this chapter's title? Anyone who didn't blurt out *A Tale of Two Cities,* go to the back of class and read your Dickens. This is one of the most famous openings in literature, and it continues to hold its power: "It was the best of times; it was the worst of times." With this seemingly paradoxical statement, Dickens announces he will work on a large canvas, that he will range from best to worst, that he will speak from high omniscience about times and historical eras. With this line, we pass into a novel of grandeur and high stakes that concerns the lives of a great many people.

A good opening suggests the nature of the story about to be told. It locates the reader, if not in the story's place and time, then in the approach of the story—its tone and narrative stance. Otherwise, there are no rules about what constitutes a good opening. If it works, it works. The reader is engaged and moves forward. If not, the reader stops reading or, if the writer is lucky, continues reading but already has lost a bit of faith in the piece and will abandon it if he is not engaged very soon. Writers need to rely on their judgment when assessing their opening sentences and paragraphs.

GREAT OPENINGS

One way to develop criteria for judging the effectiveness of your openings is to review ones you especially like, ones that resonate in your mind, ones that, when you first read them, carry you into the pieces. As you review openings, look for patterns. Try to determine what ingredients you tend to enjoy and admire. Here are a few of my favorites:

> When I was a windy boy and a bit,
> And the black spit of the chapel fold,
> (Sighed the old ram rod, dying of women),
> I tiptoed shy in the gooseberry wood . . . .
>
> —DYLAN THOMAS, "LAMENT"

> You had to get out of them occasionally, those Illinois towns with the funny names: Paris, Oblong, Normal. Once, when the Dow-Jones dipped two hundred points, the Paris paper boasted a banner headline: NORMAL MAN MARRIES OBLONG WOMAN. They knew what was important. They did! But you had to get out once in a while, even if it was just across the border to Terre Haute, for a movie.
>
> —LORRIE MOORE, "YOU'RE UGLY, TOO"

> In a little house, in a little village, not far away from Thunderbolt City, lived a whistle fixer named Lunchbox Louie. He had a wife named Bigfoot the Chipmunk, and a little son named King Waffle.
>
> —DANIEL PINKWATER, *THE WUGGIE NORPLE STORY*

> Lolita, light of my life, fire of my loins. My sin, my soul. Lo-lee-ta: the tip of the tongue taking a trip of three steps down the palate to tap, at three, on the teeth. Lo-lee-ta.
>
> —VLADIMIR NABOKOV, *LOLITA*

Once I got started writing, more favorites flooded into my mind, but these few will do to start. Notice that all have a striking use of voice; all have a certain playfulness of tone and language. If you asked me before today what I liked in an opening, I don't know that I would have rattled off those qualities, but that seems to be true. What qualities do you notice as you think about your favorite openings?

PROMPT: List ten openings you like. Look for patterns. What qualities do many of your favorites exude? Then look at the openings in your own work. Do they take a similar approach? Do they exude similar qualities?

PROMPT: Rewrite a few of your openings, striving to achieve the qualities you noticed in your favorites list. Or, if you prefer, write a few lines that could be used as openings in pieces of writing. Again, strive to achieve the qualities you admire most.

PROMPT: Steal an opening line or sentence from one of your favorites. Cut away the next lines and substitute lines of your own. Try to match the tone and voice of the authors whose work you're borrowing.

PROMPT: Let's do the previous prompt again, using a line from a published piece of writing, but don't start with the opening. Instead, pick a line from somewhere in the middle and use that as your opener, moving on from there.

TYPES OF OPENINGS

Just as there are no rules for what constitutes a great opening, there are no rules regarding what type of opening works best. Your opening must perform a few functions to be effective, one of which is to match the story that follows. An opening can do any of the following:

- set the scene
- create mood
- introduce characters
- introduce situations
- establish place and time
- introduce conflict

It needn't do all of these, but it had better do more than one. Most of all, it must interest the reader, as we discussed in the previous section of this chapter. It can do this in a variety of ways. Let's try some of these approaches.

PROMPT: Find a collection of pieces—stories, essays, poems, whichever form you prefer—and read the opening of each piece. Choose five to seven that you especially like. Using the same approach as the author, relying on description or drama, narrative or dialogue, setting scene or jumping into conflict, write five openings of your own.

PROMPT: Open a story with dialogue. A famous model for this approach is the opening of Ernest Hemingway's "The Snows of Kilimanjaro":

"The marvelous thing is that it's painless," he said. "That's how you know when it starts."

"Is it really?"

"Absolutely. I'm awfully sorry about the odor though. That must bother you."

"Don't. Please don't."

The first speaker is dying while camped in the plains of Africa. The opening brings us immediately into the story, its characters and conflict.

PROMPT: If you have an ongoing project, consider moving a scene that appears later in the piece to the opening. Does it work?

PROMPT: Write an opening dialogue in which one character asks a question of another character or characters. The response will move the scene forward and, with luck, get you rolling on a piece. *A Clockwork Orange* by Anthony Burgess opens with four "droogs" sitting bored in a milkbar, trying to think of a bit of mischief to undertake. The novel begins with one droog asking the others, somewhat ominously, "What's it going to be then, eh?"

PROMPT: Begin in the middle of a scene or event. Keep pushing forward rather than stopping to inform the reader of background details. Known as beginning in medias res, in the middle of things, this opening supplies a quick start to your story. As Richard Hugo writes in *The Triggering Town*, "When the poem starts, things should already have happened." Myriad examples of this type of opening exist. It's especially plentiful in movies and action novels.

PROMPT: Write a few paragraphs in which a character introduces himself as though beginning an autobiography. Don't directly state any conflicts, any hardships or situations, but try to imply what hardships the character has suffered or will suffer in the story ahead. For example, consider this opening from Marilynne Robinson's *Housekeeping*:

> My name is Ruth. I grew up with my younger sister, Lucille, under the care of my grandmother, Mrs. Sylvia Foster, and when she died, of her sisters-in-law, Misses Lily and Nona Foster, and when they fled, of her daughter, Mrs. Sylvia Fischer.

Though this character does not directly state her young life has been filled with tragedy and abandonment, the point comes through clearly. Her not saying it makes the opening powerful. Can you use your paragraph as an opening for something longer?

PROMPT: Use the same approach as in the previous prompt, but try it in third person, as if you're writing a biography.

PROMPT: Begin with a statement, a general observation that you or a character makes. Remember Tolstoy's statement about families, mentioned in a previous chapter. Or consider this statement that opens the memoir *Blue Highways*, by William Least Heat-Moon:

> Beware thoughts that come in the night. They aren't turned properly; they come in askew, free of sense and restriction, deriving from the most remote of sources.

Try to move quickly from the general statement to specifics of your story. In *Blue Highways*, for example, by the end of the first paragraph, the narrator has lost his job and found out his estranged wife is seeing another man. Tip: Find a general statement somewhere in your writing. Move it to an opening and begin the piece there.

PROMPT: Begin with a statement of fact. Scan earlier prompt writings for a simple statement, nothing monumental, perhaps a line that appears in the middle of a longer piece. Freewrite or cluster using this focus. Mark Richard began his story "Strays" with a line that kept nagging at him, though he had no idea what it meant: "At night stray dogs come up underneath our house to lick our leaking pipes." To write the story, he put the statement in a character's voice and pushed forward.

PROMPT: Mark Richard began his story "Her Favorite Story" by picking a single word and deciding, arbitrarily, to start there. He chose the word *in* and created his first sentence: "In Indian this place is called Where Lightning Takes Tall Walks." Begin a sentence with a preposition: *about, above, after, at, below, by, for, from, in, of, on, over, to, up*. Then follow that sentence with at least one paragraph. If you feel a spark, keep going. If not, pick a different preposition and try again.

PROMPT: Begin with a statement that addresses the reader, as if you are speaking to someone and beginning to tell that person a story. Here's the opening from Don DeLillo's masterful novel *Underworld*:

> He speaks in your voice, American, and there's a shine in his eye that's halfway hopeful. It's a school day, sure, but he's nowhere near the classroom. He wants to be here instead, standing in the shadow of this old rust-hulk of a structure, and it's hard to blame him—this metropolis of steel and concrete and flaky paint and cropped grass and enormous Chesterfield packs aslant on the scoreboards, a couple of cigarettes jutting from each.

DeLillo uses several techniques for engaging the reader with this opening. The direct address—calling the reader "American"—creates a sense of intimacy, as if the novel will be a one-on-one conversation. Using the word *American* also suggests an attitude, one that's a bit confrontational. That word also implies that the "he" is *not* an

American. The reader gets to reach that conclusion and therefore is participating in the story from the very first sentence. Finally, the paragraph goes on to describe what obviously is a baseball park, and yet DeLillo never specifically names it as such. Again, he lets the reader reach this conclusion. And so, in the first paragraph of what is a long novel, the reader is involved, filling in gaps that the author intentionally creates.

PROMPT: Begin with a paragraph of description. Set the scene for the drama to follow. Be sure your description introduces an element of tension or conflict, or achieves something beyond mere scene painting. Focus on details that will bring the setting quickly to life.

PROMPT: The Bible opens with "In the beginning ..." Let's use that, but rather than following with "God created the heavens and the earth," use something different, something that creates a situation you want to explore. The sentence should suggest that whatever occurred "in the beginning" is about to change. For example, "In the beginning, Dave really didn't care for Andrea" or "In the beginning, Charlie was sure no one would find out who was siphoning money from the employee 401(K) fund."

PROMPT: Begin with a cliché and then immediately contradict it, setting up a piece that will offer a new perspective on life. For example: "Wiser people than I am have said 'Haste makes waste' but that isn't always true . ..."

A FEW TIPS ABOUT OPENINGS

Openings can be tough. Sometimes you can block yourself by trying too hard to get them right. A commonsense tip: Don't begin with the beginning. Start with a scene or idea you planned to introduce later. Then, when you have a draft or when you're really cooking on the piece, come back to the opening.

Sometimes we put too much pressure on the opening, sweating out every word until we've forged an absolute zinger. By trying too hard, working and reworking it, we end up with a stiff, overwrought paragraph, or we lose the momentum of our idea. If your opening is labored and forced, read your piece and look on page two for a better place to start.

PROMPT: Write a paragraph or two to open a story. Really work those paragraphs, establishing character, plot, setting, tone, voice, and atmosphere. Then put those paragraphs aside and begin again, simply telling the story.

PROMPT: For fear of losing the reader, we sometimes hype the opening, shooting off all sorts of narrative fireworks—arguments, fistfights, lovemaking, guns blazing,

THE WRITER'S IDEA BOOK

life decisions made and announced in rhetorical flourish. The questions then become: How do I top this? Where do I go from here? So much noise also can put off the reader. The writer appears too eager for attention, like a slick salesperson or a child showing off. Rather than intrigued, the reader is repelled. Find an opening of this kind in your files and rewrite it, taking a more natural, more subtle approach. If you don't have this type of opening, write one, as an exercise in what not to do.

PROMPT: A variation on the previous prompt: Write in an exciting tone about something that is quite ordinary. In his article "Butcher," Tom Chiarella works in a butcher shop—not the most glamorous of professions—and yet his opening pulls the reader in immediately through powerful language:

> "The sink is full of tongues. Beef tongues, each as big as a man's shoe, frozen into one icy clump the size of a propane canister, defrosting for an afternoon pickup. ... But right now the guys in back are breaking cows. ..."

PROMPT: Begin a story with the blare of an alarm clock. Your protagonist awakens for the day, showers, dresses, eats breakfast, and heads out to begin his day. Sometime early in the day, a conflict arises. Drama begins. Now, cut all the paragraphs leading up to the moment of conflict. In her book *Building Fiction*, Jesse Lee Kercheval warns writers about the "alarm clock" opening, noting that too often this approach delays the start of the story. If your story opens with the character in any way getting ready for the drama to begin, cut to the drama. This is not a hard-and-fast rule; some of the openings I cited earlier don't begin with action. But dramatic openings are the easiest for many writers to achieve, and they are the least risky. However, if you can begin with a powerhouse voice or compelling language, and you feel confident that with that approach you can carry the day, go for it.

PROMPT: Find an unfinished piece or one that has never satisfied you. Write a new opening, beginning in a different place. Write the piece from that point forward, filtering in scenes and description from the earlier work.

PROMPT: Try the cut-and-paste method. Find an unfinished piece or one that has never satisfied you. Cut your piece into sections or paragraphs and rearrange them. Look for interesting juxtapositions.

PROMPT: To come full circle, let's end with our beginning. Start a piece with the famous opening from *A Tale of Two Cities*. Explain why the story you're about to relate was both the best and worst of times, emphasizing its contrasts. Now cut the Dickens line and move forward for at least a few paragraphs, exploring the ideas you set up in the first paragraph.

CHAPTER TWENTY-NINE

A SORT OF MIRACLE

Most writers enjoy two periods of happiness—when a glorious idea comes to mind and, secondly, when a last page has been written and you haven't had time to know how much better it ought to be.

—JOSEPH PRIESTLEY

A number of years ago, I interviewed writer and teacher Rick DeMarinis for an article on the writing craft. At one point, I asked him for tips on endings. "I can't really say much about how to write endings," he said. "For me, they're always a sort of miracle." This statement, from a man who had published many short stories and a handful of novels? But if you've ever struggled to find the right ending for a piece, you probably did feel like you'd need nothing less than a miracle.

Endings are hard.

People can't live happily ever after. All the characters can't die. Your protagonist can't wake to find it all a dream. Even the sacred epiphanic moment, when the character comes to some type of realization, is feeling a bit shopworn these days. The mystery can be solved, the lovers united, the foe vanquished, everyone sadder but wiser; but still, striking that last note in a way that will give it depth and resonance, that will make it sound like just the right note, as satisfying and surprising as it is inevitable, ain't easy.

How many times do we read stories that engage us only to feel disappointed at the end? How many complaints about endings have you heard in workshops and writing groups? Years ago, there was a popular joke about the unpleasing open-endedness of stories in *The New Yorker*: "Why do they put the author's name at the end of the story? So you'll know it's over." Then there are the "endings are hard" legends, such as the one about Hemingway rewriting the final paragraphs of his novel *A Farewell to Arms* forty-seven times. But we are writers, and even if it takes "a sort of miracle," we must write our endings.

PROMPT: Write about an ending you struggled to complete. What problems did you face? Are you satisfied with the ending as it stands? If not, consider ways to revise it. Does the problem exist in the ending, or does it lie elsewhere in the piece?

PROMPT: If you're struggling with an ending at the moment, put the piece away and force yourself not to look at it. If possible, don't even think about it. Don't work on any other sections of the piece. Nothing. Forget about that piece. After a week (and you should wait longer, if possible), read the piece from start to finish. Have you discovered any new possibilities for endings? Does the problem lie in the ending?

Before moving on, I must admit that even discussing endings in a book of this kind is difficult. By ending, do we mean the climax of the narrative or the last paragraph or the last sentence? Though the age of the epilogue appears to have passed, the denouement remains with us. In choosing "favorite endings," I have, for the sake of simplicity, reprinted final paragraphs. But even the power of these wonderful literary pieces is lost without an understanding of what came before them in the piece, without the steady accretion of event in language, without the tingle of exhaustion still alive from the resonating climax. The topic, however, remains important, so on we go. Endings are hard.

GREAT ENDINGS

As we did with beginnings in the previous chapter, let's look at a few endings that work. Begin by finding and writing down your favorite endings, at least five or six. Here are a few of mine:

> And with Footers beside him, and Martin trailing with an amused smile, Billy went out into the early freeze that was just settling on Broadway and made a right turn into the warmth of the stairs to Louie's pool room, a place where even serious men sometimes go to seek the meaning of magical webs, mystical coin, golden birds, and other artifacts of the only cosmos in town.

—WILLIAM KENNEDY, *BILLY PHELAN'S GREATEST GAME*

"Well, darling—" he began. His right hand came up and touched the middle button of his shirt, as if to unfasten it, and then with a great deflating sigh he collapsed backward into the chair, one foot sliding out on the carpet and the other curled beneath him. It was the most graceful thing he had done all day. "They got me," he said.

—RICHARD YATES, "A GLUTTON FOR PUNISHMENT"

He gave her the answer he had planned. He told her his name. Then he told her who he was and what he had done.

—TOM CHIARELLA, "FOLEY THE GREAT"

There are, of course, many others. Classic ones, such as the endings to "Araby" by James Joyce, and Fitzgerald's *The Great Gatsby.* There are more contemporary examples, such as in Lorrie Moore's "People Like That Are the Only People Here," Norman Mailer's *Ancient Evenings,* and Don DeLillo's *White Noise.*

PROMPT: In the same piece of writing you chose as a favorite, flip back to the climax or the dramatic moment to which the piece has built. Does it satisfy you? Write about the connection between the climax and the end of the piece. How are they complementary or different?

PROMPT: Sometimes an ending doesn't satisfy because you simply don't want to leave the piece. You want to remain in that world. Allow yourself this pleasure by continuing the story on your own. What happens next?

PROMPT: Rewrite a famous ending, or one you know well. Save the character who dies at the climax. Get those loves together. Change a bittersweet ending to a happy one, or change a happy one to tragedy.

PROMPT: If you're having trouble with an ending, study how the endings on your favorites list work. Imitate a few of them in tone, language, or approach. Now, go back to the ending in your own piece. Have any of your favorites sparked an insight or idea that helps your own ending?

PROMPT: Write an ending for an unwritten piece. In other words, write the ending first. A number of writers do this on a regular basis, using the ending as a destination to guide the writing of the piece. Katherine Anne Porter, for example, used this approach:

If I didn't know the ending of the story, I wouldn't begin. I always write my last line, my last paragraph, my last page first.

THE WRITER'S IDEA BOOK

WHY ENDINGS WORK

In the previous section, you examined why you like the endings on your favorites list. You tried to discover why they work. I tried to do the same with the endings I cited. I like the rhetorical flourish of the first one, from William Kennedy's novel, because the lyricism provides a nice counterpoint to the mundane details being described. There is a fine mix of notes in the paragraph, celebratory yet sad, mystical yet gritty. These tones fit the novel up to that point and provide a compelling music with which to leave the story behind. In the Yates story, the final note is harder, more closed-ended. The story recounts a man's struggle at work, his attempt to find a place for himself in the world. He doesn't share his struggle with his wife. The "they" have been after him since the start. In the end, they get him. Like a sharp crack, the story ends. There is no denouement, no trailing off. Both endings fit what has come before.

PROMPT: Read the endings you've written in the past—your favorites and ones that never quite satisfied you. Why do some work and others not? Do they seem organic to the piece or do they strive too hard for a final impact? Try to rewrite at least one of the endings that you don't particularly like. Look for ways to more clearly mirror the language and tone of the piece as a whole.

PROMPT: Choose one of your endings that you've never really liked and add one more sentence to it. The sentence should flow naturally out of the previous one. Do you like the new ending better? Endings sometimes are a matter of taste. A magazine editor who I wrote for always said he wanted "one more note" when I turned in an article. Since he was the editor, I added that note, but rarely did I feel that the piece needed it. I prefer endings that resonate by giving the reader just a bit less than expected. The editor, however, preferred a strong sense of finality in the last line. If this experiment interests you, try deleting a sentence or two from the ending. Does it work better?

THE ENDING FITS

A good ending provides closure in which character, plot, theme, and tone match what precedes them in the story. If the star-crossed lovers in *Casablanca* had hightailed it across the tarmac, leaving Ilsa's husband behind, we would not be happy. We have watched the characters make sacrifices for a larger good throughout the film. To fight the Nazis, they have put themselves at risk and have grown from the experience. They have cast aside their personal desires for more significant goals. Their final parting is inevitable, and we feel the sadness of that parting even as we admire its nobility. The ending fits the characters.

The movie *Rain Man* also closes with a parting. Charlie must watch as his autistic brother, whom he has fought to keep with him in Los Angeles, returns to Cincinnati. In the film, we watch Charlie grow from selfish and defensive to open and caring. That new openness allows him to let his brother go. If he had tried something foolish or sneaky to keep his brother, we wouldn't believe it or enjoy it.

Throughout John Steinbeck's *The Grapes of Wrath,* we are aware of the theme of resilience. Though the Joads lose everything and endure many hardships, their spirits remain alive. When Rose of Sharon feeds the starving man with milk from her breast, we see the theme of the resilient human spirit once again. Her action fits the theme of the novel (which should appear on any list of great endings).

PROMPT: In an ongoing piece, determine if your ending fits what has come before it in plot, character, and theme. Ask: Would the character I've presented do this? Does my theme change, presenting a new perspective at the end?

THE READER'S EXPECTATIONS ARE MET

Sometimes an ending doesn't work because you haven't been leading the reader to this moment, or line. The reader is confused about the story or has taken a completely different path. When you've written a draft you feel has the right ending, reread the piece to be sure you have led the reader to this point. Inexperienced writers are sometimes surprised to learn that readers have not been following the lines the writers think they've drawn through their narratives. Writing a story can be like dropping popcorn to mark your trail through a forest: You have to know what clues the readers are finding and that they are following you. This does not mean the ending can't hold a surprise. But the reader's reaction should be, "Aha!" rather than, "Huh?" The surprise should delight, not mystify. The reader should not feel manipulated or tricked.

PROMPT: Outline a story that leads to a surprising conclusion. In your outline, put in clues that could lead the reader to this conclusion. If you choose to write the piece, work to conceal those clues.

You can prepare the reader through foreshadowing—lines, details, scenes that suggest what is to come. Again, you're not "giving away" the ending. People still come to stories of all kinds for the purpose of finding out "what happens." But foreshadowing what happens unifies the story, gives the reader that sense of "I think I know what's going to happen," which you can control and shift and change. A friend and I read a mystery a few months ago, and we were both a little irritated to learn that we could not have predicted the murderer. A few key clues were not mentioned or were buried so deeply that instead of feeling pleasantly surprised, we were both annoyed.

THE ENDING UNIFIES THE PIECE

One way a writer creates good endings is by bringing back images and details that appeared earlier in the piece. This technique adds a satisfying sense of recognition and pulls the piece together, amplifying its unity. The most common method for nonfiction writers is to refer back to the opening. This approach creates a full-circle effect, though through much use, this can seem forced and obvious. But it can work if it is used well. It can even work in fiction. Many of us saw it for the first time in S.E. Hinton's classic young adult novel *The Outsiders,* in which the last line repeats the first. Quentin Tarantino uses a variation of this approach with startling results in his film *Pulp Fiction:* Characters planning a robbery in the opening scene disappear from the film until the final scene, during which they attempt the robbery.

PROMPT: Read a piece in progress with an eye toward image and detail. Find one or two that can be used at the end to unify the piece and amplify the themes.

PROMPT: Read the opening paragraphs of the piece with an eye toward picking up something to use at the end. Is a question raised that now can be answered? Can a line of dialogue be echoed? Can a statement be restated with new meaning?

As Rick DeMarinis told me, endings require "a sort of miracle." They are rarely easy. Writing about endings isn't easy, either. (Notice the repetition of the opening remarks with which I'm making an obvious and very clumsy attempt to end this chapter.) If you're having problems with your ending and the earlier prompts haven't helped, try a few more.

PROMPT: Change your approach to the ending. If you're fading out, try to be more abrupt. End at the climax. Try ending with a line of dialogue. If you're already ending with a scene, try description, handling the final action in a narrative rather than a dramatic way.

PROMPT: Write at least four possible endings to your piece. End in different places in the piece, or try different methods as you did in the previous prompt.

PROMPT: Look for the ending a few paragraphs prior to where you're trying to end. The piece may be finished already, and you're trying to force it further than it needs to go. This approach also can end the piece in a nice way because when you wrote the line, you weren't envisioning it as part of the ending.

I really will end now, by leaving you with an anecdote about endings. John Cheever was struggling for an ending to his story "The Country Husband." He had wrapped up the action and resolved the themes of the story but could not think of a good last line with which to end. Nothing seemed to work. Then, when he was walking through his home, not even thinking about the story, the last line came to him in a flash. He used the sentence exactly as it came to him. Here is the final paragraph of the story:

> "Here pussy, here, poor pussy!" But the cat gives her a skeptical look and stumbles away in its skirts. The last to come is Jupiter. He prances through the tomato vines, holding in his generous mouth the remains of an evening slipper. Then it is dark; it is a night where kings in golden suits ride elephants over the mountains.

CHAPTER THIRTY

RUBIK'S CUBE

We are all apprentices in a craft where no one ever becomes a master.

—ERNEST HEMINGWAY

To end this section of the book, let's discuss putting all the elements we've covered into motion. Because that's what you have to do when writing a creative piece. Books on writing—including this one—divide topics into chapters, covering structure, characterization, and so on one at a time. That way, each element can be covered at length and with a certain amount of clarity.

But when you're writing, you can't divide the elements so easily. The growth of your character, for example, influences the arc of the narrative. The point of view you choose affects your character and the reader's relationship with the unfolding drama. The process is a lot like working a Rubik's Cube. From a quick bit of research, I discovered that those maddening little puzzles are still around, but readers of a certain age will recall when Rubik's Cubes were all the rage. Everyone, it seemed, was working on one—or bragging about having solved one. The goal with the cube is to make each side all the same color by turning the various layers within the cube. Sounds simple enough—but by turning a layer to match the color on one side, you then change the color on a different side.

I admit, I was never a big fan of the cube, finding plenty in my life to frustrate me without spending precious free time adding to those frustrations. But it makes an apt metaphor for the writing process. When you make a change to solve one problem, you automatically create another. That's why I used Hemingway's quote to open this chapter: As writers, our apprenticeship lasts a lifetime. There are no quick fixes that work every time or with every project. With each new project comes new lessons to learn, some that will carry over to other projects while others are suited only to that particular piece. The great Gustave Flaubert once admitted, "I am irritated by my own writing. I am like a violinist whose ear is true, but whose fingers refuse to reproduce precisely the sound he hears within."

Of course, the challenges of a piece—and of the craft in general—are part of its appeal. The affects we manage to achieve and the powerful feelings we manage to impart to our reader would not be possible without the efforts of twisting and turning those elements so that they fit together as well as we can make. So let's get started on our own twisting and turning.

PROMPT: Choose one of the prompts from Part II and write the exercise. Then choose a prompt from two different chapters in Part III. If you've already responded to prompts then you can use what you've written. The next step is to write a piece that fuses the three prompts. A piece from the chapter on writing about your family, for example, could be shaped with an exercise from chapter twenty-three and set in a place you created in chapter twenty-six.

PROMPT: Respond to a prompt in the chapter on openings (chapter twenty-eight). When you've completed that exercise, continue the piece by responding to a prompt in chapter twenty-one on characters.

PROMPT: Write about a secret someone told you that you have never told anyone—but create a fictional situation, changing the particulars of the secret so your trust will not be betrayed. Then continue to explore this situation by changing the point of view—rather than a secret someone told you, it's your own secret.

PROMPT: Recall the piece you wrote about your own fifteen minutes of fame—a time when you were in the spotlight. If you haven't done one, do it now. Then, create a fictional character who has the same experience and tells of the experience in first-person point of view. Allow that voice to be strong and to take liberties with the facts. For example, you could write about the time when you were on the homecoming queen float at your high school. Give this experience to a woman who makes far more of the occasion than you would give it.

PROMPT: In chapter nine, you wrote about your travels. Recall one of the trips you've taken, but fictionalize it, adding a made-up detail that changes the experience significantly. For example, your chronicle of your trip to Italy, during which you visited many ancient landmarks, could include meeting a beautiful stranger,

THE WRITER'S IDEA BOOK

who acts as your guide. Who is this person, and what happens as a result of her entering your life?

PROMPT: In a prompt early in the book you wrote about a favorite object—a souvenir from a special time in your life or just something you own that you truly value. Write about that object from the point of view of someone who has no emotional attachment to it. How do they see it? Then let's say that you are forced to sell that object at a yard sale (I guess you need the money or someone in your family insists you get rid of it). Begin a story with that person buying the object at your yard sale. What happens next?

PROMPT: In several of the chapters, we've explored experiences of loss: the death of a loved one, or the ending of a marriage or friendship. Revisit that topic, but handle it in a new way. Write about it using three different points of view. You might use third person, for example, or you might explore the loss from the point of view of a third party who was not directly affected.

By now, you've got the idea. Try a few more combinations on your own. Don't choose only the ones that most obviously match each other. Explore possibilities. Move past the most likely ways to handle the material and stretch for more innovative solutions.

BRICK BY BRICK

One of my favorite books on writing is Anne Lamott's classic *Bird by Bird*. Her title came from advice she heard her father give her brother when they were kids, and he was feeling overwhelmed by a school project in which he had to describe quite a few birds. To help the boy feel less overwhelmed, her father told his son to simply take one at a time. Lamott advises writers to take a similar approach when they're feeling overwhelmed by a writing project.

We'll change her metaphor a bit for our purposes here and say that creating a strong piece of writing requires putting together the various narrative elements we've covered in this section. And, as mentioned above, there's no formula that works every time for achieving that goal. We must simply build our story brick by brick, creating the blueprint as we go along.

But I can offer some general advice about storytelling that you can keep in mind as you develop your idea. Some of that advice is scattered through earlier chapters in this book, but let's bring it together here. I've condensed the process to ten points to keep in mind. Some involve structure, others characterization, still others point of view, still others beginnings and endings.

1. **Begin with conflict.** Someone wants something. Forces exist that impede the character from getting that thing.

2. **Begin as close to the end as possible.** You might need to write more than necessary at the beginning to get the story going, but go back and cut as much as possible. Be ruthless in leaving only the bare minimum. So many manuscripts I see include prologues; so few actually need them.

3. **Expunge exposition.** Err on the side of telling too little. A good editor will let you know when you need a bit more information to clarify a point. Better to risk confusing a reader than boring her.

4. **Know your character's goal.** See Rule #1. Your protagonist wants something. No doubt other characters have their own goals. Know what each one wants. To create conflict, character goals should sometimes oppose each other.

5. **Let your reader participate.** Here we come to the classic advice for telling stories—show don't tell. Let the reader make the discoveries rather than spoon-feed them to her.

6. **Focus on scene, not summary.** A corollary of "show don't tell." Put people in action. Create drama that the reader can see and feel. Allow the action to tell the story rather than you telling it.

7. **Every dramatic moment should do more than only advance the story.** As we've discussed in this chapter and elsewhere, your dramatic elements need to be working in concert.

8. **With dialogue, only present the important parts.** Don't include every word of a conversation—just the good stuff.

9. **The story is a matter of point of view.** What happens in your story—even what seem to be the basic facts—can change according to who is telling the story.

10. **The ending must resolve the reader's expectations.** At the beginning of every story, the writer makes an implicit promise to the reader. Make sure you fulfill that promise.

These "rules" are not particular to me or to this book. They are the fundamentals that writers have used for generations. To keep our metaphor going, they are the bricks of storytelling. Many writers through the years have touched on these basics, presenting them in a different way, perhaps, but offering similar advice. Playwright David Mamet said, "The job of the dramatist is to make the audience be interested in what happens next, not to explain to them what just happened, or to suggest to them what happens next." And we create that interest for the audience by keeping these fundamental principles in mind as we write. One of the best pieces of advice I ever heard on telling a good story came from Kurt Vonnegut Jr. who said, "Make sure your audience members do not feel like you're wasting their time." That pretty much sums up what every writer should do.

Of course, these "rules" can be bent when necessary because, as I mentioned earlier in the chapter, each piece makes its own demands on us. There's no one-size-fits-all formula we can follow. Furthermore, writers aren't usually conscious of these rules as they work. Early on, we internalize them and then do what is necessary as we tackle each new piece of writing.

To illustrate that point, here's the opening of Sean Flynn's brilliant article on the soul singer James Brown. If you asked the writer if he kept in mind all the fundamental "rules" listed above, he'd probably say he wasn't aware of a single one of them in a conscious way. But he certainly puts a number of them to good use.

> The day he buried his mama in the big cemetery on Laney Walker Boulevard, in the row where he'd buried his daddy and his third wife, too, James Brown draped an arm around Roosevelt Royce Johnson's shoulders and pointed at a plot of unturned earth.
>
> "Well, Mr. Johnson," he said, "that's my spot right there. What you gonna put on my headstone?"
>
> Johnson grunted. Mr. Brown talking foolish, headstones and all that. Like he might actually die someday. What's a man supposed to say to that.

A tour de force of dazzling prose? Not really. But Flynn manages to employ a number of the elements we've discussed, working them in concert with each other to pull the reader quickly into the piece. First, he introduces the narrative voice while also setting the scene. Though we are in a third-person point of view for this scene, simply observing it, note that Flynn establishes that we will mimic the voices and present the thoughts of the characters. Brown has buried his "mama" and his "daddy." Johnson says "Mr. Brown talking foolish," using ungrammatical phrasings. Flynn also establishes a unique formality among these old friends, who refer to each other as

"Mr." The one line of dialogue not only develops the dramatic moment in the cemetery, but it also speaks to the theme of the piece—James Brown's legacy. How will he be remembered? In three short paragraphs, much is happening, many elements are working together to draw in the reader and set the piece in motion.

PROMPT: Reread a piece you're working on and write down the goals of each character. You probably knew these goals in a general way as you were writing, but try it now in a more specific, conscious way.

PROMPT: Follow the previous prompt but focus this time on conflict. What is the essential conflict of the piece? What is the essential conflict of each scene? Is the nature of the conflict clear to the reader? Is it, in fact, clear to you?

PROMPT: Reread a piece with an eye toward scenes. By thinking in terms of scenes, you keep the focus on dramatic action rather than on explanation—on showing rather than telling. Find one scene that you summarized and render it dramatically. Then ask yourself if the scene should stay in the piece. Of course, not every moment of a story needs to be rendered dramatically, but if you have a tendency to tell rather than show, or to summarize in long passages, consider shifting to a more scenic approach.

UNITY AND BALANCE

When you have basic elements in place in a piece, you then need to work on creating a pleasing sense of unity and balance. These are somewhat abstract concepts and not as easy to explain as, say, point of view or plot. They are elements of writing that readers tend to feel unconsciously—and usually will mention only when they're not working. Readers often won't know the true nature of the problem but will feel something is just not right.

One method for creating a sense of unity in a piece is the use of selective repetition. A detail or remark, or even just a unique word mentioned early in your piece can be echoed later, creating a sense of unity and wholeness through the reader's recognition of the previous mention. That recognition in the reader's mind also imbues the repeated element with a resonance, not unlike a coda in a musical composition. The reader enjoys a satisfying sense of progression, of having moved from one literary moment to another. To try out this strategy, reread a piece you're working on with an eye toward finding that element you could repeat in a subtle way, and then look for a place later in the piece where you could drop it in. If you are unsure which one would be most effective, experiment by trying several. Another strategy would be to ask yourself, if you had to cut all the details or images

THE WRITER'S IDEA BOOK

and retain only one, which one would you keep? Which one is essential to the core of the piece? That's the one you want.

We covered the use of patterns in the chapter on theme, but let's explore it more deeply here.

PROMPT: Reread a piece you've developed into a draft, looking for images that are repeated—or that could be repeated. Perhaps you've mentioned a time or two that your character taps his foot restlessly during conversations. Does this foot tapping suggest an underlying impatience in the character or perhaps signal impatience with the conversation itself. When that character appears later, can the foot tapping be used again?

PROMPT: In a description of a place, choose the detail that best suggests its atmosphere—a tacky chandelier that jars the otherwise understated décor, for example. Now repeat the process of the previous prompt, looking for a place later in the piece to revisit that image again.

Creating a sense of balance in your piece is similar to creating unity, but the repeated element is even more clearly—and obviously—connected to its earlier use. A classic example: In *The Great Gatsby*, as F. Scott Fitzgerald introduces us to the Buchanans in early summer, he emphasizes the breeze blowing through the room, billowing the curtains and the women's dresses. Later in the novel, the same characters seated in the same place are shown in the heat of summer as weighted down, dispirited, languid. The connection between these descriptions creates balance in the story and gives the reader a keen (if not necessarily conscious) sense of progression, of time's passage. Fitzgerald also implies that the characters are weighted down by the circumstances that have arisen in the novel. They are no longer free and airy but encumbered.

PROMPT: Spend a writing session rereading your piece, looking for a description or scene or metaphor that you can repeat later, changing some aspect of it so that it serves as a counterweight to the first usage.

Part IV

EVALUATING
ideas

CHAPTER THIRTY-ONE

THE WATER'S FINE

If I waited for perfection, I would never write a word.

—MARGARET ATWOOD

By now, you have responded to some of the prompts in the previous chapters and are moving forward on at least one writing project. I hope you've also created a file for the ideas you've developed and for the pieces you've written so far.

At this point, try to narrow your focus to a single project. Sometimes having too many ideas can be more of a distraction than a useful bounty of riches. We find ourselves jumping from one project to the next, making little progress on any one of them. My advice is to commit to one, for now. And that's not easy. In fact, it's often the case that as soon as we commit to one project, the others we've put on hold seem to offer so much more potential, seem much riper with possibilities, far more publishable, far more fun. Don't fall for this "grass is greener" syndrome. In most cases, it's simply a way to keep yourself from committing to a project, from taking the emotional, intellectual, and literary risk of going down deep in your creative explorations.

A good friend of mine, for example, has been juggling several projects for years—a memoir, a self-help book, and a screenplay. Now and then, he'll also be consumed with an idea for a novel. When I talk to him every few months, he provides an update on all of his projects. Usually one of the projects is generating the most enthusiasm at the moment, but when next we talk, he's put that one on hold, and one of the other projects occupies his writing time. He's sustained this juggling act for as long as I've known him—at least five years—and has yet to finish a full draft of any of the projects. If I were inclined to place a bet, I'd put my money on his never finishing any of them. He definitely suffers from the "grass is greener" syndrome.

As creative people, we're all prone to this syndrome, and having multiple projects in various stages of development is normal, even desirable. But at some point, we need to pick one and stick with it. That commitment can be scary. But if you hope to complete a project and to learn the lessons that can only be learned by battling a project all the way to the end, you need to focus on just one. To make this choice easier, you can give yourself a deadline or end point for that commitment. Tell yourself you will commit to working only on the chosen project for one month or six weeks or for the remainder of whatever season you're in at the moment. (Give yourself a long enough time for this commitment—a couple of weeks, for example, is too short.) After that date, you can assess whether you want to continue the commitment. If so, you might want to make another commitment—another six weeks or whatever. These interim commitments can help you manage a long project as well as your writing time.

PROMPT: When you have a project in motion, commit to it for a specific period of time. In fact, put it in writing. If it sounds like fun or if you feel it will help, create a contract for yourself stating that during the next number of weeks, you will make Project X your writing priority. After that time, you will assess whether or not you want to continue the commitment.

With your focus now clear, keep moving, keep writing. At this stage, we're just playing. Don't put pressure on yourself or judge the project as good or bad. You don't know what it is yet, so there's no point in trying to determine if it's any good. Just keep going, making that leap of faith we discussed in the first section. Also, don't spend hours trying to write a perfect first sentence. That's way too much for now. You're a kid playing in a mud puddle. Swirl the water with your finger, and watch the dirt roil from the bottom. Jab a finger down deep and feel the tug of suction as you pull the finger out. Splash around. Play.

I'm not being intentionally vague or poetic here. At this stage of the process, it's tough to offer much in the way of specific guidance. You're discovering an idea, following it intuitively, waiting for characters to assert themselves, a conflict to reveal itself, a shape to begin to form, a voice to rise from the page. Allow these things to happen, but try not to force them.

The key, for now, is opening up to possibilities. The piece is quite fragile. It requires a gentle touch. It also requires attention. When a piece is getting underway, return to it often—every day, if possible. If you leave it for too long, you risk losing inspiration for it. As Annie Dillard suggested very insightfully, "you stop believing in it." The magic of the piece disappears because you can no longer feel its rhythms as intuitively as when you return to it frequently. The Editor kicks in and you find yourself questioning every aspect of the piece, doubting its validity. My advice is to follow the advice of the poet William Stafford: "Lower your standards and keep writing." Another poet, Maya Angelou, explained the process a bit more poetically: "What I try to do is write. I may write for two weeks 'the cat sat on the mat, that is that, not a rat.' And it might be just the most boring and awful stuff. But I try. When I'm writing, I write. And then it's as if the muse is convinced that I'm serious and says, 'Okay. Okay. I'll come.'"

PROMPT: Choose one idea from your file or notebook. It need not even be your favorite. Write the first page or, if you have it pretty well underway, write the next page. At your next writing session, circle the phrase or detail or action that engages you most. Rather than continuing from where you stopped at the previous session, begin with what you've circled and write a new page.

PROMPT: Choose an idea from your file or notebook, and work on it at least ten minutes per day for one week. If you can go longer than ten minutes, keep going, but don't let a day go by without spending at least ten minutes on the piece. Write something—even if it's just a list of character names or random images somehow associated with the idea. Every day. At least ten minutes. This approach will keep the piece alive in your mind. Your subconscious will continue to work on it even beyond the time you spend at the keyboard.

PROMPT: Keep writing. Do Not Stop. Remember to trust the process. Also remember that you are not qualified at this point to decide on the quality of the piece. It is just beginning to reveal itself to you.

PROMPT: After each writing session, write a congratulatory note from your ideal reader to you. The reader should tell you he or she loves your idea and is eager to read more. Or you could write the note to yourself. Just a short one, a literary slap on the backside or high five for sticking to your schedule.

TECHNIQUES FOR EXPLORING

There are many ways to explore an idea when it's beginning to form. None is more right than another. Through experience, you'll find what works for you. One way is to approach it from a variety of angles, as we did in the earlier prompt involving "A Family Gathering." We wrote personal reflections about the subject, and we wrote opinion pieces. We wrote about it as fiction. We looked for relevant quotes and photographs and responded to them. We tried to fuse these approaches into a single piece. This strategy keeps us open to possibilities.

Allow the point of view to shift. Allow characters' names to change. If you want to write a reportorial or academic piece but personal stories keep creeping in, let them. If you're writing a memoir of a childhood incident, allow yourself to shift from your adult perspective to a present tense account from your view as a child. In fact, play with that shift, moving back and forth until one establishes itself. If you're writing a screenplay, capture lines of dialogue in whatever order they come. Don't pour your story into the three-act formula before developing its possibilities outside that formula.

Sometimes we get bogged down at the start because we're not sure where to start. We have a sense of the story, but we're not sure where to begin. If you've just begun putting it on paper, start anywhere. Get something on paper. In the previous chapter, we discussed starting as close to the end as possible, and that's good advice, once you know the ending. For now, allow yourself to move around. And if you're too sure of the ending, you may be stalled by the fact that the story is already neatly resolved in your mind. It feels stale from the start. If that's the case, start with a new ending. Begin by writing your ending or conclusion in a fresh way.

Like many writers, I try to focus on characters at this stage, when I'm writing fiction. Usually my idea for a piece begins with a character or two. I follow them to their jobs, try to figure out where they live, try to get into their heads for a while. When I move too quickly to The Story, they sometimes are swallowed by it, becoming pawns of the plot rather than fully realized characters. Some fiction writers, however, move first to the situation. The energy of a conflict drives the early stages of the story, and characters are discovered and developed as the plot unfolds.

For personal essays and memoirs, the early stages of a project can be fraught with self-consciousness. We think: Who cares what happened to me? We wonder if the personal story and ideas we're relating are of any interest to readers who don't know us. Trusting your impulse to write the piece is crucial. Delay The Judge. Or agree that the whole thing is silly and self-indulgent, but you're going to do it anyway rather than plop in front of the television or linger on Facebook. The other concern is what to put in and what to leave out. If you're being completely open and not censoring, how do you know which details about an event or situation to include? The fact is, you don't. That's why early drafts of memoirs tend to seem unfocused. One memory leads to another, and before you know it, you're off on a tangent. Later in this book, we'll discuss ways of deciding between important details and extraneous ones. For now, put in whatever relates to the idea you're developing.

In his book *Lessons from a Lifetime of Writing*, David Morrell explains his method of interviewing himself in order to explore a new idea. When beginning a novel, he writes extended question-and-answer interviews with himself to better understand the nature, scope, and possibilities of an idea and his interest in it. He asks basic questions about the characters or about the reasons behind his inspiration. His responses to the questions allow him to write down his thoughts without the framework of chapters and opening lines and so on. At some point, a response to a question grows into the novel itself, and he's underway.

In *Writing the Blockbuster Novel*, Albert Zuckerman explains how Ken Follett, a very successful client of Zuckerman's literary agency, develops a series of heavily annotated outlines for a novel before he begins writing it in earnest. The outlines can be changed while the writing is in progress, but mostly he sticks close to them. Some writers would find such a method confining. Others couldn't live without it.

Years ago, literary disciples of renowned editor Gordon Lish focused on finding the first sentence of a story. They believed the rest of the story would flow naturally from it. This approach was successful with a certain type of literary short story, but most writers would never complete a single project if they had to hone a perfect first sentence before moving on. I had a friend in graduate school who would think about an idea for weeks before writing it. Then he would revise and revise the first page over and over. As poor graduate students in the early 1980s, we didn't have computers. I remember seeing more than a dozen typed versions of that first page on his sawhorse desk.

Some writers need to carry an idea around in their heads for a while or doodle it on the page, knocking it around a bit, before it comes pouring out. You'll find what works for you, and maybe you've found the approach already. The key is finding a way of gently guiding a piece through its infancy, nudging it along in the direction it seems to want to take, and remaining open to shifts in direction.

At this stage, make a deal with yourself: You'll explore the idea for a specific number of pages before abandoning it. Give it a chance to grow. If you're a runner, you probably know that feeling of being tight and tired early in a run. A friend of mine calls it "feeling junky." Your breath is short and your legs are leaden. You think you'll never make your full course today. But usually, you find that if you keep running, you'll break through the junkiness and have yourself a good run. The same is true for writing. The going can be a little tough at first, but stay with it. Don't give up on a piece before it's had enough time to establish itself.

PROMPT: When your project is underway—at least a few pages on paper—write several paragraphs from a new point of view. If you're writing fiction, change the focal character. If you're writing an essay, change your authorial stance.

PROMPT: If you're working on a poem but are stalled at the start, focus only on the images themselves. Forget about thematic intentions. You could be blocking yourself from what you want to say by trying too hard to say it. Let the images dictate the direction.

PROMPT: If you know what you want to write about but aren't sure where to start, begin with a line of dialogue, something you know is going to be said at some point in your piece. Write that line of dialogue and follow it, developing a single scene.

PROMPT: Write at least a page from an omniscient point of view, in the godlike voices of nineteenth-century novelists. Introduce the reader to your setting and situation, to the characters. For examples, check out Charles Dickens, Jane Austen, or William Makepeace Thackeray. You'll probably ditch that voice later, but for now use it to usher you into the story.

PROMPT: Begin with the moment or detail or image that excites you most. Ignore that old rule about not getting your dessert until you eat your dinner. Start with dessert. For example: You want to write an essay about the breakup of your romantic relationship, but you keep getting strangled by the endless details of backstory. Jump right to the climax. Give us the moment when somebody says he wants to leave. Develop it fully. Assume you'll do the explaining later.

PROMPT: Shift to a different form. For example, if you're trying to write the break-up essay but are beginning to feel like you're off the mark, shift to fiction for a session or two. Write it as a short story. Or, you could shift perspective. Rather than telling it from the perspective of rueful-but-wiser you, the more innocent victim of the breakup, tell it from the perspective of the other person.

PROMPT: When you're stuck on where to go next, write a general statement about the subject. For the breakup story, write a statement about the nature of breakups. Then move to specific examples to show that what you've said is true. You could use these statements as section heads. Allow yourself to move away from the particulars of the breakup you were trying to write about.

PROMPT: If you have an idea and know where to begin but find yourself struggling with the first couple of paragraphs, skip them. Start on page two. Assume you've written those opening paragraphs and simply continue. We sometimes block ourselves by trying to perfect our openings, and sometimes we never get

THE WRITER'S IDEA BOOK

beyond that opening. Allow yourself to leap over it and get the story moving. You can go back later and create that wonderful opening sentence or paragraph that for the moment eludes you.

PROMPT: As you work every day on the piece, it will begin to occupy your thoughts even when you're not writing. You'll begin to make connections between the piece and your daily life. Write down these thoughts and ideas. For example, when you're at the grocery store you overhear someone make a statement that fits your character. Write it down. On a day, when you don't feel inspired, focus on one of these thoughts, exploring its connection to the ongoing piece.

PROMPT: Surprise yourself. When you're feeling uninspired to write but want to stay on your schedule, brainstorm about the piece, writing down all the thoughts that come to your mind, even if they don't seem to be related to the piece at all. Then pick one of the unrelated pieces and explore it. You'll probably find there's a connection after all.

As should be obvious, the theme that connects these prompts is that, in the first stage of development, we don't know what we're writing. We have an inkling or an urge, but often we have no more that that. We have to rely on faith, confident that if we put in the time and stay true to the piece, we'll find out where we're going. And that act of faith can involve a pretty long leap of faith, sometimes. That's why it's so important to do something on the project every day. Take too long a break from it and the natural doubts that arise will convince you it's not worth continuing or will bring in The Judge and The Critic and all those voices that will just confuse the process at this stage.

One of my favorite writers, Tobias Wolff, also offered some of my favorite advice about this early stage of the writing process. He writes:

> If you're looking over your own shoulder all the time, crossing every other sentence out, and holding every other word up to the light as you're composing, that can lead you to become kind of constipated as a writer. Later on, you have to look at your work with a very cold eye, as if you were editing someone else's. But in that first blush, why not enjoy it?

Also keep in mind an oft-quoted statement attributed to James Thurber: "Don't get it right, just get it written." At this stage in the process, that is our one clear goal. If it helps, use that goal to gauge your progress. Your focus is simply to get it written. You're not concerned with whether it's "good" or "bad" or "hackneyed" or "ground-breaking." It's not your job to deal with those judgments. Your job: "Get it written."

CHAPTER THIRTY-TWO

STOKING THE FIRE

Often I'll find clues to where the story might go by figuring out where the characters would rather not go.

—DOUG LAWSON

As we move deeper into a project, we sometimes sense it going flat. It lacks the inspiration that kept us going through the early stages of creation, and even though we're willing to suspend judgment, as we discussed in the previous chapter, we can't shake the notion that the piece needs more of something. Sometimes we don't make this discovery until we've finished a complete draft. Our great idea that sent us racing to a notepad in the middle of the night, the one that scorched our fevered brains through exhilarating sessions at the computer, now lies on the page, a ghost of what we hoped it would be.

For an idea to work well, it needs to grow, to complicate itself with more ideas. By complication, I mean a second idea that extends or enlarges the first. A very basic example:

Idea: Boy meets girl. They fall in love.
Complication: Their families have a long-standing feud and hate each other. Their parents would forbid a marriage. And so the lovers get married in secret.
Complication: The boy gets into a fight with the girl's cousin, who is killed. The boy must run away.
Complication: The girl's father, unaware she has married the boy, orders her to marry the son of a well-placed family.

You get the idea.

Shakespeare could have pushed the single conflict between the families to its natural conclusion, but he complicates the story of star-crossed love by bringing in larger questions about human nature and society. Meanwhile, he pushes his lovers further and further away from each other.

It's tough to know all of these complications when we first sit down to explore an idea. We discover them as we write. That's why it's important to work on a promising idea long enough to explore its possibilities and why we need to commit to a single piece so it can occupy our conscious and unconscious minds. That's how we're going to make the necessary discoveries, adding new ideas to the generative idea.

Here's another example. We're working on a story about a woman whose boss is making her life miserable. His demands are impossible to meet. We create several scenes showing the boss unfairly and caustically criticizing the protagonist. Then we write a few more. And a few more. She works harder, but the fatigue caused by the pressure and the shaky judgment caused by her lessening confidence make her prone to error. She talks to a colleague, then to a friend or two, about the situation with the boss. Then we have another scene with the boss that mirrors previous ones. The story progresses in this way, but the conflict is, for the most part, flatlining.

I see this type of story time and again when I read for conferences and contests. A strong idea that is full of drama and conflict becomes a one-note wonder, in which the writer presents the same conflict between the same characters in largely the same way and with the same tone until the story has lost its punch. The initial conflict is played to its inevitable conclusion. It's the kind of story that makes inexperienced readers fumble for what to say. They often question the pace, saying, "It seems slow in the second half." And, indeed, it does. But the problem isn't the pace. The problem is a lack of invention. The initial idea isn't developed with more ideas. There are no surprises, no complications.

Think about it: At any one time, we feel a range of emotions, and aspects of our lives can be at any number of stages: Work is going well, the kids are sick, health is fine, money is tight, the marriage could be better, we have many wonderful friends. That's why the question, "How's it going?" is so pointless. Which "it" does the person want to know about?

In stories, we try to streamline the lives of our characters, giving some sense of order to the chaos. We focus on a single "it." Sometimes, however, we focus too narrowly, and a good idea doesn't develop into a good piece. These one-note wonders fail from too heavy a reliance on the generative premise. We lock into the first idea and fail to push beyond it. In his essay "On Defamiliarization," writer and teacher Charles

Baxter discusses this point with his usual insight. In the excerpt that follows, he reflects on why a competently written story, submitted by a student in his workshop, is dull, despite interesting situations. After the story's strong opening, Baxter finds:

> [T]he story's initial surprises began to seem less wonderful, even though its details were excellent, and the story was never anything but truthful. But the story had begun to read itself too early, and before long it was always and only about one thing, with the result that all the details fit in perfectly. All the arrows pointed in the same direction. When all the details fit in perfectly, something is probably wrong with the story.

What's wrong with perfectly fitting details? Nothing, of course, unless they fit so well because we're not digging deeply enough. The story skates along the surface. The reader knows where we're headed and may or may not be interested in joining the inexorable march to the end. As writers, we, too, might get bored, putting the idea away for a while, and maybe never coming back to it. We think that, in the end, the idea just wasn't good. The real problem, however, lies in settling in too quickly, in not pulling, as Baxter writes, "something contradictory and concealed from its hiding place."

For example, a few years ago I read a story for a contest. It began well. The writing was crisp, the details nicely chosen. The situation was interesting: A marriage was crumbling under the weight of the wife's new high-paying job that demanded more of her time and energy, and was changing her values in significant ways. By page three, the situation was in place and the couple confronted the change in their lives with an angry scene. In the next scene, the couple argued again about this issue. Next scene: more issue, husband angry and confused, wife changing. Next scene: the same. You get the point. One note.

If you feel a piece starting to become a one-note wonder, read it again, looking for dramatic possibilities, places to add new elements, ways to push beyond the familiar or what "really happened." Try to surprise your reader—and yourself.

PROMPT: Brainstorm a list of complications for your work in progress. Make it a big list—at least fifteen items. Go crazy with it. At least three of the complications must be preposterous, requiring of you (and your reader) huge leaps of faith.

ADDING IDEAS

If you're feeling your piece go stale, or if readers aren't responding to it in the way you hoped, step back and evaluate how you've developed and complicated the idea. How

THE WRITER'S IDEA BOOK

many pages—or scenes or lines of the poem—are spent making the same point or eliciting the same response from the reader?

PROMPT: Spend a writing session playing "What if?" Challenge some of the basic elements of your work in progress. What if your poem about traveling to Japan included a moment from the trip you hadn't thought to include—the hotel clerk who supplied you with directions, for example? What if your memoir about your mother's death included scientific facts about her illness? What if your screenplay about an unlikely superhero included a meeting with another superhero? You get the idea. Brainstorm a list of answers to the "what if" question, and choose one to focus on for the rest of the writing session.

PROMPT: Grab some colored markers and underline in a single color all the sentences dedicated to one conflict in your piece. If the conflict shifts or if it's complicated by new information, grab a different marker and keep underlining. When you've finished, step back and see the result in living color. Perhaps the problem with your "dull idea" or "bad idea" is simply that it hasn't taken the next step into something larger or deeper. The problem at the end exists in the same place as when we started. In the example of the piece in which the woman is having trouble with her boss, we continue to come back to the same situation presented in the same way: boss=bad; protagonist=good; conflict=stay or go.

PROMPT: Do the same thing as in the previous prompt, but instead of using your piece, use one that has been published. Mark the turns in the story, the deepening of character or theme, the shifts in conflict, the complications, the surprises, the passages that build suspense. Use the same color scheme you used in the previous prompt, in which you marked your own story. How well do they match? Does the story you've read have a greater variety of colors than the one you wrote?

If you conclude you've got a one-note wonder on your hands, it's time to add ideas. Getting ideas at this stage is much the same as getting the generative idea for the piece. You imagine possibilities. You ask "What if?" What if the woman in our story about the tyrannical boss has quit her last two jobs, having disliked or failed at them for various reasons? By adding this complication, her staying at this job and satisfying the tyrant takes on greater importance. The stakes have been raised. Or, what if she's raising children on her own, or her husband is in law school and she's the only breadwinner? Her pressures at work spill into her relationships at home, expanding the range of the story. Or what if you gradually show that the boss's complaints are at least partly justified, reversing the reader's expectations? Suddenly, we have a more complicated story than before, one with the power to surprise. Or what if she discovers the boss's marriage is failing or that he's working through some personal grief? Now there's a matter of humanity involved, a question of how much sympathy she'll allow to excuse his behavior. Or what if you changed the relationship between the characters? What if the tyrannical boss is her father? Now we have a new element, a father-daughter theme that complicates the initial idea of a workplace story.

You see my point. Imagine new possibilities. Push the story to its next logical step. Deepen the characters. Imagine the situation from a new perspective. Raise the stakes. And raise them again. How can the situation be more distressing for your protagonist? How can the outcome be of greater consequence? How can she, in attempting to extricate herself, plunge herself even deeper into confusion or misery?

Here's another example: We have an idea for an article about a grand, old building scheduled for the wrecking ball in our hometown. We research the building's history and talk to the people involved in the demolition. We find nothing especially surprising, and there seems to be no conflict about whether or not to tear it down. In the story, we rhapsodize about the building's former glory, even as we admit that the old sometimes make way for the new. We end up with a nicely written yet utterly predictable elegy that never rises above our initial conception of the piece. It's a one-note wonder.

A complication would have helped. We needed another element, perhaps a new building going up elsewhere in town that could supply a comparison. Instead of interviewing only the city planners, we could have rounded up stories from elderly people who remember the building's glory days. Perhaps these stories could be contrasted by reactions of local teens who think the old place was pretty much a dump. Perhaps we could have written an extended piece of satire, in the tradition of Swift's classic "A Modest Proposal." We could have called the piece "Good Riddance."

Again, the point is clear. By sticking too close to the original idea rather than adding new ideas, we ended up with a predictable bit of one-note nostalgia. As with the story about the woman's conflict at work, we needed to ask "What if?" Raise the stakes. Consider new approaches, perspectives, and tones. Place the idea within the context of something larger.

Another way of finding these ideas is to search your feelings about the piece. Ask yourself: Is my idea fresh? Have I read pieces like this before? How is mine unique? Does the piece reflect my true feelings about the building? What *are* my feelings about the building? Am I truly sad, or am I conjuring a somber tone simply because I feel it's expected? How can I more accurately reflect my true feelings about the subject? What ideas could be added to this idea to make it fresher, more engaging so that readers will enjoy the experience rather than be run through the standard grid of emotions and ideas?

Sometimes we must be willing to go way beyond the initial conception. The generative idea took us to a certain place, and now we must move from there. For example, in our story of the woman and her boss, we may need to ask, "What if she quits? Where does the story go from here?" Though our initial idea focused on the situation at work, leading up to an anticlimactic showdown at the end, the situation with the boss could be condensed into a few opening paragraphs, sending us boldly on our way into a completely different story, one involving the search for a new job or one focusing on the character's need for a more significant life change.

Keep your mind open to shifting the story in a new direction. When you read interviews with writers about how a book evolved, often, you'll learn that the generative idea is only a tiny part of the completed project. That idea was simply an avenue toward others. And the writer was willing to explore those others, to consciously pursue them.

PROMPT: Create a new element of the story that is being kept secret by one of the characters. Allude to this secret somewhere in the first scene. As you move ahead, slowly reveal the secret, one that adds another complication to the story. You needn't know the secret yourself when you start writing. Allow yourself to discover it as you write.

PROMPT: Take a day off from the work in progress and brainstorm ideas for a new project. Again, make it a long list. Put the list away and return to the work in progress at your next writing session. At some point, pull out the list of ideas for a new project. Choose one item from the list and find a way to weave it into the work in progress.

PROMPT: If you feel your scenes are too similar in their objective, add a random element. The more random the better. Brainstorm a list of possibilities. Or, if you feel you won't be random enough, consider these possibilities: a fortune cookie, a necklace, pruning shears, a flat tire, a grocery receipt, a ferret, a negligee, a park bench, a glass of water, M&Ms.

WHY JUST THE ONE NOTE?

Sometimes our stories are limited because we really don't want to broaden their range, but for various reasons, we can't admit this fact to ourselves. One reason we don't want to consider other possibilities is our rush to publish. We finish a draft of a story, massage it a bit, give it a quick edit, a polish and a proofread, and it's out the door, sailing to the doors of magazine editors. We haven't lived in the world of the story long enough. We haven't imagined its possibilities, taken risks with it. The most common complaint I hear from friends who edit magazines is that they see "too many early drafts." They reject these stories, leaving the writers to wonder where they went wrong.

The solution is simple: Don't be so quick to declare a story finished. We all enjoy getting published, but make sure you're sending out fully realized work. Give yourself time to live in the world of the story, to carry your characters around in your head. If you're writing an essay or memoir, give yourself time to know for sure you've said what you want to say, that your piece is developed to its potential.

Some writers send stories off too quickly because they suffer from commitment phobia. When the generative idea has been pushed to its natural conclusion, the story is finished. They have no desire to break it apart or start over after page three, thank you very much. These drastic measures require more commitment than they're willing to make. They either file away the story as a bad idea or do a quick, nip-and-tuck edit to superficially address the reader's concerns. The question then becomes: How important is it to these writers to tell this story? Is the problem a lack of invention or a lack of commitment, a passionate need to put these words on paper? These are questions we must ask ourselves.

We also might block a story's emotional and thematic range because broadening that range requires us to venture into psychologically troubled waters. Here's an anecdote to illustrate. In a workshop at a conference, my group read and discussed a student's short story about a woman whose distant, critical mother carps at her constantly throughout a weekend visit. The protagonist rolls her eyes at these complaints, occasionally shooting a wry rejoinder at her mother before, in the end, the mother leaves, and the daughter sighs with relief, a bit sad that the relationship isn't more loving. The story was well written, full of sharply observed details. The group praised its strengths, as groups tend to do. It was clear to me, however, that the story was not fully realized, that after all the clever exchanges and interesting details, it didn't amount to much. The story wanted to be more.

I asked the writer about her intentions for the piece and about the relationship between the mother and daughter. The writer said she simply wanted to present the relationship and to show the daughter putting up with the mother's constant criticism, which she had lived with all her life but which, now, lacked much meaning for her. It was the story of a daughter's triumph, of her reaching a new level of maturity.

"Why don't the criticisms bother the daughter anymore?" I asked.

"Because she's older now," the writer answered. "She's outgrown the need for her mother's approval." (This writer, a smart, dour woman in her early sixties, didn't much care for me, and, like the daughter in the story, rolled her eyes at any critical comments, however kindly phrased, I made in the workshop.)

"I'm just not sure if that's enough to move the story forward," I said. "She doesn't care at the beginning, and she doesn't care at the end. What do you want the reader to take from that?"

"I'm just showing a relationship," the writer snapped.

I said, "What if the daughter did care? How would the story be different if the mother's criticism hurt the daughter deeply? What if the daughter is just pretending not to care and secretly would love to have her mother's approval?"

The writer burst into tears.

When she regained her composure, she told us that the story was based on her relationship with her own mother, who is very critical, and though the writer doesn't show how much those criticisms have hurt her through the years, she has the emotional scars to prove it.

I wish I could tell you that I knew all of this, and with the cunning grace of Socrates I guided her through my questions to discover the true nature of her story. But I would be lying. I was just fishing around, trying to open the writer to various possibilities, trying to find out what made the story worth telling for her, looking for the chaos beneath the polished exterior. That's what we do when a story needs more, an extra *something*, but we're not sure what it is. We fish around. We ask ourselves questions. We experiment. The workshop student had decided from the start that the story was about a daughter putting up with, while no longer caring about, her mother's hectoring comments. She closed the door on the possibility that she really needed to write about how much the daughter did care, how much she resented her mother's lifelong emotional stinginess.

Again, sometimes our first idea is simply a way to get at a better one. Sometimes it's simply a single facet of a larger jewel of writing. When we don't explore and discover the other facets, our story doesn't end up as a diamond. It ends up as a flat rock.

If you feel a piece you're writing is starting to go flat, don't abandon it. Instead, ask yourself if there's an aspect of it you're hesitant to explore. Is the one note simply the first note of a song you're afraid to sing? If so, you have a decision to make. I'm not telling you to sing that song. That's your choice. But you've found the reason why a story with a good strong idea isn't lifting to great literary heights.

I'd like to end this section by telling you that after the beautiful moment in the workshop, the writer and I became good friends. We had a good-bye hug, she returned home and revised the story, which she then sent to me. It was great. But that would be too obvious and familiar a note to strike. (It also wouldn't be true.)

I don't know if she revised the piece or if she went home from the retreat and confronted her mother. I'll leave that next step in the tale to you. What do you think might happened?

PROMPT: Describe your story in two sentences. Now add a third sentence, introducing a new element, even one that may not seem appropriate. For example, the workshop student could write: "This story focuses on a weekend visit by a woman's mother, who has always been very critical. During the weekend, the daughter realizes she's outgrown the need for her mother's approval." As a third element, she might add, "As the mother loads up her car to leave, the daughter insists that they go shopping together." Try this prompt several times, playing with possibilities for the third element.

PROMPT: Outline your piece as you see it now. No need for long annotations in your outline. Just use a word or phrase to describe each part or scene. Then outline a piece with the same subject or premise but change the approach—its structure, its events, its outcomes, its point of view, etc. Outline it again, this time with yet another approach. And again. Allow the piece to be illogical, even outrageous. When you're finished, review your outlines, looking for elements that can be added to the original outline.

PROMPT: Play "Raise the Stakes." Add a new element to your piece that makes the premise or situation more significant in some way. More dire for the protagonist. More meaningful. More life changing in its outcome. If you're working on a personal essay or memoir, look for greater consequences in the situation. Is the experience you're exploring a pivotal one in your life? Does it resonate beyond your life in ways that may touch the reader's own life?

PROMPT: After you've raised the stakes in the previous prompts, look ahead in your piece for a place to raise them again.

PROMPT: Rewrite a scene from the work in progress to change the tone in a significant way. If the scene is fraught with anger, for example, present that anger in a humorous tone. Experiment with ways to make the scene funny. Or, if your scene involves a shocking revelation, emphasize the beauty of the moment.

PROMPT: Make a surprising move. If your character reacts in a predictable way to an event, change the reaction. A man driving home from a wonderful first date doesn't whistle a love song or dance in the street. He stops at a grocery store, carefully selecting his items. Or, in an essay, rather than summarize your response to an event you've just finished dramatizing, shift to a new subject, bringing in some fresh element.

THE WRITER'S IDEA BOOK

PROMPT: Describe a process. This exercise is a standard in technical-writing courses. Students explain the steps involved in doing something, such as fixing a flat tire or installing a water heater. Spend part of a writing session describing a process. Then look for ways of weaving this process into the work in progress. For example, in her essay on how to write the lyric essay, Brenda Miller describes how to make challah bread. She uses the process to enlarge the essay and make her points about craft in a more lyric way. In fiction, describing a process can have the same effect, the most famous being the chapters in *Moby-Dick* that describe the techniques of whaling. Your fictional character, rather than react to his wife's leaving in the typical ways, might carefully wax his car. Don't look for obvious parallels when deciding on which process to describe. Choose one you know well or one you can research.

PROMPT: Spend a page or two with a minor character or, in nonfiction, a minor person. Expound a bit upon her or him. Give us background details and a detailed physical description. Look for ways to expand the role of this person in your piece.

PROMPT: Choose your favorite part of the piece you're working on—a line of dialogue or detail or a sentence that strikes you as especially good. Freewrite about this part, letting yourself take off in a new direction. You may decide after you finish that the part needs to remain exactly as it is, or you may discover a new mine of inspiration.

PROMPT: Change a relationship in the piece. If your character is having a problem with a neighbor, for example, make that neighbor a high school sweetheart of your character's wife. If you're writing a personal essay, explore a new attitude about one of the people in the piece. If you've showered your sister with loving praise throughout the essay, for example, admit that her habit of deciding where everyone must sit at Thanksgiving dinner bothers you. Explore that feeling a bit. Or, if your essay involves plenty of snipes at an ex-spouse, spend a few paragraphs mentioning the spouse's endearing qualities. (Surely there's at least one!)

PROMPT: Give your character some surprising news that shifts the natural course of the story. It could be good news or bad news, but it must be news that requires a new plan of action for the character. If you're writing nonfiction, add some type of news to the mix, even if it seems unrelated at the moment. Your task will be to expand or deepen the piece enough to accommodate such news.

PROMPT: Qualify or contradict a statement that you or a character made in the opening pages. For example, if your character claims to be content with the life he's chosen, have him explain what he means and add a note of doubt.

PROMPT: Add a new piece of information about a character or person who appears in the opening pages, a piece of information that contradicts or amplifies the reader's understanding of the character. For example, if the opening focuses on observations about your mother and her lack of tact, tell the reader something that characterizes her in a different light.

PROMPT: Adjust the tone of the piece by adding a different note. If, for example, your opening is loaded with high-energy drama, shift to a quieter mood, for at least a paragraph. If your opening is somber, add a sentence or two of humor.

PROMPT: Add a new element to a relationship. If your pair of detectives has been focused on news about a case, suggest—or state—that they were romantically involved at an earlier time. If your character is struggling with a tyrannical boss, for example, make the boss an old rival from high school or a distant relative.

PROMPT: If you know what comes next in your piece but can't seem to build the bridge to get there, skip to that part, jamming it right up against what you've already written.

PROMPT: Add a new person to the piece. If you've been focused on two characters in a situation, for example, bring in a third. Allow that character to change the personal dynamic in some way, entering with her own agenda. For example, if your memoir of a family picnic has focused on you and your brother, show us what Uncle Dave is doing over there on the volleyball court.

PROMPT: If you're writing a memoir or personal essay, say something that surprises you about the subject you're exploring. Or, if you're feeling nervy, say something that reveals a detail about you or deeper feelings about the subject.

PROMPT: Slow the pace at which you're introducing characters or people. We sometimes move too quickly in the early pages, feeling we must get the piece moving as fast as possible. Take time to linger, giving the reader a richer beginning.

PROMPT: Shift the narrative mode. If you've begun with a page of description to present the setting, move right into a scene. If you've explained the situation and presented the background information, move to the present time of the story. If you've begun with a scene, move to narrative summary. If you've begun with characters speaking, move into the mind of a character and present his thoughts.

PROMPT: Add a seemingly unrelated object, one that comes quickly to mind (and therefore probably has some connection in your unconscious mind to the piece). For example, if you've been discussing how your lover left abruptly, introduce the potted corn plant standing next to your front window.

PROMPT: Make a general statement or have a character make one—a sweeping statement, along the lines of "people always work to undermine their own best interests," or "Jill will never be a happy person as long as she keeps dating engineers." It should be a statement that adds a new tone or moves the piece in a new direction. By that I mean, the first scene might have shown Jill coming home aglow from a first date with a man she met recently.

PROMPT: Ask a question. Or have a character ask a question. Surprise yourself and just write one down. Even if the question seems unrelated to what has come before, follow it, find out where it goes or where the answer to the question (or the lack of an answer or the struggle to answer) takes you.

PROMPT: Shift the time. If you've opened with a night scene, take us to the next afternoon. If you've opened in the present, shift us back to 1992.

PROMPT: If you know what comes next but can't seem to build the bridge to get there, change course, inventing or choosing a new direction.

PROMPT: Shift the character's goal. Your opening probably makes clear this goal, either directly or indirectly. Write a page in which the character is not focused at all on achieving this goal. If you're writing a memoir and you've focused on coming to terms with an experience in your past, nudge yourself away from this focus.

PROMPT: Add a second thread. If the opening of your novel concerns the theft of a priceless painting, move to a bar where customers argue about the chances of the Red Sox winning the pennant. If your opening concerns a woman walking home from a job interview and worrying about money, have her stop at a grocery and concentrate on finding fresh oranges for her kids. In her essay "That's What Dogs Do," Amy Hempel opens with a brief discussion on why she writes, then adds a second element, her attempts to train her dog.

PROMPT: Sustain the action of the opening scene. If you planned to end at a certain spot and move to flashback or summary, stay focused on what happens next in the dramatic present and maintain your focus, even if you're not sure where you're headed.

PROMPT: Show your character doing something uncharacteristic. For example, your soft-spoken accountant could fold a wad of bills from the petty cash drawer into his pocket. Or, you may want to show that your character doesn't perceive herself in the way others perceive her. Isaac Singer's Gimpel, in the short story "Gimpel the Fool" is often bullied and manipulated by those around him. They think he's a fool. But he sees himself much differently, and his voice in the story has a quality of strength.

PROMPT: Change the atmosphere. If your opening is light and straightforward, add a note of eeriness. If your story opens in a silent, empty house, shift the scene to a carnival full of crowds, noise, and excitement.

PROMPT: Shift the setting. If you've opened at the family picnic, shift to a new location. If you've described the sun rising against a cityscape, move us inside, to a diner for breakfast.

PROMPT: We've explored many ways in this chapter to add new ideas to the initial idea, ways to enlarge and complicate the piece you're working on. What new possibilities haven't we covered yet? Review the prompts in this chapter and then brainstorm a list of other ways you can add notes to your story.

PROMPT: Picking up from the previous prompt, now brainstorm other ideas for the piece itself. Be bold, be inventive, have fun.

CHAPTER THIRTY-THREE

A MATTER OF PERSPECTIVE

If you see a whole thing—it seems that it's always beautiful. Planets, lives ... But up close a world's all dirt and rocks. And day to day, life's a hard job, you get tired, you lose the pattern.

—URSULA K. LE GUIN

The cliché about hindsight being 20/20 hangs around because there's a lot of truth in it. We look back on decisions we made five, ten, twenty years ago and can see with often rueful clarity the errors we made. If you've been writing awhile, you've had a similar experience with your work, I'm sure. Oh, the sweet pain of reading that story from college, the one we were sure would soon turn us into the literary scene's next Young Turk. It so clearly embodied our poetic souls, put forth such a sad yet triumphant lyricism that it would bring readers to tears throughout the world. When we read it now, however, it sounds like the pretentious gibberish of the ambitious sophomore who wrote it.

Unfortunately, that distance gained by years is difficult to achieve in other ways, but unless you are content to finish a piece every decade or two, you'll have to find some ways to help you gain a clear perspective on your work, clear enough to make the necessary assessments. Assessing your ideas as you develop a piece requires a level of objectivity. The closer you are to the material emotionally and psychologically, the more distance you need to see clearly and assess the piece. An idea that moves you profoundly is worth investigating in a piece of writing, but it may require more refined ideas to make it come alive for the reader. You could be deeply moved while writing an early draft and believe it has a power that is not yet on the page.

A case in point: In graduate school I went to a reading by a respected writer who had published several collections of short stories. He read a long story that he'd written recently. (Our most recent work tends to be our favorite work.) The story was—at the risk of being unkind—excruciatingly dull. One person, a teacher in the program, even fell asleep, jerking awake with a loud bang of his foot against the back of the seat in front of him. And yet, as the story reached its climax, the writer began to fight back tears. His throat closed, and he had to pause for a few seconds before reading the ending. By that point most of us had lost the thread of the story, and we were aghast that what seemed to be an uninspired tale held such power for the writer.

The story in his mind was not yet on the page. From what I recall, there seemed to be some autobiographical threads running through the story. The writer was responding to those personal memories. He needed more distance from the material to notice that the story, though deeply moving to him, was not yet moving to others.

Let's assume you have developed a piece of writing to the point where you have begun assessing and evaluating it—where it's working, where it needs help. What is the piece trying to tell you? What is it trying to be? What are its possibilities? To begin answering these questions, you need to gain some distance, some perspective. Let's explore ways of doing that.

GAINING DISTANCE

Seasoned writers develop their own methods of gaining the distance necessary to effectively assess their ideas. My favorite is one I heard years ago from a professor, though I've never been able to validate. The professor told us that a best-selling author found that he couldn't see a piece with fresh eyes until it appeared in print, especially in a glossy magazine. Something about the shiny paper, I don't know. He would consider a piece finished, then send it to his editor. When he read the published version, he saw all the wrong turns and missed opportunities, as well as the less-than-perfect phrasings. And so the author would type a draft, then tack it to a corkboard hanging on a wall in his office. He hung a wall light with a bendable neck above the corkboard, positioning the light to shine directly onto the tacked pages. He then walked to the other side of his office and read the piece through binoculars. The glare of the light simulated glossy pages, and he gained the distance he needed to assess the piece.

THE WRITER'S IDEA BOOK

I'm not recommending this approach. I'm simply showing the lengths to which authors will go to objectify a piece in process, so that they can see it anew. Without that freshness of perspective, it's tough to assess what's going well and what needs help.

From my own experience, I do read a piece differently when the published version arrives in the mail or in the bookstore. It does always seem a bit different from the version grown so familiar on the computer screen. Once, I even cursed the magazine editor who obviously had rewritten entire passages, substituting a number of awkward phrases and clunky transitions for my crystalline prose. The nerve! I rushed to my computer to gather evidence to cite in the vitriolic letter already taking shape in my mind. I was stunned as I reread the piece in the Word document I'd sent. Other than a word or two and some minor punctuation, she hadn't changed anything. The clunkers, alas, were my own.

Other times I've seen places that might have been more fully developed, thought of ideas that seemed so obvious and yet hadn't occurred to me. I don't know that it's a matter of the glossy paper so much as the distance between the time the piece is submitted and its final publication. It's also the writer's mind-set. When you read your published work, you read it through the eyes of all the readers who will find it in the magazine or the book. They provide a wonderfully useful (and sometimes heartbreaking) distance that's tough to conjure on our own.

I had a writing professor who typed (this is going back some years) on three typewriters, using one for the first stage of the work, a second for the next stage, and so on. Each typewriter had a different color ribbon. This approach worked for him, helping him see the piece with fresh eyes. It also helped him relax and explore on the first typewriter. He knew that on the second or third typewriter he could change something that wasn't quite right.

Such strategies work for you or they don't. Experiment. The most common advice on the matter is to file a piece and move to something else for a while. Sometimes a few weeks or a month is all you need to gain the right distance. Meanwhile, the piece percolates, consciously as well as unconsciously. You think of new ideas or ways to refine earlier ideas. However, as I said in an earlier chapter, when you put away a piece, give yourself a time limit. That way, it won't be left untouched for so long that it loses its pull on your imagination. All writers have too many fragments in their files, half-written pieces that have been filed as "failures" or ones to which we hesitate to return, thinking that someday we will, but these pieces languish beyond the time when we actually can return.

Yet another strategy for gaining the necessary distance is to change the time when you write or the place where you write. If you write early in the morning, before heading for work or school, make time in the evening to read the work in progress. Or if you write in the evenings, read your piece in the morning, before heading out for the day. We tend to be in different emotional, mental, and psychological states at different times of the day. Many writers are sharper in the morning but a bit more regimented, too. In the dreamy glow of evening, their minds are looser, more adventuresome. Reading a piece in progress at an unusual time of day can provide some objectivity. Do the ideas still work? Does the new mindset provide new inspirations?

Reading in a different place from where you write also can help. If possible, get out of your living space. Go to a library or coffeehouse or to a park. You'll find that you'll see the piece differently. Your awareness of different surroundings adds a fresh element to your conscious mind, altering the way you perceive what you're reading. You'll understand the piece in a new way.

Yet another method is to send it to a trusted reader. This approach gets the piece out of your hands for a while, which is good, especially when you're feeling stuck or indecisive or have begun to lose faith in your idea. You also may find that by giving it to the reader, you are able to see the piece through his perspective even before you receive any comments. You gain a new sense of what's working.

PROMPT: When you feel you're stuck or just want a fresh perspective, put the piece in an envelope and mail it to yourself—snail mail style. Commit to not reading the piece on your computer until it arrives in the mail, probably a couple of days later. When it arrives, read the hard copy you've pulled from the envelope. This is one way to gain distance from it.

PROMPT: Read what you've written so far into a recorder. Then play the recording, listening to it as if someone else was reading to you. Don't read along as you listen to the recording. Instead, keep your ears open for surprises, and jot down any new ideas that arise as you listen.

You might want to imagine giving it to a reader. In other words, read the piece yourself but conjure, if you can, that reader's viewpoint. How would she see the piece? What would make her laugh? What would surprise and delight her? If you have the good fortune of working with a gifted writing instructor, imagine sending the piece to him.

I advise you not to actually give a piece to a reader until you have it well underway. If you're simply looking for some validation on a raw idea, it's better to work through the idea first. You might detect a note of doubt in your reader's voice, causing you to doubt the idea in a significant way and abandon it, when the reader's

THE WRITER'S IDEA BOOK

doubt might be imagined or might result from the idea needing refinement rather than abandonment. If the reader loves the idea, you might feel inspired to continue or you might have received your reward for it and lose your desire to develop it. You may not realize either of these feelings on a conscious level, but they still can be there—and they're dangerous to a project in the early stages. Save your trusted reader for something more developed. Imagining your reader's comments might be enough to give you some distance.

Consider reading the piece aloud. You should read your work aloud when you're in the proofing and editing stage, but try reading it even in first-draft form, even if certain sections are still not finished. How does it sound to you? Where do the ideas need to be stronger, and which ones are working well?

If you're really brave, ask someone you trust to read it to you. Their voices won't give the piece the same inflections and emphasis that you would give it, but that's okay. Sometimes we supply emphasis that isn't there. And, at this stage, we're simply trying to assess the ideas and the ways they've been executed on the page. It doesn't matter if the character cries out "I *love* you" or "I love *you*."

PROMPT: Change the time when you write for the next few sessions. As we discussed earlier in the chapter, the change in time will produce a change in mindset, allowing you to assess your ideas from a fresh perspective.

PROMPT: Change the place where you write for the next few sessions. The shift in geography can supply a fresh perspective.

PROMPT: Spend a writing session rooting through old files and notebooks. It's probably been years since you looked at some of what you've written. Use that distance to reevaluate abandoned projects. Look for patterns among the ideas. Look for ideas that can be moved from stalled projects to ongoing ones.

PROMPT: If you've taken time to do the previous prompt, choose one idea from your files that appeals to you and make it the focus of your next writing session. Explore and develop the idea, bringing to it all you've learned since the time you first put that one on paper.

PROMPT: Extending the previous two prompts, write a page or two in which you respond to what you've discovered in your cache of earlier ideas, fragments, and drafts. What patterns run through the work? What themes run through the work? What do these fragments suggest about you as a writer—your interests and inspirations?

PROMPT: Shift the distance you feel from the piece by reading it as if it were someone else's story. This shift may be difficult, but give it a try. Imagine that you discovered the piece in a magazine or a book. From this perspective, does the piece work? What advice would you offer this writer in revising the piece?

PROMPT: Have you given a piece enough time in the drawer so that you can see its possibilities? If so, read it again with fresh eyes. Make one change to the piece.

PROMPT: Go on a treasure hunt or, if you prefer, go geocaching. In the piece as it stands, there is a single image or detail that unlocks the literary door and holds within it the next step you need to take. Your job: Find it. The goal of this exercise is to find a new way to read the piece—to read it from a fresh perspective. Often, we reread our work with the same mind-set, noticing the same things time and again. This time, you simply want that one detail. After you've picked one, spend a session pushing the piece in whatever direction the detail or image suggests.

PROMPT: Let's do the reverse of the previous prompt—find the one image that must be cut. If all seem perfectly suited to the piece, pick one arbitrarily, then make a brief case for why it needs to go. Again, our goal here is not so much to find an actual new direction as to read the piece with a new goal and mind-set, which might suggest new ideas that you hadn't considered before.

When you've found a way to create enough distance to assess your ideas as they are manifest on the page, ask yourself the basic questions first: How meaningful is this idea, and, therefore, this project? Is the idea merely clever or has it yielded greater and varied depths? Does the idea deliver its basic goal? By that I mean, if the idea is essentially comic, has it led to a funny or entertaining draft? If the idea is essentially a melancholy reflection, does the piece that embodies it evoke that tone and those emotions? If so, what new ideas will take the piece even further in that direction? If not, what's missing? Are there flaws in the executions holding back the idea, or does the idea seem to want to go in a new direction?

As we've discussed, sometimes the generative spark, the first idea, is simply a way into material that might be quite different from what you expect. Does the draft, for example, lack humor, despite the comic nature of the initial idea, because the humor was leading you to darker material than you anticipated?

PROMPT: Though the conventional wisdom tells us to try to forget about a draft while it's gestating, odds are it's going to surface in your mind from time to time. You'll think of a new idea—a fresh stanza, a line of dialogue, a description of a place. Take time to write these ideas on paper and put them in the file with the draft. Feel free to forget about them afterward. When you pull the draft from hibernation, you'll discover any number of little scraps of paper with ideas for developing the piece, ideas you may have forgotten entirely.

PROMPT: Spend a session recasting the piece in a new point of view. If it's a first-person piece, shift to third, for example. You need do this only for the first few pages. Has your perspective changed? Can you read it with fresh eyes?

PROMPT: Read the piece as if you plan to burn it as soon as you finish reading it. No other person will ever read it. You need not be concerned, therefore, with the glory and fame it will bring you. You need not squirm at the thought that it reveals some slightly unsavory thoughts. You need not please or displease anyone else with the piece. Seen in that light, what do you want to change? What do you want to keep at all costs? Does the piece please you? Was it worth writing despite the fact that no one but you will ever read it? Would you have written it knowing no one will ever read it?

LETTING GO

A student once told me, "The only time I can think of ideas is when I'm not trying to think of ideas. As soon as you tell us to 'brainstorm' my brain shuts down." She was exaggerating her claim—in fact, she produced some excellent ideas in the workshop—but there's an element of truth in her statement. We can force ourselves to write and to assess and develop our ideas, to the point where we kill any fun or creativity that might help make the ideas better. We put pressure on ourselves, blocking ourselves from thinking by repeating a silent mantra of "Think, think, think."

As we've discussed throughout this book, writing is an intuitive process. It doesn't submit to formulas or guidelines. It requires, instead, a level of faith on the part of the writer, using her craft to give shape to the ideas while also allowing them to take their own shapes. That approach goes against the way we try to order our lives. To keep up with bills or get the kids to activities on time, to remain efficient and productive at our jobs, we make lists to follow. We prioritize. We work to keep things under control. It's tough, therefore, to let go when it's time to write.

We structure our days to allow for an hour to write, a sacrifice that makes us demand production from that hour. We've got to have something to show for it.

This approach can make us reject our ideas too quickly. We think of an idea, writing furiously over the course of days or weeks, but when we feel the first surge of disappointment that our idea on the page doesn't look like the idea in our minds, we declare it "stupid" or "unworkable" and ditch it. Spending more time on it, we think, would simply be a waste. Or, we ride our initial inspiration by trying to rein in the idea, to capture and control it on the page. We know what the piece is supposed to be, and, by gum, we're going to make it exactly that.

PROMPT: The world ends tomorrow. There's no hope of publishing the piece you're developing and no point in publishing it anyway because no one will be around to read it. With that mind-set, spend a session working on the piece. Go crazy with it. Add whatever ideas come to your mind.

PROMPT: Spend a writing session changing the form or genre of your piece. And make that change significant. If you're writing a memoir, for example, turn it into a musical. If you're writing a science fiction novel, turn it into a narrative poem.

PROMPT: Turns out the world is not going to end after all. But you are. You have five minutes left to tell the story of your piece. Edit it down to the nub, keeping only the essentials. Everything else must go because there's no time left. What parts do you keep?

EVALUATING

When evaluating your ideas as they're manifest on the page, the first step is to assess without labeling. Your goal is not to declare what's "good" or "bad." You're trying to discover the nature of the idea. When you begin exploring your ideas on paper, you're figuring out what it is. What's the story here? What clues are appearing within the descriptions or the characters? How is the material manifesting itself? Which characters are moving in directions you didn't foresee? Which ideas spark still more ideas? What shape seems to be emerging from the piece? What new possibilities occur to you as you read and reread?

The process of assessing ideas should be creative. It should inspire ideas as much as sort through them. You are trying to find the hidden nature of your idea rather than judging whether it's worthy of further pursuit. You are not shutting down your creative self; you're opening it. Your first passes through the draft should be ones of discovery. Focus on what's on the page rather than bemoaning what's not yet there.

In her essay "Lost in the Woods," Cathy Ann Johnson compares the creative process to wandering in the woods:

> There is an art to wandering. If I have a destination, a plan—an objective—I've lost my ability to find serendipity. I've become too focused, too single-minded. I am on a quest, not a ramble. I search for the Holy Grail of particularity and miss the chalice freely offered, filled full and overflowing.
>
> There are times when I go to the woods to find specific wild-flowers or plants or animals, to illustrate an article or a book, armed with sketchpad and pencils. At those times I set my inner viewfinder for plants, or animals, or whatever—and my larger vision is as limited as if I were looking

> through the wrong end of a telescope. I've preconceived a notion and closed
> my mind and my eyes to whatever else may be offered free, gratis.

Many of us manage to use Johnson's process of wandering in the very early stages of a project, but when it's time to step back and see what we've done, we grab that "wrong end of a telescope." Instead, as we move deeper into a project, we can put to use the critical skills discussed in the previous few chapters by allowing those skills to inform an open-minded reading. As we assess a project, we'll make better decisions if we keep our minds open than if we limit ourselves by taking on a "quest" mentality.

That mentality hampers your vision, and it can stall the project that began with such great promise. One of my favorite pieces about the process of writing is the film *Barton Fink*. If you haven't seen it, treat yourself. It's brilliant on many levels, but let's discuss it from a writer's view. As you may know, Barton is a successful playwright in pre-World War II America. He writes about, as he loves to say, "the common man." And yet he grudgingly leaves Broadway to write in Hollywood, where he hopes to make a lot of money. The studio assigns him "a wrestling picture." Throughout much of the movie, we see him struggle with the project, barely writing any words at all. He is stalled by his desire to please his Hollywood bosses, despite the fact that he knows next to nothing about the form. Though he spouts passionately about his love for the common man, he knows little about the common man's reality. And he's too busy spouting to realize that his neighbor, a beefy insurance salesman named Charlie Meadows, is a potential fount of stories and is eager to tell them. At the climax of the film, Charlie gets to the heart of Barton's problem when he roars, "You. Don't. Listen."

When they began writing *Barton Fink*, Joel and Ethan Coen were struggling with the screenplay for what later became their film *Miller's Crossing*. I wonder if the admonition about listening was targeted in some ways at themselves. We're all guilty of not listening from time to time. The idea Barton struggles to find is right in front of him, but he doesn't hear it. As you move through your draft, take time to listen. Free it from the expectations of some vague and fickle audience. Free it from your own hopes that it will verify your creative genius to the world.

If you feel the piece is not working the way you want or simply seems to be running out of gas, ask yourself if those expectations are blinding you or making you deaf to the more authentic idea contained within the one you're struggling to develop. Or, perhaps, the idea lacks vitality because it's dishonest from the start, or is a way of cashing in on commercial trends or a way of eliciting praise from your writers' group or workshop. It's not dishonest, of course, to write commercially, but understand that that's what you're doing and find the place inside you that's invested more deeply in the project. Even the most commercial writers have to believe in the efficacy of their work at some level.

Or, perhaps, the idea is working better than you think, but you're pressuring it to be something that it's not, for the reasons mentioned above. Or, perhaps, the idea is growing larger and, in some ways, messier than you expected when you began developing it. For some writers, this would be good news: "I thought I'd caught a little fish, but the weight on my line shows I've hooked a much bigger one!" For other writers, the hard and heavy tug on the line is scary. What monster of the deep have we accidentally hooked? They cut the line in fear they'll lose their line, rod, and boat.

The key, of course, is listening.

PROMPT: Write a brief review of the piece as it stands, as if you were reviewing a published piece by another writer. Include examples to support your points. Quote your favorite parts directly in the review.

INFORMED LISTENING

You might be wondering why we discussed developing and honing critical skills in the opening chapters of this section if the evaluation process is so passive. Good question. The answer is that you're not passively listening. You're actively listening. Compare it to the process of meditation. In a meditative state, we are, ideally, both relaxed and alert. We lose ourselves by being utterly conscious of the moment. We empty ourselves in order to fill ourselves.

When evaluating your work, try to find a similar balance. Your critical skills will inform your listening. The more you develop the critical skills, the less you will need to be aware of them in a conscious way. You have read the masters. You have studied your genre. You have taken part in workshops or writers groups, learning from writers at your own level. You have listened to experienced writers critique submissions. You have worked hard at your craft. With the skills you develop in your training, you can *listen* to your drafts in an informed way. The confidence you gain through hard work will help you let go and allow your ideas to be what they want to be. You can trust yourself to let go. The skills you've learned will be there, even as you open yourself to all possibilities.

Evaluating ideas, therefore, requires a balance of critical skills and passive openness. As you read your draft, be alert to possibilities. Read and reread. Then read it again. What patterns emerge? What do these patterns seem to suggest about the piece? How might the patterns be explored more fully?

While reading, be mindful of where you trip. If you tend to trip at the same spot whenever you take a pass, make a quick mark in the margin. Ask yourself why this idea or phrase or image stops you. Is it not organic to the piece? Perhaps it needs to be cut or perhaps it's trying to assert itself more fully into the story.

As the piece develops through successive drafts, keep asking these questions and keep your mind both relaxed and alert. As the piece continues to develop, it will be clear which ideas don't fit, which ones are redundant, which ones belong elsewhere, perhaps even in a different piece. It will be clear if a line in a poem or a scene in a short story is not working, because those around it now are working. It also will be clear which details are relics of an earlier draft and no longer fit the piece, because now you have a better understanding of where you are going.

You can use this method from the first tickle of inspiration through the final draft, developing some ideas, discarding others, seeing all the stages in the process as equally creative, ones that require a balance between the critical skills you've developed and an openness to possibility and discovery. As you listen, be mindful of destructive or distracting self-talk: "This is stupid, because I'm a lousy writer." "This will be a failure like all the other things I've written." "This is great because I am a genius!" "Readers are going to weep in their chairs when they read that line!" "Is this idea great or lousy? Am I just wasting my time, or is this idea worth pursuing?" "This is going to be good, damn it, I don't care what it takes."

Those statements create noise that makes it difficult to hear the piece in progress. They have nothing to do with what's on the page. They're symptoms of the insecurity and grandiosity we all share. They profess faith in an empirical grid of "good" and "bad." They upset the balance we've discussed in this chapter. When you're listening as you read, you'll hear these thoughts. They may even try to take over. Recognize them and push them aside. They're not on the page, and they're really not even about what's on the page. They are born of fear—of failing, of succeeding, of hard work, of committing to a long project, of exploring emotions and ideas we'd rather not face. Keep your focus on the page. Keep your ears open to the ideas and the words on the page. The other stuff doesn't matter. It's simply you trying to get in your own way. Instead, like Cathy Johnson, wander in the woods and be open to what is there for free.

PROMPT: As you work on your piece, listen to what's on the page rather than trying too hard to control it. Try to balance passivity and activity, critical skills with stillness.

PROMPT: As your work on the piece, listen for any thoughts that reflect on you—how the piece proves that you're a genius or a loser or anything in between. Then tell yourself that, well, no it doesn't. It is simply one of many pieces you will write in your lifetime because that's what you do—you write. The piece probably isn't a turning point or a disaster or the most inspired work you'll ever do. Divest it of all those trappings and labels. Sometimes we have to do that in a conscious way.

PROMPT: Underline the main ideas: the primary conflict, plot, emotions, characters, themes. Rather than labeling them or assessing if they're "good" or "bad," write each at the top of a blank page, then brainstorm any possibilities that spring to mind, even if they don't seem to be related. Put the "storms" aside for a day, then read them, noting which ones draw you in most. Use these ideas as the basis for at least a page of writing.

PROMPT: Return to a piece you've abandoned and read it with the balanced listening approach we've discussed in this chapter. Circle or highlight the lines, phrases, images, or anything in the piece that grabs you in some way. Read the piece again, this time focusing only on the highlighted passages. Is there a pattern running through them? An image motif? A character? A thread of action? Now read the sections that aren't highlighted. Is there a pattern here too? Explore the pattern of the highlighted passages. How can it be developed? What might be discarded from the sections that didn't engage you?

PROMPT: Expanding on the previous prompt, write one of the highlighted passages at the top of a page and begin exploring it as a separate entity rather than as part of the work in progress. Allow yourself to create new ideas around it, knowing that you can return it to its original home later. For now, see what else it might reveal.

PROMPT: Write down all the destructive and distracting self-talk statements you usually make while evaluating your work—all the statements you use to create noise and thereby deafen yourself to the piece in progress. Now read the piece and immediately discard any thoughts that your list contains.

During the "evaluating" stage, we are still in a creative mode. In fact, I'd say that it's even more creative than the first stage when we're full of passion and energy, the idea exploding onto the page. We are listening and trying to gain distance, to see through the illusions created by the first explosive stage. We are less concerned with labels like "good" and "bad" than in finding what fits, what is organic to the piece and what might work somewhere else—in a different piece down the road.

CHAPTER THIRTY-FOUR

OCCASIONS AND OPPORTUNITIES

Revision, once well done, becomes a sort of automatic itch which you scratch in the next work without thinking about it.

—ROMULUS LINNEY

Does the name Edd Roush mean anything to you? Most of you probably answered "no." I once asked that question during a conference lecture and, of the more than fifty people in the session, only one person raised a hand. (After the lecture I asked her how she knew, we talked for a while and have been good friends ever since.) Edd Roush was a baseball player, a center fielder for the Cincinnati Reds, and was one of the best in his day. But his day was nearly a hundred years ago. He's in the Hall of Fame, but the average person, even serious fans of the game, do not know him.

So when his granddaughter approached me about publishing a biography of Edd, my initial thought was to turn it down. She had interviewed him many times decades before and had used the tapes to write the manuscript. Her personal access to the subject did intrigue me. She also had published articles on the era in which he played, so she knew her stuff. I simply couldn't imagine wide enough interest in this mostly forgotten player. We talked for a while and exchanged e-mails about the project and, from those discussions, we hit on an idea: Readers don't know Edd but they do know about the 1919 World Series, in which some players on the Chicago White Sox were accused of throwing games to collect money from gamblers and eventually were banned from the game forever. The classic book *Eight Men Out* had covered that story and was later made into a film, which has become a classic in its own right. Shoeless Joe Jackson, the most famous of the banned players, became something of a national icon after the film *Field of Dreams*. The author told me that there was another side to the World Series story, part of which she told in a chapter of the biography. I suggested reframing the manuscript, focusing on that untold story of the infamous World Series, and weaving Edd's personal story throughout. The new approach required a lot of work from the author, but she rose to the challenge, and over a year later, we published the book, which earned excellent reviews and created a bit of a stir among baseball historians.

This experience offers some valuable lessons to writers. You need to be committed enough to a project to make significant changes to it. Those changes might require a significant amount of work. They might involve cutting some of your favorite passages. You must be willing to see a project in a whole new way, and you must possess the nerve to go forward with this new vision. Beyond the willingness to reenvision a project, we need the ability to execute the changes we have decided are necessary.

When evaluating an ongoing project, you need to see it clearly, as we've discussed in the previous two chapters. After you step back—metaphorically speaking—you need to make decisions about the nature of the piece and its possibilities. What is working well and where you've gone off course. At the Writing It Real conferences, we don't label what's not working as "bad" or "stupid." Instead, following Sheila Bender's lead, we call them "occasions" and "opportunities." Now, this isn't some misguided double-talk or tenderhearted euphemism. In fact, "occasions" and "opportunities" actually articulate the true nature of evaluating your piece. Some parts might be working better than others, but do those that aren't working hold the key to the piece's full potential? Do the parts that are working provide a path you can follow as you continue to explore the piece?

In chapter thirty-two, "Stoking the Fire," I mentioned a writer who had written a perfectly acceptable piece about a carping mother and a daughter who had learned to carp right back. The writer, however, failed to realize the true nature of the story, relying instead on snappy dialogue to characterize the relationship, which fails to progress throughout the story. Using the good/bad approach, a reader would say that the early pages work well, moving quickly and riding a wave of clever exchanges between the mother and daughter. But things start to drag in the middle so you might want to cut some of that part. Keep the "good" dialogue and images but cut the "bad" ones. The ending ties things together as the mother leaves after the visit, but somehow leaves the reader feeling a bit empty. The piece doesn't resonate. The ending, therefore, is flat. Work on the ending, keeping the "good" parts. I circled all the parts I really like and the ones that I think you should cut.

Sound familiar? In workshops and writing groups, we hear such evaluations all the time. If, instead, we use an "occasions/opportunities" approach, we improve our chances of discovering the piece's possibilities. When we took that approach with the mother/daughter story, asking questions and wandering through the piece, the writer discovered that the daughter was hiding behind a sardonic façade in the scenes—and the writer was hiding behind a similar façade in the story itself. After that discovery, the story could become a much more powerful piece. The revisions would be far more productive.

PROMPT: Review your piece with a pen in your hand. Circle all your favorite details, images, turns of phrase, whatever brings a smile to your face as you read. Mark these as "occasions," meaning that they might hold even greater potential. Then go through the piece again, circling all the parts that you don't like. Circle them as "opportunities." Ask yourself why they're not working.

As we discussed in the first section, resistance to a work in progress isn't always cause for alarm. It's a sign the piece is beginning to assert itself. It's part of the process. But when a piece begins to assert itself like a concert of angry gorillas, you're going to feel . . . a bit concerned. If things get completely out of control, or simply grind to a halt, it's time to focus on what's working and build from there.

Read what you've written so far, and mark the parts that you like, anything from a single word to an entire scene or stanza. Don't question why you like it or try to categorize it, just note it. A dot of your pen in the margin is all that's necessary. When you've finished reading the draft, put it away for a day or two. Let it simmer in your mind. Then ask yourself, every now and again, what comes to mind when you think of the piece. With luck, it won't be the skull-scalding rage at the piece's failings. Instead, one of those images you noted will come to mind. Or the way a character snaps out a line of dialogue.

When you come back to the piece, begin with the image or event or whatever you first think of. Think about what makes that idea so prominent. Does it embody, in some way, the piece as a whole? What qualities make it unique, resonant, and memorable? Are these qualities apparent throughout the piece? If not, think of ways to expand them. If the element you've chosen doesn't seem to be emblematic of the piece as a whole, explore its relationship to the piece. Does it belong there? Also consider possible connections that you may be missing. Perhaps it is emblematic, but you haven't yet realized the connection. You may not yet understand the piece well enough, and this image or detail or whatever is sending signals to you. Even if you don't believe there's a connection, imagine the possibility. If this image were central to the piece, how would the piece change? Focus a writing session or two on exploring possible connections.

PROMPT: Read the piece again and choose three elements—images or descriptions or parts of scenes—that you like, even if they don't fit the rest of the draft. Just liking them is enough. Spend a writing session on each one, brainstorming ideas to develop these elements. Write one or two pages focused on each of the three elements, based on the ideas you created while brainstorming.

PROMPT: Building on the previous prompt, try to pull the previous brainstorms into a somewhat unified piece, fashioning transitions and making connections. Feel free to add new ideas to the piece to harmonize the elements.

CONNECT THE DOTS

As you review your draft, note where you've placed a dot in the margin to signify an element that is working well. You may even want to list these elements on a separate sheet of paper. Look for patterns that emerge as you study these elements separate from the larger piece. It's easier to see the connections between the elements when you separate them from the larger piece. It's also easier to see how much of the troubled draft is going well. Some writers tend to "catastrophize," unable to see that a troubled draft contains much that is good. This exercise will help you see those elements more clearly.

After you can see them, compare them to the piece as a whole. Why are these elements working and why is the overall piece not working, or at least not working as well as you'd hoped? How do the working elements compare in terms of tone, focus, theme, and story to those that are less successful. For example, do your favorite parts tend to involve one character or one place or situation? Do they focus on the main idea of the piece or on what you had thought were subordinate ideas? If the latter, consider changing the emphasis of the piece, foregrounding what you had thought was less important but now seems to be the stronger element. If the "good parts" do tend to derive from the piece's primary ideas and goals, what makes you feel the piece is not working? Are there too many elements that distract from the main idea? If so, can some of them be cut or condensed?

Can the ideas or approaches that are working best be expanded? For example, if your essay is a humorous look at today's workplace but seems to be strongest when evoking the sad state of employee morale, perhaps the humor simply was a way into the subject, a way for you to approach a subject about which you had stronger feelings than you wanted to face. Now that you have a draft in progress, perhaps the humor needs to be shed or at least become a minor, complementary tone rather than the primary thrust of the piece. It can be used as a counterweight rather than dominating the piece. Maybe the piece is feeling constricted because you're not allowing yourself to face less comfortable feelings. You're trying to avoid allowing the piece to become a raging polemic, but in doing so you're hiding behind the humor.

Or perhaps you're writing a screenplay but your efforts to keep the plot moving swiftly along have left your characters undeveloped. And yet, your favorite parts are the moments when the characters reveal themselves in some way. Your list of elements that work mostly contains items pertaining to these moments. If so, you might be forcing the story in directions it doesn't want to go, which is why it feels flat and empty to you, despite a dynamic plot. Expand the moments you like best. Look for ways to explore the characters more deeply without significantly slowing the plot. Consider that the story you want to tell may not need such a fast-moving plot. Are you being too heavily influenced by what you perceive as the expectations of movie producers?

I could offer a dozen more examples, but you get the point. Focus on what's working and use those elements as guides for revising, even reconceiving, the entire piece. When you strip away the elements holding back the piece, you may end up moving forward with something vastly different from the draft you have now. Allow that to happen. Some pieces have slower evolutions than others and require more time to reveal their true natures.

PROMPT: Reduce the piece to its frame, its skeleton. If necessary, outline it. Examine how the pieces work together. Isolate those elements that don't fit and brainstorm ways of making them fit. If they still don't fit, outline the piece again without those elements and see if the piece still works.

PROMPT: Using the outline from the previous prompt, look for redundancies. Are two characters doing the work of one? Can the characters be fused somehow or can one character be eliminated? Are two image motifs producing the same effect? Eliminate one and decide if the piece works better that way.

PROMPT: Write a "bizarre" version of the piece, using the same basic elements—setting, characters, plot—but allow yourself to achieve completely different results. Can a melancholy character, for example, perform the same actions but in a comic way? Can a moody atmosphere be made frightening or energetic?

PROMPT: Is there a flaw in the premise of your piece? Look closely at the core idea and decide if it still works for you. If you feel confident in it, brainstorm new possibilities for it, new ideas and new directions.

PROMPT: Spend a writing session interviewing the principle person or character in your piece. If you're writing a memoir, interview yourself during the time in your life you're writing about. If you're writing a novel, interview your protagonist. Ask him or her about the piece—its challenges and possibilities. Just freewrite their responses, noting whatever comes into your mind. If a second person or character begins to intrude and interrupt, by all means let them.

STARTING OVER

Sometimes you'll find that by isolating the good ideas, you're not left with much. Ten pages of prose might contain only an image or two that you really like. Before abandoning the piece, run through the strategies we've explored in recent chapters: Put it away for a while; listen to the piece and allow it to go its own way; give it to a trusted reader for comment; examine the expectations you have for the piece, the various personal issues that inform your work; try to be objective about the piece and about your expectations, trying to see it clearly. If you're still convinced that the premise is good but your execution poor, consider starting over, this time focusing on the elements that are working in the current draft.

For example, you believe your idea for a short story is a good one and the first few pages work well. Then the piece loses its energy and its focus, it drifts off into dullness and confusion. Okay. Cut everything after those first few pages, and start from there. But before moving ahead and possibly frustrating yourself or feeling blocked, read those first pages several times. Why are they working and how are they working? What do you like about them that's missing in the rest of the draft? Try to get back to that initial burst of inspiration. What was it about that burst that started the piece so well? What goals were you foreseeing? What strengths did you hope the piece would possess? In short, take the one-step-back-two-steps-forward approach. For whatever reason, the piece has lost some of its juice. Try to recover that juice by returning to a place—in your mind as well as on the page—where you still had it.

Perhaps that process is more difficult than simply stripping away pages four through ten and returning to three. Perhaps, as mentioned, you're left with only a few scattered images, an opening situation, a brief exchange in dialogue. That's okay. If you still believe in the generative idea, we have these few elements to build upon. Isolate each of them and brainstorm, taking them together or separately, one at a time. Use them as the core around which to build a new piece, one more reflective of the strengths of those elements.

Apply the method we've discussed earlier in this section of the book: Add new ideas to ones already on the page; stay creative and open as you continue to develop the draft; listen to the piece and look for patterns that hold the key to a deep understanding of the piece. As you continue to build around the core ideas, you'll find that some of the images, sentences, descriptions, and bits of drama that you cut will make their way back. Not all of them, of course, but more than you planned to salvage. Seen within the context of a reenvisioned draft, they will take on a fresh appeal. You'll also have a richer understanding of the piece itself, gained from the hours of work and struggle you put into the earlier draft. At the risk of sounding like Pollyanna, the time spent on the "failed" draft was not wasted. You'll reap the rewards of those efforts in the next drafts, even ones that are far different from the first.

As you move forward with the salvaged draft, you'll find the piece takes on new energy. More ideas will occur to you and flow into the piece. It's not likely that you'll ride the mad rush that produced the first pages of the piece, but Hemingway talked about the advantages of turning down the burner to a low, steady flame. Within that approach, you'll work more productively. You'll live more completely in the world of the piece, rather than roaring ahead outside of it. Overheard lines will find their way in. Images will appear in your mind as you drive. Characters will speak while you're in the shower. The story will take on a life of its own.

PROMPT: Ask yourself if the piece *really* is not working or if your expectations for it are off the mark. Are you failing to achieve your goals for the piece, and if so, do those goals need to be evaluated and revised? Perhaps you are trying to force the piece to be something it doesn't want to be. Spend a writing session exploring these questions.

PROMPT: *Don't* write anything on the piece for at least a week. Do new ideas for it continue to pop into your mind? If so, you've put the project to the ultimate test. If the ideas keep coming, or if you're simply nagged by an urge to keep searching for ideas, write about your quest. Try to focus on the source of your desire to move forward with the piece. Elaborate on your interest in it, your goals for wanting to complete it.

PROMPT: This is a tough one: Spend a writing session or two literally starting over. Open a fresh Word doc and begin the piece again. Of course, you can include bits from the current version but don't even copy and paste them. Retype them. You cannot even have the other document open on your computer. Write them from memory.

Thinking in terms of occasions and opportunities rather than good and bad can open up a piece and help you realize its full potential. Allow the piece to grow and shift as it takes shape. As writers, our role is to guide the piece while allowing it to be what it wants to be. If it begins asserting an identity different from the one you envisioned at the start, that doesn't mean it's "bad" or not working. That assertion could mean you're onto something special, that the piece holds within itself far more opportunities than you could have foreseen at the start. Don't abandon the piece. Be willing to risk letting go.

CHAPTER THIRTY-FIVE

GOOD COP, BAD COP

I can't write five words but that I change seven.

—DOROTHY PARKER

As we move into the nitty-gritty of the piece in progress, you should be congratulated on making it this far. Most writers don't. They keep starting over with new ideas, and maybe that's what they need to do at their point in the lifelong apprenticeship of writing. But some lessons can only be learned by pushing deeply into a piece.

At this point, our level of commitment must be strong. We have spent quite a bit of time and effort on the piece, and odds are good that we have far more ahead of us. And so at this point, we start to wonder if it's worth it. Does this project warrant that level of risk and commitment and obligation? Are we just kidding ourselves? This part isn't as much fun, we might think. Long gone is the time when we were exhilarated by the concept, when we fancied ourselves geniuses to have created such a wonderful idea. Now we're hunkered deep down in the literary trenches, hoping that the final product will justify our blood, sweat, and tears.

Revision, however, doesn't have to be a painful task. It really can be fun. And it's definitely just as creative a process as those first freewrites that led us to this point. To get a better view of revision, consider this statement from writer Naomi Shihab Nye:

If a teacher told me to revise, I thought that meant my writing was a broken-down car that needed to go to the repair shop. I felt insulted. I didn't realize the teacher was saying, "Make it shine. It's worth it." Now I see revision as a beautiful word of hope. It's a new vision of something. It means you don't have to be perfect the first time. What a relief!

Focus on that relief as well as on that hope. Those feelings will help you to get through the final stages in the process. We now have to see the piece with cool objectivity, to assess its possibilities as we have done in the previous few chapters. In this chapter, we're going to focus on questions you can ask yourself about the piece as you revise it. Think of them as part of an interview, or even an interrogation, in which you are both the good cop and the bad cop. The questions offer new ways of looking at the piece and can lead to stronger revisions.

WHAT'S AT STAKE?

This question is raised often in writing workshops, usually after several people seated at the table have made fumbling attempts to articulate why the competent story in question doesn't quite grab them. Following these attempts to get at the source of everyone's discontent, one member of the group will ask the dreaded questions: "What's at stake in this story? Why should I care about what happens?" Editors and agents ask these questions, too, usually while issuing rejection slips. The question speaks to a fundamental issue in the piece. It tells us that even though the piece is well written, the reader doesn't care enough to find it interesting.

How important is the conflict to the characters in the story? What consequences does your character face if the colliding forces don't resolve themselves to his advantage? In short: What if he doesn't get what he wants? What does he lose? As Stanley Elkin once wrote, "I would never write about someone who was not at the end of his rope." The outcome of the poem, screenplay, story, memoir, or whatever you're writing must be of great significance to the people in the piece. To give your story the tension it needs, the stakes must be high. The outcome must matter to someone—and matter a lot.

PROMPT: Review your piece and ask yourself what's at stake for the people involved. Are the consequences high enough to sustain tension? Is this one of the most significant moments in a character's life? Is the decision, event, action, or dramatic element crucial to the future of the character, changing her life forever? If you're not sure what's at stake, dig deeper by writing about the character and exploring the situation.

THE WRITER'S IDEA BOOK

If you find that the stakes are not high enough, assess your choice of this story. Why is it important that you tell it? Why is this moment important in the lives of the characters? Is this the most important moment? Is the character, "at the end of his rope"? Then ask yourself how you can make the situation more significant. For example, your character is sick of his job and decides to quit. This decision means he will have to find a new job to support himself and his family. Quitting a job without having another one is always cause for some anxiety. Will the new job be even worse? Will he have to change himself in some way to make the new job work? Important questions. But are these questions significant enough to the character? Maybe.

But what if the job he's leaving had been The Dream Job when he landed it three years ago? His disillusionment with a sought-after career path has left him confused, and searching for direction. He now not only needs a new job, he needs a new life plan. The stakes are a little higher. And what if right after he makes the decision to leave the job behind, his wife tells him she's pregnant? Money will be tighter than ever. And what if the person who hired him is a beloved uncle who risked his own position to bring in the favored nephew? Quitting will break the uncle's heart. Or what if he must quit because of improprieties that sometime soon may come to light? I could go on, of course, but you get the point. We have raised the stakes, added new and powerful forces to the initial conflict.

PROMPT: Write about the primary conflict in your piece, the primary dilemma that drives it. What is the protagonist's goal? What does she want, and what forces are preventing her from getting it? Now, raise the stakes by changing the obstacle, making it larger in some way.

PROMPT: Change a relationship with another character (preferably the protagonist) in some way, as we did in the example above by bringing in an uncle. Would a conflict with a friend be intensified if the friend were changed to a sibling? Would a conflict with a friend be intensified if the friend also were a neighbor or colleague? Would the conflict be intensified if you introduced an element of rivalry?

PROMPT: Use the process again, this time changing the character in some way— her age, gender, or level of income. If she is single and childless, give her two children and an ugly divorce. If he is thirty years old, consider how the conflict would change if he were forty-five.

PROMPT: Use the process again, this time adding a new obstacle. If the conflict focuses on love, add a financial element. Now the conflict involves love and money. If the conflict focuses on money, add a love element or one involving the threat of violence.

PROMPT: If your piece has gone flat, find the place where the character is "at the end of his rope." If many pages precede this moment, consider cutting or condensing them. If you can't find such a moment, consider how you can create one. In both cases, focus on that moment, expanding and deepening it. Your interest in the project may return.

WHAT'S AT STAKE FOR YOU?

Why do you want to tell this story? Why are you writing it? Are you writing to understand a personal experience? Are you exploring an issue that fascinates you? Are these characters running around in your head, begging to be put on the page? Whatever your reason for writing, be aware of its influence on the piece itself. The greater the need to write the piece, the greater the urgency in telling this story, the more energy the piece will possess. The playwright Marsha Norman once said, "When I have ideas for plays I try to dismiss them so that I only end up writing the plays I *have* to write."

When I'm asked by writers to assess whether or not they should continue working on a project, my first response is, "Do you feel like you have to write it?" If you could easily let it go, then maybe you should. The piece lacks the personal urgency for you that will make it powerful for the reader. Give yourself permission to let go of the piece. If it still calls to you, still nags at you, then it's worth pursuing.

PROMPT: Explain your reasons for writing a story to an imagined reader. Tell him why the story is important to you, why you feel compelled to write it.

PROMPT: Try to make the story more important to you by assessing how much you care about the people involved. What might you change that would make you care more? What change would give the story greater urgency for you? Can you add an element that reveals something about you or focuses on a subject that is important to you?

HAVE YOU HEARD THIS ONE BEFORE?

No matter what subject you're exploring in your piece, odds are very good that it's been written about before. You need to make the material fresh for the reader as well as for yourself. You also need to pull against the tug of influence from the other work that you've read on the same subject. Some writers consciously avoid reading other work on the subject they're exploring, fearing that they will be influenced by it and lose the originality of their piece. They also fear that they might be disheartened through the realization that "it's been done."

THE WRITER'S IDEA BOOK

I once worked with a writer who was in such a position. She wanted to put her experiences during the Holocaust into a book, gathering the stories she would write for her family into a single collection. No end of books have been written about Holocaust experiences, and hers, though powerful in themselves, were not particularly unique. The one element that drew me most to her manuscript was the relationship between the teenage daughter (the writer) and her mother. The pair remained together throughout the ordeal of being imprisoned in concentration camps. I suggested that the writer move that relationship to the foreground and use it to connect the various stories she had written already. That relationship became the broader theme of the collection—a powerful mother-daughter story set within the horrors of the Holocaust. It was published as *My Mother's Eyes*, and the author has read from it throughout the country.

If you're feeling that you're trying to harvest literary fields that already have been overly worked, look for a fresh way to approach the material, a theme that is more closely connected to you. Know that everything has been said by writers of the past, but you have your own particular experiences to bring to that subject. Focus on those particulars, and you can make the well-worked fields sprout a new bounty. As Mark Twain wrote, "Adam was the only man who, when he said a good thing, knew that nobody had said it before him." And a whole lot of great stuff has been written since then!

PROMPT: Review your piece with an eye toward what is most fresh, most unique about it. Spend a writing session exploring that part. Look for ways to expand the role of that part in the piece.

PROMPT: If you've read a good bit on the subject you're exploring, look for opportunities to incorporate some of that reading into your piece. Earlier in the book we discussed Joan Didion's *The Year of Magical Thinking*, which chronicles her grief after the sudden death of her husband. The death of a spouse has been written about extensively in memoirs as well as in self-help and psychology books. Didion uses what has been written about grief to give new dimensions to her own story.

HOW DOES THE READER CONNECT?

Here we come back to the theme of showing vs. telling. Though we feel we have a great story to tell, we need to avoid *telling* it. We must present it in a way that allows the reader to connect to it. To do this, we rely on subtext and inference, allowing the reader to fill in the gaps of what is *not* said. Let the reader solve the mystery, reach conclusions, know more than the people in the story know. Resist the urge to explain.

Have faith in your reader's ability to make the connections and be sure that you have included enough details to guide the reader.

The most powerful stories will lay flat on the page if the reader doesn't get the chance to participate in the action. I have seen this occur many times in workshops. The writer is shocked that his tale of international intrigue and brushes with death has not riveted the group. People around the workshop table offer suggestions as to why they found the piece slow or somehow not engaging. The problem in most of these cases is that the piece relies too much on telling. The reader sits passively outside the drama, simply having everything explained to him. There's no connection.

PROMPT: Look for opportunities in your piece to shift from an explanatory to a dramatic presentation. In fact, pick one and change the mode. You can always change it back if you feel the information should be delivered in summary rather than through scene. But take the time to try the experiment.

PROMPT: Read one of your all-time favorite short pieces—a poem or short story or essay. Analyze the piece from a writer's perspective. How much is shown as opposed to told? What can you take from this analysis and apply to your own work.

A key strategy for connecting the reader is called "indirection." We don't directly state how a character feels. Instead, we show it. To get at the truth of something, to summon the emotions we want on the page, we can't always take the direct approach. We must experiment, try new angles, new voices. To this end, Emily Dickinson gave us some great advice:

> Tell all the Truth but tell it slant—
> Success in Circuit lies
> Too bright for our infirm Delight
> The Truth's superb surprise
> As Lightening to the Children eased
> With explanation kind
> The Truth must dazzle gradually
> Or every man be blind—

This poem pretty much says it all. As writers, our goal is to present our piece in a way that the reader gets to discover, and enjoy, that "superb surprise."

For example: A pair of men wait to die, stranded in the snow, perhaps their car has broken down, they have no radio or telephone, and no way back. Maybe someone will come along to save them, but probably not. Probably they will freeze to death. This scenario holds many dramatic possibilities. It offers conflict, tension, suspense. If you have done your work as a writer, you have developed these characters enough that the reader knows them well and cares about them. Your first impulse may be to have them talk about their impending death, to admit to each other their fear, their regrets, their dreams that will never be realized.

Or they could talk about hot dogs. Really. That would probably be a better approach. Maybe they could debate the chances of their college football team having a winning season next year. This approach is an example of indirection. If you follow your first impulse and allow the characters to voice their concerns, you defuse the tension in your story. You're pointing too directly at the source of the tension. But by using indirection—or, to use Dickinson's words, by telling it slant—you allow the tension to build beneath the surface. The tension informs every word the characters say, and the reader participates. She knows what these guys are feeling and brings that knowledge to the discussion of hot dogs. She is more engaged in the narrative because she is interpreting it. She is playing a part in it.

PROMPT: Create a scene in which two characters face a significant conflict. It need not be life or death, as in the scenario I created above, but it should be important to the characters. Let the reader know the conflict through detail and description. Then create dialogue in which the characters don't directly address their conflict. They speak on a completely unrelated topic.

PROMPT: Revise a scene you've already written by relying on indirection. Choose a scene in which the characters directly address their concern. For example, if you have a scene in which a couple argues about a problem, allow them to argue, but don't mention the problem. Or, you may not even allow them to argue, keeping the tension beneath the surface.

PROMPT: Write about a relationship in your life—or make up a relationship between two characters—by showing the characters doing something together. They could work together to fix a car, or they could attend a concert, or they could zip a Frisbee back and forth. Suggest the nature of the relationship by how they do the thing. Who leads and who follows? Who knows what he's doing and who doesn't? Do they talk to each other and share the experience in a positive way, or does it lead to disagreement? Take this one wherever it wants to go. The only rule is that the pair can't make direct statements about themselves or the relationship.

PROMPT: If you're blocked on a scene in your ongoing piece, step back and try to decide ways to approach the drama through indirection. Perhaps your feelings of frustration with the scene rise from it seeming flat and predictable. You may be right. Work to find a fresh point of entry and keep the tension beneath the surface.

CAN WE TALK ABOUT SOMETHING ELSE?

> Fun was a different kind of thing in the 1950s, mostly because there wasn't
> so much of it. That is not, let me say, a bad thing. Not a great thing, perhaps,
> but not a bad one either. You learned to wait for your pleasures, and to ap-
> preciate them when they came.

Bill Bryson opens a chapter with this observation in his memoir *The Life and Times of the Thunderbolt Kid*. The book loosely chronicles his childhood and adolescent years growing up in Des Moines, Iowa. His early years weren't particularly eventful, and so you wonder if at some point he wondered who would care about the story. He uses his signature humor to engage the reader, but he also expands the scope of the story through extensive research and observations about the 1950s in America. This narrative thread acts as a counterpoint to Bryson's personal anecdotes, giving them a sharp context and a larger resonance.

If your piece has begun to feel too narrow, too tightly focused on only one theme or dramatic thread, look for ways to expand it. A new element can add meaning and impact to the main thread, like adding a harmony line in a musical composition. For example, as mentioned in an earlier chapter, I got an idea for a magazine piece about a museum commemorating the famous outlaws Bonnie and Clyde. I would visit the museum, talk to the colorful caretaker, soak up some local flavor, and provide a bit of background on the gangsters. I told a friend, who is also a gifted writer, about my plan. In researching the museum, he found out about an annual Bonnie and Clyde festival held in the tiny Louisiana town where the museum is located. The festival featured a bizarre mix of small-town Americana—funnel cakes, kiddie rides, a parade—and bloody reenactments of the famous ambush in which Bonnie and Clyde were killed. We decided to collaborate on a piece combining the festival, the museum, and the caretaker. We pitched the idea to a magazine.

The editors liked the idea but wondered if we could frame it with details from the 1967 film about Bonnie and Clyde to fit an upcoming theme issue. We said fine. But the editors still felt the piece lacked a certain gravity. Could we add a more topical element? Something a little weightier? At that time, the news was full of stories about high school students shooting each other. In such a climate, should a festival be dramatizing gunplay to attract visitors? We added this element, which also complicated the tone of the article. How could we mix the wackiness of the festival with the tragedy of dead teens? And we later learned that the festival itself was held by good folks desperately trying to keep their little town alive. This element had to be included.

The article turned out far better than if I had kept to my original, much more narrow premise. It was noted in the next year's edition of *The Best American Travel Writing*, and I doubt it would have earned such an honor if I'd stuck to my original focus.

PROMPT: Return to your piece and add a new element to it, one that does not seem to be related. Try the mix-and-match approach, choosing two dissimilar elements from two lists. Look for connections within the topics as you write about them. Allow yourself to see both topics in new ways. The connections may not be apparent at first, but the topics could resonate on a deeper level. If you find that the topics simply don't gel in your mind, try two others, but don't give up too quickly. In her book *Refuge*, Terry Tempest Williams combines dissimilar topics: breast cancer and the fight to preserve a wildlife refuge. In her book *Hawk Flies Above*, Lisa Dale Norton combines her search for spiritual wholeness with a study of the ecology of the Nebraska sandhills.

PROMPT: Use the same approach as in the previous prompt, but this time add an element that's more closely related to the triggering idea. For example, the elements in the Bonnie and Clyde piece are related. For another example, in his book *Far From Home*, Ron Powers writes about the decay of small-town America as exemplified by Cairo, Illinois. After a section on Cairo, he shifts his focus to the upscale town of Kent, Connecticut, showing how it has grown from an insular community to a commuter village dominated by people who work outside the town. He then moves back and forth between the towns, enlarging his thesis and creating a richer book than a focus on either town would allow.

PROMPT: Add a third element to either of the two pieces you created in the previous two prompts. If using the first piece, which combines two different topics, add a third element that is closely related to one of the topics. If using the second piece, which combines closely related topics, add a third element that's vastly different. Work to enlarge the piece, striking even more notes than you could have struck before. For an example, let's look at "Safe Forever," a short story by Rick DeMarinis, in which several elements are combined into a unified whole. The story concerns an eleven-year-old narrator who is coping with life, with his mother and her live-in boyfriend. The boy vends ice cream for the boyfriend, and this arrangement is a further source of conflict. In one scene, the boy discovers his mother and her boyfriend in bed with another woman. The boy has a strange little scene with the woman as she leaves their house. Certainly these elements give the author plenty of material with which to create a richly textured story. But DeMarinis also includes a friend for the narrator. The boys go swimming, see a ball game, build models, and even explore sex together, through reading medical textbooks and spying on a girl in their neighborhood. Late in the story, the friend contracts polio. The narrator visits his friend in the hospital, sees him encased in a hideously clicking iron lung. The story is set in the weeks following V-J Day, when the country was undergoing an awkward yet heady transition to postwar life. Soldiers were returning and life was changing. DeMarinis uses all of these elements to create a powerful story that is thick with detail and incident but doesn't seem dense. He uses the elements to complicate and enlarge each other.

Can a story be too complicated, too heavily nuanced? Absolutely. And simple stories can work very well. But many more stories suffer from being too familiar and too thinly imagined than suffer from too many complications. The point to this discussion is to explore the dramatic potential of an idea. Strive for freshness and surprise. When you find your piece simply has too many elements, subordinate or cut one. Look for ways to balance the elements. This can be difficult, but it's worth a try.

WHOSE STORY IS IT?

As we discussed in the chapter on point of view, the protagonist—or point-of-view character—should be at the center of the piece. The reader's primary interest focuses on that character's fortunes. As you assess your piece, ask yourself if that's the case. Sometimes our first idea needs to change and grow. The character who introduces us to the project sometimes turns out to be merely a way into the piece. At some point, we need to discard that character, deciding that the story truly belongs to someone else. That's a major decision, of course, that could change the piece completely.

Sometimes you're working on your piece, following the main idea, when you notice a minor thread beginning to assert itself. This thread could be a minor character in your screenplay or novel, perhaps a subordinate subject in a poem, a secondary subject in your memoir. You feel a growing interest in this character or topic and find yourself lingering there longer than planned. Perhaps you even let a few people read the piece, and they all comment on that aspect of it. What does this mean?

You may need to shift your focus. How would your piece change if you moved that character to the foreground? Does the character provide an interesting complication, or does the character warrant a major change in the design of the story?

Of course, minor characters sometimes possess a certain charm within a limited role and draw attention to themselves, even drawing the reader's interest away from the main characters. In her wonderful book *Get That Novel Written!*, Donna Levin calls this "the Barney Fife Syndrome," named after the bumbling deputy on

THE WRITER'S IDEA BOOK

the old *The Andy Griffith Show*. If the show were recast to feature Barney, however, it would have become a slapstick farce rather than a homey, feel-good comedy. Small doses of Barney worked better, giving the show a comedic range without making it a completely different type of show.

To extend Donna's point by returning to television, the show *Happy Days* began as a quirky and somewhat textured evocation of the 1950s. It had a quiet charm and an ideal protagonist to render that charm: Richie Cunningham. A minor character named Fonzie added a nice note of rebellion, a counterpoint to good-guy Richie. Fonzie was 1950s-cool, and yet his obvious personal limitations added an element of melancholy. The audience sensed this was the heyday for such guys, and life would never be so good for them again. The audience loved the Fonz, and so the writers shifted the focus to emphasize him. But he was a stereotype, really, not a character who offered a lot of range. The new approach constricted all the other characters, turning them into broad stereotypes, too. The show lost its quiet charm and became a caricature of itself.

The point is that shifting your focus will have consequences for your story. Try to determine if this character requires you to explode the original idea, or if you've simply happened upon an engaging character who adds a new layer of charm to the story. Keeping the character in a limited role can be difficult, especially when readers laud the character. "I love the woman who smokes on the train!" they'll say with delight. What writer can resist such delight from readers?

If a minor character is drawing the most attention but you're sure it's not his story, examine your protagonist. Is he compelling enough? Perhaps the minor character is simply spilling into the story's missing center. It may be time, as we discussed earlier in the chapter, to raise the stakes for the protagonist.

It need not be a character drawing attention. It could be a theme, a subplot, a place. Your drama set in the Rockies is dwarfed, literally, by the setting. Perhaps the setting needs to be pushed to the foreground, made a character in its own right. Perhaps the story has less to do with the conflict between your characters than a conflict between the characters and the place they live.

The same situation can occur in essays and memoirs. You want to focus on a particular person, and yet another person keeps wedging into the spotlight. And readers seem to respond to this person. They're curious about her. You find yourself responding, too. Perhaps your essay is a recollection of a particular place where you played as a child—a grove of trees or the sprawling backyard of a long-forgotten friend. It's also a meditation on childhood, and on the power of imagination that dims with time. You have children of your own now and conceive of your essay as a comparison between where they play and where you played, using the place as a metaphor for childhood itself.

Except that the long-forgotten friend keeps butting in. You find yourself describing the friend for pages, recalling specific summer days and the games the two of you played. You remember in sudden, sharp detail, the look on the friend's face when it was time for you to go home to eat dinner. You find yourself struggling to get back to your idea about the play areas and watching your own kids. Every time you end a passage about the friend, you sense a need for more. Perhaps it's time to put aside the essay about childhood places of play and focus on an essay about a long-forgotten friendship.

PROMPT: Let's go back to television for a moment. You have been called in to create a spin-off of your work in progress or from a completed piece. Your new show focuses on a single character or setting or event from the ongoing work. Choose the focus of your spin-off and write a few pages. Do you find it more or less engaging than the longer work?

PROMPT: Spend a session exploring your piece with a different thematic goal in mind. For example, if your story seems to be about people struggling with the tenets of their conservative religious training, push these folks and their situation forward with a new focus, perhaps their struggle with the mores of the small, southern town where they live.

PROMPT: Look closely at the piece and try to answer the question about whose story it is. If you're convinced the protagonist should remain at the center of the piece, how can you continue to draw power and pleasure from the "Barney Fife" character while keeping him in subordinate role?

PROMPT: Spend a writing session focused on the "Barney Fife" element. Allow it to be its own story. Explore its possibilities.

The broad-ranging questions speak to the essence of the piece. Your answers will determine its ultimate success. Of course, there are other questions you can ask, ones we've mentioned throughout this book, about particular elements in the piece. Is the point of view the best one for the material? Are the characters fully realized in a way that draws the reader's interest and sympathies? Are the details rich and vivid, drawing the reader into the world of the piece? Have you sustained dramatic tension throughout the piece, keeping the reader's interest—and the pages turning? All of these questions must be answered as you step back and evaluate how well the piece is working and where new opportunities for improving the piece are calling to you.

If you can gain enough distance to see the piece's possibilities and evaluate it with a cool eye, you can answer these questions successfully and reach a level of contentment with what you've managed to achieve. Sometimes we lock into a piece too soon, feeling that it must be told in a particular way. We limit the possibilities of our ideas before exploring them and experimenting with them. This syndrome can be especially tough to break through when we have finished a first draft. The words take on a certain inevitability, as if the piece can only take that form and no other. Let's try some ways to see a piece in a new light. In the words of Rachel Carson, "The discipline of the writer is to learn to be still and listen to what his subject has to say." The answers to all of these questions, in other words, are there on the page. It is up to us to hear what they're telling us.

CHAPTER THIRTY-SIX

UPS, GPS, AND WTF

You write to communicate to the hearts and minds of others what's burning inside you. And we edit to let the fire show through the smoke.

—ARTHUR POLOTNIK

It's now time for the serious troubleshooting. Maybe you've worked your way methodically through the book and have a piece well underway as a result. Or perhaps you already had a piece in motion and have come here in order to figure out what type of piece you've been developing. It may have begun on one subject and somehow evolved into something else. Perhaps it began in a different form or genre but keeps tugging against you to switch into another one, like a dog straining at its leash as you walk along the sidewalk. Perhaps it has simply grown dull for you. You've put in enough hours that you want to finish it, but you're wrestling with how to do that. When you read the piece, you find it boring. Or, worse, you've given it to a few other readers who also seem to think it's boring. We feel like chucking the whole thing and taking up a different artistic medium altogether. Pottery, we've heard, can be a lot of fun.

Maybe the problem lies in the storytelling rather than the story. If you're struggling with a piece of writing, take time to think about the issue. Is it a matter of UPS, GPS, or WTF? In this chapter we'll look at all three to evaluate the piece in hopes of shedding light on its nature and possibilities.

UPS

Consider method of delivery, which can be as important as what you're trying to say (much like choosing the right parcel service to insure your package arrives). Sometimes we're so intent on getting the point across that we can neglect the storytelling.

I see this dilemma most often with writers working on memoirs. The writer knows the focus of the piece because she *is* the protagonist. The story is about her. In some ways she knows the story *too* well. Let's say we have a writer who is working on a memoir about her battle with breast cancer. The subject obviously is very serious and well worth exploring. The writer knows what she wants to say about it. She has learned the hard lessons that such a formidable challenge can teach. She begins with the day she hears the terrible news and walks the reader step by step through the various medical procedures. She tells the reader how the illness changed nearly every aspect of her life. She tells us what the illness has taught her about herself and offers advice to other women about surviving such a dreaded disease. She tells the reader to support breast cancer research. In fact, even before she sat down to write the first page, she knew that her goal was to spread that message of awareness.

The problems from a writing perspective should be clear. First, you'll notice that I use "tells" rather than "shows" to describe her approach. When we already know what we want to say, the message we plan to deliver, we tend to rely on an expository approach rather than a dramatic one, and we've discussed how this approach undermines the reader's experience. The memoir becomes more like a lecture than a story—the reader passively listening to, rather than engaging in, the story.

Next, the writer concentrated on delivering a message tends to be too narrowly focused. She knows the goal of every page and does not stray from it—leading to what we called in an earlier chapter a "one-note wonder." We hear about the situation and feel immediate sympathy for the protagonist—such a tough challenge for her to face. We then learn and accept the message of the piece. But the writer continues, telling us what happened next and on and on. We soon find our interest waning. There will be no discoveries for us because there will be no discoveries for the writer.

When taking the memoir to her writing group or to agents and editors, this writer is surprised that readers aren't bowled over by her manuscript. She's a competent writer and she has remained true to her subject, achieving her goal of writing about this difficult time in her life and even delivering her larger message about the need for greater awareness. She's confused about why readers aren't more engaged and struggles to improve the manuscript, cutting a bit here and adding a bit there. She's told that the story is slow, so she trims some material to speed the pace.

The problem is not as much that it's too slow as that it's boring. Despite the serious and genuine nature of the material, it is too narrow, too controlled. There's no interesting subtext to engage the reader because the writer knows exactly what she wants to say and never deviates from saying it.

Hannah Arendt speaks to this situation when she writes, "Storytelling reveals meaning without committing the error of defining it." Reveal your meaning and let the reader define. That's where the connection is made. And allow the story to reveal its own meanings. To quote the writer Sharon O'Brien, "Writing became such a process of discovery that I couldn't wait to get to work in the morning. I wanted to know what I was going to say."

As we've discussed, in our first drafts we're often telling the story to ourselves. But that draft should allow for discoveries, for our own revelations, for the piece to take its own direction. Rather than delivering our message, we need to focus on evoking the moments and the people in our story. We then must pull back.

PROMPT: Go through your current draft and highlight all the instances of narrative summary—where you're telling the reader what happened rather than evoking places and people and scenes dramatically. Pick one event that is summarized and dramatize instead. Turn it into a scene. Give us the details and the dialogue. Capture and evoke the moment.

PROMPT: To extend the previous prompt, dramatize another scene that is summarized in the current draft. And another and another until you surprise yourself at least once. By "surprise" I mean that you discover something in a scene that you didn't expect—an observation about a character or, if you're writing from personal experience, a detail that surfaced from your memory. For example, I worked with a writer who was writing a book-length memoir about a lingering medical issue that had caused significant changes in her life. Though she was a good writer, she was succumbing to the "one-note wonder" syndrome. The piece was told in an unrelieved tone of somber acceptance. When she began (grudgingly) to present some of the story in scenes, she was surprised at a rising tone of anger—at life, at her family and friends, at the illness, even at herself. She hadn't allowed herself to express that emotion on the page, maintaining a wise, well-informed, almost clinical stance. That stance was part of the message she wanted to deliver right from the start. The piece, needless to say, took on new energy when she abandoned that stance and began dealing with less controlled emotions.

PROMPT: Write the history of the project so far, focusing on your initial goals for the piece. Was there a message you wanted to deliver? Are you trying too hard to

THE WRITER'S IDEA BOOK

deliver it? Have you allowed the piece to grow and change or are you guiding it too forcefully?

PROMPT: Write down all your initial goals for the piece. Note which ones involve theme—such as "I wanted to write about the importance of parenthood"—as opposed to drama—such as "I want to write about a man struggling to be a good single father." Focus on the latter, cutting away all passages that speak to theme rather than story. Can you begin moving forward with the piece using only these parts?

PROMPT: When you think about your theme, what two or three details or characters come to mind? Take time to freewrite about it, just writing whatever comes into your mind. Let the images pour out, even if they don't seem related—in fact, *especially* if they don't seem related. I tried this strategy with a writer who was working on a piece about his very difficult experience weaning himself from pain medication he had taken for years to treat a serious back injury. The piece, though passionate and heartfelt, was suffering from UPS. At first he listed details already related in the draft, but by continuing to focus on whatever images came to mind, he surprised us. A couple that I recall: When he woke in the morning, he would see his hand gripping tightly to his pillow—white-knuckling it. The image gave him—and the reader—a keen awareness that the pain was inescapable, that even while asleep he was fighting it. He also noted his doctor's eyeglasses, which he said he'd never really thought about before. The frames of the glasses were unique and obviously very expensive. The lenses exaggerated the size of the doctor's eyes, giving him a quizzical, almost stupefied look as he continued to dispense prescriptions for the addictive medication. The writer said they embodied his anger at the helplessness of the medical community and the blithe way his doctor kept the writer addicted while making money off his injury. By adding images like those two, the writer added dimension and engagement to his story. The reader understood his meaning implicitly, without being told, and the meaning thereby deepened.

PROMPT: Do the previous prompt, but this time focus on dialogue—on what your characters say. If you're writing from personal experience, focus on what people actually said. If you're writing fiction, focus on a single character and let them pour forth. Don't limit him to speaking only about the subject of the story. Then choose another character and do the same.

GPS

Let's look at the structure and direction of your piece and try to find ways to clarify it—or to determine if you've taken a wrong turn somewhere. Perhaps your literary GPS keeps saying "recalculating" in an annoying tone of voice. Sometimes we know the story we want to tell but struggle with how to present it. The default structure, of course, is simple chronology—this happened and then this happened and then this happened, etc. Other times, we get mired in flashbacks, which tend to be delivered in summary and can shift the narrative from showing mode to telling mode.

We discussed structure in a couple of earlier chapters, so let's focus here on troubleshooting a structure that's not working. Have you started as close to the end as possible? Have you whittled away the nonessentials, presenting only the most necessary and engaging moments in the story? Leo Tolstoy speaks directly to these questions by saying, "Drama, instead of telling us the whole of a man's life, must place him in such a situation, tie such a knot, that when it is untied, the whole man is visible."

Focus on that situation and on tying that knot. Show us how the character struggles to untie that knot. Question with the skepticism of a steely judge anything in the piece that doesn't pertain to the essential conflict. Keep the dramatic heat on high by trimming away anything that cools the piece, such as long flashbacks or exposition. Think in terms of digging deeply rather than ranging widely.

Think, too, in terms of causal connection between events. The piece shouldn't be built on "this happened and then this happened"; it needs to be "this happened *because* this happened." The lack of causal connection is why many pieces fail to keep the reader engaged. A writer, for example, wants to work on a book about a fascinating trip abroad or a stint in the military. After hearing the writer relate a few tales of the time, everyone tells him "You need to write a book about that." The book, however, becomes a series of loosely connected anecdotes that lack causal connection. The piece lacks tension and momentum. The writer grows confused by the apathy of people who read the piece because when he told the same stories at dinner parties his audience was completely engaged. Well, a story on the page needs to be more than a tossed salad of anecdotes. The stories need to have a causal connection. Now, you might raise an exception, citing great travel writers such as Bill Bryson or Peter Mayle, whose travelogues engage us without such deep connection between events. Those writers, however, rely primarily on their powers of voice and observation. They entertain us with their unique perspectives. In short: We enjoy the trip. It doesn't have to be pushed by a dramatic situation. The writer need not struggle against a knot or be revealed by the knot's unraveling. We look forward to the next trip we can take with these writers, no matter where we're headed. For the rest of us, however, the rules apply.

PROMPT: Harold Ross, the colorful founder of *The New Yorker* magazine, once quipped, "I asked Ring Lardner the other day how he writes his short stories, and he said he wrote a few widely separated words or phrases on a piece of paper and then went back and filled in the spaces." He's joking, of course, but let's try that approach. Outline your piece and then pull from the outline the main events. Then look for ways to more effectively fill in the spaces, with an eye toward making those causal connections.

PROMPT: Picking up from the previous prompt, look for places in your outline where you note scenes or events that lack a causal connection. Have you taken a wrong turn and now need to double back? Have you included scenes that have no business being there?

PROMPT: Picking up from the Tolstoy quote, try to define the "knot" with which your protagonist is struggling. Spend a half hour or so writing about it. When distilled to its essence, what conflict is your piece exploring? Then read your draft with an eye toward tightening that knot.

PROMPT: If you feel the piece is wandering too far, give it a clear temporal or spatial frame, as we discussed earlier—a distinct shape created by, for example, a season of the year, a holiday, a road trip, and so on. The compression and shape created by the frame can supply a greater sense of control and of unity in your story.

If any and all attempts at giving shape to the piece fail, perhaps the problem isn't structural. Perhaps, instead, the piece wanders aimlessly because it's looking for itself. You don't yet know the dramatic question you're hoping to answer. In that case, read on.

WTF

Sometimes we simply don't know where we're going or what we've got. We have piled up quite a few pages by this point, but the piece remains a mystery—or maybe more like one hot mess. Though you have worked on it faithfully and consistently, it has yet to reveal itself to you. New characters emerge and take center stage and then fade away as newer characters grab the spotlight. New complications arise to push the story forward but lead to dead ends. You change the point of view, but after initial promise, it solves nothing. Neither UPS nor GPS will help. You are simply lost.

First: Don't despair. If you remain engaged by the piece, you have some valid and valuable connection to it—you just need to understand it. At these times, writing truly is an act of faith. In fact, faith might be all we have. If you're tired of the piece and have no energy for or interest in it right now, put it away. If you remain interested, however, then that is a sign it's worth pursuing.

Begin by trusting that feeling of engagement with the material. Then let out some line on your literary fishing rod; allow the story to set out for deeper water. In other words, don't try so hard to control it. Allow it to be what it wants. Maybe the struggle you're having results from your pushing it in one direction when it really it wants to go in another. If that's the case, there's little you can do to make it work.

The piece might have begun, for example, as a story about a couple struggling with their marriage due to their inability to conceive a child. The writer drew the idea for the story from a friend who is in that situation and confided in the writer. (Silly friend to have confided in a writer, I know.) The writer fictionalized the situation but stayed true to the basics of it. The early pages came easily, but then the piece began to lose steam. The writer added a few fictional complications but none seemed to fit the piece. She tried writing through to the end, but all the resolutions strike her as hackneyed, lacking invention or nuance. And so she continues to plod through draft after draft but is ready to give up. She needs to go back to the start, to figure out her own connection to the piece. Why is she intrigued by it? She doesn't face the dilemma personally so why does she want to write about it? What's the personal connection?

The great Eudora Welty wrote, "Writing a story or a novel is one way of discovering sequence in experience, of stumbling upon cause and effect in the happenings of a writer's own life." The key word in this insight is "discovering." We need to reveal to ourselves our connection to the situation and then reveal the connections among the events.

The writer of the marital discord story might discover that what began as her friend's story has become her own. That's why she feels such a strong connection to it. At some level, it speaks to her own fears of separation from a mate due to forces beyond her control. It might speak to her deeper fear of isolation, of being alone. With those ideas in mind, she can refocus the story—she might even start over. In the foreword to this book, I quoted author Annie Dillard speaking to the need to abandon the generative idea after the piece has taken on a direction of its own. "Tear up the runway," Dillard says. "It helped you take off, and you don't need it now."

Or, maybe you can salvage the story of the struggling couple. With a greater understanding of your personal connection to it, you can shift the emphasis. Instead of focusing on the couple coming to terms with their inability to have a child, the story becomes one of a woman who fears a life of loneliness, worrying that her marriage will fall apart, wondering about her identity in life if she cannot be a mother.

THE WRITER'S IDEA BOOK

PROMPT: Read what you've written so far. Try to determine your personal connection to the piece. Why are you engaged by it? What thoughts, ideas, and emotions within you does it touch?

PROMPT: Look for image patterns within the piece—recurring references to nature, for example, or to styles of clothing. What clues to the true nature of the piece do those patterns suggest? Rather than just thinking about these clues, write about them. Often, we make our best discoveries about our writing through writing.

PROMPT: Pick one pattern of images—or simply one image that stands out for you—and spend a session writing a new piece focused on it. Don't feel the piece must extend or be closely connected to the troubled draft. Let it go where it wants to go. Then put it away for a few days before rereading it, looking for those connections—a similarity of tone, or perhaps a noticeable difference in tone. The new piece, for example, might involve a lot of humor and whimsy while the troubled piece is serious and direct. How would that piece change if you added humor to it?

PROMPT: Sometimes a piece we've worked on for a while takes on a certain inevitability, as we've discussed in previous chapters. Experiment by cutting a few of the elements—lines of dialogue, images, character actions—that have been in the piece since its early stages. How does the piece change without these elements?

This scenario illustrates how we can get back on track when we're completely lost. The key is to begin with what you do know—that you believe in the piece and want very much to write it. Then try to gain a better understanding of your connection to it. Use that awareness to guide the piece. We'll look at a few more strategies for confronting and moving past the WTF stage. Take heart in the words of John Steinbeck who admitted, "I have written a great many stories and I still don't know how to go about it except to write it and take my chances." And he won a Nobel Prize in Literature! Sometimes taking our chances is all we can do.

CHAPTER THIRTY-SEVEN

BLOW IT UP

Be willing to have it so. Acceptance of what has happened is the first step to overcoming the consequences of any misfortune.

—WILLIAM JAMES

Pablo Picasso said, "Every act of creation is first an act of destruction." I wasn't there when he said it, and I have no idea what he meant. He may have been in a bad mood. But I've always thought the statement sounded pretty cool. It makes the creative artist seem powerful and iconoclastic, smashing with the hammer of artistic vision the statues of conformity. As writers, we do have that power, if we're willing to use it.

For our purposes, however, we're going to use the quote to begin a discussion of destroying our initial idea. As we've discussed in previous chapters, sometimes the generative idea for a piece is more an avenue to richer ideas than an end in itself. At those times, we must be willing to let go of our initial premise. We have to explode the idea. In some ways, to echo Picasso, this is the first act of creation.

There are few comments more deflating than when your readers agree that your twenty-five-page story "really begins on page twenty-four." We've worked hard on those first twenty-three pages. They're honed and crafted and have a lot of good lines in them. And now we're supposed to believe they're only so much throat-clearing? A mere prelude to the *real* story? Sometimes the answer is yes.

At such times, we must remember that we wouldn't have achieved the real start of the story if we hadn't written what came before. Our initial premise led us to literary gold, even though now it must be discarded. I had this experience with a story I wrote a few years ago. It concerns a mother and daughter who are lost in Los Angeles, far from their Ohio home. I worked hours on extended dialogues between the characters, took great pains to deliver the exposition in an unobtrusive way. I had conceived the story much like a play, focusing on subtle shifts of character as the mother and daughter conversed. Near the end, two rough-looking guys enter the doughnut shop where the story takes place. My plan was to have a brief encounter with the men and for the foursome to leave together at the end. Several readers said they felt the story spark to life when the two guys enter. But that was at the end! This was a Beckett-like story of tightly woven dialogue, not some tale of women being picked up by truckers. *Hel-loo.* Tightly woven Beckett-like dialogue here. You folks are missing the point.

I let the story sit for some months. Then I read it with a fresh view. Then I re-read the readers' comments. They were right. My pages of tightly woven, Beckett-like dialogue were cut extensively. I now could see that much of it was self conscious and tiresome anyway. The tension between the mother and daughter as they sat in a doughnut shop wasn't enough to carry the story. After five pages or so, the story felt static. In the revised version, the men enter the doughnut shop on the top of page two. The foursome is out the door by page seven. But those weeks of working the dialogue helped me get to know the mother and daughter, and my knowledge of them led to surprising turns in the revised story, turns I don't know I'd have imagined if I hadn't had such a rounded understanding of the characters.

When you find yourself in a similar place, listen to your readers. If only one reader advises to start with the ending, give the piece to a second reader or put it away for a while. Your first reader may be imposing her own vision of your story world and is stating the way she would handle the material. If a second reader offers similar advice, it's worth considering. If the second reader says something more like, "It seemed kind of slow to me," ask for specific places where it seemed most interesting. If the reader points to the place the first reader suggested to begin the story, you have a decision to make.

Lopping away a big chunk of story isn't easy and requires consideration. Put the piece away and move on to a new one for a while. Give the piece at least a month to cool off. Set a date for rereading it. Put it on your calendar. The date will ensure you don't read it sooner than is helpful, and it also reminds you the piece is waiting. We sometimes forget about our projects for so long that we have trouble bringing them back to life. And so the deadline works in two ways, making sure you don't return too soon or wait too long.

When you return to the piece, note in the margins where it's working and where it needs help. Are the readers correct in their assessment of the sections that could be cut or be significantly condensed? Read the piece again, beginning at the place where it might be made to start. Does it make a strong opening? What needs to be pulled from the cut material and how much can be set free?

LETTING GO

It takes a certain amount of courage to cut away pages of a project. Don't forget to put these pages in your idea file or in a separate document. They may contain the seed of another idea or lines that you don't want to throw away. But when you've cut the pages, they're gone. Don't agonize over them or rationalize ways of returning them to the story.

As we've discussed earlier, it's tough to let go of this material because it has taken on a sense of inevitability. It's been in the piece for so long it seems organic. We've read and reread these passages. We expect them to appear, and we recognize their rhythms. In fact, in some ways, we don't even see them anymore. We take their presence for granted.

Putting a piece away for a while can lessen that sense of inevitability. When we can read with a fresh vision, the story loses its familiarity. At that time, ask yourself if this or that section is necessary, if this or that event signals a new and better course for the piece. Are there places where you must, to paraphrase Faulkner, kill your darlings? Scenes and sentences can overstay their welcome because they are favorites. Usually, we like them because they possess a brio that reflects well on us as writers. They make us sound good. But are they relics of an earlier vision for the piece? Are they there *only* because they make you sound good? If so, they must be killed.

Letting a piece go where it wants to go also can be difficult for us. Our initial premise dictates a certain structure, a clear narrative path. And yet, when a piece is well underway, it takes on a will of its own. I don't talk a lot about characters taking over or telling the writer what to write. I've always found such talk a bit fallacious and self-aggrandizing, turning the creative process (and therefore, the creative artist) into an inspired genius in touch with mysterious forces beyond the powers of normal folk.

At the same time, I don't agree with Nabokov's famous comment about characters being his "galley slaves." The creative process isn't just a mechanized act of will, an application of learned techniques. Our subconscious minds, the myth-making power of our imaginations, do come into play. Conscious craft and subconscious artistry unite in a piece, granting it a power we can't always control. I don't know that it's a matter of characters taking over. I think it's that, at some point, the story moves along its own path. It knows what it wants to be, even when we have different ideas about what it *should* be.

Creative writing is such an intuitive act that it's tough to make this point in a concrete way. To recognize when you're forcing a piece away from its natural course, look for places where it begins to sound awkward to your artistic ear. Do you find yourself, at some level, asking if the character would really do that? Does a scene end with one character having the last word in a way that seems false? Does the analysis of a key event in your personal essay serve more to make you look innocent than to provide an authentic insight? Is your poem more mysterious than is necessary, straining for a resonance it doesn't truly possess? Trust your instincts. Perhaps you're working against your own piece. You've moved beyond your initial premise into territory you may not want to visit, but your uneasiness is suggesting you have to explode that generative idea and move on. Responding to that uneasiness, even consciously feeling it, requires spending enough time on a piece to really hear what it's telling you.

At first, we may feel uneasy about an aspect of the piece in a faint way. We may feel it sometimes as we read, but at other times, it feels just fine. Sometimes it takes another reader to point it out, causing us to say, "I sort of wondered about that part. It never seemed quite right to me."

For example, we're trying to end a scene but nothing works, nothing feels like the natural place to stop. Whatever final lines we write don't have the ring of finality. If you want to say that the characters have taken over, that they've decided they don't want to stop talking, fine. I would phrase it more along the lines of the story asserting its own course. The falseness enters because we are sticking too closely to our idea of where the story must go. We say to ourselves, "This isn't an important scene. It's just a transition, taking me from this event to that event. I can't spend ten pages on a transitional scene." And yet, something about that transitional scene remains unresolved. If we trust our intuition, we allow the scene to find its own resolution. Perhaps a better idea is emerging, but we stick stubbornly to our original concept of the piece, trying not to notice that something about the scene bothers us every time we read it. Something just doesn't quite feel right.

Try not to see the need to explode your idea, blowing it up and beginning a new course, as a failure. It's not. It's another way of perceiving and building upon the possibilities of the original idea. The explosion creates all sorts of wonderful fragments that can be new ideas in themselves. In his book *Revision: A Creative Approach to Writing and Rewriting Fiction*, David Michael Kaplan writes of *re-vision*, seeing a project in a new way. The revision stage, as I mentioned earlier, involves just as much creativity as the earlier stages.

PROMPT: Review your work in progress, looking for places that concern you, ones that don't seem to be working. Rather than cutting them, explore them by writing another page or two. You could extend them, writing beyond what you have done so far. You could write *about* them, explaining why you find them troublesome. Don't put pressure on the pages you write. Use them as a way of spending more time on a place in your piece that needs more attention.

PROMPT: Review your work in progress, looking for places that particularly interest you. Explore them by writing another page or two. As with the previous prompt, you could extend them or simply write about why you like them.

PROMPT: Where does the piece seem to be working best? Where is it most genuine? Do these sections grow out of the original idea or do they hint of better ideas, ones that move beyond the original idea? If the former, spend a session pushing ahead on that original idea. If the latter, spend a session moving past it, following the lead of the sections working best.

PROMPT: Is one aspect of the piece trying to dominate or even take over the piece? Is it possible that the original idea needs to be discarded or perhaps refocused to allow this aspect to surface or develop in the foreground? Spend some time exploring this possible new focus.

PROMPT: Imagine that you've lost—due to a computer failure or a literary burglar—the entire work in progress. If necessary, hide anything you've written on the piece from yourself. Begin again. Write a few pages. Some you'll be able to write from memory, while some you'll have to create afresh. When you finish, compare the new version to the "lost" one. How do they differ? What discoveries did you make in the new version?

PROMPT: Go through work you've done in the past, whether or not it's finished, that you feel didn't quite work in the way you hoped. Choose one piece and reread it. Can you find places where the piece goes awry? Are there places where you made a wrong turn? Focusing on those places, write new material, allowing the piece to push off in a fresh direction.

PROMPT: Pick another piece from your pile. Try to read it without thinking about the goals for the piece, your intentions when you wrote it. Read it, if possible, as if

THE WRITER'S IDEA BOOK

someone else wrote it. Then write an analysis of the piece, its strengths and weaknesses. Sometimes we find that a story we thought was about one idea was truly about a different idea.

PROMPT: Spend a session on an alternative scene or version of the piece in progress. For example, if your piece leads to a climactic scene in which the protagonist reaches a new level of insight, deny her that insight. Have her reach a completely different conclusion. For example, in the classic story "Araby" by James Joyce, the protagonist goes to a carnival to buy something for a girl with whom he is smitten. The story leads to the moment when the boy reaches a booth where he hopes to find the right gift. While standing there, he realizes he has been foolishly romantic in his quest and walks away empty-handed. As an alternative, the author might have allowed the boy to select a gift and bring it home without having reached any conclusions about his emotional state.

PROMPT: You've been told to condense the piece to two pages. Everything must go but the best, most essential, parts of the piece. Choose what remains. The two pages need not be self-contained or even make sense when read from start to finish. You might choose six lines of dialogue from one scene, a one-sentence description from another page, and so on. When you have made your selections, write a short explanation to explain them. As you're doing this exercise, be mindful of what you value most in the piece and look for ways of building on those elements so that the entire piece reaches that level of interest for you.

PROMPT: Loosen the reins on a character by writing a scene (or recalling a time, if you're writing nonfiction) in which the character acts in a way that contradicts what you've presented already. Your father figure, for example, who has shown patience with a difficult situation could be seen throwing a fickle toaster against a wall. The point of this exercise is not necessarily to show many sides of a character. Our goal is to relax our own assumptions and expectations about a character, to let them act on their own.

WARNING SIGNS

For a variety of reasons, an idea sometimes just doesn't quite work. It may be a large idea—for a book-length project or a screenplay. It might be for a smaller piece. It might even be an idea for a character or a situation within a piece. At some point, we have to let go. Smaller ones, of course, are easier to give up. A sixty-page start on a stalled novel is a lot tougher to put aside.

But how do we know when it's time to let go—to blow it up and move on to a new project? Of course, there's no rule of thumb or step-by-step formula for answering that question. However, there are warning signs that an idea is in trouble. Let's explore a few of them.

SUCCESSIVE DRAFTS DON'T HELP

Sometimes an idea resists our attempts to develop it. As we've discussed, listening to the idea can help. It may be resisting because it doesn't want to follow our prescriptions for what it needs to be. It wants to be something different, and it's up to us to figure out the nature of the idea. But despite draft after draft and days and weeks and months of work, the idea isn't becoming clearer to us and it isn't working on the page. It may be time to let go.

For example, a writer wants to write about a family picnic, held many years ago, that speaks to the nature of her childhood. Images of the event have been seeping into her mind—half-remembered comments, the geranium-colored dress her mother wore and the startling look of sadness in her eyes when, briefly, she took off her sunglasses. The writer begins writing about everything she can remember, trying to capture the mixture of innocence and melancholy, the joy of a sunny summer day in childhood and the inkling that life has less carefree days in store for us. But on the page, the event feels pedestrian, anecdotal. Who cares about any of this stuff? The writer adds new dramatic elements, turning the memoir into fiction in hopes of energizing the piece while capturing a deeper truth. With those changes, however, she drifts further away from her initial vision. Now there are moments bordering on melodrama. There's a strain, a false note running through the piece that's tough to pinpoint. She switches the point of view, changes characters and actions. She tries a lighter tone, then a darker one. She introduces an entirely new context for the event. She brings it to her writers' group, hoping for some insight. She puts it away for a month, but upon returning, her sense of the piece is even more remote. It seems wooden and self-conscious, and she can't quite grasp the feeling that inspired her to develop the idea in the first place.

As writers, we hear that genius is mostly a matter of hard work, and that's true. But this writer can make herself crazy trying to develop this idea, or she can admit that, at least for now, it's not going to happen. Continued work, rather than shedding light, seems to move the piece further away from its possibilities.

ENTHUSIASM WANES

Sometimes we come up with an idea that seems great, especially to anyone we tell about it. We convulse people at parties with the story about our uncle Dave and his bizarre kleptomania. "You've got to put him in a story," people tell you time and again. And so you try, giggling away at the keyboard, the imagined sounds of a laughing reader inspiring you forward. But as the story develops, it rings false. Uncle Dave, transferred to the page, refuses to be funny. Instead, he seems dull, even a bit tragic. As we work on the piece, we find ourselves less and less interested in it. We return to the piece with a sense of duty, with the belief that other people have found this a funny tale, but our hearts and minds aren't truly engaged. It may be time to let go, to let Uncle Dave be a party favorite, a role that suits him better than literary stardom.

You'll know when you reach the point of diminishing returns, when the piece is no longer a struggle and has become a forced march, one for which you have no passion, not even anger. It has become a bore, and until you find a way to muster new energy for it, continuing is hopeless.

I suffered this problem while trying to write an essay about a runaway cow. While waiting for its turn at a slaughterhouse in an urban area of my hometown, the cow somehow escaped during the night and ran away and eluded her pursuers for more than a week. National news shows covered the attempts to capture the cow, which hid in a city park. Friends from other parts of the country sent e-mails to me saying they loved hearing about the cow on the news. What a great story! So I wrote and wrote and wrote some more. But I failed to bring the story beyond the level of anecdote. I tried to use the cow as a foil for a deeper essay about the national recession and my own little piece of it, but that approach felt contrived. I tried to use the cow's escape as a metaphor for my own escape from a difficult career situation. No luck. So I tried to use it as a sort of parable in an essay about animal rights. The piece sounded preachy, and the cow story never quite connected with the other elements of the piece. So I tried to fictionalize the cow story, changing the setting and occasion, creating characters. The piece felt strained and obvious, taking on a broadly humorous—or coy and clever, depending on the draft—humor that strained to please without ever feeling natural. After any number of drafts, I realized that I really didn't care much about that cow and was trying to force a cute human-interest story to be more than it could ever be, at least to me. Another writer, with a different connection to the story, might have done well with it. For me, it was time to let go and move on.

A GROWING SENSE OF DISCONNECTION

Thoreau warned us many years ago about undertaking enterprises that require "new clothes." He meant, of course, we should avoid situations that insist we become someone we are not, that force us to be untrue to ourselves. Some ideas require the same approach. We set out with motives that are not tied to the idea itself. We want to sound wise on the page, to be admired by readers, to look hip or scholarly or empathic or any of a hundred things. Often we're not conscious of this desire. We feel we're burning to write about a subject, but what's really burning is our desire to appear to be a certain way. As we develop the project, we find it moving further away from who we are. The material continues to distance itself. Our words on the page ring false. The ideas themselves grow vague and indistinct. And we find ourselves, more and more, bluffing our way through.

If you find yourself in this situation, you may need to let go of the idea. It may be right for someone, but it's not right for you. The situation is common in the early stages of apprenticeship, when we try on various identities, speak in various voices. In college, I loved the work of F. Scott Fitzgerald and tried to mimic his long, lyrical sentences, and I tried to put his lush cadences on the page. Unfortunately, I also tried to write about what he wrote about. As a twenty-year-old college student in the Midwest, I knew nothing about being an alcoholic writer in Hollywood coping with an institutionalized wife and fading memories of a glorious past. But I wrote a few stories about such characters. The stories were terrible. And I suffered many false starts. I wondered what was wrong. Why did the ideas always seem so stupid when I put them on the page? When I conceived the ideas they seemed great, worthy of F. Scott himself. The answer to my questions lay in the material itself. When I began to write about a less literary world, one far less glamorous but one that was mine, a world I understood instinctively, I suffered fewer false starts. I was no longer bluffing. Along the way, I did pick up a bit of Fitzgerald's cadence and rhythm, I think, and I really, really, really hope you've noticed.

ENDLESS BEGINNINGS

Earlier, we discussed how the generative idea might simply be the conduit that leads us to the truly inspired idea. We must have faith and move forward, allowing the idea to evolve. However, sometimes we find ourselves shifting from one idea to the next in an endless series of discoveries. These discoveries change the piece in significant ways. Unfortunately, they don't lead to progressive development. They lead to starting over in an endless chain of new beginnings.

If you find yourself in this situation, it may be time to let go. After a while, the nature of the core idea should reveal itself. If it doesn't do that, you don't fully understand the nature of the idea and may need to give it a rest, at least for a while. A friend of mine worked on a novel over the course of years. Every few months, she'd update me on the project, and each time it sounded completely different

THE WRITER'S IDEA BOOK

from the time before. A minor character would emerge to take the novel in a new direction. Instead of a dark study of one subject, it would become a campy look at another subject. The next update would bring new subjects and treatments, a new protagonist. I couldn't help feeling that it was time for her to let go of the project, which had become an aimless amalgam of false starts. The more she invested her time and energy in the project, the higher her personal stake in it rose. The piece gathered a greater and greater need to be, well, great, in order to justify the enormous effort she had invested in it. A project that had started with an engaging premise had evolved into a magnum opus that absolutely needed to set the literary world on its ear.

When you realize you're caught in a similar web, step back and consider your motives and approach. Have you invested too much personally in the piece to see it clearly? Are you trying to force new layers upon an idea that, for whatever reason, doesn't contain such layers? Is it time to let go of such endless work?

PROMPT: Ask yourself a series of questions, and write down your answers. Are you still interested in the idea? Does it continue to reveal itself, if only in elusive bursts of inspiration, or has it become a matter of habit to continue? Is the idea evolving or is it simply becoming a different idea in a succession of different ideas? Have you lost the thread of the initial impulse to develop the idea? What would happen if you abandoned the idea, at least for a while? Can you begin a new project or does the current one still consume you? What are your motives for developing this idea? Are they focused on the idea itself or are they more linked to impressing readers, advancing your career, capitalizing on a trend, landing a contract, unburdening yourself of difficult emotions, or making yourself look smart, profound, or worthy of sympathy? Do your answers reveal any insights or give you a clearer understanding of the project? Is it time to let go?

PROMPT: Spend the next five writing sessions approaching the troubled idea from new angles, changing the point of view, dramatic context, tone, setting, or some other significant element. After these sessions, read what you've written. Have any of these approaches revealed new ideas about the idea or new energy for developing it? If so, keep going. If not, allow yourself to let go for a while.

PROMPT: Write a few pages about the idea, its meaning and interest for you, your connection to it. Be as honest as you can be as you analyze the connections. Is this idea right for you? Is it clear? Are you bluffing?

PROMPT: If the idea in question is a small one, a new character in a story perhaps, pull the character from the narrative and review how the absence affects the story. Is the character necessary? Is the scene extraneous? Does the stanza call attention to itself or shift the poem into a less appealing direction? If so, let go of the idea. If you're still drawn to it for its own sake, explore it in a page or two of writing. It might be the start of a different project.

PROMPT: Take a week off from developing the idea. After the week, review the idea, reading the pages you've already written. Spend a writing session using the energy the time off has given you. Are new possibilities presenting themselves, or do you find you have little new energy or interest. If the latter is true, it's time to let go.

PROMPT: Develop the idea in a writing session from a different persona. Create a writer who is not you, and make that writer the author of the project in progress. Have fun with this one. Write from a different persona every day for a week, sometimes using the ghost of Jane Austen, other times imagining that a close friend is exploring this idea. This approach can reduce any self-consciousness that might be blocking you. If the idea eludes the likes of Jane Austen or Mark Twain or whomever else you've imagined, perhaps it's not right for you.

HONORING THE IDEAS THAT DON'T WORK

We've discussed avoiding labels for your ideas, and we've discussed ways to revive ideas and ways to strip away what's not working to save ideas. But sometimes an idea just isn't going to work. Though de-clutter experts would chide me for saying so, I advise you *not* to throw your idea away. I've heard a number of writers tell me how one night they realized their story or poem or novel wasn't working, and so they burned the pages in some ceremonial way. The organizational gurus would applaud such an act—a ritual cleansing! A symbol of your letting go of the project and of the past! A rite of passage that allows you to move on! These opinions are not without validity, and such symbolic acts might be necessary if you do find yourself unable to let go of a project or find that the project blocks you from starting something new. But burning the damn thing strikes me as foolish and egotistical.

If you must get it out of your field of vision to forget about it, put it in a P.O. Box and have someone else hold the key. Put it in your mother's attic. Mail it to a friend in a faraway city and ask him to hold it for you. I say this because an idea that's fundamentally unworkable now may speak to you in two years or five years, revealing itself in new ways. You'll want to be able to go back to the manuscript with your fresh inspiration.

THE WRITER'S IDEA BOOK

In the meantime, it really is time to move on, and that's not easy. As in relationships, breaking up is hard to do. We try one strategy after another, but still the relationship isn't working. We read books, surf Internet sites, seek counseling. Nothing helps. Something essential is missing, and all the advice and effort in the world won't bring back the love you once felt. At some point, we need to tell the piece to sit down. We need to summon the courage to say, "Honey, we need to talk."

Part V

BETTER
ideas

CHAPTER THIRTY-EIGHT

STUCK AT THE START

Writing is not hard. Just get paper and pencil, sit down, and write what occurs to you. The writing is easy—it's the occurring that's hard.

—STEPHEN LEACOCK

In this chapter and the ones that follow in this final section, we'll narrow our focus solely to putting words on paper. The prompts in this section will help you through the various stages of building a piece, from getting started to improving a completed draft. I hope that the instruction in this book has been helpful, but at some point, we must put away the books and sit down to write. There are lessons to be learned about writing that only can be taught by writing.

The prompts in this chapter will help you begin a project. If you're feeling uninspired, you might find something here that will spark you. If you're feeling inspired but don't know where to start, try a few of these prompts. If you've recently finished a project and are casting about for a new one, you might discover it here. If you've been blocked for a while, you might find the way to break through that block. If you just want to warm up with an exercise or two, you can do that, too.

Remember what we've discussed about the first stages of a new project: Don't put pressure on it. Don't be quick to label what it is or whether or not it's "good." Play. Wander. Let it go where it seems to lead you. But don't let it wander too far away by not writing regularly. Consistency, as in most things, is the key. When you're feeling uninspired, do it anyway. One of my favorite remarks about getting started, even when you feel blocked or blah, comes from one of my favorite writers, Nicholson Baker, who advised, "Feel panic at how quickly life slips by. Get to work." Another great one comes from the poet Cynthia Ozick, who said, "Prescription for writer's block: Begin."

PUT IT ON PAPER

PROMPT: In this book, you have hundreds of prompts to choose from. Open to any page, point your finger at it, and respond to the prompt nearest your finger. If you're reading the electronic edition of the book, zip through the pages and stop at random. Perhaps destiny brought you to that page and to that prompt.

PROMPT: Play "speed creating," a variation on "speed dating" that I developed for workshops. Pick seven or eight prompts at random in the book. Type them and print them, leaving a few extra spaces between each one. Then cut them into seven or eight strips, one prompt each. Fold them and put them in a hat or jar—something to hold them together. Then pick three or four without unfolding them. Then set a timer. Open the first one, read it, and respond with five minutes of writing. Then go to the next one, unfold it, respond with five minutes of writing. And to the next and so on. When you've responded in five-minute writing sessions to all of them, pick the one that most interests you and give it your phone number—or, rather, spend another five minutes writing a response to the prompt.

PROMPT: Make a list of as many aspects of your life as possible, from the big, important stuff to the most inconsequential. The list could include your job, the names of your friends, the make and model of your car, your favorite food, whatever. You won't think of everything at one sitting, so be patient with yourself. Add to the list whenever you think of something. Anything that's an ongoing part of your life, such as "enjoy the smell of tulips," "can't sleep on Sunday nights," "love watching reruns of *The Office*." Nothing is too small or unimportant. You're creating a life inventory, of sorts.

PROMPT: Pull an item from the list you made in the previous prompt and write a few pages about it in whatever way seems most natural. You could explore the subject in a personal essay or fictionalize it in some way. Focus a writing session on this item. Then choose another item from the list and spend a session focused on it. Any time you're feeling stale or uninspired, take an item from the list and write about it.

THE WRITER'S IDEA BOOK

PROMPT: Choose two items from the list you created and write a piece using both items. For an even bigger challenge, choose three items. Try to find a way to bring the items together by looking for connections between or among them.

PROMPT: Still using your "life inventory" list, arrange some of the items under headings—such as "passions" and "gifts" and "habits I want to break." Then pick an item from each column and create a piece that brings those things together.

PROMPT: Write about a hobby or avocation that used to play an important role in your life but that no longer is a part of your life.

PROMPT: Find a title in a collection of stories, essays, or plays that you've not read. Write a page of narrative that would fit the title.

PROMPT: Put three characters in a room. Each character thinks the other two are aligned against her. Write a dialogue. If you want, write the scene three times, each time from the point of view of a different character.

PROMPT: Write a scene in which a character shows up at an event wearing the wrong type of clothes.

PROMPT: Have you ever had the common dream of showing up too late for something? The most common is a dream about showing up for school too late to take a test, but there are many variations. Usually the dream wakes us with a start. Allow yourself to keep dreaming (on paper, of course) and continue the scenario. How do you, or how does your character, resolve the situation?

PROMPT: Recall a family situation or event that went wrong or turned out badly in some way. Write about what happened, shedding light on the event, or fictionalize it and change the ending—making it either happier or more disastrous.

PROMPT: Write a scene in which some type of sound interrupts (or triggers) a heated discussion. Consider a barking dog, a ringing telephone, a blaring television, a creaking staircase, a rumbling car, a dripping faucet.

PROMPT: Your character wakes in the morning and goes to a window to see an unlikely animal—a moose, ostrich, or something similar—staring back. What happens?

PROMPT: Explore the cliché "from the mouths of babes." Write about a time in which something a child said made you see something in a new light or inspired you to take some type of action. If you've never had this experience, fictionalize one.

PROMPT: Read the local section of your newspaper every day for a week. If possible, keep the sections in a pile. Choose two stories that interest you and find a way to fuse them into a single situation, then explore it. If possible, bring both elements into a single sentence and use that to begin the story. For example, you might find a story about a house fire and another about an annual Easter egg hunt held in a local park. Your opening sentence could be—"On the day of the annual Easter egg hunt, an event my brothers and sisters wouldn't miss for the world, our house burned to the ground."

PROMPT: Fill in the blanks in the following sentence: "All during that time I ate too much _____, listened to too much _____, and thought far too much about _____. When you've filled in the blanks, use the sentence as the opening for a narrative—a personal experience or maybe a piece of fiction. Was this a summer of mourning lost love? The first year of a new career? Perhaps a time in your childhood?

PROMPT: Write about a time when someone gave you a piece of bad news in an insensitive or inappropriate way. If you want, fictionalize the experience, changing it to fit your needs. Either way, get even with the lout who needs a lesson in manners.

PROMPT: What is your least favorite way to travel? Are you afraid of flying? Do you hate buses? Write about your feelings for this mode of transportation, exploring the reasons you feel this way. If you prefer, send a character who shares your feelings on a trip involving that type of travel.

PROMPT: Make a confession. Open with the words, "I admit that I . . ." and take it from there. Come on. You can do it. No one else has to see it. You can burn the pages afterward if you want.

PROMPT: Write a scene in which no one talks. You must convey all the meaning through silent action.

PROMPT: Make a list of your deepest passions—the subjects that are nearest and dearest to you. Odds are good that you have written about them before. But odds are even better that you haven't written about them in every possible way. Pick one from your list and freewrite. As usual, no rules. Write about why it's a passion or write about how this passion plays a role in your life. Keep going from there.

PROMPT: Write about the passion you chose in the previous prompt, but create a fictional character who shares that passion. Begin a narrative with this person engaged in your passion—playing music or blogging or shopping or whatever it is.

PROMPT: Play a round of creativity roulette. (For this one you'll need actual print magazines rather than online versions.) Cut twenty pictures from magazines. Use a variety of magazines, so you'll have lots of tones and subjects. Crumble the pictures into balls and throw them in a box or vase or some type of container. Pick three of the balls and straighten them. Write a few pages involving all three images. One tip: Don't cheat. Use the first three you pick.

PROMPT: As writers, we're told time and again that we must hook our readers with the first paragraph. To that end, we try to open in a dramatic or surprising way. Try the opposite approach. Open with a character sitting and thinking quietly. Focus on observations. Put us into the mind of the character.

PROMPT: Open with a character saying he is the world's greatest something. It could be something the character brags about—world's greatest softball player or world's greatest decorator. Or it could be something said in a self-deprecating way—world's greatest whiner or world's greatest spoiler of a fun evening. Then have the character tell an anecdote to support his claim.

PROMPT: Describe a place you know, or one you imagine, by focusing on smells and sounds. Continue your description until a person or fictional character appears, then shift the focus to the character. Then introduce a second person or character. Keep going.

PROMPT: Pick a minor detail or minor character (or living person) from a piece you've already written in the past. Put that detail or character at the center this time. Open a piece with the focus on that person and move ahead.

PROMPT: Who do you miss most in your life? A loved one who has passed away? Perhaps a child who has grown up and moved away? Maybe a former mate who you no longer see due to a break-up. Begin a piece focused on that person. Begin with an anecdote—a story of something that happened to the two of you. Withhold any explanations of your feelings for that person.

CHAPTER THIRTY-NINE

STUCK IN DEVELOPMENT

Ideas are easy. It's the execution of ideas that really separates the sheep from the goats.

—SUE GRAFTON

We've talked at some length about the importance of adding ideas to your initial idea. You need to complicate and expand your premise, to augment and amplify it. In this chapter, you'll find prompts to help you do that. You have an idea for a piece and have developed it in at least a few pages of writing, probably more. You may have written your way through the initial burst of inspiration and are unsure how to move forward. Or, you may have explored the initial idea in a limited way and are looking for ways to develop the idea. Or, you may have begun with a burst of inspiration, but you've hit a creative wall. You're not only unsure how to proceed, you're feeling blocked.

The prompts in this chapter speak to all of those situations. Use them for those reasons, but keep them, and the thinking behind them, for this stage of any project you begin in the future. Remember what we've discussed about sometimes needing to move past the initial idea. Sometimes that idea functions simply as the booster rocket to get the space shuttle of your idea beyond the grip of gravity. Having served its purpose, it must fall away. Conversely, you might discover a great idea in this second stage of the process that pulls you in a direction so different from the initial conception that it doesn't fit at all. The author Jeffery Deaver speaks to this situation when he says, "When I find myself frozen—whether I'm working on a brief passage in a novel or brainstorming about an entire book—it's usually because I'm trying to shoehorn an idea into the passage or story where it has no place." You then must decide which project more passionately engages you and move forward with that one.

Finally, with these prompts feel free to add or alter the instruction in a way that suits the particulars of the piece you have in progress.

PUT IT ON PAPER

PROMPT: Qualify or contradict a statement that you or a character made in the opening pages. For example, if your character claims to be content with the life he's chosen, have him explain what he means and add a note of doubt. Or have him illustrate his contentment with an example that implies the contentment is a façade, that beneath the surface he feels restless or angry or sad.

PROMPT: Shift the location. If your piece up to this point is focused in a single place, move to a new place. Give the new setting a role in the drama. For example, if your lovers have been battling at home, move them to a coffeehouse where they are less free to fight, where the people around them suppress the argument.

PROMPT: Change the conversation. If in your opening the people have focused on a conflict, switch to a different one. Perhaps they're dealing with how to handle their rebellious teen daughter. Bring in their concerns about finances.

PROMPT: Slow the pace at which you're introducing characters or people. We sometimes move too quickly in the early pages, feeling we must get the piece moving as fast as possible. Take time to linger, giving the reader a richer beginning while giving yourself a better sense of the piece. You can always go back later and condense.

PROMPT: Shift the narrative mode. If you've begun with a page of description to present the setting, move right into a scene. If you've explained the situation and presented the background information, move to the present time of the story. If you've begun with a scene, move to narrative summary. If you've begun with characters speaking, move into the mind of a character and present his thoughts.

PROMPT: Ask a question. Or have a character ask a question. Surprise yourself and just write one down. Even if the question seems unrelated to what has come before, follow it, find out where it goes or where the answer to the question (or the lack of an answer or the struggle to answer) takes you.

PROMPT: If you know what comes next but can't seem to build the bridge to get there, change course, inventing or choosing a new direction. After you've taken that direction for a while, look for ways that it connects to the earlier direction.

PROMPT: Shift the character's goal. In an earlier chapter we discussed ways to use a character's goal to structure a story. Your opening probably makes clear this goal, either directly or indirectly. Write a page in which the character is not focused fully on achieving this goal, but instead has a deeper purpose. Your character, for example, has established her desire to reinvigorate her marriage, but we learn she already has given up and is looking for ways to leave. Or, if you're writing a memoir and you've focused on coming to terms with an experience in your past, nudge yourself away from this focus or connect it with a current conflict.

PROMPT: Sustain the action of the opening scene. If you planned to end at a certain spot and move to flashback or summary, don't. Stay focused on what happens next in the dramatic present and maintain your focus, even if you're not sure where you're headed. You can go later to insert the exposition or flashback. For now, move forward. You may find you don't really need to stop the forward progress of the piece and can sprinkle the backstory into the drama.

PROMPT: Use repetition. Have a character repeat a line he said in the opening pages. He might say it to himself while thinking about the earlier scene. Or he might say it while telling a new character about what happened in the scene. Or, to give the prompt a twist, have another character say the line to him, repeating what he said.

PROMPT: Fast forward to a new time. Don't fret the transition. Simply write "Two months later . . ." and keep moving. You can go back later or summarize what has happened in between.

PROMPT: Shift the role dynamic. If one person or character has been dominant over another, for example, show a situation in which their roles are reversed.

PROMPT: Raise the stakes. As we discussed earlier, the outcome of the situation must be extremely important to the main character. After you've established the basic conflict, add a new element that makes the conflict even more vital and urgent.

PROMPT: Shift the point of view. If the meeting of friends has been presented through the eyes of one person, follow a different member of the group home from the meeting.

PROMPT: Shift from dramatic mode to expository. For example, if you've begun with a scene showing a divorced couple getting together to discuss their children, move to a general exploration on the nature of regret.

PROMPT: Use Jack Kerouac's automatic-writing approach. Spend a few sessions writing whatever comes into your mind, based on your vague sense of the nature of the piece. Don't censor. Just keep piling up details and events.

PROMPT: Technology intrudes on our lives every day. Use that to add a new element to your opening. A couple's discussion of their rebellious teen daughter could be interrupted by or woven through local news stories blaring from the television. Or, perhaps, you open with the parents sitting down to address their concerns to the daughter, whose cell phone erupts every thirty seconds with incoming text messages.

PROMPT: Shift to a different communication mode. If you've been writing an essay, for example, change it to a series of e-mails or blog posts.

PROMPT: Change the narrative distance. If you've begun with a scene between two characters in a single place, for example, pull back to relate the history of that place. Earlier I mentioned how Bill Bryson, in his memoir *The Life and Times of the Thunderbolt Kid*, moves back and forth between memories of his own childhood to observations about the 1950s in America.

PROMPT: Take a personal risk by wandering into uncomfortable territory. Follow the initial burst of inspiration by pushing it to a place where you feel somehow exposed. The protagonist of your novel, for example, might make a confession of reckless behavior. Your memoir could introduce an unseemly side of you or one of the people you're writing about.

PROMPT: I know I've advised against following your opening with a flashback, but if you're struggling with the question of how to proceed, write a prequel to your opening. What happened right before that point in time?

CHAPTER FORTY

STUCK IN THE MIDDLE

What is written without effort is in general read without pleasure.

—SAMUEL JOHNSON

One of the worst times for a writer is when a project has been moving along for a good while and then stops moving. We've made a commitment to the piece and spent much time and effort developing it to this point. Try as we might, we can take it no further. We curse and fret, enjoy an occasional moment of false promise, then find ourselves struggling again.

As I mentioned earlier in the book, struggle is a natural part of the process. There's a truism about this struggle that you've probably heard: Writin' is fightin'. But when a piece is going well, we win the fights, or at least most of them. When it's going bad, we're always on our backs, a striped-shirted referee counting us out or asking us how many fingers he's holding up.

The reasons for shutting down in the middle are varied. We lose our energy or interest in the project. We've grown bored with it. Or we've written ourselves into a corner and feel we have no way to get the piece moving again. The direction and nature of the piece inevitably changes as we write, and we might be confused about the shape and direction the piece is telling us to take. We may have taken an unfortunate turn early in the piece, the results of which confound us.

Sometimes the block is linked to our nonwriting lives. Pressures from our jobs or families sap the energy we had been reserving for our creative work. We're struggling with a crisis. Or sometimes we're having too much fun and don't want to retreat into the solitude of writing. We've gotten out of the habit of writing. F. Scott Fitzgerald struggled for years with the novel that became *Tender Is the Night*, squandering his talent on the high life in the south of France, then struggling with Zelda's breakdown and his own alcoholism. His writer's block had little to do with writing.

If you're stuck in the middle of a project, consider what's happening in your life and observe if some new situation is sapping your energy and creative drive. If not, if the problem truly is on the page, then accept that such problems are part of the process. They're inevitable. Resist the urge to quit or to conclude that you're a failure. Read some of the quotes from writers that open all the chapters in this book. If you need more, go to a website that offers some. Many will talk about the difficulties of the craft. A few even call it "hell." In other words, you're not in unfamiliar territory. In fact, the territory would be far less familiar if you whipped through a piece without feeling stuck a time or two.

Also, take comfort in knowing that such times are when the most learning occurs. Just as in life, these rocky periods require our greatest focus and awareness. The lessons that derive from getting through these times stay with us for the rest of our lives. Seen in this way, we should feel a certain amount of gratitude for these challenges. Of course, when we're in the middle of overcoming that challenge, it's tough to see it in a positive light, but know that persevering through it truly will help you develop as a writer.

To get yourself unstuck, try some of the prompts in this chapter. One caveat: Don't fight the prompts. If you've been stuck in the middle for a while, you're probably feeling frustrated, even helpless. Your impulse might be to read a prompt and think "*That won't work.*" Take the leap of faith and give it a try.

PUT IT ON PAPER

PROMPT: Read what you've written so far, highlighting the lines and the sections that are working well. Try to determine what quality these parts possess, such as humor or insight or a certain energy in the voice. Notice if you find yourself highlighting fewer parts as the pages progress. In the next page that you write, don't focus as much on what happens as on bringing that quality or qualities back into the piece.

PROMPT: If you haven't already, determine your destination for the piece, not so much the final conclusion you hope to draw as where you plan to end in terms of time and place. In your mind, or on a piece of paper, draw a line between where you are now and where you want to be at the end. You may want to outline the steps you'll need to take to reach your destination. If you don't like outlines, simply write down your thoughts about how to get to where you want to go. Then write one page that moves you a bit further toward your destination, a page that takes the next step, so to speak. Then write another.

PROMPT: As an alternative to the previous prompt, read what you've written so far, keeping in mind the destination you've noted. Is this really your destination? Sometimes we begin writing with a particular destination, goal, or purpose in mind, but as we've discussed, a creative project will assert a will of its own. The destination for the piece you're developing may have changed, and your efforts to push toward the old one could block you. It may be time to determine a new destination or, scary as it sounds, write for a while without a destination in mind.

PROMPT: Once again, and especially if you haven't done so already, read what you've written so far. Often writers frustrate themselves by focusing on the next step when they're blocked. They try a number of options, sending the piece in one direction, then another, but nothing seems to work. The problem might be that they're focused on the wrong spot in the piece. The problem doesn't reside in the pages they wrote right before they began to feel blocked. The problem resides in an earlier passage. For various reasons, the problem didn't assert itself fully on the piece until later. Read your piece with an eye toward a wrong move, a shift that may have seemed natural at the time, but upon close reading, pushes the piece toward an inevitable block.

PROMPT: Sometimes we need to leap out of the middle and go to the end. Spend a session or two sketching your ending. If you feel comfortable and confident, write the ending. Then, with that ending in mind, return to the middle and begin writing toward the ending you've completed already.

PROMPT: Put the piece away for a specific short period of time. Dive right into something new. Don't even miss a single session. Concentrate on the new piece. The distraction can release the block on the other piece.

PROMPT: A variation on the previous prompt: Put the piece away for a specific period of time but make it a longer period than the previous one. But do give yourself a deadline. Otherwise, you could drift away and never finish.

PROMPT: Try the reverse of the previous prompt. Rather than put it away, spend at least twenty minutes on it every day for a week. Don't struggle against it. Write about the people in a general way—not about their actions in the piece. Write short biographies of them, for example. Describe the styles of clothing they wear. If you're working on a memoir, write about other things they've done that don't fit into the piece you're writing. The key is to stay with the project. Often writers will struggle briefly with a stalled piece and then abandon it. Keep it in your subconscious mind—where problems can work themselves out when you're doing other things during your day—by visiting the piece frequently.

PROMPT: With a long project, we can fall into a rut, moving in an uninspired way through our paces. This feeling also can occur with shorter projects that are protracted by interruptions. We lose the zest of the initial inspiration. If you're stuck in this way, go back to the beginning and spend some time reading the first pages, trying to recapture some of that early energy. You may find yourself editing a bit, changing lines and words, adding some details.

PROMPT: Add a surprising element—surprising to you as well as to your reader. It could be a small detail or a significant announcement. The point is that it gives you something new and something you didn't expect. When we're blocked, we sometimes hammer on the same spot, trying new approaches that really are just variations on the same approach. It may be time to step back and reconceive the piece.

PROMPT: The writer Philip Gerard once told me, "You're not really revising until you cut something that hurts." It may be time to do that to free you from the blocked middle. Review what you've written, looking for a turn or a passage that you like but that doesn't serve the piece. Often, this is a passage with which we're quite pleased, one that involves some type of cleverness or showing off. It calls attention to us and to itself. If it doesn't serve the piece, however, it needs to go. It could be causing the block that's holding up your momentum.

PROMPT: Sometimes a narrative thread isn't so much tangled as frayed. We've grown a bit tired of it. Our energy and enthusiasm have flagged. In this case, look for a spot in the piece that does interest you, even if it plays a minor role in the grand plan. Explore it for a while. It could end up playing a larger role, or it may renew your interest in the piece as a whole.

PROMPT: Find a place in the piece that makes you curious to know more. It could be a single image or perhaps a line of dialogue. Maybe it came to you during the first rush of inspiration and you moved past it quickly. Take some time now to explore it more fully. Why does the character make a statement with such a strangely formal phrasing? Why does your friend twist the ring on her finger as she tells you about her divorce? Where did she get that ring?

PROMPT: Build rumination time into your writing schedule. If, for example, you try to spend an hour per day on writing, stop after a half hour and do something else that doesn't require your full attention—go for a walk, load the dishwasher, take a shower. Allow your mind time to wander without the computer screen or blank notebook page staring at you and without jumping into the duties of the day. Do this for one week.

PROMPT: If you've been working intuitively on the piece to this point, following its development on faith rather than on a clear notion of your intentions, it may be time to stop and review what you've done so far. Working intuitively, allowing a piece to develop of its own accord, is a fine way to work, as we've discussed throughout this book. But as we write in this way, we can't help but make certain conclusions about it. We can't help but begin to sense its nature and direction. Perhaps your sense of the piece needs adjustment. As you read it, try to put out of your mind the conclusions you've drawn already and allow yourself to find fresh clues. Your unconscious mind has planted them, and they're waiting to be discovered.

PROMPT: If you've been working from an outline, it may be time to assess your plan. An outline can be an effective tool for keeping us on track, but we must be willing to revise it as the project develops. It's difficult to know what a story will reveal to us before we've begun writing it. Adhering too closely to an outline developed at the start can lead to blocks when the piece is underway. As you review your outline, look for ways to revise it that will create possibilities for moving forward.

PROMPT: At a writers' group meeting, I overheard a guy say, "I've written the first half of three novels." He went on to admit that, although he'd been writing for years, he'd yet to finish a novel. He probably had specific reasons why each project stalled and could explain them in detail. But clearly there's a pattern at work in his writing life that is undermining his success. If you find yourself facing a similar pattern, it's time to step back and evaluate what's stopping you. Rather than focusing on the particulars of the blocked project, try to recognize the pattern of not completing projects. Some projects are better left uncompleted. However, if project after project ends up in the dead-end file, there's a problem. We can't begin to cover all the psychological possibilities for such a pattern right now, but I highly advise spending time to explore those tendencies on your own. Focusing on the latest block, when many have preceded it, would be fruitless. Take some time to explore—in your mind and also on paper—the pattern of half-finished projects. Write about it at length.

PROMPT: Write your characters' names on strips of paper and put the strips into a container. At the start of the next writing session, pick a strip and focus the session on that character. Don't feel as if you have to write about that character within the context of the stalled project. You could write an unrelated sketch or scene involving the character. The point is to return to a free-spirited sense of play. A project, as we all know, can begin with inspiration and exhilaration but then turn into a grind. This is particularly true of long projects. After a while, they can lose their energy. We eventually stop writing, not because we're blocked on the piece so much as we're exhausted from it. That exhaustion, however, can feel like a block.

THE WRITER'S IDEA BOOK

To get yourself going again, return to that sense of play. This prompt and the next ones offer ways to do that.

PROMPT: Place two characters who don't share a scene in the ongoing project into a scene. Have them meet and discuss the conflict at the heart of this project. Buy them a few drinks or find some other way to induce them to speak candidly. If you want, insert yourself into the scene, explaining your problems in writing the piece.

PROMPT: Spend a session writing about your setting. Do a little research and write a brief history of the place. If it's a fictional place, write a brief fictional history.

PROMPT: Brainstorm a list of possibilities of what happens next in the piece. Be as imaginative and illogical as possible. Risk some flights of fancy. Don't worry that you would have to change what you've written already to allow for these possibilities to be, well, possible. Have fun with it.

PROMPT: We've discussed letting your characters guide you, but let's try a different approach. Let's use the guidance of writer Doug Lawson who said, "Often I'll find clues to where the story might go by figuring out where the characters would rather not go." Do your characters—or maybe it's their creator—seem to avoid certain actions or subjects? Think about it for a while. Follow your instincts and spend a session writing the piece toward a place it "would rather not go."

PROMPT: How are you feeling about the piece in its current state? Have you fallen out of love with it? Perhaps it's not the wonderful work of genius it seemed to be when you first started, just as people we meet eventually show their quirks and flaws. And yet sometimes these flaws make them even more interesting. Take a leap of faith and pledge to love the piece no matter what it turns out to be. With this mind-set, make a list of the qualities you love about the piece. Then pick one quality and write about it in detail. Then pick another and do the same.

PROMPT: Take your block to Writer's Block Anonymous. Surround yourself with your favorite writers, and create a scene in which you explain your struggles, seeking their advice. No doubt they have struggled to complete plenty of projects. What do they tell you to do?

PROMPT: Interview yourself about your struggles with the piece. Use this approach to get ideas for moving past whatever is hindering you. Your interviewer should be ruthlessly insistent, continuing to probe for answers, even if you're resistant or confused. Your interviewer shouldn't be chiding or deprecating—not giving you the third degree, but definitely is seeking answers to the questions.

PROMPT: Spend a writing session on a scene or a passage from the piece that you would never show anyone because it's far too revealing. In fact, you probably should pick a very private place to spend this writing session. The passage should reveal something about a character or about yourself that you wouldn't want people to know.

PROMPT: A variation on the previous prompt: Highlight the most revealing passage in what you've written so far. Spend a session exploring that passage—expanding and deepening it. Pick a word from the dictionary by opening to a page at random and dropping your finger onto a word. Use that word as part of the next sentence you write. Draw the remainder of the paragraph from that sentence. If you're stuck for the next paragraph, choose another word in the same manner.

PROMPT: Speaking of drawing, spend a writing session actually drawing the people and places in your piece. Even if you are not a gifted artist, the point is more about observation, fun, and discovery than in creating museum-worthy art.

PROMPT: Sometimes we're stalled by too much material and have lost our way because the core is buried. Spend a few sessions cutting away everything that isn't essential to the piece. To do this exercise, create a second document so you don't lose any of the cut material. Then ruthlessly strip away all the descriptions, details, scenes, asides, summaries, and whatever else, leaving only the bare bones of the piece. Then read that decidedly thinner version for clues as to where it needs to go.

The writer John Hersey declared, "To be a writer is to throw away a great deal, not to be satisfied, to type again, and then again and once more, and over and over." And when you reach the middle of a piece, that process is very often inevitable. I don't offer this observation as inspiration so much as a means to accept the naturalness of the process. If you're struggling and throwing away "a great deal" and typing over and over, know that you're right where you need to be, and you're where countless writers have been before you. Do not let that inevitable stage of the process sap your energy and interest. Rather than stepping away, you need to stay close to the piece, to keep it fresh in your mind. Find a way to engage with it on a regular basis. Sure, a few days off can give you a fresh perspective and renewed energy. But wait too long and you risk losing it completely. The regular engagement will allow your subconscious mind to work through the struggles and provide new ideas. Keep in mind an observation made in an earlier chapter: That's not writer's block. That's writing.

CHAPTER FORTY-ONE

STUCK AT THE END

… telling the truth in an interesting way turns out to be as easy and pleasurable as bathing a cat.

—ANNE LAMOTT

You've made it through the middle and can see the end in sight. You're happy, for the most part, with how the piece has developed. And then you find yourself struggling with the best way to end the piece, to pull together the narrative threads. In this chapter, when I use the word "ending," I mean the concluding part of the piece—the climactic moment or the resolution of the drama that has been carrying the reader. We'll also address the final lines, but most often the struggle occurs with pulling those threads together and resolving them in an appealing way rather than simply writing the last line or two.

Struggles occur at the end for a variety of reasons. Perhaps you made some changes in the middle, and now the ending you had foreseen no longer is appropriate. Questions have been raised that the planned ending doesn't resolve. Perhaps when you wrote the ending, which had seemed wonderful in your mind, you found that it doesn't work on the page. You need a different ending.

We struggle with endings because endings are tough. They may be the toughest stage of the process. In all the earlier stages, we can assume we'll resolve problems of character, structure, design, or whatever at some later time. Endings don't offer that luxury. Not only must problems be faced directly and immediately, all those earlier problems to be solved later have come home to roost. *Later* is *now*. We also tend to put a lot of pressure on our endings. We want them to be brilliant. We want to hit the perfect note that will move the reader in a powerful way. If we're writing a humor piece, we want the ending to be hilarious. If we're writing a darker piece, we want the reader to embrace our depth of feeling or profundity of thought. We want the ending to resonate. In short, we want the ending to be perfect. With those goals in our minds, it's no wonder we have such a tough time with endings.

I exchanged e-mails recently with a good friend, the writer Mark Garvey, about his own experience with endings. He has published a number of books, most recently one titled *Stylized*, which presents the history of many writers' favorite little book, *The Elements of Style*. Here's what he had to say:

> "I did struggle with the ending. It's such an important moment in any book, I think, that putting it together just naturally brings on the anxiety. With *Stylized* in particular—since it was a book for writers and about writing—I was concerned about drawing together my themes in a way that was both natural and conclusive while at the same time (in the spirit of Strunk and White) not overblown, sentimental, or too fussy. It was very much a matter of getting the tone right—or getting it to sound right to my ear, at least. I rewrote the last paragraph probably two dozen different ways and played with it for at least two days. I asked a trusted friend to read and critique it. And all that prolonged focus on it, of course, then introduced an additional concern about whether or not I was fiddling with it too much for its own good. It's easy to get trapped in that kind of anxiety loop. Once I began to feel that way—that I was spending too much time tweaking it—I wrapped up the version that I thought sounded best, and then I let it sit for a week or so. After that, I came back to it with relatively fresh eyes, and with one or two small adjustments, I finally satisfied myself that it said what I wanted it to say in the way I wanted to say it."

As I mentioned in the previous chapter, we also might be struggling for reasons that have nothing to do with writing. The blocked ending results from stress about your job or a relationship, about money, about dozens of other things that affect our lives. Or you may be undergoing some personal transition, and for the moment, lack clarity and direction in your life, and therefore have little to offer your writing. Or you might be simply too busy at the moment to write often enough to maintain momentum. The demands of daily life are sapping your energy, and the lack of regular writing is disconnecting you from the mind-set of the piece in progress. All of these factors are reasonable and common.

THE WRITER'S IDEA BOOK

Another common reason for feeling blocked at the end is the fear of finishing. As much as we look forward to the end, we also approach it with trepidation because we can no longer imagine the piece within the glow of the initial vision with which we began it. The beginning is fueled by that vision—our excitement that we have begun a truly special project. That excitement—and that vague but energizing sense of the project's quality—can carry us through the tough middle section. But at the end, we have what we have. It is what is on the page and nothing more. We must accept it in that way, which always involves a sort of compromise with ourselves, a sort of settling for less than what we had foreseen when we started furiously writing down our first ideas. Oscar Wilde once said that projects are never finished, just abandoned. We always feel that with one more crack at it, we could attain the level we had vaguely envisioned at the start. Seen in this light, for the writer, there are no truly happy endings.

The prompts in this chapter, however, are designed to get you closer to what you want—and to finishing the project, which is a wonderful accomplishment and a happy ending in its own right.

PUT IT ON PAPER

PROMPT: Sometimes we struggle or feel blocked at the end because the endings we've written don't satisfy the expectations we've raised in the reader's mind. To satisfy those expectations, you have to know what they are. Read the piece with an eye toward the expectations you've raised. What implicit promise have you made to the reader throughout the piece? Finding the killer? Requiting the love? Bringing the protagonist to a new level of insight about a situation? Apprentice writers in workshops and groups often say "I liked the story except for the ending." This sends the writer of the piece back to the ending for revision after revision, which never satisfy because the problem is not in the ending. It lies earlier in the piece, when expectations were raised unintentionally in the reader's mind. Find that spot and begin revising there.

PROMPT: Perhaps, as Mark Garvey mentioned, the problem lies in the pressure you're putting on the ending. Read the final four or five paragraphs of a narrative, the final pages of a script or screenplay, the final lines of a poem. Do you need them all? Perhaps your piece will end more naturally if you cut some of the closing material. When you wrote the next to last page, for example, you weren't trying to strike a note of finality. That page may have a more natural eloquence, free of the self-consciousness writers feel in trying to strike a powerful last note.

PROMPT: In endings, we sometimes shift from *show* to *tell*. We want to sum up the piece, to tell the reader what he or she is supposed to think. If the endings you've written, and rejected, take this approach, shift to dramatic mode. End with some type of action.

PROMPT: If you've ended with an action, perhaps it's too final, too close-ended. You can't find the resonance you seek because that action stops the reader with a bang. Open up the ending by using an ongoing action, along the lines of "We got back in the car and began driving toward Denver, using the Rockies in the distance as our guide." Though surely your ending will be more graceful than this example of driving off into the sunset, it shows characters in motion. It suggests a possible future rather than abruptly slamming a door on the narrative.

PROMPT: To extend our discussion in the previous prompt, consider that your ending may be too pat. Its simplicity undercuts the thematic layers of the piece. For example, a writer has developed a personal essay about her struggle with bulimia in which she investigates the sources of the problem, its manifestations, and the ways it affected her life. To pull the piece together at the end, she offers a reductive statement about life being a learning experience or "what doesn't kill us makes us stronger." Readers complain that the ending is unsatisfying, or the writer senses that it's not quite right, though she's not sure why. The reason it fails to satisfy is that she has treated the experience with thought-provoking sophistication that the ending doesn't match. She's created an expectation in the reader's mind of a thought-provoking, sophisticated conclusion but hasn't delivered it. In her attempt to end with a quick summing up, she has not done justice to her theme.

PROMPT: Another way to avoid telling the ending is by using an image, a specific, concrete detail. In my own writing, my first ending tends to be very expository. Maybe I'm telling myself the ending that first time through. I then try to find images that capture the point I had made in an expository way. In a recent essay about playing a rain-soaked football game with my sons when they were young, I ended in an expository way, wrapping up the theme of the piece. Oh, it was a beauty that made my eyes mist just reading it. Then I realized that my eyes were misting at the memory of that game rather than at the ending I'd written. And the reader didn't have that memory. So I put myself back in the game and recalled the slosh of shoes on the wet field and the whispered plays concocted as I huddled with my son. Out went my effort at profound insight and in went the details that would make the reader experience that game. See if that strategy works for you.

PROMPT: I read many stories for workshops and conferences that shift away from the protagonist or the main conflict at the end. The writer pulls back to give some universal insight about life and the human condition. If you've taken this approach, put the focus back on the central character or situation.

PROMPT: The problem may be a matter of tone. At a recent conference, I read a story about a woman's attempts to meet a man. The story was witty and sharp, with a light note of despair that added dimension. Then, in the last few paragraphs, the light note erupted like a bomb, changing the tone in a way that jarred the reader. The writer hadn't prepared the reader. If your ending suffers from such a shift, you can either change the ending to fit the earlier tone or foreshadow the shift by modulating the tone throughout the piece, dipping into the darker tone from time to time, so that when it appears in full force at the end, the reader has been prepared and the ending feels organic to the piece.

PROMPT: Maybe you feel that the ending doesn't unify the piece. The easiest way to remedy this problem is to return to a key image or two from earlier in the piece. You might also return to a line of dialogue or recall some earlier event. By returning to these earlier elements, you bring a sense of wholeness to the piece, creating a resonance that ties the piece together.

PROMPT: If you're concerned that the ending is too open, that it doesn't supply enough closure, see the previous prompt. By recalling an element from earlier in the piece, you give the reader a sense of having come full circle. Of course, you'll need to choose the right element to recall. It needs to be one central to the intention or meaning of the piece—not necessarily the one on which you lavished the most attention when it appeared earlier but one that speaks to the core themes.

PROMPT: If your ending doesn't feel right because you've not prepared the reader for it, go back to earlier sections in the piece where you can add details that foreshadow the ending or make it feel more organic. Of course, you want to blend these additions into the earlier sections so they don't call attention to themselves or too obviously signal the ending.

PROMPT: One way to circumnavigate the temptation to overthink your ending or overwhelm it with rhetorical flourish is to set a technical challenge for yourself. Decide you're going to end with a line of dialogue. Or with a gesture. Or a description of an object. Or anything else that occurs to you. Choose something appropriate to the piece, of course, but the key point to the exercise is to find a way to end in a natural way with whatever you choose. By concentrating on the challenge of the exercise, you'll free yourself from concentrating too much on perfecting the ending. Straining for perfection may be blocking you.

PROMPT: Read the first few paragraphs of your piece. They may hold the key to your ending. In them you suggested—explicitly or implicitly—the direction of your piece. You pointed the reader to the path that leads to the final paragraphs. The technique of returning directly to the opening is a bit shopworn, and though it still may work, I'm not suggesting you be so obvious in your approach. After reading the first paragraphs a few times, and, as best you can, putting out of your mind the piece that developed from them, decide on where the opening would lead. In other words, given this opening, where would the piece inevitably end? Use that marker as the basis for your decision on where you now must end the piece. Perhaps you haven't reached the end, and that's why you're blocked. Perhaps the ending doesn't offer a suitable destination for the opening as it stands, in which case you can either change the opening or write a more suitable ending.

PROMPT: Let's look at another way to use the beginning to find the ending. Read the first few paragraphs looking for ways to echo them in the ending. The technique of returning directly to the beginning in the ending has been done so often and continues to be done in workmanlike nonfiction that I'm not suggesting you do it. Instead, look for more subtle ways to echo the opening. Is there a word you can repeat, an implied question you can answer, a tone you can bring back, a method you can use again? For example, did you open with a statement? A line of dialogue? A quip? An anecdote? A character's thoughts? A description? Use the same approach to end the piece. The reader won't be conscious of what you're doing but will feel a sense of closure on an unconscious level.

PROMPT: Have you considered that you might be struggling with the ending because you're not ready to end? If you're writing genre fiction and the plot has climaxed—the lovers united, the killer caught, the villains vanquished—you're probably sure it's time to wrap up, but if you're writing a piece less dependent on plot, perhaps you're not happy with the ending or are unsure how best to end the piece now because there is more to say. Spend a few sessions pushing beyond the point where you decided to end and find out what happens. Many writers, myself included, have struggled with an ending because it opened more doors than it closed. And so we were off on a novella or a novel. I wrote a novella in graduate school, bringing the piece to a rousing conclusion that I'd planned early in the process. When I reached that point, I realized that the scene pushed the protagonist into a deeper conflict than the conflict that had driven the piece from the start. I struggled for a while to enlarge and deepen the scene, to give it a stronger closure, but the new conflict kept asserting itself. I realized in time that my struggle with the ending was really a struggle against the piece itself and against the realization that I would have to commit to a longer project. Consider that possibility.

PROMPT: Consider the opposite approach to the previous prompt. Maybe the best place to end is before your current ending. The piece may have reached its natural conclusion, and yet you have continued the piece, reaching for something else that isn't organic to the story you're telling. Look for places earlier in the piece where you can end.

PROMPT: Read the endings of ten published pieces in whatever form you're working. You need not read the entire piece. Study the endings as self-contained pieces, trying to determine the technique the author is using. Experiment with several of the techniques—dialogue, statement, thoughts, action, detail, or whatever—applying the particulars of your own piece.

PROMPT: A variation on the previous prompt. Reread the endings of your five favorite pieces—novels or poems or whatever form you're working in. Analyze the techniques used in the endings while keeping in mind everything that has come before. You might even try copying a few of the approaches to see if they can work for your piece.

PROMPT: Shift the goal of your ending. If you're trying to end with a quiet gesture, try a sharper, more abrupt approach. If you're trying to end with a summary of the character and events, take a more dramatic approach. In short: Do something different, even the opposite, of what you've been trying to do. We can suffer tunnel vision in trying to make our endings work, limiting our possibilities and frustrating ourselves in a never-ending cycle of revisions.

PROMPT: If you're stuck on what happens in the end, in terms of plot or event, spend the next five session exploring five alternatives. Make each different from the others in a significant way. Tell yourself you're not going to choose from among them until you finish all five.

PROMPT: If you're stuck on what happens in the end, in terms of plot or event, chart the actions and events that occur in the piece to the point where you're blocked. If it helps, make an outline of the piece as it stands so far. Study the outline or sequence or whatever you've done to strip away the other elements of the story. Is there a natural, interesting, compelling flow to the events? Is there a logical system in place? If the answer is no, then the problem isn't the ending. It's what has come before. If the answer is yes, extend the outline to include the next logical event. You may have found your ending. If that event leads to others, you're not yet ready to end the piece.

PROMPT: If the problem is one of resolving a question of character, use the method in the previous prompt, but apply it to character. Strip away the other story elements and determine if you've developed the character and her conflict in the way you intended or a way that pleases you. Perhaps your character needs more time on the page and in your imagination before you're ready to end.

PROMPT: Simplify your ending. Sometimes we try to reach for the stars to wow our reader at the end. Eager to reward the reader's interest, we shoot off the rhetorical rockets red glare. Often, this means we're trying too hard, and it shows. We sense the ending's bombast. Simplify it. Work to make the ending satisfying. That is all your reader wants.

PROMPT: At our Writing It Real conferences, we always have a "bad writing" contest, in which everyone writes a terrible love scene or opening to a memoir or whatever we decide will be a fun assignment. One year, the contest focused on writing a "bad ending." The conferees submitted no end of hilariously contrived endings with one deus ex machina after the next. Give that approach a try: Write at least three terrible endings to your piece—ones that surprise with sudden introductions of new (and very convenient) details or take sudden and unreasonable turns or pile on the pomposity. Have fun with it. This approach can loosen you up and put you in the frame of mind to find a much better ending.

PROMPT: Instead of continuing to struggle, declare the draft complete and move to a new piece, setting a deadline for when you'll return to the current piece for revision. During the time away, try not to focus on resolving the ending. Know that you have more work to do but move your conscious mind away from the struggle for solutions. Your unconscious mind will continue to play with ideas, and the ending will come.

CHAPTER FORTY-TWO

WHEN YOU'RE STUCK IN REVISION

When I finish a first draft, it's always just as much of a mess as it's always been. I still make the same mistakes every time.

—MICHAEL CHABON

Unless you're working on one of your first pieces, you've probably had the experience of writing a draft, and after finishing it, feeling that it's not the piece you had hoped to write. To some extent, every project has a bit of that feeling. Against the hard black-and-white reality of the page, we struggle to place our visions, and rare is the time when the result equals our initial passion and inspiration. Of course, if we did succeed, we might quit writing, so let's try to perceive the struggle as a positive force in our lives.

We'll accept that a finished piece won't quite equal the piece we conceived in our minds at the start. Some pieces, however, will be closer than others. In this chapter, we'll focus on those pieces that fall considerably short. We have a completed draft that somewhere, somehow went wrong, and yet we remain intrigued by its possibilities. There are very good passages in it—perhaps a great conflict or situation or characters—and we don't want to lose them. We want to find a way to resurrect those passages that are not yet working.

When you find yourself facing this challenge, don't despair. It is part of the writer's life. All writers face it. Successful writers develop a level of resilience that allows them to persevere, to accept the good news—and good stories—with the bad. Cultivating resilience takes time. It's rooted in experience and in perspective, in the ability to see each piece you write as just one of an ongoing development of your art. Some projects come easily, gifts from the muse that appear almost miraculously on the page. Other projects, no matter how hard we try, will not be tamed. Despite wonderful ideas and inspired passages, they never quite work. Some remain unfinished and will remain that way, awaiting our return like the toys of childhood. Others will succeed because we have the fortitude to persist. We work on those pieces with a mixture of tenacity, ambition, frustration, invention, and blind faith. If you're ready to apply that mixture to your completed draft, try some of the prompts in this chapter.

When we talk about revision, however, we don't mean simply line editing. Many apprentice writers feel bored by revision. The fun part, they think, is over. When someone suggests the need for a change, they take the quick-fix approach. They're told, for example, that a character's motives remain confusing. They slap on a three-sentence explanation of the motives and they're finished. Revision complete. That's really not the way it works. Revision calls for much more engagement with the piece. The poet Rita Dove once said, "In working on a poem, I love to revise. Lots of younger poets don't enjoy this, but in the process of revision I discover things." The revision process is just as creative and full of discovery as the initial draft. In fact, I'd say it's even more creative.

A quote I like to use in workshops comes from Romulus Linney, who said, "Revision, once well done, becomes a sort of automatic itch which you scratch in the next work without thinking about it." It becomes organic to the process—not a final wrap-up stage at the end to tidy things a bit before shipping off the piece to agents and editors. Much can be learned about the piece and about writing in general during the revision stage. If you're struggling to get through it, don't take that struggle as a bad sign. It may be the best sign you could see.

PUT IT ON PAPER

PROMPT: If you've finished the draft recently—within the past week or two—put it away. Try not to think about it. Your frustration with it might be simply the postpartum depression we often feel after finishing a draft we've worked on for a while. The elation that drove us to write the piece has passed. Our belief that we have

THE WRITER'S IDEA BOOK

written a masterpiece has curdled into the belief that we're nothing more than a self-deluded failure. The piece sucks. It's terrible. Who are we kidding to think we can write anything worth reading? Sound familiar? These feelings tell you that you can't see the piece clearly yet. It may not be the masterpiece you hoped it would be, but those feelings are the result of the loss of elation you used to finish it. Accept this drop in enthusiasm as a natural part of the process. When it has passed, when you find yourself thinking of new ideas or itching to tinker, it's time to read the piece with a fresh vision.

PROMPT: After following the first prompt and putting the piece away for a specific period of time, take it out and recommit to it by working on it every day for at least a week. The break will refresh you, but you need to reinvest in the piece, to hear its rhythms and get it back into your mind again. If you don't feel ready to make large decisions about the piece while working on it every day, focus on the small stuff. The key is diving in again. Stick to that schedule.

PROMPT: Be willing to cut anything in the piece—and that means everything. When you achieve this mind-set, question the largest issues, such as the structure of the piece, its voice, and protagonist. Make a list of several alternatives for every major element. For example, think of three or four distinctively different ways of structuring the piece. Think of several other characters who could be the protagonist.

PROMPT: Commit yourself to at least one significant revision of the piece. In his classic book *Fiction Writer's Workshop*, Josip Novakovich makes a keen observation about how computers have changed the way writers revise. He notes that writers were willing to make larger revisions when they were forced to retype their pieces. Now that computers spare us that drudgery, we tend to tinker with the first draft rather than recast it. There are many advantages to working on a computer, but if you have a serious concern about how well a piece is working, taking time to retype it could lead to the larger revision it may need.

PROMPT: Spend a session writing about the piece. As we've done in earlier prompts, you could do this one as an interview with yourself, framing it in a question-and-answer format. Address your concerns about the piece. Why do you feel it's not working? What seems to be missing? What *is* working? If you can, express your intentions of the piece when you began writing it. Try to capture the essence of the piece in its current state. Compare your intentions with the results and ask yourself how they differ.

PROMPT: Spend a session writing the history of the piece, its evolution from initial idea to its current state. Read what you've written about the piece with an eye toward significant turns or changes. For example, I struggled off and on for several years with a story involving an eccentric character based on someone I met in real life. In early drafts, I made him the story's narrator, but his voice overwhelmed the piece. And his eccentricities were such that he was a character who was easier to take at a distance. I switched to third person, but there was still too much of him. I invented a son and told the story through the son's viewpoint, gaining the distance the story needed and making the father more sympathetic. I continued to revise and felt I'd found the answer. After finishing the story, I still wasn't happy with it. For some reason it just didn't work or, rather, it didn't approximate my original hopes for the story. After putting the story away for a while, working on it from time to time, I mapped its evolution and realized that by introducing the son, I had moved too far from the character who most interested me. I had made it a story of fathers and sons rather than one about a man's self-destructive tendencies. Though I was loath to do it, I moved the focus back to that man, subordinating the son. The story regained some of its early magic, and the most compelling character was back at the center again. Having viewed that character through the son's eyes during those drafts, he had grown more sympathetic and more human to me, and so the time spent on those drafts wasn't wasted. By charting the story's evolution, I could see where I'd taken a turn that turned it into a different story, one that didn't possess the wallop of invention that I wanted.

PROMPT: Read the piece aloud and, if possible, record yourself. Play the tape several times, listening for passages that work and those that don't. Take notes as you listen, scribbling any thoughts and impressions that occur to you. If the sound of your own voice on tape makes you squirm with self-consciousness, ask someone to read the piece aloud to you, and record the reading.

PROMPT: As a variation on the previous prompt, tell the story to someone rather than reading it directly from the page. Use the same basic structure you used in the written version—including flashbacks, asides, etc.—but don't strive to use the same words you've written. You're trying to gain a sense of the story's logic and clarity, its interest. Does your listener laugh? Cry? Is your listener confused by parts of the story? By telling it in this way, you'll gain objectivity, and you'll be able to gauge more clearly your own grasp of the story.

PROMPT: Give the current draft to a trusted reader or two and ask for their opinion. By now, the piece has been worked to the point that you don't really risk losing its energy by showing it to someone. After the piece is in your reader's hands, take a break from it. When you hear the reader's critique, listen closely. You may not agree at all with the reader's assessment, but listen for comments such as "I was confused here" or "I didn't understand when . . . ." You're too close to the piece to notice these issues, so such comments will be very helpful. Be willing to ask your reader specific

THE WRITER'S IDEA BOOK

questions about concerns you have for the piece. Take notes on his critique and then put the piece and the notes away for a week. Then ask yourself what you recall from the critique, which comments resonated for you—clarifying or confirming issues you had considered already.

PROMPT: Distill the draft to its essence by summing it up in one sentence. You may want to sum up in a paragraph and condense the paragraph to a sentence. This process won't be easy, and even after you have your one-sentence statement, you may feel you haven't done justice to the piece. But the exercise will force you to consider the fundamental nature of the piece. If you aren't able to arrive at some type of statement, perhaps the problem with the draft is that you're not sure yet what you're trying to accomplish.

PROMPT: Look for sudden and dramatic shifts in tone in the piece. Do they need to be modified—perhaps cut? Or do they need to be explored? Years ago, I wrote a short story that didn't quite work. After struggling with it for quite a while, I gave it to a trusted reader, who said the problem was a broadly drawn, boisterous character I introduced near the end. "The light changes when he comes in," the reader told me. I considered cutting the character but muted him instead. The story then worked but I moved on and forgot about it. Not a bad story; just sort of blah. A few years later, I recalled that story and had a revelation. Perhaps the larger-than-life character wasn't the problem. Instead, he was my unconscious attempt to inject energy into the story—a clue to my feeling that the story lacked passion, that it was too muted. I went back to the early draft and resurrected that character and infused the earlier pages with a similar energy. The story immediately became much more engaging and powerful. If you see similar shifts in tone, perhaps a wild bit of humor in what had been a somber story, you may want to mute that humor or find other places in the piece to add humor.

PROMPT: Sometimes starting small can lead you back into the story. Look for small changes you can make. They can help you past feelings of frustration and failure that block you from seeing the possibilities for improving the story. Spend the next few sessions focused on the little things, telling yourself that you'll confront the larger ones later. For now, fix a line of dialogue, sharpen a description, correct errors in grammar, punctuation, and spelling.

PROMPT: If the piece is based on a real-life experience and you're writing nonfiction, check to be sure you've captured that experience. Are all the key elements on the page? Have you evoked the experience sharply enough for a reader to share your thoughts and feelings about it? Add one more element about the experience that, for whatever reason, you chose to exclude in the draft.

PROMPT: If you're writing fiction based on a real-life experience, have you moved the experience far enough from its real-life inspiration that you feel free to change and edit the parts that don't work? Add one more element to the story, an element that is entirely fictional. Your problem with the draft could be that the piece hangs in an awkward middle ground between a self-contained fictional story and your memory of the real-life experience.

PROMPT: Spend a session focused on characters, asking yourself questions about them. Are they compelling? Sympathetic? Are the events in the piece meaningful and significant to the characters? How many characters appear in the piece—write down all the names. Are there too many characters? Too few? Should several characters be condensed into one? Which characters interest you most? Why? Which ones interest you least? Why? What qualities do the characters share? How are they different? Do you know the characters well enough? Are all aspects of the characters on the page or do some remain vague? Are they all described? Are they all described in the same way or do you vary your methods of presenting them? What is the goal of each character in the story?

PROMPT: Spend a session introducing a new character. Describe the character. Use him in a scene. How would the piece change if you inserted this character into it?

PROMPT: Check your scenes. How many do you present and how long is each one? Have you varied the length? Are the scenes generally long or short? Is the length of each scene appropriate to its significance to the piece? If you had to cut a scene, which one would you cut? Spend a session writing a new scene. How does the scene affect the piece?

PROMPT: Check the pace of the piece. Does it move quickly or slowly? Have you modulated the pace, creating a pleasing rhythm? Is the pace appropriate to the content of the piece? Does it match the intentions you had when you began writing the piece?

PROMPT: Check the structure of the piece. Do you offer a pleasing mix of scene and summary? Have you provided clear transitions between scenes, chapters, and sections? To do this prompt, you'll need a printed copy of the piece. Lay the pages across a table so you can see them all. Highlight scene and summary. Use a different color for transitions.

PROMPT: Add a new sentence to every page. If it's a short piece, add a new sentence to every paragraph. You can cut the ones you don't like at a later time. For now, you're trying to extend. Go wild. Push your imagination.

THE WRITER'S IDEA BOOK

PROMPT: Reverse the previous prompt. Rather than adding sentences, cut a sentence from every page or every paragraph. Determine what has been lost and what has been gained. Put back only those sentences that add something important to the piece.

PROMPT: Add a detail, trait, or quality to every character, preferably one that enlarges or makes the character more vivid and complex. Don't neglect even minor characters. If the guy from room service appears only for a sentence, to deliver a bottle of champagne, add some stains to his uniform or give him an odd accent.

PROMPT: Do the opposite of what you did in the previous prompt—that is, cut any details and asides and explanations that aren't essential to the piece. In early drafts, we tend to load up a narrative with more than it needs. Cut, cut, cut. I learned this lesson again a couple of years ago at a reading. I brought a published story to read but, upon arrival, was told that each reader would get only fifteen minutes. I hadn't brought a backup story, and the one I brought would take a good twenty minutes to read. As the first readers took their turns, I cut the story, trimming words here and there, lines of dialogue, even leaving out an entire stand-alone section. The story withstood these cuts—and probably was better as a result.

PROMPT: Go back to the chapters in the previous section on evaluating ideas. Ask again the questions we posed there: What's at stake? Whose story is it? Am I using the appropriate point of view? Have I made the dramatic goals clear enough? And so on.

PROMPT: Spend a few sessions pushing the language. Read each sentence with an eye toward making the language more interesting and more vivid, more particular and more specific. Your concern with the draft may not have anything to do with the big elements, such as character or structure. Instead, you may be sensing, at some level, that the language is uninspired or that it's merely competent. Force yourself to improve a sentence in every paragraph. Look for language that is vague or dull. Make it sparkle.

CHAPTER FORTY-THREE

TILL WE EAT AGAIN

The beginnings and endings of all human undertakings are untidy.

—JOHN GALSWORTHY

One of the great moments in the writing life occurs when we declare a piece finished. If it's a short piece, the writer has lived with it for weeks, maybe months. If it's a longer work, the process may take years. As we've discussed throughout this book, writing can be a struggle. Finishing a piece may require starting over several times, cutting long passages of a draft that was fundamentally flawed. Finishing a piece usually includes a handful of turning points when the piece reveals itself and sets the writing in motion in an exciting new direction. The process can require dozens of revisions. It can mean putting the piece away to simmer for a while, then pulling it out and starting work with a fresh eye and spirit. When all the big blocks are in place and the tough early drafts are complete, the writer begins editing and refining. New little bursts of inspiration create interesting details and language. We polish and we polish and we polish. And then, we're finished.

And then, we must begin again.

As a writer, you probably know this feeling. You've just finished spending weeks, even months, in the editing and polishing phase of a piece whose larger issues have been resolved long ago. In the final stages, you've watched a good piece improve at the microlevel. You've worked with the confidence gained by having spent so much time in the world of the piece. You can flip to the passages you like best, the ones that came from hours of work or were born from a flash of inspiration at four in the morning.

When the work is finished, and the piece is off in the mail to agents or editors, we must return to face the blank page again. Though the prospect of working with new material can be exciting, it also can be a little scary. The confidence of the previous weeks evaporates. You face the unknown. The victories, large and small, of the previous piece mean little now because a new piece sprawls before us.

Many writers feel blocked at this time. It's a natural feeling. Sometimes we slide into a postpartum depression, or a similar psychological state, and lack the energy and will to start anew. As we were writing the previous piece, the one that now stands so lovely and complete, we were concocting the next one. In fact, we had to fight the urge to dive right into it. But now that we don't have to fight the urge anymore, we don't feel the urge anymore. The piece that shimmered like candy in the distance—"I can't wait to start that one!"—seems far less shimmering. We want to keep writing the finished one, to stay in that world.

The prompts in this chapter address the time in our writing lives after we've finished a piece but struggle to begin again. As a general principle, expect and accept that this time will come. If you've engaged yourself deeply with the finished piece, you will suffer a bit of depression in letting it go. During this time, you might feel enervated and stale. If you're proud of what you've been able to accomplish in the previous piece, you may feel that you can never quite hit that level again. The completed piece will be your best, the result of luck or fate or some unique mingling of circumstance that will happen only once in your life. Or, you may simply feel tired. You may be emotionally and creatively exhausted. The silos of inspiration stand empty. Some of the prompts speak directly to this mind-set, while others offer new ways of beginning that you can use at any stage of your writing life.

PUT IT ON PAPER

PROMPT: Here's the easiest prompt in the book: Don't write anything. Give yourself a specific amount of time away from writing. When we try to push through exhaustion by using will and determination, we usually end up frustrated and unproductive. Our imaginations need time and care. We have to feed them with new possibilities, new images. And that takes time. However, do give yourself a *specific* amount of time off, based on your natural rhythms and work habits. If you're a writer who needs time to recover and begin thinking about a project before starting to scribble words on paper, give yourself what you need. If you're a writer who needs less time, who can begin with energy and vigor after only a short pause, honor your ability. If you're not sure how much time you need, set a specific start date anyway and adjust to how you feel when that date arrives. Do set that date. Time off is essential, but too much time erodes the habit of writing that you've worked hard to create, and before long, you'll need to develop the habit again. Set the date. Take some time off. Enjoy. Let life wash over you and through you.

PROMPT: Another easy one: Spend a session with a stack of magazines and scissors. Cut out at least ten pictures of people. Cut ten more of events—some type of action, anything from a couple entering a room to firefighters battling a blaze. Keep your piles of people and events separate. Shuffle them a few times. Close your eyes and pick three from the people pile and three from the event pile. Paste them together into a collage and study it. Let your mind begin to draw connections among the pictures. Spend a session exploring these connections and allow a story to develop through those connections.

PROMPT: Go someplace you've never been and don't bring your notebook or tape recorder. The place can be as accessible as a shop in your neighborhood, or it could be a nearby town. The key is discovery—filling your senses with new information. Keep your senses open. Talk to people. Ask questions. Do whatever it takes to connect with the place. If you're visiting a clothing store, try on a dress or a pair of pants. Touch things. Close your eyes and focus on sounds. When you return home, you can write down your impressions but don't force yourself to write. Our goal here is not research or to fill new pages of our notebooks. Our goal is to feed our imaginations, to experience a fresh environment outside the context of writing.

PROMPT: Visit a museum and spend some time focused on a single exhibit or show. Use the method we discussed in the previous prompt (except for the directive to "touch things"). Your goal is not to record the experience. Instead, linger long enough to interact with the exhibit, studying its nuances and subtleties.

PROMPT: One more visit—spend at least an hour in a natural setting where you've never been before. The place can be as accessible as a park in your town, or you may want to drive into the country. Walk around. Scoop dirt into your hands and feel its texture. Close your eyes and listen to the sounds around you. Linger long enough to connect with the place.

PROMPT: Let's focus on words. Flip at random through a dictionary and write down the first ten concrete nouns you find. You're making a list of things. (On my search, I pointed to *reef, penguin, concertina, infield, hemp, rain, snorkel, pie, water-hole, cornet*.) If your finger falls on a word that's not a concrete noun, find the closest one or flip to a new page. When you have your list, search for ten abstract nouns, words that name ideas, feelings, and beliefs. (On my search, I found *religion, justice, enthusiasm, outrage, dislike, truth, sentiment, misery, agitation, ambition.*) Compiling the second list may take longer than it took you to compile the first one, but stay the course. Allow yourself to enjoy skimming through the dictionary. Linger on words you don't recognize. Write them down on a separate sheet of paper and add them to your vocabulary. When you've finished both lists, write them in two adjacent columns on a single page. Then begin pairing them in various ways. You might try writing sentences using a pair in similes, such as *Truth is like a snorkel* or *Misery is like a concertina.* Write a page to support your simile, either in an expository or narrative mode. Or you could pair the words in a description, such as, *Throughout the evening, Abbey played her concertina of misery.*

PROMPT: Pick a place where you've spent time in your life. Draw a map of it, noting the places where various events occurred. They need not be significant events. You might mark, for example, the grocery store near where you lived and chart the route you took from your home to the store. Have fun with the map. Use markers and highlighters of many colors. Allow the process to spark memories of people, situations, events, details. Spend a few sessions writing about this place. If you feel inspired, keep going.

PROMPT: Follow the same process described in the previous prompt but focus on a fictional place or simply allow yourself to fictionalize elements of a place you remember from your life. The key: Have fun with it. Go nuts with the map, and when you're ready, begin writing.

PROMPT: Spend several writing sessions paging through reference books, particularly guides to specific subjects, such as trees, historical figures, architecture, transportation vehicles. Writers need to know the names of things, so spending time with reference guides is essential. Also, the names, descriptions, and pictures of things can feed your imagination. Write the names that particularly interest you in your notebook. Use one or two as the basis for a writing session. For example, I opened a reference book and found information about the Hudson Hornet, a car made in the early 1950s. I searched the Internet for a bit more information about it, then wrote a sentence in which a character pulls up to a house in a Hudson Hornet. Why is he there? What is the nature of his visit? A quick flip through a guide to birds gave me the Louisiana heron. I opened a guide to Americana and the first entry that caught my eye was Tabasco sauce (which has been bottled and sold since 1868, a fact I didn't know). And it's bottled in Louisiana, home to the Louisiana heron. Perhaps there's a case of Tabasco sauce in the backseat of that Hudson Hornet as it pulls up to the house. Why is it there? Is it a peace offering brought by the driver to the people who live in the house? And how does a heron figure into the scene? You see where I'm going. Reference guides can give you specific information that can lead to your next piece of writing.

PROMPT: Here's a variation on the previous prompt. Pick a page from a visual dictionary, a reference guide that provides the names of the parts of various things. If you don't have this type of dictionary at home, you can find one in any library. Spend a session writing a short piece in which you use most of the names of the thing you found. If possible, create a scene, dropping the descriptive words in at appropriate intervals rather than simply writing a description in which you use the words.

PROMPT: Let's focus on cutting the cord with the piece you've finished recently by consciously doing the opposite of what you did in that piece. For example, is the finished piece a dark study of character? Freewrite by focusing on humor and action. Is the previous piece set mostly indoors? Freewrite a scene or two set outside. Is the protagonist in the previous piece a solemn introvert? Freewrite about a character who is gregarious.

PROMPT: Did you have a specific place and time for writing the piece you finished recently? If so, make a change for the next few sessions. Create a new routine. You can always return to the old one if it's more convenient, but let's break the old routine for a while.

PROMPT: Try a new form. If the piece you finished recently is a novel, spend a few sessions creating scenes for a play. If you've just finished a play, try a personal essay. If your previous piece focused closely on the lives of a few characters, explore a national issue. If your previous piece was based on a real-life experience, write about an experience that's made up from start to finish.

PROMPT: In the opening of this chapter, I mentioned the familiar situation in which a writer, while working on one piece, is distracted by interest in a different piece. When he finishes the first piece, however, the new one seems far less interesting than before. The new one existed in his mind mostly as a distraction, a device he created to relieve him from the burden of completing the piece he was writing. If you have experienced this type of situation and have resisted the urge to hop to the new piece, good for you. If the new piece now doesn't interest you, let it go. If it still interests you but you're feeling blocked at the beginning, schedule the next three writing sessions to work on it. You may be blocked because you're expecting the piece to possess the level of invention and particularity of the previous one, forgetting that achieving that level in the previous one took a long time. Have patience. Allow the new one to find itself, to begin to reveal its own qualities.

PROMPT: If you've been keeping an idea notebook, open to a page at random and point to an entry. Make that entry the focus of your next three sessions. The key is that it's a random choice. There's no pressure to make it a masterpiece, and the choice is not guided by a desire to continue the thread of the piece you've completed recently. It's important, furthermore, to explore the piece in at least three sessions before moving to something else. When we finish a piece that took some time to complete, we tend to hop among a number of new ideas, which is not a bad approach in itself, if you want to play and experiment for a while. However, if you find yourself getting frustrated by beginning a new piece with every session, try spending a little more time on each one and allowing it to grab your interest.

PROMPT: If you're feeling stale, seeing your new ideas as clichés, let's push into that feeling. Begin a piece in which you prove a cliché wrong. First, write a list of a half dozen clichés, such as "Cheaters never prosper," "Ignorance is bliss," "You get what you pay for," or "A penny saved is a penny earned." Then recall an event or create a fictional event in which a cheater prospers or ignorance is decidedly not bliss.

PROMPT: When we begin a new piece after finishing one, we often feel tired, bored, frustrated, impatient, anxious, or confused. Let's push into what you're feeling by creating a character who is feeling the same way but for different reasons. Come up with some reasons. If you're writing nonfiction, write about the emotion itself or write about another time in your life when you felt the same way, though not in connection with your writing.

PROMPT: Let's use the final prompts in this chapter to move beyond the previous piece by creating some new situations and conflicts. Write about a character who is by nature an introvert but for some reason is forced to act in an open, friendly way. For example, your introvert is forced to host a reception for his boss and must create a festive atmosphere.

PROMPT: Reverse the previous prompt—your outgoing character is in a situation in which she must be silent and passive, observing the people and action around her rather than leading the action.

PROMPT: Place a character in a place that rubs against the character's nature, where she feels exceedingly uncomfortable. The character works very hard to hide or mask the lack of comfort but eventually is exposed.

PROMPT: Make a list of expressions we use to communicate that we're in trouble such as "up a tree," "between a rock and a hard place," "in hot water" "at the end of my rope." Place a character literally in such a place.

I took the title of this chapter from Lorrie Moore's wonderful short story titled "How to Be an Other Woman." In the story, the protagonist is having an affair with a married man and struggling with issues of self-esteem and identity. Moore mixes in much humor. The couple meets mostly for lunch and dinner, and after one lunch, the protagonist calls out, "Till we eat again." It's a clever line that also speaks to the sadness of the situation. Now that the book is finished, I feel a similar feeling. And that seems to be the way it is with books or with any long writing project. It becomes part of our daily life, and when it's finished, there is a sense of loss.

Revisiting work I wrote more than ten years ago brought back many memories for me and increases that sense of loss, though maybe in ten years, I'll be doing it all again. I do hope you find much of use in your own writing. When you're feeling blocked or maybe just stale and need a spark, you've got quite a few to choose from here. The key is to keep writing. And I very much hope that you do. The hundreds of prompts in this book are designed to make it easier for you and also more fun. But as we've discussed throughout the book, there are no shortcuts, no formulas, no easy answers. As the writer Gabriel Fielding wrote, "The mere habit of writing, of constantly keeping at it, of never giving up, ultimately teaches you how to write." And that's the way it is. To that lifelong apprenticeship, we bring our individual experiences and observations, our talent and our passion and our desire, in the end, to create something beautiful.

INDEX